TWO WEEKS

TRANSFORMING SOCIAL INQUIRY, TRANSFORMING SOCIAL ACTION

New Paradigms for Crossing the Theory/Practice Divide in Universities and Communities

OUTREACH SCHOLARSHIP

Editor:

Richard M. Lerner
Tufts University
Medford, Massachusetts, U.S.A.

TRANSFORMING SOCIAL INQUIRY, TRANSFORMING SOCIAL ACTION
New Paradigms for Crossing the Theory/Practice Divide in Universities and Communities

edited by

Francine T. Sherman
Boston College Law School

William R. Torbert
Boston College School of Management

KLUWER ACADEMIC PUBLISHERS
Boston / Dordrecht / London

Distributors for North, Central and South America:
Kluwer Academic Publishers
101 Philip Drive
Assinippi Park
Norwell, Massachusetts 02061 USA
Telephone (781) 871-6600
Fax (781) 871-6528
E-Mail <kluwer@wkap.com>

Distributors for all other countries:
Kluwer Academic Publishers Group
Distribution Centre
Post Office Box 322
3300 AH Dordrecht, THE NETHERLANDS
Telephone 31 78 6392 392
Fax 31 78 6546 474
E-Mail <services@wkap.nl>

 Electronic Services <http://www.wkap.nl>

Library of Congress Cataloging-in-Publication Data

Transforming social inquiry, transforming social action: new paradigms for crossing the theory/practice divide in universities and communities/ edited by Francine T. Sherman, William R. Torbert.
    p. cm. -- (Outreach scholarship; 4)
   Includes bibliographical references and index.
   ISBN 0-7923-7787-7 (alk. paper)
    1. Community and college--United States. 2. Social Action--United States. 3. Social sciences--Research--United States. 4. Research--United States. I. Sherman, Francine T., 1955- II. Torbert, William R., 1944- III. Series.

LC238 . T73 2000
378.1'03--dc21

                                    00-020446

TABLE OF CONTENTS

FOREWORD

John F. Kerry
United States Senator

If we are to reinvigorate and reinforce civic participation in this country at a time when our society is increasingly fragmented and highly technologically based, we must find a way to unite distinct communities, such as universities, regional and non-profit organizations, and families. We must find ways to link academicians, students, teachers, and professionals with the reality of events and circumstances so that theories and ideas mightily pursued within the "ivory tower" are connected to social reality and useful. As the editors and contributors in this volume point out, the way to bridge theory/practice divide is not merely to interpret and report on circumstances of the real-world; but rather, to deconstruct the separate and distinct communities that exist within our society and actively engage other communities to realize a continuum of mutual understanding, collaboration, and action.

It is crucial to include our nation's public schools in this new approach of social inquiry and social action. Improving and creating educational opportunity for all children in the United States has been an ongoing critical federal issue. We know that when children achieve in school they have a much greater chance of living healthy, productive adult lives that will benefit themselves and society, and we know that increasing the base of stakeholders in children's education yields those positive results. In 1999 alone the Senate is considering bi-partisan bills to provide ongoing federal funding with corporate matches bringing together multiple sectors in local, collaborative education projects with proven track records (Senate 824, 1999) and to provide incentives to schools at the local level so they can adopt the best practices of our nations best schools (Senate 1068, 1999). We must renew the concept in American life that schools are a focal point within our society and that every stakeholder must be engaged to collaborate for the benefit of our children.

This work describes specific case studies and supporting theories for university based initiatives that do just that—engage communities and universities to promote educational achievement for our nation's youth. From the case study in Chapter 6 of the seven year development of an extended-service school in Boston; to the analysis in chapter 14 of ethical issues in action research to understand children's attitudes about learning through their drawings; from the description in chapter 8 of a self-study of perspectives on social justice among professors in a teacher education program; to the description in chapter 10 of multidisciplinary service learning programs training counseling psychologists in practice relevant to communities; to the analysis in chapter 12 of a model for clinical legal education that incorporates the voice of delinquent girls into their representation: this work is rich with examples of engaged research and practice holding promise for children and youth.

In a 1981 overview of university-community partnerships, Peter Szanton reflected general disillusionment with universities' roles in solving problems faced by local, state and national communities and sought to determine " . . . why analysis and proposals offered to local public agencies by consultants of many kinds so often seem to be useless, or at least go unused." (Szanton, 1981). The failure of so much university generated research of the 60's and 70's to provide relevant solutions to social problems is well-known (Cardozier, 1987). But current federal investment in university-community collaborations reflects a confidence in the efforts of universities who, like Boston College, are committed to relevance and citizenship, to move beyond this history. For example, in partnership with universities the U.S. Department of Education supports a Title XI program for applied research and outreach activities by universities in distressed communities. Similar partnerships are supported by the Community Outreach Partnership Centers Program (COPC) at the U.S. Department of Housing and Urban Development (HUD) which was re-authorized in 1999 at twice its original 1992 level (Fleming, 1999). These programs are examples of federal-university collaborations investing in the power of university –community partnerships.

This work, edited by Francine T. Sherman and William R. Torbert, exemplifies the work of engaged universities (Boyer, 1990; Kellogg, 1998) and transcends the rhetoric of any one institution as the center of a community. In doing so, it develops a new paradigm for reaching out to communities and assuming some responsibility for their success. Building on research and the growing presence of the Boston College Center for Child, Family and Community Partnerships, the authors in this volume blaze a trail for universities and schools, teachers and academics, and, in the best sense of the word, "citizens" to follow a path of "outreach scholarship" that makes a positive contribution to our communities. This book offers a vision for spanning the rigid and artificial divide between the "ivory tower" world of research and the world beyond the university's walls. The divide between the university and the community is a false one—the truth is the academic expertise of our universities and the real-world experiences within our communities can compliment each other in a synergy that can benefit us all. That is a notion we must all embrace—and work to instill across our nation.

REFERENCES

Boyer, E.L. (1990). *Scholarship reconsidered: Priorities for the professoriate.* Princeton, NJ: The Carnegie Foundation for the Advancement of Teaching.
Cardozier, V. (1987). *American higher education: An international perspective.* Aldershot, U.K.: Gower Publishing.
Fleming, J. (1999). Unpublished doctoral dissertation. *A typology of institutionalization for university-community partnerships at American universities and an underlying epistemology of engagement.*
Kellogg Commission on the Future of State and Land-Grant Colleges (1998). *Returning to our roots: The engaged institution.* Washington, DC: National Association of State Universities and Land-Grant Colleges.
Senate 1068, Early Childhood Development Act of 1999.
Senate 824, The Comprehensive School Improvement and Accountability Act of 1999.
Szantan, P. (1981) *Not well advised.* New York, NY: Russell Sage Foundation.

FOREWORD: THINKING AND HITTING AT THE SAME TIME

Martha Minow[1]

It's an old joke about economists, but it could be told about so many academic fields: a senior colleague deflates a younger one's enthusiasm for an idea by saying, "Sure, it works in practice, but will it work in theory?" But the problem is not only that practice too seldom plays an important part in theory-building. Even when it becomes vital in academic study to examine community action or to evaluate a program in use, the very methods of research reinforce the distance between scholar and community members who are imaged as "subjects," rather than partners in learning and action. Indeed, the conventional methods reinforce the distance between the academic player—faculty or student—and his or her own self as a person capable of emotions, at risk of self-delusion. Even students preparing for professional roles such as lawyers, psychologists, and educators imbibe the culture of distance and cut themselves off from self-reflection and collaboration with those they are supposed to assist.

The conventional methods also strengthen the assumptions that those who research and teach have no connections or responsibilities to larger communities, except in the production of conventional research and the arc of individual career achievements. The usual view treats university and college scholars and students as having no further community involvement even when scholarship and teaching addresses vital social questions such as poverty and racism. Action, including actions to redress such problems, lies in a different realm, for other actors; academics must remain objective and sufficiently distant to analyze. A slogan for the conventional approach could be Yogi Berra's classic: "You can't hit and think at the same time."

This book demonstrates that it can be otherwise. Each of the chapters grows from engaged efforts by scholars and teachers to join in partnership with others to be reflective about the work of social inquiry and its connections to social action. The very variety of the chapter topics reveals how many aspects of the conventional thinking hampers relationships that could connect academics with students, universities with communities, and criteria of rigor with topics of genuine human concern. Thus, chapters consider when and how a researcher should participate as an collaborator in the very community organizing activity he chooses to study (Fairfax, Chapter 2); how multidisciplinary research centers can reach out to generate work that benefits communities under study (Lerner, Chapter 2); whether a college with a religious mission and a secular research university can effectively collaborate (Bruyn, Chapter 4); how a university can join in a community school's efforts to change (Walsh et al., Chapter 6); and whether university ethics rules intended to protect the subjects of academic research require revision when scholars and community members become partners in social inquiry (Haney and Lykes, Chapter 14).

Other chapters address the complex relationship between the academic training of professionals and the capacities of the individuals to address the needs of clients and communities more fully than in the past (McMorrow, Chapter 7; Cochran-Smith, Chapter 8; Kenny and Gallagher, Chapter 10; Waddock and Spangler, Chapter 11; Sherman, Chapter 12). To enhance the abilities of professionals to collaborate with community members in preventing and redressing social problems, universities need to develop new approaches to service learning, executive education, collaborations across professional training programs, and even to place of the author's voice in scholarship.

It should not be surprising that each of these undertakings yields frustration and also identify enduring tensions. Thus, the researcher may learn that joining in as a colleague in the effort of community organization lends richer insights as well as more trusting relationships with community organizers who are under study but also potentially jeopardizes the enduring aspiration of objectivity (Fairfax, Chapter 2). A faculty team devoted to collaborative self-study and research confronts the difficult questions about whose voice is presented when they write and talk about their efforts (Cochran-Smith et al, Chapter 8); indeed, whose name should be cited here, when the collaborative writings are mentioned? A scholar committed to creating a doctoral program bridging knowledge and action is shocked to learn that Donald Schon, an pioneering advocate of reflective practice, finds the work unscientific (Torbert, Chapter 13). More generally, the chapters collected here may trouble some because they do not make findings, disprove hypotheses, or even move in authoritative, univocal directions. Instead they include self-criticisms, dialogues, and honest disclosures of troubles and hopes.

Ironically, perhaps, it is Donald Schon whose work best predicts such problems. He described the topography of professional practice as including a high hard ground overlooking a swamp. On the high ground, manageable problems lend themselves to solution through the application of research-based theory and technique. In the swampy lowland, messy, confusing problems defy technical solution. (Schon, 1987, p. 3, quoted in Walsh et al, Chapter 6). Yet, Schon continues, the problems on the high ground are relatively unimportant to individuals and society, "while in the swamp lie the problems of greatest human concern."

Cultivating a tolerance, if not an appreciation, for messiness and complexity may be the most crucial requirement for each effort to connect theory and practice, university and community, professional and person. Law professor Thomas Grey turned to the work of poet Wallace Stevens to advance a pragmatist aesthetics, one that resists dichotomies and cultivates appreciation for paradox and messiness.[1] Certainly the book in your hands asks for such acceptance and, for the willing reader, rewards it.

I admit, though, that even such talk of ambiguity and complexity risks the remoteness and temptation of the technical that perpetuates divides between theory and practice, thought and action, as well as roles and persons. Putting human beings and our relationships at the center of social inquiry and action requires mindfulness of actual people in the ways we work as well as in the purposes of the work. Interrogating our practices, regularly, in this light is uncomfortable but essential. Thus, Richard Lerner poses a question worth pondering precisely because it is likely to seem so preposterous to both academics and community members: of what

---

[1] See Thomas C. Grey, The Wallace Stevens Case: Law and the Practice of Poetry (1991).

benefit to the life of "a crack-addicted, teenage single mother, who is jobless and a high school dropout" is the leading research and teaching institution in her neighborhood? (Lerner, Chapter 3). For her to believe that the university has anything to offer to her would require even more enormous changes than it would take for professors to view her seriously as both audience for and collaborator in their work. For then the professors would have to treat this individual—who has a name and her own dreams and aspirations—at the center of their map of what matters in how they teach, write, organize their departments, create lecture series, seek funding, recruit students, hire faculty, think, and hit at the same time.

And then, appropriately, academics would have to address who is on the team: who contributes to and benefits from the processes of social inquiry and action. I hope this book will have sequels reflecting the shifts in perspective and team membership the authors have so vigorously started.

---

[1] Professor, Harvard Law School.

ACKNOWLEDGEMENTS

We have thoroughly enjoyed and deeply appreciated the colleagueship of our co-authors during and after the Barat House Seminars from which this book has emerged. It has been inspiring to work so closely with colleagues from different disciplines and professions who all share a dedication to collaborative inquiry "on the ground."

Our thanks also to the Schools of Law and of Management for their generous support in completing this project. Finally, we are especially grateful for the unstinting and absolutely essential contributions that Linda Raute and Jennifer Leigh offered in translating manuscripts into the final camera-ready copy.

AUTHOR BIOGRAPHIES

Severyn T. Bruyn is professor of Sociology at Boston College and former director of the Program in Social Economy and Social Policy. An early participative and actively observant researcher in Guatamala in the 1950s, Bruyn is considered a father of social economic thought. Among his many books and articles are *The Social Economy* (Wiley, 1977), *The Field of Social Investment* (Cambridge University Press, 1987), and *Beyond the Market and the State* (Temple University Press, 1987).

Marilyn Cochran-Smith, one of nine authors of Chapter 8, all whom are faculty members in the Department of Teacher Education, Special Education, and Curriculum and Instruction at Boston College. Marilyn Cochran-Smith, chair of the department, has research interests that include teacher education, research interests overlap into three areas: pedagogical implication of writing to learn and understand mathematical problem solving; practical applications of Vygotskian Psychology; and social justice education. **Phil Dimattia's** interests include classroom management and assistive technology for individuals with multiple disabilities. **Sara Freedman** does research on urban education, the privatization of public education, the political economy of education and the intersection between critical pedagogy and multicultural education. **Richard Jackson's** interests include assistive technology, functional use of low vision, and children with disabilities. **Jean Mooney** is engaged in research on cognitive and metacognitive learning strategies, service models within remedial education, collaborative consultation, and strategies for learning disabled college students. **Otherine Neisler's** research interests include multicultural curriculum, education and technology, qualitative and survey methodologies, social studies education, and the experiences of minority members of the educational professoriate. **Alec Peck's** interests include technology and education, families of children with special needs, and accessibility. **Nancy Zollers** is engaged in research on urban schools, inclusion, disability, and transition from schools.

Allen Fairfax is currently on the faculty of Bowdoin College and is completing his doctoral dissertation in Sociology at Boston College. He has served as a community organizer and community researcher in Atlanta and Valdosta, Georgia, as well as in the Merrimack Valley Project in Massachusetts.

Timothy Garvin is Executive Director of the Allston-Brighton YMCA. He is a lead member of the school-community-university partnership involved in the Gardner Extended Services School.

Walter M. Haney worked as a teacher in Vientiane, Laos, from 1968-71 and is currently Professor of Education at Boston College, as well as Senior Research Associate in the Center for the Study of Testing Evaluation and Educational Policy. Haney is the author (with Madaus and Lyons) of *The Fractured Marketplace for Standardized Testing* (Kluwer Academic Publishers) and has published widely in scholarly and wide-audience journals. He has also served on several editorial boards and on the National Advisory Committee of the ERIC Clearinghouse on Assessment and Evaluation.

Kimberly A. Howard is a doctoral candidate in the Department of Counseling, Developmental, and Educational Psychology in the Lynch School of Education at Boston College. Her research examines the development of children's' conceptions of jobs and careers.

Richard M. Lerner, currently at Tufts University, has earlier served as director of centers for child, family and community partnerships at Pennsylvania State, Michigan State, and Boston College. A widely published advocate of contextual developmental psychology and founding editor of *Applied Developmental Psychology*, Lerner advises several foundations. His titles include *Concepts and Theories of Human Development*.

M. Brinton Lykes is Professor and Chair of Psychology at the University of the Witwatersrand in Johannesburg, South Africa, and is on leave from the Lynch School of Education at Boston College. An activist scholar and teacher, she has lived and worked among women and child survivors of state-sponsored violence and war in rural Guatemala since 1987. She has published extensively and is co-editor of *Myths about the Powerless: Contesting Social Inequalities* (Temple University Press, 1996), *Gender and Personality* (Duke University Press, 1985), and *Your Daughters Shall Prophesy: Feminist Alternatives in Theological Education* (Pilgrim Press, 1980).

Judith A. McMorrow is a professor at Boston College Law School, where she teaches torts, professional responsibility and related topics. She has written many articles on topics of professional responsibility and age discrimination (with a focus on retirement policy). Professor McMorrow is active in pro bono activities, including representing women in Massachusetts seeking commutation based on Battered Woman Syndrome. She has also been active in promoting the interdisciplinary practice of law. After graduating from University of Notre Dame Law School in 1980, Professor McMorrow clerked for the Hon. Gilbert S. Merritt (United States Court of Appeals for the Sixth Circuit) and Chief Justice Warren E. Burger (United States Supreme Court.) She practiced with the Washington D.C. law firm of Steptoe and Johnson before entering teaching in 1985.

Catalina Montes is Principal of the Gardner Extended Services School in Boston. She is a member of the Holmes Partnership and has presented her approach to integrating curriculum and student services at several national conferences.

Francine T. Sherman is the founder and Director of the Juvenile Rights Advocacy Project at Boston College Law School as well as Co-Director of the Boston College Center for Child, Family and Community Partnerships. She is an Adjunct Clinical Professor at Boston College Law School where she has been teaching Juvenile Justice for the past ten years. She speaks widely about girls in the justice system in, academic, continuing legal education, bar association, and foundation forums and is currently conducting research for the Annie E. Casey Foundation to contextualize the pathways girls take through state systems and develop advocacy techniques for girls in the justice system. Her publications include, "The Role of Context in the Representation of Children," In *Who Speaks for this Child? A Dialogue About the Legal Representation of Children*, 3-16 Boston, MA: MCLE, 1999; "Law in the School-Linked Services Model: Problems and Possibilities" In *Collaborative Practice: School and Human Service Partnerships*, edited by R.W.C. Tourse and J.F. Mooney, 201-218 Connecticut: Praeger, 1999; and "Thoughts on a Contextual View of Juvenile Justice Reform Drawn from Narratives of Youth," 68 *Temple Law Review* 1837 (1995).

Eve Spangler is an associate professor of Sociology at Boston College and faculty chair of the Leadership for Change executive program. An internationally known contributor to the field of occupational health and safety, Spangler is editor of *New Solutions*, a journal for labor and public health planners. She is also a founding and active member of the International Exchange for Environmental and Ocuupational Health, chair of the advisory board to the Center for Women in Politics and Public Policy at Umass/Boston, and a Fellow at the Harvard School of Public Health.

Nora Thompson is a doctoral student in the Department of Counseling, Developmental, and Educational Psychology in the Lynch School of Education at Boston College. She is currently coordinating an empirical evaluation of the Gardner Extended Services School in Boston.

William R. Torbert is Professor of Management at Boston College's Carroll School of Management, where he earlier served as Graduate Dean and Director of the Ph.D. Program in Organizational Transformation. Still earlier, he served on the faculties of Southern Methodist University and Harvard University, having received his BA and Ph.D. from Yale. He is the past-chair of the Academy of Management's Organization Development & Change Division and a widely published author (e.g. award winning *Managing the Corporate Dream* and Terry Award finalist *The Power of Balance: Transforming Self, Society, and Scientific Inquiry*). He also currently serves on the Boards of Harvard Pilgrim Health Care (#1 ranked HMO in 1998) and Trillium Asset Management (the original and largest social investing advisor). A founding research member of the new Society for Organizational Learning, he engages in a research practice called "developmental action inquiry" that, unlike purely third-person social science research, integrates first, second, and third-person research and practice in real time.

Sandra A. Waddock is Professor of Management at Boston College's Carroll School of Management, where she teaches strategic management and social issues in management. She received her MBA (1979) and DBA from Boston University (1985). She has published extensively on inter-sector collaboration and corporate social performance in journals such as *The Academy of Management Journal*, *Strategic Management Journal*, *Human Relations*, and *Business and Society*, among others, and served as program and division chair of the Social Issues in Management Division of the Academy of Management. Her book on collaboration for school reform in the United States entitled *Not By Schools Alone* was published by Praeger in 1995 and her 1997 paper with Sam Graves entitled "Quality of

Management and Quality of Stakeholder Relations: Are They Synonymous?" published in *Business and Society*, won the 1997 Moskowitz Prize. She is currently co-chairing an Academy task force on service learning.

Mary E. Walsh is a Professor in the Department of Counseling, Developmental, and Educational Psychology in the Lynch School of Education at Boston College and Co-Director of the Boston College Center for Child, Family, and Community Partnerships.

1 ENGAGING NEW FORMS OF SOCIAL INQUIRY AND SOCIAL ACTION

Francine T. Sherman
Boston College Law School

William R.Torbert
*Boston College
School of Management*

During the twentieth century, the scientific enterprise, enshrined primarily within the world's great research universities, has increasingly come to be viewed as the central hero of modernity. The university itself has become, in Robert Pirsig's (1974) phrase, the church of modernity. With the advent in the 1990s of global capitalism, along with the Internet and the World Wide Web, scientific inquiry has paradoxically become the primary source of economic creativity and growth. We say this is paradoxical because the most authoritative paradigm of modern science—empirical positivism—attempts to divorce "value-free" scientific observing and theorizing from "value-driven" social action (see Torbert, Chapter 5). We are transitioning from national industrial economies to a global information economy, and at the same time our urban centers are concentrations of poverty, marginalization, and despair (Fleming, 1999). Ignoring this context, our dominant paradigms for research, thought, and action are still based on mechanistic, technological, uni-directional causation and unilateral power.

At the beginning of the twenty-first century, we are faced with questions that no longer yield to the paradigms of modern science, modern politics, and modern economics. Indeed, we are faced with questions that have been caused by the very successes of modern science, modern politics, and modern economics. Our challenge is to transform science to engage human experience so that it reflects and is relevant to the reality of most of the world's population. Only if research universities become "engaged universities" will they be able to continue the scientific enterprise to impact world problems in all their natural complexity (Boyer, 1990; Edgerton, 1996; hooks, 1994; Kellogg Commission, 1998). Correspondingly, it is that engagement that will allow universities to grow in their mission to train the next generation of scientists and professionals so that they are capable of continually pushing the boundaries of their and other disciplines in a way that is relevant to the increasing number and complexity of world problems. The task is not to somehow rescind the advances of modernity, but rather to preserve them while simultaneously transforming beyond their limitations.

The authors of this book are exploring this new, engaged, participative science in their community commitments, their teaching, and their scholarship. Our task, in which we invite readers to partner with us, is to learn how to practice new forms of social inquiry and social action that engage scholarship, curriculum and finally the entire university in partnerships with communities, making science relevant and alive (Fleming, 1999). Our path focuses more on human development than on material wealth, more on mutual transformation than on unilateral power to achieve one's current preferences, and more on spiritual communities of friendly inquiry than on fundamentalist communities of conviction. Our results, reflected throughout this book, challenge universities to push the boundaries of discipline, profession, status, and geography in a search for scientific engagement working toward a fundamental social justice (see Lerner, Chapter 3).

An example of the limitations of modern science and the need for engaged science and universities concerns the field of health care. The United States has the most advanced medical and drug research in the world and devotes a larger proportion of its wealth to health care than any other nation in the world. Sounds great! Yet its health care system is in crisis. Doctors, patients, nurses, hospital and HMO administrators, and the constantly growing proportion of uninsured citizens are anxious, frustrated, demoralized, and in pain about the system.

Why? Because a science that separates inquiry from action tells each of us very little about the ongoing first-person action inquiry we each need to conduct in our daily lives to make and keep ourselves healthy over our lifetimes (Torbert, 1997).

Why? Because a science that concentrates on physical causes of illness and physical causes of relief (pills, operations) gives us little purchase on the intersubjective causes of disease in dysfunctional families and workplaces (Karasek & Theorel, 1991).

Why? Because a science that separates objective fact from subjective meaning gives us no purchase on how to face death, so doctors and patients collude in spending one sixth of all health care dollars on preventing unpreventable death during the last two years of life.

Why? Because the expert, scientific rationality of doctors does not converge with the opportunistic, economic rationality of for-profit, market insurers. Moreover, our political representatives during the 1990s have not succeeded in articulating and enacting a publicly shared framework for health care policy (partly because so many voters currently distrust all logic other than that of the market).

University researchers bound within single disciplines and isolated from practice cannot develop analysis and proposals relevant to the multidimensional complexity of critical societal issues such as health care. "Wicked" real world problems exist in real time, across categories and require universities organized to support the multi-directional transfer of knowledge across disciplines and between researcher and practitioner (Huberman, 1999; Waddock, 1999). When medicine engages with psychology, sociology, education and economics we will address life long issues of maintaining individual and family health. When law engages with medicine, psychology, and business we will explore the dilemma of death and dying in an age when science can prolong life well beyond prior expectations. By interweaving action and research through the types of "outreach scholarship" and "action inquiry" described in the following chapters, universities will satisfy their moral and functional responsibility to generate and transmit knowledge relevant to the surrounding community (Fleming, 1999).

Universities engaged with communities in action-oriented research give voice to the disempowered in our society, promoting equity by including perspectives of those marginalized by history, class, race, and status (Freire, 1990). Nowhere is the need for an engaged science that is empowering more apparent that across the myriad issues that continue to keep children in poverty and achieving far less than is just in an increasingly global and affluent society (Kozol, 1991; 1998).

Despite the economic boom of the last decade in the United States, in 1998 14% of children lived in "high risk families" as defined by four or more of the following: 1) children not living with two or more parents; 2) children living in households headed by a high school drop out; 3) family income below the poverty line; 4) children living with parents who do not have steady, full-time employment; 5) families receiving welfare benefits; or 6) children without health insurance. Thirty-nine percent of fourth graders in 1998 scored below the basic reading level and 28% of eighth graders scored below the basic reading level (Annie E. Casey Foundation, 1998a). The United Stated leads developed nations in teen births (Annie E. Casey Foundation, 1998b). In 1997-1998, 3,024 children in America died from gunfire (Donohue, Schiraldi, & Ziedenberg, 1998), and the United States continues to defy the world human rights community by imposing the death penalty on minors, by prosecuting about 200,000 children a year in adult criminal courts and by incarcerating more than 11,000 children in prisons and other long-term adult correctional facilities (Amnesty International, 1998).

University supported engaged science, bridging the divide between research and practice, is the only paradigm with the potential to yield results relevant to children in the United States. Their problems engage medicine, law, psychology, sociology, history, economics, education and business (Kozol, 1996). Their problems require research and models of practice that fully incorporate their voices in a multi-dimensional and ongoing sharing of knowledge among community, practitioner and academe (Lopez, 1992; Kenny & Gallagher, Chapter 10; Sherman, Chapter 12; Walsh, et al., Chapter 6).

On a personal level, the path toward increased engagement between science and the reality of their lives and the lives of those with whom they study, brings with it the potential for transforming the lives of engaged scholars, professionals, and managers. All of us, are experiencing an accelerating work speed-up, generated by e-mail, the web, and the more general point that innovation in all industries depends, more than ever before, on access to new knowledge. Detached scientific study of this phenomenon is not going to solve each one's first-person issue of how to reconfigure our daily priorities in order to retain that sine qua non of creative research and professional development, leisurely free time. Nor will detached scientific study resolve our second-person issues of how to continue to invest more deeply in our most challenging and sustaining professional and personal relationships, in the face of the access that anyone now has to us through the web and e-mail. While many of these contacts are themselves creative opportunities, their sum total threatens our hard-won independence of thought and action.

In order to continually reshape our time alone, with others, and in relation to larger institutions, we require a type of scientific inquiry we can practice in each moment of living (Orlikowski & Yates, 1999; Torbert, 1991). We require, not just the detached, third-person science of modernity, but a science that spans self (first-person), face-to-face others (second-persons), and colleagues, clients and strangers at a distance (third-persons) and that integrates inquiry and action in each present moment (Reason, 1995; Torbert, 1999). All this is necessary if we wish to be able to go beyond merely entraining ourselves to the rhythm of the herd, or to persist in lonely deviance. All this is necessary if we wish to be able to act in a truly timely, transforming fashion within our particular social nexus.

By engaging in a mutually transforming way with communities in knowledge generation and transmission, universities become citizens contributing to power equalization and social justice. As seen in the chapters in this book, this engaged science tackles "wicked" real world problems and in doing so transforms individuals and universities in their missions of research, teaching and service.

THIS BOOK

This book illustrates, throughout its chapters, the humble hard work involved in moving beyond unilateral, expertise-based paradigms that separate detached ivory tower inquiry from messy, real-world action. The work is humble and hard because it aims at interweaving action and inquiry in real time. The work is humble and hard because it involves engaging oneself and ones own actions in the inquiry, and because it involves inviting others to influence the direction of action. Action becomes not just a matter of achieving a certain pre-conceived goal, but also of inquiring with others in real time about whether the initial vision is shared and whether there are incongruities among a given person's, team's, or organization's vision, strategies, performances, and assessments.

Through mutual vulnerability, mutual imaginativeness, mutual accountability, mutual self-correction, and mutual empowerment, trust is built, valid information about real-world conditions that matter to people is generated, and persons, teams, and organizations gradually transform. But such mutuality cannot be achieved simply by invoking it and advocating it. It must be learned by transforming beyond our current personal, economic, institutional, political, and scientific assumptions about how to inquire and how to act.

In Chapter 2, Allen Fairfax, a doctoral student in Sociology at Boston College who is currently on the faculty at Bowdoin College, demonstrates the years of work and self-questioning involved in gaining the trust of communities whose work he wishes his research to support, but whose previous experience of researchers on "data raids" he must overcome. At the same time, he struggles to discover what kind of research at what time can serve the communities' development. (A striking feature of mainstream scientific research that is not concerned with its direct contribution to the community or persons studied is that no theory of timing is necessary. Hence, it is not surprising that very little theorizing about what constitutes timely action has occurred [for recent exceptions, see Albert, 1995; Ancona & Chong, 1996; Torbert, 1984, 1991].)

In Chapter 3, Richard Lerner, formerly Director of the Boston College Center for Child, Family and Community Partnerships and currently at Tufts University, reflects on the challenges of, and the necessary conditions for, successfully establishing and sustaining interdisciplinary "outreach scholarship" centers at universities. Success in these ventures is particularly difficult to achieve today because such scholarship and community partnerships violate the departmental and reward structures of contemporary research universities.

Five centuries of unparalleled institutional success and longevity make university norms today difficult to change. Nevertheless, at the outset of the third millennium, universities are threatened as never before by for-profit teaching institutions (e.g., the University of Phoenix, Motorola University, etc.) and by for-profit research centers (e.g., at Microsoft, at Xerox Park, and so forth.). We can expect many consolidations and transformations within higher education itself over the next quarter century.

The question arises, "How can research and practice best interweave as a college or university faces the decision of how to reorganize itself?" In this case, it becomes unavoidably clear that research and practice become conjoined in the same persons. In Chapter 4, Severyn Bruyn, a member of the Sociology Department at Boston College and one of the original practitioners of the participant observation method of research at the United Fruit Company in Guatemala in the 1950s, imagines a future scenario in which the faculty of "Alpha Omega College" in the Midwest participates in determining the fate of their own institution.

The self-study process that Bruyn describes is brought to life in a different way later in Chapter 8. There, nine authors from the Teacher Education Department at Boston College collaborate to describe a two-year process of meeting to explore what they mean by "social justice" and how their evolving understanding should influence their curricular offerings. This chapter illustrates, not only the ongoing self-questioning and the surprising productivity that such self-study generates, but also the special rigor required to craft a document that validly and fairly represents the multiple voices of the community engaged in the study.

Chapter 5 is arguably the most abstract chapter of the book, offering a model of seven different paradigms of social science. Most scholars tend to be socialized into one or another of these paradigms during their graduate school years and to work from that paradigm for the rest of their careers. But this chapter shares the stories of two scholars who believe they have evolved through several of the paradigms during their careers. The chapter highlights the fundamental differences between twentieth century social science and new paradigms of inquiry that are emerging today. The dominant twentieth century social science paradigms (named Behaviorism, Gestalt Sociologism, Empirical Positivism, and Multi-Method Eclecticism in the chapter) have all separated scientific inquiry from social action in order to increase validity. The new paradigms of inquiry (Postmodern Interpretivism, Cooperative Ecological Inquiry, and Transformational Action Inquiry) explore how action and inquiry, as well as first-person subjectivity, second-person intersubjectivity, and third-person objectivity, interweave in everyday life. As the chapters in the second section illustrate, research in the action inquiry mode challenges and transforms the researchers themselves.

THE DIFFERENT AND TRANSFORMING MEANINGS OF COMMUNITY

In the action inquiry mode, researchers represented in this volume are not distant and disembodied from the communities they are researching. They are not merely studying tapes of stock market transactions or surveys filled out by anonymous hundreds of subjects. Nor are they merely participant observers, present on the scene of action, but not truly a member of the community in action. Instead they are observant participants seeking to join with the other participants in creating a community of inquiry where all are both participating and inquiring. Chapters 6 through 9 illustrate the process by which scholar/practitioners participate in co-creating "communities of inquiry within communities of social practice" (Argyris, Putnam & Smith, 1985; Torbert, 1976, 1991).

Chapter 6, co-authored by Mary Walsh and her colleagues at the Boston College School of Education and the Gardner Elementary School in nearby Allston-Brighton, wonderfully illustrates this point. It documents the seven-year evolving collaboration among social agencies, a local elementary school, and university researchers in developing a true "community school." During this period, each constituency changed its view of what it and the other constituencies had to offer and how good work could be done together. And they created an ongoing community of inquiry together, as indicated in small part by the co-authorship of this chapter by the school's principal.

Chapters 7, 8, and 9 describe other mini-communities of inquiry between lawyers and other professionals, among scholar-consultants helping one another study and increase their effectiveness, and within a teacher education department, as already mentioned. One way of thinking about the four chapters in this section is that they focus with increasing intensity on increasingly shorter moments of action inquiry, until, in Chapter 9, the reader is offered extensive portions of the actual transcript of a particular meeting, along with intensive interpretive analysis of particular comments.

This sequence can highlight for the reader how third-person, second-person, and first-person research/practice interweave. These four chapters are all written for third-person readers like you and usually rely on some third-person research methods, such as archival materials and tape recordings of meetings. Also, Chapter 6, in particular, describes the interaction over many years of a number of large, third-person institutions. At the same time, the chapters are all about developing second-person communities of inquiry and of practice, of which the authors are members. Moreover, the validity, not just of the data, but of the points of view, is subjected to second-person tests either by co-authorship among various participants, or by seeking feedback from other community members about what has been written.

Finally, the first-person challenges, vulnerabilities, and rewards of participating in such second-person communities of inquiry are well illustrated. These are no mere "academic" exercises. They are profound personal exercises that do not necessarily end in harmony, as Chapter 9 illustrates. More than this, both Chapter 8 and Chapter 9 offer impressions of the kind of awareness-and-moment-to-moment-action challenge that participating in such second-person dialogues offers each member. The engagement that such action generates is anything but an authoritative, self-satisfied, "professorial" contentment.

TRANSFORMING TEACHING AND SCHOLARSHIP

Although none of the first nine chapters directly describe how or how much the authors themselves or the communities with which they have interacted have been transformed by the experiences they describe, we can certainly tell, in at least Chapters 2, 6, and 8, that both the authors and the community in which they participate have been changed. So, the reader will not be surprised upon reaching Chapters 10 through 14 to find that, in offering more specific examples of teaching and research that open toward engagement, these authors describe change, not only in their students and the organizations in which their students participate, but also in themselves.

Chapter 10 describes members of an Education faculty developing service learning opportunities for their students. Chapter 11 describes a partnership among Sociology faculty, Management faculty, and business partners in creating a unique executive program called "Leadership for Change." Chapter 12 describes how a law clinic supports students interfacing with delinquent young women and the social systems that they, in turn, face.

Chapters 13 and 14 turn from teaching to research in this action inquiry mode. Chapter 13 describes a research project on the ten-year history of transformations of a Ph.D. program in Organizational Transformation, including some of the effects of the research itself on the department and on the researcher. Finally, Chapter 14 describes the history of developing ethical standards for research, as well as the very different political and ethical dilemmas that participatory action research in Guatemala or in elementary schools generates from those envisioned by current codes of research ethics.

Readers will notice strong commonalities among most of the book's chapters. Repeatedly, in different settings and within different disciplines, we read about an interweaving of teaching, researching, and creating communities of inquiry. Also, all of the experiments in this book have occurred at Boston College, where the development of the six-school Center for Child, Family, and Community Partnerships and the two-school Leadership for Change program, have engaged faculty and students in a cross-university sense of community of purpose that has, in turn, generated this book.

We hope that the following chapters communicate, not just descriptions, concepts, and programmatic structures that may be of use to readers, but a deep spirit of committed inquiry too. How to interweave inquiry and action—passion, compassion, and dispassion—subjectivity, intersubjectivity, and objectivity—will never be a technical question that someone can answer for others. This will be a question that more and more persons take on as an aspect of their own living inquiry, if it is to transform persons, organizations, and scientific inquiry on a society-wide basis.

REFERENCES

Albert, S. (1995). Towards a theory of timing: An archival study of timing decisions in the Persian Gulf war. *Research in Organizational Behavior*. Greenwich, CT: JAI Press. 17, 1-70.

Amnesty International (1998). Betraying the young: Human rights violations against children in the US justice system. New York, NY: Amnesty International USA.

Ancona, D. & Chong, C. (1996). Entrainment: Pace, cycle, and rhythm in organizational behavior. *Research in Organizational Behavior*. Greenwich, CT: JAI Press. 18, 251-284.

Annie E. Casey Foundation (1998a). *Kids count data book*. http://www.aecf.org/cgi-bin/kconline.cgi.

Annie E. Casey Foundation (1998b). *Kids count special report—When teens have sex: Issues and trends*. http://www.aecf.org/cgi-bin/kconline.cgi.

Aristotle (1984). *Nichomachean ethics*. Grinnell, IA: Peripatetic Press.

Argyris, C., Putnam, R. & Smith, D. (1985). *Action science: Concepts, methods and skills for research and intervention*. San Francisco, CA: Jossey-Bass.

Boyer, E.L. (1990). *Scholarship reconsidered: Priorities of the professoriate*. Princeton, NJ: The Carnegie Foundation for the Advancement of Teaching.

Castells, M. (1996, 1997, 1998). *The information age: Economy, society, and culture*. London: Blackwell.

Donohue, E., Schiraldi, V., Zeidenberg, J. (1998). *School house hype: School shootings and the real risks kids face in America*. Washington, DC: Justice Policy Institute.

Edgerton, R. (1996). Learning, teaching, technology: Putting first things first. *AAHE Bulletin*. 49(1) 3-6.

Fleming, J., (1999). Unpublished doctoral dissertation. *A typology of institutionalization for university-community partnerships at American universities and an underlying epistemology of engagement*. Berkeley, CA: University of California Graduate School of Education.

Freire, P. (1990). *Pedagogy of the oppressed*. New York: Continuum.

Hooks, B. (1994). *Teaching to transgress*. New York: Routledge.

Huberman, M. (1999). The mind is its own place: The influence of sustained interactivity with
        practitioners on educational researchers. *Harvard Educational Review.* 69 (3), 289-318.

Karasek, R. & Theorell, T. (1991). *Healthy work: Stress, productivity, and the reconstruction of
        working life.* New York: Basic Books.

Kellogg Commission on the Future of State and Land-Grant Colleges (1998). *Returning to our roots:
        The engaged institution.* Washington, DC: National Association of State Universities and
        Land-Grant Colleges.

Kozol, J. (1991). *Savage inequalities: Children in America's schools.* New York: Crown Publishers.

Kozol, J. (1996). *Amazing grace: The lives of children and the conscience of a nation.* New York, NY:
        Harper Perennial

Orlikowski,W. & Yates, J. (1999). It's about time: An enacted view of time in organizations.
        Cambridge, MA: MIT Sloan School Working Paper #4055.

Pirsig, R. (1974). *Zen and the art of motorcycle maintenance.* New York, NY: Morrow.

Reason, P. (1995). *Participation in human inquiry.* London: Sage.

Torbert, W. (1983). Executive Mind, timely action. *ReVision.* 4(1), 1-23.

Torbert, W. (1991). *The power of balance: Transforming self, society, and scientific inquiry.* Thousand
        Oaks, CA: Sage.

Torbert, W. (1997). Developing wisdom and courage in organizing and sciencing. S. Srivastva & D.
        Cooperrider (Eds.). *Organizational wisdom and executive courage.* San Francisco, CA: The New
        Lexington Press.

Torbert, W. (1999). The distinctive questions developmental action inquiry asks. *Anagement Learning,*
        30(2), 189-206.

Waddock, S. (1998) Educating holistic professionals in a world of wicked problems. *Applied
        Developmental Science,* 2(1), 40-47.

2 FROM DATA RAIDER TO DEMOCRATIC RESEARCHER
Learning To Become An Academic-Activist With The Merrimack Valley Project

Allen Fairfax
Boston College

Over the last several years I have been volunteering with the Merrimack Valley Project (MVP), researching this extensive community coalition as the subject of my doctoral dissertation for the Social Economy/Social Justice program at Boston College. The MVP is a neo-Alinsky community organizing effort working across four historic industrial cities in northeastern Massachusetts (Lowell, Lawrence, Haverhill, and Amesbury). As an institution-based coalition, the membership consists of congregations, labor unions, and other community groups. These organizations have provided hundreds of grassroots leaders who have conducted local and regional issue campaigns across the Valley. The MVP has been a place for me to research democratic process and institution-building dynamics at the community level (the academic focus of my dissertation) as well as a place to participate with a large group of citizens working for a more just and civil society.

However, my involvement with the MVP also represents part of my journey toward becoming what I understand to be an *academic-activist*. On this journey, I have been guided by the following kinds of questions: What does it mean to participate in community organizing *as an academic researcher*? What does it mean to do research in a community organizing context *as an activist*? Can the skills learned in a Ph.D. program be directly relevant to the practical world of day-to-day organizing? Or is the academic a relatively unwelcome guest at the table of community activism?

BECOMING AWARE OF THE PROBLEM

Before beginning graduate work at Boston College, I had been a community organizer in Atlanta and Valdosta, Georgia. My academic background in economics and social ethics had provided a broad general and abstract understanding of the problems of housing discrimination, homelessness, and poverty which I encountered in these organizing contexts. My interest in participatory democracy had led me to volunteer on an Israeli kibbutz and to read such books as Benjamin Barber's *Strong Democracy* (1984) several times through. I was fascinated by how to organize ways for ordinary people to have a regular voice in local issues that impacted their daily lives and I was very aware of the language/conceptual gap between academics and local practitioners. Local politics, I was discovering in the above settings, had "briar patch" qualities that are often difficult for academic research to fully conceptualize and communicate.

This gap between "what was written" and "what was practiced" was illustrated for me when I had the opportunity to discuss these issues with Michael Harrington, author of such books as *The Other America* (1962) and *The New American Poverty* (1984), who had come to Valdosta to speak to political science classes at the local college. Afterwards, in the living room of one of the board members of the community-based coalition for which I worked as the Organizer/Director, several of us discussed with him his understanding of poverty in the United States and talked about the situation of the poor in Valdosta and south Georgia. As the evening wore on, I asked him a question about what he thought it would mean to put some of these democratic principles into practice in a small southern city like Valdosta. He quickly responded "Oh, you know much more about that than I do." I was a bit taken aback, as I was aware of how much difficulty I was having thinking through how to implement participatory practices and how limited the possibilities seemed to be. I did not feel as though I knew all that much, and I found it a little disconcerting to think that this "expert" did not venture to outline a model for us to consider.

Contrary to the feelings of most activists (cf., Nyden & Weivel, 1992; Perkins & Wandersman, 1990), at that time I really was hoping that Michael Harrington would provide us with some mix of conceptual and practical guidance. To his credit, he did not even pretend to know how to really implement his understanding of democracy in our context. Nevertheless, I was left with the feeling that in reflecting on our local actions, we could have benefited from his historical and comparative knowledge as well as his conceptualizing abilities. Had the approach we were taking been effective in other places and times? What were some possible models for understanding small city southern politics? How could we research some of these issues in a timely and efficient manner?

Michael Harrington seemed to be resisting the role of expert. However, I believe we did need someone like him to be part of an ongoing dialogue. Luckily, I had had some of this dialogue in personal conversations with two local faculty members who participated in the organization as board members. Yet, even though I benefited personally from these discussions, their direct participation and impact was limited to the normal roles of the organization. They were mostly participating as concerned citizens, not as academics. Was the academic role really limited to "observing" in the midst of actions, and then sitting back and discussing/writing up a "case study" which "evaluated" what went right or wrong? Was there a voice for academia in the midst of the action itself? It seemed to me that there were quite a few potential roles for academics to play, but it would require a different, more direct involvement in the organization. This role would need to be one that was away from the "outside observer" (or even participant observation) model so prevalent in academic research. (Though I did not know of it at the time, I was angling toward the notions of "observant participation" and "action inquiry" discussed in Chapters 5, 8, and 13 of this volume).

Such questions and reflections eventually led me to the Social Economy/Social Justice (SE/SJ) program at Boston College. I wanted time to reflect on what I had experienced as an organizer and to learn about building participatory democratic institutions at the local/regional level. In particular, I hoped to learn how to integrate academic and activist roles and to bridge the gap between the world of the discipline and the "thorny" world of the local polity. While the emphasis on participatory democracy in the program has provided the academic training I desired, the Merrimack Valley Project provided the advanced community organizing model in which to participate. My time in the MVP has involved a re-naming of my role by the grassroots leadership from that of "student intern" to that of "senior intern." It is that transformation of my role that is the subject of this paper—a story of building trust with the grass-roots leadership and staff of the MVP and it is also a story of progress toward a discovery of my own voice and role *as an academic* in the midst of a community organizing effort.

COMMUNITY MISTRUST OF DATA RAIDERS

A major obstacle for academics who are trying to find a useful role in community organizing efforts is a pre-existing basic mistrust by community activists. Many organizers have had negative experiences with academics who offer to help/research a community group. Clark (1980) characterizes these forays into community settings as "data raids":

> The traditional primary task of the university is the disinterested pursuit of knowledge. Unlike the physical and biological sciences, however, the social sciences cannot be indifferent to their objects of study. People, both individually and collectively, will reject social science, and deny access to critical settings unless they see some overlap of purpose or interest between themselves and social scientists. *Data raids* [emphasis added] are too clearly one-sided and instrumental; they are unlikely to be tolerated for long, other than in trivial areas. (Clark, 1980)

Data raiders, then, are those researchers who come into a situation appearing to offer some type of expertise to a community group that is committed to *solving a social problem.* The assistance may be welcomed (and the academic is often personally committed to solving the social problem as well), but when the research work is complete, the data raider returns with the plundered knowledge to be processed at the academic gristmill. If an analysis is given back to the community group at all, it is likely to have been written in academic jargon inaccessible to those who have been "studied," and also to have a critical quality which may leave communities with the feeling that they were an object of experimentation like rats in a maze (which to some extent they were). The researchers may feel they have performed an invaluable service by offering an "objective" scientific analysis of the situation while the "objects" of the study may not even recognize themselves in what they read. By what methods were the questions framed? Was there an opportunity for dialogue about what the researcher was observing? Did the research provide a valuable learning opportunity for the community group? Were they simply being "evaluated"?

After presenting this concept of "data raiders" to a gathering of Boston College academics and administrators discussing civil society, I was asked to offer a more in-depth appraisal in a seminar setting. While I had used the term "data raiders," what was inadvertently published in the advertisements for the seminar was the phrase "data rapers." While I do not agree with the violence explicit in this label, it does suggest something about the relationship that organizers and community leaders fear might develop when they "date" an academic! Are the rights and purposes of the community organizing effort going to be respected? Are they going to be "used" in order to further the academic's own career? Will they end up afterwards with a subjective sense that they were violated? Did they lose their voice by not being able to respond to the critique? While the researcher may adeptly use their own words, did they lose their voice when it came to how those words were finally framed?

THE MVP EXPERIENCE WITH OUTSIDE RESEARCHERS

The Merrimack Valley Project has had some experience with journalistic and academic researchers. One article, written for *The Nation* (1994), carried some hope, from the leadership's perspective, of providing some welcome exposure about many of the positive aspects of the work of the MVP. In addition, there have been two academic-based research efforts. The first was a master's thesis (written during the early history of the MVP) focusing on how and why the MVP organizing model was not immediately connecting with some of the ethnic/immigrant groups in the Valley. The second academic effort has been my own dissertation research in which I have sought to understand how the organizing efforts of the MVP are affecting the practice of participatory democracy in the local/regional polity.

The article written for *The Nation* (1994) is more than a simple journalistic account of a single public event in the MVP's experience. It resembles academic research in that its author/researcher came to a number of actions, meetings, and leadership training events over a several month period in addition to interviewing some of the leaders. He asked for access to the MVP to write an article on the tough economic circumstances that poor people were up against, creating some expectation/hope by some of the leadership that this was also an opportunity to portray the MVP as a stellar example of how people were successfully addressing these tough circumstances.

In my own reading of the article, I found that to some extent these expectations were met. There were some good things written in the article about the work of the

MVP. The staff and executive leadership of the MVP, however, voiced significant concerns about both the general tenor of the article and some specifics. Immediately after its publication one of the Executive Council members, Paul Dettman (a retired urban planner quoted in the article), wrote a draft letter in which he comments: "try as [the author] may, the picture that he paints [of the MVP], taken as a whole, is not a positive one." He criticizes the author for portraying the MVP as a

> fragile institution operating in a fragile economic and social environment. The reality is, however, that, even though it is relatively new, the Project already has a solid base, and it faces a Valley which, although it will certainly change for the worse as well as for the better, is not going to do so radically overnight.

In regard to statements in the article about the strong role of the Staff Director, Ken Galdston, in training the leadership and guiding the organization, Dettman comments:

> To be sure, the Project's Staff Director does all these things in a very skillful and effective way, but the picture of the volunteer members which emerges from the author's description is that of a troop of trained dogs who jump through the hoops which Ken Galdston holds in front of them. And the picture of the Project which emerges is that of an organization which has a presentable front but nothing behind it but the Staff Director and, therefore, one which would presumably collapse if he were not there to keep it going. The fact of the matter is, however, that, although the Staff Director does provide a considerable share of the Project's energy and direction, its members are not mere "tabula rasas," but a group of thinking people who provide solidity to the organization by bringing to it a substantial amount of experience, skill, and vision of their own.

Dettman was particularly incensed by the final assessment of the MVP at the end of the article. In this, the author, George Packer, writes:

> It is difficult to imagine a better organization or better people emerging from the battered Merrimack Valley. The project has already won some battles and prevented total loss in others; if it doesn't arrest a decay that's almost as old as the century, it will have done no worse than anyone could expect. And it will leave behind fifty or a hundred or 300 people who at least share an idea that their destinies in the valley are somehow connected (Packer, 1994, p. 904).

Dettman contests this conclusion and the general tenor of the article by pointing out that Packer fails to distinguish between "problems" (which are more than the MVP can "deal with") and " issues" ("something that is wrong but which the organization can do something about"). Thus,

> The Project deals in "issues," not in "problems," and its success or
> failure should be judged by the standard of what it seeks to do.
> George's article makes the mistake of assuming that we deal in
> "problems" and takes the position that, because we cannot reverse
> the Valley's "de-industrialization" or stamp out its crime, we are
> fighting a losing battle. The truth is that the Project is not trying to
> solve either of these "problems." Rather, we are seeking to make
> the lives of Merrimack Valley residents better than they are now by
> making them more secure, more decent, more fulfilling than they
> would otherwise be. This is the standard by which the Project's
> success or failures should be judged. By this standard, we are not a
> bunch of ineffective "do-gooders" who are engaged in
> strengthening our inner characters by courageously fighting a
> losing battle against insurmountable odds, but members of an
> outgoing and effective organization which is having a significant
> impact for the better in the struggling world of the Merrimack
> Valley.

This view seems to have been shared by most of the leadership who read the article.
However, this letter did not get sent to the "Letters to the Editor." After discussion, a
less critical and more "civil" version was eventually sent from the MVP President in
which she focused on various aspects of the Project's work which were not covered
in the article. Unfortunately, this letter was sent too late to be published in a timely
fashion.

Six months after the article's publication, another letter was sent to *The Nation*
by the succeeding MVP President. He expressed his "surprise and disappointment"
that their "Letter to the Editor" was not published. He comments that,

> we believe that the article missed the heart of the Merrimack
> Valley Project's structure, power and work. Failing to publish our
> letter has meant a lost opportunity for your readers to get the full
> picture of what we do and the importance to the lives of thousands
> of Valley residents.

The comment back from the Letter's page editor about why it was not published
expressed regret and noted that the "letter came a full two months after the
publication of our article, and was a bit long." Though these observations from the
Letters editor are true, it does illustrate the essential source of the problem when
outside researchers offer to write about a community organization. That is, that there
is very little opportunity for dialogue and feedback to the researcher and even when
a letter which goes through proper discussion in the participatory framework of a
community group is complete, it may be sent "too late" to be included in the only
dialogue space available (i.e., the Letters to the Editor). And then the letter must also
not be "too long." In this loss of voice, the institutional constraints of the journalist's
deadline and of the particular format of letters in response gives a power to the
outside researcher which seems to be at the heart of the problem of community

mistrust. There is a sense of having been the victim of a "data raid." This dynamic is similar to that encountered by academic researchers in being able to provide a dialogical voice to those who have been the "objects of research."

Community mistrust toward outside researchers can also stem from the researcher going into a situation and (probably unwittingly) looking for evidence which supports a pre-conceived notion which is motivating the write-up. Thus, perhaps the original motivation for *The Nation* article was to paint a picture of how de-industrialization was wrecking everything in its path, and to show how even this large community group could not arrest its path of destruction. Perhaps this was fulfilling a political perspective expected by the editor/readers of *The Nation* but was unfair to the work of the MVP leadership. As illustrated above, many community members were feeling relatively empowered by this organizing effort and were not feeling disempowered by unrealistic expectations of what could be accomplished (i.e., stopping deindustrialization in a few short years). Thus, the article as written reflected back to the leadership an "evaluation" which they did not share. The outside researcher certainly has the right to his/her opinion, but by not giving the leadership an adequate chance to engage in a collective dialogue with the author, a "distorted picture" may have been painted, which went out across the "nation" and potentially could have had a negative impact on funding sources and the collective identity of the MVP leadership.

In contrast to *The Nation* article, the master's thesis written about the MVP and also my dissertation work have represented a different approach to research with a community group. In an interview with Ken Galdston, he comments:

> Laura Buxbaum [author of the master's thesis] came to us as someone who could be helpful to us in a research intern role. Now that's different from someone who comes in and asks if they can do a thesis. You could have somebody coming from an academic department saying "I want to study what you are doing, and ultimately, why should you let me do it? Well, because you will learn, people will learn, etc." What we have in Laura and you, is someone saying I can be helpful to you in an internship role in carrying out some things, and by the way, I'm also writing this paper, and this will allow me to get to know you better, and then I'll be able to take it over to the academic side, and maybe at some point by the effort I put into reflecting on the organization and comparing it to other things that will help you too . . . With you, with Laura, there's just been some assumption that you are sort of kindred spirits that want to see this done, to develop, that you have some knowledge of this, have done something like it, and want to use this experience to go out and do more, that you are not "voyeurs," you're not simply doing this because you got a grant, and you're trying to find out something "sexy". And not to be harsh, but George Packer is a novelist and a journalist and was not presenting himself as somebody who is doing this because he was going to go on and do other organizing or popular education.

Laura's participation in the MVP led to an analysis that was "right on" according to Galdston and was instructive to the way the Project was organizing with recent immigrant groups. Laura and I have both participated as "volunteer organizers" and thus created a mutually beneficial social exchange relationship with the MVP. In addition, my role has expanded through my most recent research in which I have convened leaders to reflect on the role of their member organizations to the MVP as a whole (case study, discussed below).

These kinds of research roles represented a way of doing "relational research" (in contrast to that done for the article in *The Nation*) which apparently have overcome the problem of community mistrust. Through this "relational" method, a basic trust with the leadership and organizers was established. Of course, this type of research took time, just as any relationship does, but it did provide the context through which Laura Buxbaum and I could judge the meaning and validity of various actions and comments in the MVP experience. The leadership could trust that our observations were grounded in the knowledge of them as real people growing along with the MVP as citizens in an expanding civil society. As Galdston has said: "You were not simply standing on the outside observing."

ACADEMIC APPROACHES TO OVERCOMING COMMUNITY MISTRUST

What solutions have other academics offered for overcoming community mistrust? A common way to do this has been to make the research more palatable in various ways while urging the practitioner to recognize the legitimacy of the academic's research. For example, Perkins and Wandersman conducted an evaluation study of an extensive community organization in New York City. They note that the "primary end of a practitioner's work is action; that of a scientist's is understanding" (1990). This is a basic value conflict that can create "mistrustful partners" in any serious research project. Perkins and Wandersman point out that this is especially true in a study which has, as theirs did, potential personnel evaluation implications. This potential impact on personnel was a particularly significant barrier to building trust. In reflecting on their experience, they offer the following advice:

> Probably the most important lesson researchers should learn in working with community leaders, organizers and other practitioners is that they deserve a great deal of respect. They may not always appreciate the utility of empirical knowledge as much as the researcher and sometimes may feel threatened by researchers. But, in general, they can understand what researchers are trying to do and can help them do it even better. They are invaluable allies to have when planning and conducting a study. In respect for community members' understanding of the research, it is important that instead of just taking the data and running, the researcher gives something back to the setting or population being studied. It makes sense that if one gives people in an organization a hand in the research, they will understand it better, identify with the project, develop a sense of common purpose with each other and with the

researcher, and in addition they will be more likely to read and apply the results of the study.

In this evaluation approach, Perkins and Wandersman come as far as recognizing the value of the practitioners *to the study*, with a belief that this participation will make it more likely that the evaluation will be actually applied. Essentially, the advice is to forge a partnership, convincing the practitioners to appreciate the value of the research and to understand the academic's need to "conduct research in a manner that adheres to conventionally accepted research methodology" (1990). However, in return, researchers need a strong dose of realism and "must also realize that, from the practitioner's perspective, professional and organizational constraints are ultimately more important than research design considerations" (1990).

There is certainly a need for evaluation studies in certain situations, but from the perspective of overcoming mistrust, Perkins and Wandersman's advice is best described as "making the best of a bad situation." The goal seems to be to make the research "medicine" as palatable as possible, and to convince the practitioners of the objective value of the research. They clearly are accepting the legitimacy of the work of *both* the researcher and the practitioner. In other words, they are accepting the basic value conflict, and offering advice on how to ease the tensions by paying attention to each other's needs. This is a significant first step in developing a more mutual relationship between research and practice.

However, it is difficult to read the articles related to their research effort (cf., Kaye, 1990; and other articles in Wandersman & Florin, 1990) and not see the problem as one emerging from a basic barrier erected by a methodological ideology. Thus, Perkins and Wandersman, in reflecting on the issue of power in the community organizations being studied, note that:

> Since community organizations are almost inevitably as "political" internally as they are externally, their staff, clients and advocates are often suspicious of researchers' motives. Researchers, accustomed to remaining neutral, often find themselves in the uncomfortable position of being seen only as either allies or enemies. Often, organization leaders are already convinced of the importance of their group's work and cannot accept a researcher who wishes to remain nonpartisan and detached in evaluating their success. Sometimes practitioners view a study as a "test" they are at risk of failing. Group leaders may even oppose the publication of politically sensitive evaluation results (Perkins & Wandersman, 1990, p. 35-36).

It is this quest to be neutral which I suggest is a key factor in a community's mistrust of academic researchers. In this positivist approach, academic researchers seem to have an implicit notion that there is an independent truth about the organization which can be discovered. However, an approach from a constructivist epistemology would recognize that the truth, which is found in this way, is simply the truth of the researchers and less of an "objective truth" than they suppose. For example, in the above quotation the researchers illustrate their own suspicions and distrust of the organizers as they discuss the organizers' suspicions of them. Is the researchers' concern to retain unilateral control over their methodology, writing, and conclusions and to distance themselves from relational influence any less political (albeit differently so) than the organizers? Do the researchers show any greater willingness to explore the effectiveness of their approach, or are they any less certain about the importance of their work, than the organizers? While Perkins and Wandersman describe a research process which is very grounded in the daily life of the organization, one wonders whether enough "dialogue" was generated through the process which would "construct" a new collective truth for the organization or for the researchers.

One of the organizers for the community organization also contributed an article about this experience (Kaye, 1990). In it she described many positive aspects of the research effort (cf., Wandersman & Florin, 1990). However, Kaye relates:

> As the research findings began to materialize, lengthy meetings began to occur at the Citizens Committee between research team members and staff to discuss the findings and their use in our work. During these meetings, the Block Booster data began to take on an "untouchable" quality in that it could not be challenged because it was scientific. The effect of this elevation of the research findings was to constantly devalue and undermine the experience and knowledge of the community-organizing practitioners on staff. The wealth of knowledge and skills that community organizers have developed over the past 70 years through fieldwork trial and error is well documented in books, periodicals, and manuals from groups and individuals nationally. The "science" of organizing, however, became more and more submissive to the "science" of research as the project progressed. This created great antagonism and only served to further reinforce the stereotype of "ivory tower academics" versus seasoned community-organizing practitioners. Were it not for the sensitivity towards this issue of the New York research team members, it is doubtful that the project would have been as fruitful for either the Citizens Committee or the Block Booster Team (Kaye, 1990, p. 155-156).

She concludes:

> [it] is essential that community researchers continually recognize the value of community-organizing practitioners as well as grass-roots community leaders, the recipients and subjects of community research. Both parties should be actively involved in all phases of any quality research project and their knowledge, years of experience, and perspectives incorporated into both research design and implementation (Kaye, 1990, p. 156).

An openness to re-framing issues by all parties, which would have been explicit in a constructivist methodological approach, may have minimized these conflicts and created a more relational research process. Without it, it is difficult to see how at least some aspects of a "data raid" would not emerge. In this situation, fortunately, it looks like the dialogue did occur, however begrudgingly, and the research results were useful to the growth of the community organization.

Another approach, articulated by Nyden and Weivel, also assesses the relationship between practitioners and researchers as a "well-established love-hate affair" (1992, p. 43). They also point out that tensions arise because of insensitivity to each other's needs. As they see it, the problem is that the researcher fails to make the value of the research clear and, in addition, does not make an effort to teach research skills to the community leadership. Furthermore, academics are trained to study problems much more than they are trained to seek solutions, and they may write up the results of studies in academic jargon, which is often inaccessible to the "objects" of the study. Nyden and Weivel's advice on *how to make the research more palatable* is to teach research skills to the community leadership and learn how to better communicate with them:

> While it is recognized that years of training and experience as a researcher cannot be imparted to community organizers in a relatively short period of time, researchers should maximize community involvement in the research process itself at the same time as they "translate" pertinent past research knowledge and methodologies into a language and description relevant to the project at hand (Nyden & Weivel, 1992, p. 45).

This is an important step for academic researchers to take. It begins to move the methodological stance beyond the image of the objective outsider, and toward that of teacher and partner in the community enterprise. They point out that researchers typically take "advantage of a CBO's needs, doing the research, and using it for discourse-oriented ends rather than community improvement" (Nyden & Weivel, 1992, p. 47). In contrast, something needs to be done "for" and "with" the community group in question.

Thus, Nyden and Weivel clearly recognize the problems of community mistrust, and solve it primarily by making sure something tangible is offered back to the community, designing research to be about something the community needs to know (discovered through initial dialogues and ongoing participation), and teaching a collaborative/participatory form of research skills to the community leaders. They argue, however, some level of objectivity must be maintained in order to give the research results more legitimacy and perhaps become useful as a political resource for the practitioner. Thus, this model also seems to accept the "basic value conflict" between researchers and practitioners. In so doing, Nyden and Weivel's "collaborative research" also seems to be a (albeit sophisticated and authentic) way of helping practitioners swallow the research " medicine." It does not seem to offer a clear-cut way to get beyond the basic value conflict imposed by a positivist methodology.

THE PROMISE OF ACTION/PARTICIPATORY RESEARCH

In my own search I have had strong hopes that the field of action/participatory research (A/PR) would prove to be an enabling approach as I seek to weave together the roles of academic and activist. Does the "relevant" research touted by this approach offer some promise of overcoming community mistrust of academic researchers? By practicing action/participatory research, what contributions can an academic make *as an academic* to the change focus of a community organizing effort? Elden and Chisholm define *action research* as

> a cyclical inquiry process that involves diagnosing a problem situation, planning action steps, and implementing and evaluating outcomes. Evaluation leads to diagnosing the situations anew based on learnings from the previous activities cycle. A distinctive feature of action research is that the research process is carried out in collaboration with those who experience the problem or their representatives (Elden & Chisholm, 1993, p. 124).

Gaventa highlights the role of those who are researched even more in his definition of *participatory research*:

> Participatory research seeks to break down the distinction between the researchers and the researched and the subjects and objects of knowledge production through the participation of the people-for-themselves in the attainment and creation of knowledge. In the process, research is viewed not only as a means of creating knowledge; it is simultaneously a tool for the education and development of consciousness as well as mobilization for action." (Gaventa, 1991, p. 121-122)

In Gaventa's words, we can hear a different way of speaking about what Torbert in Chapter 5 of this volume calls first, second, and third person research/practice. Gaventa's "education and development of consciousness" corresponds to first person research/practice; his "mobilization for action" reflects second person research/practice; and his "creation of knowledge" parallels third person research/practice.

In these three purposes of participatory research, we can clearly see an attempt to merge/integrate the roles of the academic and activist. But this is much easier said than done. One academic who has addressed the relevance of participatory research to a similar organizing case as the MVP remarks that:

> By and large the people [that participatory researchers] not only want, but feel committed to work with, have no time, interest, or need to work with them. This is not to say that participatory research is without value; quite to the contrary *its potential is quite substantial if it reinforces an existing process of social investigation and action* [emphasis added]; but participatory

researchers must bring more to the table than their time and passion.

The *fundamental dilemma* [emphasis added] is that participatory researchers who want to work with marginalized communities must demonstrate how their work is significant for the lives, needs and aspirations of the residents of these communities (Nash, 1993, p. 54).

This is quite a dilemma. From my own experience, while I have provided research assistance (e.g., gathering socio-economic data and descriptive examples from academic literature and the news media about MVP-type issue campaigns) for the MVP at various times, and participated as a community organizer at others, most of my efforts have not been the integrating experiences between my academic purpose and activist concerns for which I had hoped.

This frustration arises from some essential differences between what I will call Organizing-Based Research (OBR) and a more Academic-Based Action/Participatory Research (A/PR). OBR is a form of A/PR, which is regularly practiced by the staff and grassroots leadership of MVP-type organizations. The methodology of OBR arises out of the concrete research questions which emerge from the immediate needs of an issue campaign (e.g., contesting the closing of a public housing project or creating a new afterschool program across a city). Thus, leaders will discuss an issue and decide what are some key pieces of information they need to have to move forward in an issue campaign. In the public housing project example, this may involve the leadership of the housing project (along with other MVP leaders) researching the availability of housing options for displaced tenants in the surrounding area and what resources would be available for obtaining this housing, as well as assessing the feasibility of the plans for the area once the housing project is gone. The leadership scramble to get as much of this information as they can within the necessary time frame. This data is then subject to collective reflection, meaning is assigned, power relations are assessed and what results is *actionable knowledge*. The leadership will then act on this knowledge and will continually reflect on the new information they learn in the process. As appropriate, this will then generate more actionable knowledge, and the process continues.

On the one hand, this is clearly a process which fits into an A/PR schema. The initial research leading to the actionable knowledge is then "tested" through actions and the results are then collectively validated. It feeds into Gaventa's (and other's) notions of participatory research in that it involves the creation of knowledge, the development of consciousness, and mobilization for action.

On the other hand, OBR never can fully satisfy the concerns of an academic-based A/PR schema. At the least, there are problems associated with sampling, with asking the right questions, and with developing appropriate ways to measure the results of actions. Moreover, there is very little time in the midst of an issue campaign to do these things. Personally, the most it seemed that I could ever contribute to these discussions was a suggestion or two. I was always frustrated thinking that I needed to have things more "controlled" and "organized" for the knowledge gained from the OBR to be directly relevant to my academic purposes (i.e., to become dissertation-worthy knowledge). The organizing/OBR process is very messy; very dependent on finding key information quickly and coming to a collective intuitive feeling for its meaning. There is generally not much time for a researcher to attend to the academic validity of the knowledge (even when collective validity is emphasized as in an A/PR academic methodology).

A second difference between OBR and academic-based A/PR is that the questions asked by academic-activists are often at a different structural/abstract level than those asked by the leadership of a community organizing OBR effort. Thus, while trying to be inductive in my dissertation research as to what I would learn from the MVP in a number of areas, there is no denying that my own "academic interest" was in gaining a better understanding of how these kinds of organizing practices might be having an impact on the institutionalized rules which govern local/regional politics in the Merrimack Valley. The questions raised through OBR were never discursively formulated in this way, and I never felt I could "impose" my more abstract questions into their very concrete discussions. While relevant in a way to what the MVP was trying to accomplish, my research "interest" always seemed secondary to the immediate needs of the issue campaign. I have had to wait for my most recent dialogical interview effort for the leadership to engage in a combination of individual and collective reflections on the range of academic concepts I had been formulating (through my participant observation of their OBR processes and general organizational practices) [see the case study below].

A third difficulty for academics trying to be involved in the OBR process is the "storied" quality of the knowledge that is generated. Stories are the language of community organizing, while academics seem to be better trained to utilize the language of abstract concepts. Larry B. McNeil, an organizer with the Industrial Areas Foundation, comments:

> My own 23 years of organizing lead me increasingly to a rather simple definition of what this is about. Organizing is the active unearthing of people's individual stories, the collective examination of the meaning of those stories in light of our shared story, and the opportunity to write new endings to both our individual and collective stories (McNeil, 1995:19; also cf., Speer & Hughey, 1995; McMillan, et al., 1995).

After an academic has finished writing up his/her research, often utilizing very processed abstract language, the leadership of a community group may not recognize themselves because they have been trained to conceptualize in terms of stories. Though community leaders may discuss such academic-friendly concepts as "interests" and "power," the analysis is often couched in a very storied language, which is not easily translatable into logical abstract concepts. The story as a whole (i.e., the full plot line) is needed in order to convey the meaning to the community group.

From my organizing and research experience, I would argue that this story-based way of conceptualizing experiences is one key to the success of community organizing because it is how people reconstitute their individual and collective understandings of themselves as citizens. In general, I would concur with Somers and Gibson that "social life is itself *storied* and that narrative is an ontological condition of social life" (Somers & Gibson, 1994). Thus, I am suggesting that academic treatises need to be very attentive to the language of story so that the "objects of research" will also benefit from the finished product.

When Nash writes that the value of participatory research is "quite substantial if it reinforces an existing process of social investigation and action" (Nash, 1993), I believe he is in essence urging academics to get involved in OBR, and forget all the ideology of a more formal A/PR. In his assessment of why "participatory researchers in the United States have been so dramatically unsuccessful" (Nash, 1993, p. 53), Nash writes:

> The problem is that participatory researchers as a group, especially those potential researchers who are new to PR, lack the time, contacts and savvy to create a community-based organization as the necessary vehicle for the unique participatory and social action requirements of their chosen form of research. *As a result they must convince an existing group of the value participatory research can bring to their current work* [emphasis added]. While many of these groups are already skeptical about research in general, participatory researchers face the additional burden of having to demonstrate the value of an approach that: 1) is relatively untried in the United States, 2) is not valued within their own profession, and 3) does not even appear to require the services of an academic. Consequently, well-intentioned participatory researchers bent on transforming academics' relationships to marginalized communities can easily find themselves in a kind of limbo between an academy that generally views participatory research with something between apathy and outright hostility *and a marginalized community that is either actively pursuing its own agenda with little time or inclination for frivolous academic research or that has no clear agenda or analysis of its needs and hence offers little immediate potential for mutual research and meaningful collective action* [emphasis added] (Nash, 1993, p. 53).

In order to deal with this situation, he offers the following advice:

> The most effective way for potential participatory researchers to [be relevant] . . . is by forgetting that participatory research exists and concentrating on identifying a community's needs, understanding its values and building relationships with its residents. *In other words, participatory researchers need to learn how to become organizers* [emphasis added]. If they are successful in this effort, concerns about isolation and the lack of a power base will become moot and they will finally be able to do the best kind of participatory research, that which is truly a process of social investigation, education and collective action (Nash, 1993, p. 54).

While I agree with much of this perspective, I wonder if there really is no place for academic-based A/PR in the world of community organizing, or does it just need to incorporate the realities of OBR into its methodology? It may be that Nash's admonition to become an organizer is at the heart of what academics may need to learn in order to engage in "actionable" research. But, questions still remain. *What does it mean for an academic to become an organizer? Is the academic role suppressed? Are the questions I was asking about participatory democratic practices and how they might be institutionalized in the Merrimack Valley simply irrelevant? Is organizing really "enough"? Is there still some need for a more organic understanding of what it means to be an "academic-activist"? Can academic-activists find ways to help with the quality of the OBR itself? Can academic-activists find ways to contribute to the extension of OBR into regular ways of reflecting on organizational or political context concerns?*

I believe that the kinds of questions I am asking of the MVP (and other academics might ask of other community organizations) may be relevant to the long-term health of the MVP. There are structural/framing/contextual questions that need to be asked, and the questions may then become "when" and "how" to address them to/with the community group in question. To a certain extent, for my research with the MVP, it may have been that I was mainly asking the right questions at the wrong time. For example, after years of experience, the leaders of the MVP have begun to define some of the ongoing structural concerns in which I was initially interested. This has led, so far, to a recent opportunity to engage the experienced leaders of the Lawrence chapter in a participatory research project which has involved a combination of stories and more abstract discussions about the "general" problems they face in "base-building" within their member organizations (see the case study below).

CONTRIBUTIONS OF PARTICIPATORY ACTION RESEARCH (PAR)

In recent years, both the epistemology and practice of an "action turn" in social science research has received increasing attention (Argyris, Putnam, & Smith, 1985; Reason, 1994; Reason and Torbert, 1999; Torbert, 1991). The search for an organic approach to academic and activist research has been best expressed through the ideals of the Participatory Action Research (PAR) approach emerging from the Third World. Fals-Borda has advocated the notion of a " people's science" which

> is formally constructed in its own terms, with its own practical rationality and empirical systematization and its own way of institutionalizing, accumulating and transmitting knowledge from one generation to the next. This science does not hinge on Cartesian or Kantian rationality (Fals-Borda, 1991b, p. 151).

Recognizing the validity and possibility of a "people's science" allows the development of a dialogical model of research which attempts to "break up the subject/object binomial" (Fals-Borda, 1991b). In this model it is the responsibility of both external (i.e., academic-activists) and internal agents of change to "contribute their own knowledge, techniques and experiences to the transformation process"

(Fals-Borda, 1991a). The goal is to create a "dialectical tension" which can only be resolved through praxis:

> The sum of knowledge from both types of agents . . . makes it possible to acquire a much more accurate and correct picture of the reality that is being transformed. Therefore, academic knowledge combined with popular knowledge and wisdom may result in total scientific knowledge of a revolutionary nature which destroys the previous unjust class monopoly (Fals-Borda, 1991a, p. 4).

This concept of *total scientific knowledge* presents the academic-activist with the opportunity to find a place at the table of community activism. On the one hand, the concept suggests that academic knowledge by itself is fairly limited in enabling effective community change. On the other hand, people's knowledge is also limited in that the ability to grasp the structural features of social change is constrained by the more tacit and immediate perceptions which constitute the "people's science." The key is to find research methods that bridge these two types of knowledge.

To do this requires the creation of a subject/subject relationship by academic-activists with the previous "objects of research," one which "reduces the differences between bourgeois intellectuals and grassroots communities, between elite vanguards and base groups, between experts (technocrats) and direct producers, between bureaucracies and their clients, between mental and manual labor" (Fals-Borda, 1991a). It is a basic matter of transforming the social relations between academics and activists. From the Gramscian tradition, Fals-Borda argues that aspiring academic-activists should become

> organic intellectuals of the working classes without creating permanent hierarchies. The proof of the success of these people's intellectuals can be seen in the fact that eventually they become redundant in their places of work, that is, the transformation processes continue even without the physical presence of external agents, animators or cadres (Fals-Borda, 1991a, p. 5-6).

It seems likely that there are many community organizers in this country who may be nearer to this ideal than most academics. If so, then it may be prudent for academic-activists (as much as possible) to participate as organizers in order to do effective action/participatory research. From a PAR perspective, the goal is for both the community organizer and academic-activist to help facilitate the construction of *total scientific knowledge* as an essential condition for moving toward long-term structural change. For various reasons discussed below, there may be organizational and time constraints as to how far professional community organizers can go in teaching/communicating these more abstract structural concepts in the midst of the day-to-day practices of the organization (even when well-versed in an academic understanding of the concepts). Thus, there may be a potential role that academic-activists can play conceptualizing by virtue of standing with one foot in the realm of academia and the other in the world of community organizing.

Constructing total scientific knowledge is certainly not easy, and one can easily argue that this notion is highly idealistic for an American context. Academics in the United States tend to be very connected to their institutions in terms of time and to their particular discipline for status and other rewards. Their conversations are primarily inward, with their own professional colleagues. Nash's admonition to become an organizer, or Fals-Borda's to become an "organic intellectual," is difficult to achieve within the current institutional patterns of American higher education. It may be impossible in most situations for academic-activists to engage in these kinds of "experiential methodology" that lead to what Fals-Borda calls a "satisfying and productive cycle of life and labor" (Fals-Borda, 1991a), a state of being that may be required for its success. It is rare when an academic has the time to make a commitment to the "subjects" of the research so fully that the line which separates the citizen from the academic blurs or disappears (although many of the chapter authors in this book play various roles that criss-cross that line). In a short-term effort, even with the best of intentions, some aspects of a "data raid" may occur. How long does it take for citizens to no longer be the "object" of a study, but genuine partners in a research process? This is also a problem from the perspective of citizens. Few of them either are able to put in the time and effort required for "total scientific knowledge" to become a "cycle of life and labor."

During my time with the MVP, the research has at times felt like this kind of "cycle of life and labor." Yet there has always been some significant tension about feeling committed to the MVP and its social justice concerns while feeling constrained by a sense that I needed to keep the MVP as a separate object of study. This experience provides a personal example of the value conflict articulated earlier by Nyden and Weivel (1992). I fear that if the construction of "total scientific knowledge" requires a sort of participatory dogmatism on the part of academic-activists and community leaders, it may be unrealistic to expect it to be a useful model for enhancing research-based social change in an American context.

In what follows, I will describe the current state of "organizing-based research" as it is practiced in the MVP and other neo-Alinksy organizations. Then, I will briefly present some reflections on my most recent research attempts with the MVP as a way to construct some measure of " total scientific knowledge." Lastly, I will make some suggestions as to how academic-activists can contribute best to community organizing efforts.

ORGANIZING-BASED RESEARCH:
THE ORGANIZER AS RESEARCH FACILITATOR

Neo-Alinsky style community organizers have become adept at practical research on issues and facilitating analytical reflection with community leaders. Thus, organizers are themselves often action/participatory research specialists and teachers in their own right. For an academic to do change-oriented research with a community group, then, it is necessary to begin with an understanding of the practices of *Organizing Based Research (OBR)*.

The primary research/organizing tool used in OBR could be classified as *Leadership Research*. The organizing practice used to generate this research is the standard One-on-One interview process that organizers and grassroots leadership use when they are first engaging a potential or existing member organization. In the initial stages, the staff organizer or trained grassroots leader will interview approximately ten individuals who have been selected as potential leaders by the pastor, shop steward or other head of the organization. In these interviews, the organizer will draw out the person's story—their basic life timeline, their hopes, fears, and so forth—as well as engage in a discussion about local issues which are of concern to that particular person. This process achieves at least two results. First, the coalition begins to hear what issues are of concern to its membership as well as some concrete stories and reflections to help in the eventual collective process of giving meaning to the issues. Second, a potential leader has been engaged, and has hopefully had an experience of being listened to by the interviewer and valued as a citizen. It is the first step toward a sense of empowerment for the potential leader. From a research perspective, the organizer has gathered data on what might be called "local theory" about several issues, as well as knowledge about what kind of leader this person might become.

A second phase in this Leadership Research process involves bringing the initial interviewees together for a collective discussion of the issues that were brought up in the interviews. The organizer acts as a research facilitator here, helping participants to discern which issues are most important and which they are willing to address at this point in time. In a full One-on-One cycle, this initial group will then agree to be trained to go out and interview other members of their organization. After this, a larger collective meeting of those interviewed (which may include all members of the organization) will be held, and momentum will be gathered for involvement in one or two selected issue campaigns. These issue concerns/campaigns may or may not already be part of the coalition's agenda.

All of this research has a flavor of what Torbert (see Chapters 5 and 9) calls second-person research/practice. The participants may also learn something about themselves (first-person research/practice), but this is not the point. In this chapter, I am contributing to third-person research/practice by describing and analyzing this type of organizing-based research, but that is also not the point of the organizing-based research itself. Its point is to study and thereby transform the relationships among all the participants.

During an issue campaign (e.g., the Prince plant closing in Lowell or immigrant rights for Cambodians and Portuguese in the Valley), the most active leaders (usually those who are showing up at chapter meetings and representing the organizations from a single city) will often organize a research action. This *Issue Research* focus involves members of a research team discussing what information needs to be discovered and the methods available for gathering that information. Research will also be done to uncover "models" as possible solutions to the issue they are addressing. Occasionally I have been asked to do library-based research in support of these efforts. This is the basic information that the leaders will need to construct "actionable knowledge" and thus formulate an action plan. As such it corresponds more closely to an a-theoretical sort of third-person research/practice (in Torbert's terminology).

A third type of research is generated through reflection on whatever organizing actions have been taken by the leadership. The MVP may invite a group of legislators to an "action" to present their concerns and press for a particular solution to the issue at hand. Afterwards, many of the leaders will gather to reflect on what they learned from the action. This reflection continues at subsequent chapter meetings and committee meetings. Two kinds of knowledge are generated. One is an evaluative knowledge about the timing, order, and effectiveness of the action itself. This constitutes a type of *"Action Reflection" Research* (or a type of "second-person research/practice"). The collective reflections are also a type of *Power Research* (or "third-person research/practice") in which the leadership gains a better understanding of the individual "targets" of the actions as well as some tacit understanding of the politics of the "target" as an institutional pattern.

Academics supposedly bring to the table a greater awareness and skill in systematizing and conceptualizing data, and thus potentially become a valuable organizing resource. But a difficulty arises when the academic attempts to stand with one foot in the systematic world of academia and one foot in the messy world of community organizing. This difficulty suggests a problem in the general rules that govern actions in each field. For the academic, definitions of what counts as valid research, along with a self-identity as the objective outsider, may create nearly insurmountable obstacles in trying to be relevant to a community organizing effort. Actions happen much too quickly for "valid" research to take place. The result is that organizers go through a hurried-up process doing enough research to instigate an organizing action, while the academic may very well still be trying to decide on the proper questions.

ORGANIZATIONAL CONSTRAINTS ON OBR

Over the years with the Merrimack Valley Project leaders who participate in OBR have gradually built up the general research and conceptualizing capacity of the coalition. A successful issue campaign seems to produce some aspects of "total scientific knowledge"—a collectively processed combination of local theory and academic knowledge. However, the leadership and professional staff in issue campaigns are not always able to complete the research/action/reflection cycles needed to achieve this goal. Ironically, the more mature the organization, the less satisfactory the research process that occurs. This many have to do with a number of organizational dynamics associated with the successful growth of these types of organizations.

Most of the interruptions to the research aspects of a community organizing effort seem to emerge as mature multi-issue coalitions such as the MVP get caught up in "fire-storm" issues which demand the leadership's immediate attention at unexpected times. The timeline for effective research as various firestorm issues emerge is squeezed ever tighter while the professional organizer's time is stretched over a wider range of issues. The role of "research facilitator" can be put aside in favor of simply mobilizing the leadership for whatever immediate protest "action" must occur. Ideally, the experienced leadership already understands much about a particular type of campaign, has built up relationships with key people in the issue area, and generally knows how to manage the given type of "fire-storm" campaign that arises (e.g., a plant closing). The leadership is thus drawing on previous relationships and knowledge gained from earlier OBR efforts. This "buildup in research capacity" is obviously an important resource for the effectiveness of the organization.

However, in this scenario, it may be difficult for newer leaders to "keep up" and continue to gain knowledge about an issue area as well as gradually feel empowered and gain important organizing skills. The focus on Leadership Research (as outlined in the previous section) seems to be a major reason for the success of MVP-type organizing efforts. Experienced leaders have already gone through a gradual process of building up their research capabilities, moving from an initial issue campaign which drew them into the work of the MVP to a capacity for involvement in multiple campaigns across the Valley. The success of the organization can be seen in how effective these leaders have become and how easy it is to get experienced leaders involved. Yet how are newer leaders to find the same opportunities for feeling gradually empowered? As life concerns inevitably begin to draw some experienced leaders away from the organization (e.g., moving out of the area, new job, or birth of a child), the organizer and remaining leaders have less and less time to devote to the "Leadership" and "Issue" research processes discussed earlier. Without these it is difficult to discover and cultivate new leadership to sustain the organization.

Another problem is that less and less time is also devoted to following up on the "power" knowledge which is generated after "actions." Rather than having a continuing influence on whatever problem area was being addressed in a specific issue campaign, the leadership (without newer leaders emerging) may be quickly pulled away to other firestorm issues. Thus, the professional organizer, who is typically very adept in teaching the leadership through the OBR action-reflection cycles more and more about the local political dynamics, finds him or herself immersed in managing the pressing issues as they arise. Leaders may begin to feel they have left something undone, even when they may have "won" the initial issue campaign. Follow-up "actions," which would lead to an ongoing influence on institutional patterns in the general issue area, are not undertaken (e.g., having an increasing influence in housing decisions in a city versus "reacting" to housing decisions made by outside power brokers).

These organizational dynamics reveal some of the ways that OBR can diminish over the life span of this type of organization. None of these organizations will ever have enough professional staff to handle all the research needs that arise and not all of the organizers will be adept in the art of OBR itself. One way academics who wish to work with a community organizing effort can do so is by finding ways to contribute to the quality of this OBR process in a timely, efficient, and language-friendly way. In part, becoming an organizer means participating in these types of research and eventually finding the time and research space to contribute to the action-reflection cycles in new ways. The following is a description of my recent experience extending the OBR process to focus on some of the MVP's organizational dynamics.

CASE STUDY:
ENHANCING AND EXTENDING THE OBR PROCESS

My understanding of the importance of participating as an organizer has increased through my recent interview effort with some experienced leaders in the MVP. In approaching the Executive Council of the MVP about this project, I framed it as a way of interviewing leaders to discover their stories of the history of the MVP (and to help wrap up my dissertation research). I also offered it as a method by which they could individually and collectively reflect on the effectiveness of various aspects of their organizing practices. From this process they could then take the necessary actions to change or strengthen whatever organizational dynamics they had discovered about themselves. A new Staff Director had just been hired and the timing seemed right for the leadership to assess themselves in this way.

The overall "dialogical/narrative" interview project (cf., Mishler, 1986; Polkinghorne, 1988) has included leaders from across the Valley. The participatory aspect of this research was enhanced by several leaders who assisted in formulating the kinds of questions/areas to cover in the interviews themselves. As the interviews have focused on a wide range of organizational issues, various parts can be drawn out in future opportunities for collective reflection on particular topics. Until now, the MVP leadership has decided to focus on the Lawrence chapter. In an interview/reflection process over a six-month period, eight experienced leaders from Lawrence participated with the specific intention to address the issue of "base-building" within their member organizations. The "action" goal has been to "rebuild" the Lawrence chapter. In essence, this has been a participatory research project on the Leadership Research aspects of the OBR process.

In addition to individual in-depth interviews with these leaders, each participated in two collective reflection sessions on the structural constraints to "base-building" which exist in their current organizing practices and resource limitations. They also explored various ways to improve these practices. From an academic perspective, this process allowed me to have more direct input (in a dialogical way) as it presented opportunities to share my own "processed knowledge" emerging from their stories/reflections. From a personal standpoint, I have felt more useful as an "academic" in these sessions. While this project is still ongoing, my sense is that these sessions have helped to generate a type of "actionable knowledge" which might approximate what Fals-Borda calls "total scientific knowledge"—an integration of local theory and academic knowledge.

From this knowledge the leadership is planning a base-building strategy which involves a more strategic focus on who constitutes the leadership research teams which are formed in each member organization. In addition, they are still assessing the nature of the roles which emerging leaders are asked to play. As discussed earlier, it is easy for experienced leaders to become immersed only in external issue campaigns and forget to do the "base-building" work that would enhance quality of participation by others in the larger congregation, union membership, or other community group. Thus, for example, the leaders have become increasingly aware of the need to build up the sense of community within a member organization before drawing out leaders for coalition-led issue campaigns. This may eventually involve a much greater focus on doing organizing "actions" within the member groups.

In sum, this current A/PR project would have been difficult to orchestrate as an "outside researcher" coming in and offering "help" (no matter how committed I was to participatory research). It is difficult to estimate how important it was for me to spend these last few years simply as a participant (as an organizer and researcher) in the work of the organization. I had become familiar with the leadership. The variety of my roles has led to an invaluable sense of trust and solidarity with the leadership enabling this recent A/PR project with the Lawrence chapter. It was clear in the interviews that my participation as an organizer also allowed me to "check" their understandings/memories of some event with appropriate follow-up questions. I had gained a significant tacit understanding of the MVP's work. Through this process I have begun to find ways to provide a research space, within their OBR framework, for addressing in a more focused way their structural/analytical/contextual concerns (beyond what normally occurs in the OBR process).

CONCLUSIONS: POTENTIAL CONTRIBUTIONS
OF ACADEMIC-ACTIVISTS TO OBR

In this paper I have related my own quest to become an academic-activist. There are drawn from this a few suggestions about some potential roles that an aspiring academic-activist can play in a community-organizing context. These roles are particularly important if an academic wishes to use some form of A/PR methodology as a means of analyzing some aspect of the community organizing effort.

Initially one can contribute simply by documenting the many issue campaigns that emerge. It is difficult for new leaders to "catch up" to the knowledge of experienced leaders, and constructing issue campaign accounts could provide valuable case studies for use in leadership training sessions. It would also be helpful to experienced leaders because often an MVP-type organization is spread out across a region and involved in multiple campaigns. It is impossible for most leaders to keep track of everything that occurs.

A second way to contribute is through becoming an "adjunct organizer," someone who can step into the organizing/research gaps which emerge as the organization grows. Academics may have to adapt some of their understanding of "valid" research methodology, but the skills are there to enhance the quality of the OBR process as long as the academician realizes the action/time constraints of the particular campaign, base-building process, and so forth. Participating in this way provides an opportunity for the researcher to learn the local theory (i.e., tacit knowledge of the leader's interpretive frameworks) and build the solidarity and trust necessary for future collective reflection opportunities. Furthermore, it allows the academic the chance to refine his/her research methods for action situations and gradually build a team of co-researchers for making a more academic-based A/PR project a viable and useful option for all parties concerned.

A third opportunity for academic-activists is to coordinate the collection and systematization of socio-economic data relevant to the work of the organization. This may include gathering hard economic data for the region, but also includes collecting the soft data conducted by leadership in various issue campaigns (e.g., what do we know about this political leader or the CEO of this corporation?). It is important in establishing such a "data bank" that it becomes what Gaventa calls a "popularly controlled research center." In such a center, while

> scientists and experts may conduct research for the people, it is
> very different from that which originates when the professional in

the knowledge system defines what knowledge should be provided to the people, or when the committed intellectual seeks to build awareness through research with the people. In a situation where the people have become active, self-conscious of their own knowledge and aware of the limitations of the experts' knowledge (that is, when they have thrown off knowledge-based domination by the experts), then they can also participate fully in decisions about the production of new knowledge, for themselves and for society. The domination arising from the "people-as-objects" of research is transformed to the "people-as-subjects," determining the directions of scientific and theoretical inquiry (Gaventa, 1991, p. 130).

People do not need to become research experts in Gaventa's model, but they do need to practice

democratic participation and control in defining the problems to be studied, in setting research priorities and in determining how the results are to be used. It means recognizing the importance of the production of scientific knowledge by scientists as one type of knowledge production that is not inherently superior to others (Gaventa, 1991, p. 129).

The key to this role is that the data that is collected be subject to the direction of the community leadership. It involves creating a partnership between the academic researcher and the people who are to benefit from whatever data is collected.

A fourth way to contribute is to find regular ways to engage the leadership in the kinds of participatory research described in the case study above. To get the leadership to this point is perhaps the closest an academic can come to helping to facilitate "total scientific knowledge." This could be the closest an academic may come to utilizing his/her training in conceptualizing social practices.

Participating in these capacities with an MVP-type organization constitutes a significant integration of academia and activism These roles help build the research capacity of the organization. They create a partnership approach to research and an increasing ability by all parties to communicate with each other concerning the purposes of research. Needless to say, this level of involvement would go a long way toward overcoming community mistrust of potential "data raiders." In these ways, the aspiring academic-activist would take on the role of *democratic researcher*, a role that represents partnership, respect, and mutual accountability in the process of social change.

REFERENCES

Argyris, C., Putnam, R. & Smith, D. (1985). *Action science: Concepts, methods and skills for research and intervention.* San Francisco: Jossey-Bass.

Barber, B. (1984). *Strong Democracy.* Berkeley: University of California Press.

Clark, A.W. (1980). Action research: theory, practice, values. *Journal of Occupational Behavior,* 1, 151-157.

Elden, M. & Chisholm, R. (1993). Emerging varieties of action research: introduction to the special issue. *Human Relations* 46(2), 121-142.

Fals-Borda, O. (1991a). Some basic ingredients. In O. Fals-Borda & M. Rahman (Eds.), *Action and Knowledge*. New York: Apex Press.

Fals-Borda, O. (1991b). Remaking knowledge. In O. Fals-Borda & M. Rahman (Eds.), *Action and Knowledge*. New York: Apex Press.

Gaventa, J. (1991). Toward a knowledge democracy: viewpoints on participatory research in North America. In O. Fals-Borda & M. Rahman (Eds.), *Action and Knowledge*. New York: Apex Press.

Harrington, M. (1962). *The Other America*. Baltimore: Penguin Books.

Harrington, M. (1984). *The New American Poverty*. New York: Viking Penguin.

Kaye, G. (1990). A community organizer's perspective on citizen participation research and the researcher-practitioner partnership. *American Journal of Community Psychology* 18(1), 151-157.

McMillan, B., Florin, P., Stevenson, J., Kerman, B., & Mithcell, R.E. (1995). Empowerment praxis in community coalitions. *American Journal of Community Psychology* , 23(5), 699-727.

McNeil, Larry B. (1995). The soft arts of organizing. *Social Policy*, winter, 17-22.

Mishler, E.G. (1986). *Research Interviewing: Context and Narrative*. Cambridge, MA: Harvard University Press.

Nash, F. (1993). Church-based organizing as participatory research: The Northwest Community Organization and the Pilsen Resurrection Project. *The American Sociologist*, 24(1), 38-55.

Nyden, P. & Wievel, W. (1992). Collaborative research: Harnessing the tensions between researcher and practitioner. *American Sociologist*, 23(4), 43-55.

Packer, George. (1994). A community fights hard times: Down in the valley. *The Nation* 258(25), 900-904.

Perkins, D. & Wandersman, A. (1990). You'll have to work to overcome our suspicions: The benefits and pitfalls of research with community organizations. *Social Policy*, 21(1), 32-41.

Polkinghorne, D. E. (1988). *Narrative Knowing and the Human Sciences*. Albany, NY: SUNY Press.

Reason, P. (1994). *Participation in Human Inquiry*. London: Sage.

Reason, P. & Torbert, W. (1999). The action turn toward a transformational social science. Manuscript submitted for review.

Somers, M., Gibson, G.D. (1994). Reclaiming the epistemological "other" narrative and the social constitution of identity. In C. Calhoun (Ed.), *Social Theory and the Politics of Identity*. 152-169 Oxford, UK. Basil Blackwell.

Speer, P.W. Hughey, J. (1995). Community organizing: An ecological route to empowerment and power. *American Journal of Community Psychology*, 23(5), 729-748.

Torbert, W. (1991). *The power of balance: Transforming self, society, and scientific inquiry*. Thousand Oaks, CA: Sage.

Wandersman, A. & Florin, P. (Eds.) (1990). An introduction to citizen participation, voluntary organizations, and community development: Insight for empowerment through research. [Special Issue] *American Journal of Community Psychology,* 18(1) 41-54.

3 TRANSFORMING UNIVERSITIES TO SUSTAIN OUTREACH SCHOLARSHIP: A Communiqué from the Front[1]

Richard M. Lerner
Tufts University

"She knows there's no success like failure, and that failure is no success at all."
Bob Dylan, *Love Minus Zero/No Limits* (1965)

Trained in developmental psychology during the 1960s, I was steeped in the "Piagetian revolution" (e.g., Flavell, 1963), that is, the cognitivization of the field that transformed Piaget's (1970) theory from a developmental theory of cognition to a frame for advancing a cognitive theory of development. The ebbing of the influence of Piaget's theory in the ensuing decades nevertheless left developmentalists with several indelible marks of its former hegemony.

Oddly, given the critiques of Piaget's methodology that flowed from both his critics and advocates, a major contribution of his theory has been a recognition that researchers can learn as much, perhaps more, from failure as they can from success. A mistake a child makes in his or her reasoning about the world may reveal more about cognitive structure—about the rules of reasoning—than the child's statement of a correct reason about why the world works as it does.

I believe, because of Piaget's influence, that I learn much more about development—of a person, a family, an organization, or a system—when I discover why there is failure: why problems emerge, why change is impeded, or why anticipated growth or transformation fall short of expectations. In my study of adolescent development (Lerner, 1995; Lerner & Lerner, 1989), for instance, I have learned that youth problems emerge when adolescents fail to meet the demands of their parents or teachers (see Lerner, 1996; Lerner & Galambos, 1998).

THE EVOLUTION OF AN APPLIED DEVELOPMENTAL SCIENTIST

In recent years, I have moved my work with youth from the realm of "basic" research to "applied developmental science" (Fisher & Lerner, 1994; Lerner, Fisher, & Weinberg, 1997). I have described the personal genesis of this career shift elsewhere (Lerner, in press). Here it may suffice to say that, perhaps like many people who enter psychology as a profession, I was always motivated to help people as well as to understand them. My scholarship in youth development proceeded at a time in history when children and adolescents in my own nation and around the world were faced with historically unique challenges to their survival, health, and positive development (Hamburg, 1992; Lerner, 1995). For instance, the comorbidity among problem behaviors and the level of youth poverty in the United States have combined to place American youth at unprecedented risk (Jessor, Donovan, & Costa, 1991; Ketterlinus & Lamb, 1994; Lerner, 1995; Lerner & Galambos, 1998).

Given my motivations and this historical context, I became increasingly interested in using my work to "matter" for the diverse children and adolescents of my nation and world. The developmental systems theory I had been developing ("developmental contextualism;" Lerner, 1991, 1996) enabled me to view interventions into the life course—public policies and youth-serving programs—as (potentially) theory-guided ways of arranging relations between individuals and their ecological settings to promote positive developmental trajectories (Birkel, Lerner, & Smyer, 1989; Bronfenbrenner & Morris, 1998). The evaluation of the efficacy of these policies or programs not only provided information about the adequacy of these interventions but, as well, data elucidating the basic process of human development, that is, the relations between changing people and contexts that constituted the developmental trajectory across the life span (Lerner, 1991, 1995, 1996; Lerner, De Stefanis, & Ladd, 1998). Thus, in the approach to developmental science I am developing there is a blending—a synthesis—of basic and applied interests.

Of course, to test one's ideas about how to arrange relations between youth and their contexts in order to enhance human development, one introduces policies or programs into the social ecology. In other words, one alters, in theory-predicated ways, the developmental system. This requires one to arrange relations between developing youth and the people (e.g., their peers, parents, teachers, and mentors) and institutions (e.g., their families, schools, faith institutions, and youth-serving organizations) of the communities within which they live. However, such community-based change requires both the permission *and* the expertise of the community.

No scholar can be expert in all the critical features of all the diverse neighborhoods within which youth live. To use one's knowledge about human development to promote positive development among diverse youth, a scholar must learn what is meaningful in, and valued by, a specific community. Members of the community have knowledge about what matters in their specific setting. Accordingly, to integrate understanding of the instantiation of basic developmental process among particular youth with actions that promote their positive development, the expertise about development in a given community, possessed by the people of that community, is required.

As such, to use knowledge about development to enhance development, the experts within the university need to collaborate with the experts within the community. Co-learning between these two groups—and humility on the part of both—is needed for such a collaboration to exist. Indeed, the ideas of co-learning and humility have become essential cornerstones of the concept of "outreach scholarship." As I explain, such scholarship is the intellectual frame for the sort of university-wide centers that, today, reflect one response of universities to the pressure to transform their approach to knowledge generation and utilization and, in so doing, the interest within universities to develop an approach to knowledge that is valued by communities.

Simply, then, in the context of such a center I have sought to use knowledge about development, in collaborations with communities, to promote positive youth development. I have now organized and led three different university units (centers or institutes) that, in different ways, have sought to foster such community-university collaborations (the Center for the Study of Child and Adolescent Development at the Pennsylvania State University, the Institute for Children, Youth and Families at Michigan State University, and the Center for Child, Family, and Community Partnerships at Boston College).

I have discovered that a common vision of, and a commitment to, taking actions that enhance the life chances of youth are necessary but not sufficient resources to deploy in order to prevent the economic, political, interpersonal, and personological impediments to success of: youth, striving to further their health and positive development; families and youth-serving organizations, attempting to contribute to these valued outcomes for young people; and university centers or institutes, working to be sustained partners of youth, families, and communities (Lerner & Miller, 1998). Indeed, even when vision and commitment are coupled with financial support for youth programs gained from successful grantsmanship, there are still impediments to sustaining effective and appropriately scaled actions serving the interests of youth.

Simply, there are still failures of scope and sustainability. It is from these failures that I have learned something about the rules of structural development that apply to university centers that seek to foster community collaborations that promote positive youth development.

UNIVERSITY CENTERS: FROM MULTIDISCIPLINARY RESEARCH TO OUTREACH SCHOLARSHIP

University centers (or institutes—terms that I will treat as equivalent in this chapter) have many functions. They can range across the breadth of the traditional tripartite mission of universities (and, in turn, the three components of the role of faculty members)—that is, teaching, research, or service—and can represent combinations of these foci. For instance, centers for service learning (Kenny & Gallagher, Chapter 10) can integrate the teaching and service missions of the university.

Centers are created for many reasons, often as, first, a "reward" to one or more faculty to recognize their scholarly productivity and, second, as a means to address a goal of the university that cannot readily be accomplished within departmental or disciplinary structures. Centers are operationally equivalent to supra-departmental laboratories, and can serve to celebrate or give visibility to the grantsmanship accomplishments of one or more Principal Investigators (PI's); in this way, they may serve as a unit making further grantsmanship more likely. Centers also allow the university to institutionalize a function (e.g., establishing a service learning capacity) or create a set of activities (e.g., through constituting a point of access for communities to interact with the university in regard to building community-based, youth-serving programs) that require resources and/or expertise that are university-wide in scope. In essence, to be university-wide entities, centers must cross (and, ideally, integrate) the disciplinary or professional boundaries of any one department or school/college. For example, the Boston College Center for Child, Family, and Community partnerships is a collaboration among the schools of education, law, management, nursing, and social work and the College of Arts and Sciences.

Indeed, an operational definition of a university-wide center is a unit that crosses the disciplinary boundaries of any given department and the funding of any one school or college. However, implicit in this definition is the idea that a university-wide center is a value-added unit that provides benefits to departments, colleges, and the university as a whole that would not exist without the center. In the lexicon of a developmentalist, a center is an emergent (or epigenetic) entity (Lerner, 1986): It creates in the integrations it produces "outcomes" (i.e., valued contributions to the university and its disciplinary and collegiate units) that would not be produced by these parts in "isolation." To legitimate its existence, then, a center must be a multidisciplinary and/or multiprofessional university-wide unit—a whole—that creates something (some value-added contributions) that is more than the sum of the parts (of the current or possible contributions of the disciplinary units) contributing to it. Simply, to be value-added contributions, the products of centers must be ones that would not occur readily through the work of independently acting departments or schools/colleges.

LABORATORY-TYPE CENTERS VERSUS CENTERS FOR OUTREACH SCHOLARSHIP

The laboratory version of university-wide centers has a long, if controversial, tradition in American higher education. These units are often at odds with departments, which contend that financial support and faculty time allocated by university central administration to such centers take resources from the disciplinary units in which the original expertise for the work of the centers derives and which, if those resources were returned, could replicate the productivity of the centers.

Despite the intellectual credibility that such arguments might have in a given case, laboratory-type centers may counter such university "turfism" through their continued grant productivity. As long as these units generate overhead return to the university, have a prestigious portfolio of grants and contracts, and publish a set of highly refereed and highly cited articles in top-tier (and, ironically, typically disciplinary-based) journals, few department chairs or deans will expect a vice president for research, a provost, or a president to actually close a laboratory-type center and reallocate its resources to individual departments or colleges. Such an act would be tantamount to killing the golden goose. Finding central administrators prone to take such actions may be a task equivalent to discovering a four-leaf clover and winning a multi-million dollar lottery on the same day that the Boston Red Sox defeated the Chicago Cubs in the seventh game of the World Series.

The value-added contributions of laboratory-type centers to the university are clear: financial returns and prestigious visibility are part of the accepted ethos of university culture, wherein research productivity and extramural funding of one's research are the *sine qua non* of the faculty role; they are the traditionally highest regarded and rewarded parts of the tripartite mission. However, the nature of the contributions of other types of university-wide centers are less clear, and the according of esteem by faculty and administrators is less certain. In my experience, centers associated with outreach scholarship are an exemplary case-in-point of this vagueness (Lerner & Miller, 1998; Lerner & Simon, 1998a).

"Outreach" involves using university scholarly expertise for the benefit of audiences and stakeholders external to the university (Lerner & Simon, 1998b; Spanier, 1997, 1999; Votruba, 1992, 1996, 1999a/1999b). The concept of "outreach scholarship" (Lerner, 1995, Lerner & Simon, 1998b) builds on Boyer's (1990, 1994) notion of the scholarship of engagement and his vision for the "new American college." Universities are in the "knowledge business," that is, they generate, transmit, preserve, or apply knowledge (e.g., in regard to their contributions to their research, teaching, and service missions). Outreach scholarship occurs when universities engage in these knowledge functions to address issues defined by community collaborators as important and/or to attain goals designated as valuable by these community partners. Outreach scholarship occurs, then, in the context of co-learning between the university and its community partners, collaborations that require that each partner learn about and accommodate to the other's culture and accept the expertise that each brings to the collaboration. Such scholarship may take the form of asset mapping, needs assessment, issues identification, demonstration research, participatory action research, program design and evaluation, technical assistance (e.g., in granstmanship or in data base management), and continuing education and training.

In response to the growing pressures experienced by universities to use their resources to add value to the communities within which they exist (Kennedy, 1999; Lerner & Simon, 1998a; Magrath, 1993, 1998; Richardson, 1996; Spanier, 1999; Votruba, in press-a, in press-b), centers for outreach scholarship have been created to provide points of access to communities and to demonstrate the university's accountability to the community. Focused on particular issues (e.g., health and human services, environmental quality, neighborhood revitalization, economic development, primary and secondary education, or children, youth, and families), or on the range of issues a community may envision as pertinent to improving the quality of the lives of its citizens, these centers draw on faculty expertise, and on graduate student (and at times undergraduate student) participation, from across the university, to holistically engage communities.

These centers seek to integrate knowledge about youth issues—for instance, about youth poverty and its behavioral sequelae; about family stress as, for instance, occurs in relation to welfare-to-work transitions; or about engaging parents, schools, the faith community, community policing, libraries, hospitals, governmental and non-governmental organizations, and the other assets present in the community to support the positive development of youth. The approach to such topics does not correspond to the way that disciplines partition knowledge (e.g., separating knowledge of the developing adolescent from knowledge of the structure or function of the family from knowledge of the legal or policy system influencing youth and families), or to the manner in which professions partition skills (e.g., maintaining a guild-like division of counseling expertise from legal practice and both of these kept separate from social work services). Rather, to transform knowledge into actions that are deemed legitimate in, and valued by, communities, these centers seek to synthesize disciplinary and professional expertise across the several levels of individual, interpersonal, and institutional organization present in the actual ecology of human development (Bronfenbrenner & Morris, 1998; Torbert, Chapter 5).

However, it is in these multidisciplinary, multiprofessional, and community collaborative integrations—syntheses valued by the community and providing the value-added access and accountability that the community is pressuring the university to provide (Boyer, 1994; Magrath, 1998; Richardson, 1996; Spanier, 1997, 1999; Votruba, 1999a, 1999b)—that the outreach center reveals its Achilles heel. The very attributes of value to the community make the outreach center a fragile unit within the contemporary American university—whether that university is a state-supported public institution, a land-grant university, an independent research-intensive institution with a large endowment, or an independent, tuition-driven, primarily liberal arts, institution.

OUTREACH SCHOLARSHIP CENTERS
AND THE DIALECTIC OF SUCCESS-FAILURE

The products of outreach scholarship centers are not only (or ordinarily) the traditional ones associated with departments and laboratory-type centers. Outreach scholarship may be realized through the creation or the enhancement of community-based programs. It may also be evidenced by the dissemination of knowledge in formats useful to the community (e.g., newsletters, technical assistance "manuals," CD-ROM, or videotape materials), but not prototypic of highly refereed, top-tier journal publications. In turn, even when journal publications are produced, they are typically multi-authored, include both university and community partners in the authorship team, and appear in journal outlets not associated with traditional disciplinary expertise. While tenured full professors can afford to publish such articles, it is far from certain whether a person seeking tenure or promotion can obtain such academic rewards through this type of publication, much less from the other types of outreach scholarship dissemination products.

Moreover, the funding produced by outreach scholarship centers may involve a portfolio of awards that are linked to few overhead-earning projects. Small contracts from community partners may support a graduate student's participation in an activity such as program evaluation but, even here, such contracts often have to be matched with university resources in order to allow the community partner to "afford" its partnership with the community. For example, the community partner may pay the student's graduate stipend but the university may be asked to match this award with tuition credits for the student. In addition, many of the grants currently awarded for outreach scholarship come from private foundations (e.g., the W. K. Kellogg Foundation, the DeWitt-Wallace Reader's Digest Fund, the W. T. Grant Foundation, the Carnegie Corporation, the Rockefeller Foundation, the Annie E. Casey Foundation, the Sloan Foundation, the Charles Stewart Mott Foundation, or the Ford Foundation), and these awards either pay no overhead or pay overhead rates much less than those provided by federal grants.

Furthermore, although an outreach scholarship center may be central in providing the grantsmanship expertise requisite for receiving an award, the university may not be the fiduciary site of the grant. Since the university and the community are equal partners in outreach scholarship projects, either collaborator may be the "PI" for the grant, assuming that both have 501 c (3) status. Moreover, since a frequent goal of these collaborations is to increase the capacity of the community to envision, enact, and sustain valued programs, it is often both reasonable and strategic for the community partner to be the PI. The university— despite its instrumental leadership in obtaining the reward—might then only be a subcontractor to the community (e.g., to conduct the program evaluation portion of the project). Thus, even when the outreach scholarship center generates grant money, the university may not be the site of the full award (but only of a small, subcontracted portion of it).

How "credit" is assigned by central administration for such grantsmanship success is not clear within or across contemporary American universities. Indeed, whether such grantsmanship performance is even regarded as a success by central administrators is far from certain. If such activity is not regarded as a valued instance of university success, then the issue of assigning credit is moot. And, if such products are not regarded as valued university successes, then the funds outreach scholarship centers use, or request, for maintaining a capacity to serve communities in the development of projects that may result in such grants (i.e., community-sited ones) would not be likely to be regarded as well-spent money.

Moreover, since not all of the *pro bono* services associated with a center's capacity to serve the community (e.g., consultation, convening meetings, or acting as a clearinghouse for information about the substance of a project) will result in a grant proposal, much less a university-sited proposal, there would be little rationale to invest university resources in such services—if it is the case that the sorts of grants that might result from such services are not regarded as university successes. Indeed, even though the rate at which *pro bono* outreach scholarship services eventuate in grants (about 10% of the time in my experience) is probably not different than the rate at which laboratory-type grant proposals receive funding, the fact that the outreach scholarship grants are not necessarily sited at the university or, even if they are sited there, earn little or no overhead, may lead central administrators to conclude that such granstmanship activity constitutes a university *failure*. Such grants may be seen as actually costing the university money. In turn, the visibility that such grants might produce (e.g., the recognition in a specific community that a greater number of youth than anticipated have been prevented from dropping out of high school because of the work of a particular program) is not necessarily comparable to the visibility associated with laboratory-type grants (e.g., the winning of a national competition for a line of research, the opportunity to, or the actuality of, producing a cutting-edge scientific discovery).

Thus, neither producing traditional dissemination products, nor associated with traditional grantsmanship or academic prestige, the success of the outreach scholarship center may easily be construed as a failure by conventional academic standards of performance. Indeed, the prototypic profile of productivity associated with outreach scholarship centers may make it an easy target for budget reduction by academic administrators seeking to save or reallocate internal resources. With none or few of the conventional indices of success that serve to protect laboratory-type centers from academic turfism or central administration budget personnel, the only meaningful assets that outreach scholarship centers may possess is the vision and commitment at the highest level of central university administration to serve the community through the center's work *and* to reward faculty of all academic ranks for their contributions to such work (Lerner & Miller, 1998; Richardson, 1996; Spanier, 1997, 1999).

Short of such leadership by a president, provost, or board of trustees, the future of any outreach scholarship center remains in "a delicate balance." Such units must, it seems, strike a functional compromise between, on the one hand, promoting access and accountability through outreach and, on the other hand, assuring its sustainability through products associated with traditional, laboratory-like center performance. In pursuing this balance several key questions must be addressed.

CAN OUTREACH CENTERS SURVIVE WITHIN CONTEMPORARY AMERICAN UNIVERSITIES?

The renowned developmental psychologist, Jerome Kagan, once explained to me that scholarship advances best when the right questions are asked. I have approached my involvement in outreach scholarship centers with this orientation by asking two interrelated sets of questions.

First, what are the relations between diverse youth and their similarly variable contexts that are associated with healthy developmental trajectories? How can relations between children and their ecologies be arrayed to promote positive development? What changes in the developmental system must be introduced to increase the life chances of young people?

Second, and given that universities are part of the ecology of human development, and are potentially significant institutional assets in the lives of children, families, and communities (Kretzmann & McKnight, 1993), I have asked how higher education can become part of the systems change required to promote and sustain healthy development of youth. What changes in university structure, and in the ways in which faculty are rewarded and undergraduate and graduate students educated, need to occur to make universities part of the solution to the pressing and historically unique problems of contemporary American youth (Lerner, 1995; Lerner & Simon, 1998a, 1998b)?

Pursuing these two sets of questions has defined my professional life for more than a decade. The outreach centers I have led have engaged in work addressing both questions. I have sought to identify the ways in which developmental systems can be changed to better serve the positive development of youth, and I have attempted to understand if and how universities, though outreach scholarship and units promoting it, can be effective and sustained parts of such systems change.

I believe that the past decade has resulted in a good deal of knowledge in support of the conclusion that changes in individual-context relations can be created in the service of both effectively preventing negative behavioral development and in the promotion of positive youth outcomes (e.g., Benson, 1997; Carnegie Corporation of New York, 1995; Damon, 1997; Dryfoos, 1994, 1998; Hamburg, 1992; Lerner, 1995; Scales & Leffert, 1999; Schorr, 1997). However, despite a great deal of activity pertinent to the development of university outreach efforts and to the creation of centers for outreach scholarship serving children, youth, and families (e.g., Lerner & Simon, 1998a; McHale & Lerner, 1996; Richardson, 1996; Spanier, 1997, 1999; Votruba, 1999a, 1999b), I think it is still far from certain whether outreach can become a core part of American universities (as opposed to relegating or marginalizing outreach through typically academically devalued cooperative extension programs, continuing education, or voluntary undergraduate service learning opportunities). I believe that it is also unclear whether university centers for outreach scholarship can be the vehicles through which outreach is woven into the fabric of the university.

Following the direction of Kagan, I think there are several key questions that must be addressed in order to understand the status and future viability of such units. These questions pertain to the role and culture of faculty, to the role and culture of the community, and to the role of leaders of higher education. A discussion of the nature of these roles provides a rationalization for the questions surrounding outreach scholarship centers.

HISTORICAL AND CULTURAL BASES OF
FACULTY, ADMINISTRATIVE, AND COMMUNITY ROLES

The questions pertinent to faculty derive from the historical content within which contemporary scholars have developed. This context has involved the elaboration within America of the nineteenth-century German model of a university as an institution disengaged from the ebb and flow of the "mundane" issues confronting the society around it. Such a university, through its faculty, was free to pursue "pure" (ethereal) knowledge in a manner unconstrained (or, perhaps better, uncontaminated) by a society focused on the concrete problems of everyday life (Bonnen, 1998; Boyer, 1990; Lynton & Elman, 1989). In America, those faculty best able to pursue ethereal knowledge were the most highly regarded and the most rewarded within their institutions, and—perhaps associated as well with the American ethos of rugged individualism—a university culture emerged wherein independent scholarly productivity by a faculty member in the development of basic knowledge was the ideal academic profile (Bok, 1982, 1990, 1992).

The cohorts of faculty that have been socialized within this culture have not been trained to or rewarded for collaboration, for example, for co-authored publications. Rather, their training and reward system have been focused on single-authored publications (derived from grants on which they have been PI's) in disciplinary journals. Collaborations with people outside of their discipline, much less with people from the non-academic community, were simply outside of the cultural frame for faculty developing within this historical context.

Given this context it is difficult, to say the least, to find large numbers of faculty oriented to engaging in community-collaborative, multidisciplinary, and multiprofessional scholarship that is supported in many cases by grants sited in the community. In my own experience, at Michigan State there were no more than about two dozen faculty (in a university with a faculty of about 2,000) who were engaged in the work of the Institute for Children, Youth, and Families. At Boston College, with an overall faculty of about 650, there are about ten faculty who work primarily through the Center for Child, Family, and Community Partnerships.

Moreover, the faculty who do have interests in working primarily through such outreach scholarship centers are typically tenured, often full professors, and of a level of accomplishment wherein there is little risk associated with pursuing outreach scholarship. However, even such colleagues find it difficult to shed the cultural influences of their historical cohort. Again in my experience, there are expectations of support and rewards commensurate with those they might accrue from participation in laboratory-type centers. While the expectation of, or even the need for, such benefits are not unreasonable stances, it is not certain whether an outreach scholarship center can, save for the presence of a large amount of discretionary, endowment income, support or reward faculty in manners equivalent to laboratory-type centers.

The final determination of the issues of support and rewards rests with the leaders of universities—provosts, presidents, and (in some cases) boards of trustees. However, these groups are also products of the same historical cohort and resulting university culture that have shaped faculty. Indeed, these leaders are also producers of the forces maintaining this culture. Their careers have been shaped by their ability to bring to their institutions higher levels of culturally-valued excellence, that is, achievement and prestige in regard to grantsmanship, publications/discoveries, and the recruitment and retention of faculty creating such culturally-valued scholarly products. No institution can enjoy the status of an elite college or university—or can claim such status, for instance in marketing itself to the best of each year's pool of undergraduate applicants—unless it can point to the stature and accomplishments of its faculty in regard to this culture.

Traditionally, there were few if any rewards within this culture to stimulate the leaders of higher education institutions to open the doors of their institutions to the voice and values of the community. Provosts and presidents did not attain their positions of leadership by sharing their stewardship of the university and its resources with non-university audiences. They did not advance in their careers if they elected to do so.

However, there is evidence that conditions may be changing, and that the current historical moment may represent a unique time within which societal conditions and reward structures align to create top level (i.e., presidential) interest in and actions promotive of community outreach. In February 1999, the Kellogg Commission on the Future of State and Land-Grant Universities, chaired by Graham B. Spanier, President of the Pennsylvania State University, issued its third report. Entitled "Returning to our roots: The engaged institution," the report concluded that community engagement, through outreach and outreach scholarship, is essential for garnering the public support state and land-grant institutions must have to survive. The authors of the report—which included 24 sitting presidents of such institutions, three past-presidents of such institutions, and the president of the National Association of State Universities and Land-Grant Colleges (NASULGC)— emphasized that "with the resources and superbly qualified professors and staff on our campuses, we can organize our institutions to serve both local and national needs in a more coherent and effective way. We can and must do better" (Kellogg Commission, 1999, p. 1).

Accordingly, a *zeitgeist* may be emerging to promote contemporary university leaders to respond to the current social pressures for greater, value-added contributions of higher education to the matters of everyday life affecting the communities within which they are embedded (Lerner & Simon, 1998b). Indeed, there are successful models of such efforts (Chibucos & Lerner, 1999), for example at the Pennsylvania State University, where technology transfer and distance education have achieved a university-wide scope and have engaged business and industry, undergraduate students, and communities around the world. Moreover, the Kellogg Commission report (1999) provides examples of other successful models involving Arizona State University; Iowa State University; Ohio State University; Portland State University; Rutgers, the State University of New Jersey; Salish Kootenai College; Tuskegee University; University of California, Davis; University of Illinois at Chicago; and the University of Vermont.

However, at this writing it is still too early to know if this changed climate for and presidential commitment to engagement will result in the widespread (nation-wide) creation and sustainability of units that are designed to promote access for and accountability to the community (e.g., outreach scholarship centers). It is still too early to know if the vision and leadership of the Kellogg Commission will result in alterations in normative cultural and career orientations of university leaders such that they will be unequivocally and sustainably committed to the creation of such units.

Indeed, a cynical view would be that if there were no external pressures for access and accountability—and if there were no external funds to be awarded for the creation of outreach scholarship units (e.g., as have been made available by the W. K. Kellogg Foundation, the Sloan Foundation, or the U. S. Department of Housing and Urban Development)—American university culture would not evolve sufficiently to lead many presidents or provosts to create such units (however, see Spanier, 1997, 1999, for an example of just such an initiative). Such a view would also predict that if external pressures or funding streams disappeared so too would any cultural "change" involving interest in such units.

Moreover, unless such units prove able to generate resources commensurate with those associated with laboratory-type centers or, at least, are budget neutral for an institution, traditional university culture would not bode well for the long-term sustainability of outreach scholarship centers. Indeed, even if we grant a changed *zeitgeist* for outreach, it may be quite difficult for the foreseeable future for central administrators to fend off pressure from departments or laboratory-type centers for the reallocation of resources given to outreach scholarship centers, *if* outreach activities are not associated with the profile of financial and scholarly generativity that is prototypic of laboratory-type centers. In the context of traditional academic culture, few presidents and provosts could continue to allocate money derived from undergraduate or graduate student tuition to outreach scholarship centers when the productivity of such centers do not embellish the reputation of the university within the domains prized by academic culture.

Together, the faculty and the administrative roles within contemporary academic culture do much to shape community culture, at least in regard to outreach (Votruba, 1992, 1996,1999a, 1999b). Most members of the university community know of the concept of "town and gown problems," that is, of situations wherein the interests and activities of the university do not fit with—or are in fact at conflict with—the interests and activities of the community. There can be many causes of such conflict, and some pertain to problems that arise when different institutions or businesses in the same community have different views about public policies, procedures, or resource distributions. Such conflicts (e.g., regarding the need for new or revised traffic or parking rules accompanying institutional expansion) may have nothing to do with university culture per se.

However, some town-grown problems arise in relation to the nature of academic culture and represent a shaping of community culture by the academic one. For instance, if faculty members' roles promote independent scholarship, then collaboration *with* communities is unlikely. Although faculty members might seek to enact their scholarship *in* communities, there would be no room for the community to partner with the faculty member in defining his or her research focus. There would be no necessary benefit of the scholarship for promoting community interests. Instead, what is typically the case is that the faculty member, in seeking to gain the permission of the community (e.g., schools or family groups) to work within it, seeks to convince the community that what he or she wants to do will be of use, if only indirectly. Moreover, even in the case of applied research, where, for instance, a demonstration project or a program evaluation may be enacted, there is rarely a commitment by faculty to remain in the community beyond the time that is supported by the funding (e.g., the grant) that enables such activity.

Given such behavior by faculty, it is not surprising that leaders of outreach scholarship centers find great skepticism in the community about the intrinsic interest of the university in the lives of the community's children and families. In my experience, many community members complain of being treated only as "research subjects" or of being regarded as of value only as objects of study (cf. Fairfax, Chapter 2). Many community members believe that the university will exploit them, that the community will be a site of university activity only so that grants may be won, publications written, or students trained. The university will "parachute" into the community for such activity and then, when the grant is over, the article published, or the training completed, the university will then "parachute out" (Lerner, 1995).

Often, because the work of the faculty may have raised hopes about, or awareness of, programs that may benefit the lives of children and families, the departure of the university makes matters worse than before the university arrived. Raised expectations have been dashed and, because there was no commitment to instilling in the community a capacity to sustain the work demonstrated by the university, frustration and anger are elicited.

Given such occurrences in the history of university-community interaction, it should not be surprising that a core feature of community culture is a distrust of the motives of universities (Boyer, 1990, 1994; Magrath, 1993, 1998). It would not be remarkable to find in the community a belief that the university was an institution with little if any interest in helping the citizens of the community in which it is located improve their everyday lives (Boyer, 1994; Spanier, 1997, 1999).

The example I often give to illustrate this situation is of a crack-addicted, teenage single mother, who is jobless and a high school drop out, living in a community wherein there is an elite higher education institution. Of what benefit to this young woman's life is it that one of the nation's leading research and teaching institutions is part of her community? And, even if it should occur to her that there were people in the institution who had knowledge and skills that could help her and other young people in life situations comparable to her own, why would she believe that these people would help? How would she gain access to these people? On what door would this young woman knock? And why, if there were people to answer the knock, would anyone there see it as in their interests to help her?

There are academics who believe that the university would respond in a helpful way to this young woman. Nevertheless, I think that most citizens in most communities across America would not share this belief (cf. Boyer, 1994; Magrath, 1993, 1998). Their culture and their experience would lead them to expect an unresponsive, disengaged institution. Indeed, on the basis of the contributions universities make to the quality of their daily life, few citizens would lobby their legislatures to add money to, or restore cut funds from the budgets of, such institutions (Boyer, 1994).

Such a community orientation to universities is one reason why pressures on higher education for access and accountability have risen dramatically in current years (Bok, 1982, 1990, 1992; Richardson, 1996; Spanier, 1997; Votruba 1999b). These pressures bring us back full circle to the rationale for the creation of outreach scholarship centers. However, a rationale for creation is not a formula for sustainability. To attain the information pertinent to creating such a formula, we must address the key questions about sustainability that derive from the historical and cultural context of faculty, administrator, and community roles.

KEY QUESTIONS ABOUT OUTREACH SCHOLARSHIP CENTERS

Several questions associated with the faculty role derive from the history that has shaped contemporary academic culture:

1)   Why would a faculty member work at or through an outreach scholarship center?

2)   Is it because such a center provides services (e.g., grant management, typing support) that are not present in the home department or school/college?

3)   Are there reasons that a faculty member should work at an outreach scholarship center that are associated with other than these benefits?

4)   Are there non-tangible benefits/rewards/incentives for faculty?

5)   If the concept of the university outreach center as a value-added contributor to the university and to the community is taken seriously, what criteria should be used to decide what faculty do for the community (e.g., facilitation of meetings, technical assistance, or consultation)?

6)   Despite the nature or formula for university funding, do faculty members have an obligation to serve the community through such work?

7)   Do faculty have any obligations to "give back" to the center, or should the center be only an instrument to provide incentives to faculty to engage in outreach scholarship?

8)   Can all aspects of the faculty/university mission—research, service, *and* teaching—be integrated in such a center? In other words, can faculty successes and rewards—and the integration of outreach into the mainstream of the university—be enhanced by not focusing exclusively on the research

(publications, grant productivity) components of the faculty role but, as well, on the role of the faculty member as a teacher of undergraduate and graduate students?

In turn, there are also questions pertinent to university administrators that derive from the history that has shaped contemporary academic culture:

9)   Can there be a difference between a laboratory-type university center and an outreach scholarship center *if* the latter type of unit is to be viable?

10) If there can be a difference, how much of a difference is acceptable before viability is threatened?

11) Should an outreach scholarship center do more for the community than is budgeted in the work funded by its grants and contracts? If so, what should be done? Who should pay for it?

12) Since outreach scholarship may lead to funds flowing into the university in only a small proportion of cases, should the university allocate resources for such activity?

13) Unless (a) there is an endowment for the center; (b) a high level central administrator creates a permanent line in the university budget in order to support the center's provision of benefits to faculty members and to the community for their involvement in the center; or (c) institutional and public policy converge to the extent that state governments fund universities to create and support outreach scholarship centers, how can a center get the resources required to provide benefits/rewards/incentives and therefore to become a sustainable part of university culture?

14) In institutions that are either tuition driven or dominated by a culture of PI grantsmanship, can or should central administration provide sustained, core funding of an outreach scholarship center?

15) Will the provision by such centers of educational opportunities for students (e.g., through offering or facilitating service learning courses or experiences) enhance the ability of central administrators to provide sustained funding?

16) Does a university have the obligation to "give back" to the community through the creation and sustained funding of centers that afford access and accountability through their scholarship?

Finally, knowledge of the culture of the community is associated with several questions, which, in many ways, are analogues to those associated with the faculty role:

17) Why would a community group work at or through an outreach scholarship center?

18) Is it because such a center provides services (e.g., grant intelligence, technical assistance regarding data base management or analysis) that are not present in the community?

19)	Are there reasons that a community group should work at an outreach scholarship center that are associated with other than these benefits?
20)	Are there non-tangible benefits/rewards/incentives for the community?

Macbeth: "If we should fail?"
Lady Macbeth: "We fail?"
Macbeth, **Act I, Scene 7, Line 59**

What is lost if outreach scholarship centers are shown not to be viable units within contemporary American universities? What if such centers fail to survive?

One response to this question involves specifying a loss in the opportunity to have such units provide what may be a unique epistemological lens for learning about the ways in which ecologically valid, lived experiences contribute to youth development (Torbert, Chapter 9). At the same time a subset of youth—those involved as university students engaged in experiential learning through center activities or as youth from community settings involved in the collaborative programs of the center—will lose the opportunity to have experiences that can potentially transform their intellectual, emotional, or social lives, and as such their abilities to contribute to civil society. Moreover, the university students will lose an opportunity to participate actively in an institutional transformation involving what Torbert (Chapter 5) terms collaborative inquiry, that is, students will miss the chance to participate in the transformation of universities from bureaucratic departments and disciplines to collaborative, boundary-crossing, knowledge-producing institutions.

William Richardson (1996), former Provost of the Pennsylvania State University, former President of Johns Hopkins University, and current President of the W. K. Kellogg Foundation, provides another answer to this question, one that is clear and compelling and that encapsulates the responses other leaders of American higher education have proffered to such questions (e.g., Boyer, 1990, 1994; Harkavy, 1998; Kellogg Commission, 1999; Lynton & Elman, 1989; Magrath, 1998; Spanier, 1997, 1999; Votruba, 1999a, 1999b). Richardson argues that American universities will, upon such a failure, become "Jurassic Parks". institutions of historical interest (or, perhaps, curiosity) but of little relevance to the important issues of our times. These issues reduce ultimately to matters of quality of life—to leveling the playing field for all people, and affording everyone the opportunity to pursue actions that may lead to their own, their family's, and their community's health, well-being, and prosperity. Either universities will become part of the solution to this problem of human systems change or they, in the words of Eldridge Cleaver (1967), will be part of the problem.

If we fail to make universities a sustained part of the assets provided to communities in support of their efforts to promote the positive development of youth we lose the incalculable power of this great knowledge "machine." We lose the best minds of our nation—both of our faculty and of our students—turning their intellectual efforts to enhancing the only real capital any nation has: the human capital represented by its children.

When Macbeth asked Lady Macbeth what would happen if they failed, she replied, as shown above, "We fail." Shakespeare provided little textual instruction to guide the reader, or actor, about how this statement should be interpreted. Literary critics have debated whether the line should reflect a Lady Macbeth who responds with a matter-of-fact acknowledgment—a vocal shrug, if you will—of the possibility of failure; with a tone of fright as she contemplates not succeeding; with a perhaps bewildered enunciation of the possibility of failure, as if this eventuality is first occurring to her; or with a remonstrating tone conveying that it is preposterous to even contemplate the possibility of failure.

Given the costs to our nation if we do not succeed in aligning the knowledge functions of universities with the assets of our communities, we must adopt the latter interpretation of the "We fail!" line. Despite the formidable obstacles to the success of university outreach centers, we must find ways to make their failure a preposterous proposition. To enable the necessitating of success in the midst of probable failure we must insist on asking two final, interrelated questions—to community members, to faculty, and to provosts, presidents, and boards of trustees:

- Who would say that the lives of our children are not worth the cost of providing them with the unique knowledge derived from sustained outreach scholarship?
- Who will stand up and assert that—despite its costs; the academic turf trespassed; the intrusion allowed for non-university people, the community, to have a say about university resources; and the revisions required in the work life of and reward system for faculty—we cannot allow the youth and families of our nation to be deprived of the knowledge functions of the university?

ENDNOTES

[1] The preparation of this chapter was supported in part by a grant from the W. T. Grant Foundation. I thank the editors of the volume and C. Peter Magrath, William C. Richardson, Graham B. Spanier, and James C. Votruba for their comments.

REFERENCES

Benson, P. (1997). *All kids are our kids: What communities must do to raise caring and responsible children and adolescents.* San Francisco: Jossey-Bass.

Birkel, R., Lerner, R. M., & Smyer, M. A. (1989). Applied developmental psychology as an implementation of a life-span view of human development. *Journal of Applied Developmental Psychology, 10,* 425-445.

Bok, D. (1982). *Beyond the ivory tower: Social responsibilities of the modern university.* Cambridge, MA: Harvard University Press.

Bok, D. (1990). *Universities and the future of America.* Durham, NC: Duke University Press.

Bok, D. (1992). Reclaiming the public trust. *Change,* July/August, 13-19.

Bonnen, J. T. (1998). The land-grant idea and the evolving outreach university. In R. M. Lerner & L. A. K. Simon (Eds.), *University-community collaborations for the twenty-first century: Outreach scholarship for youth and families* (pp. 25-71). New York: Garland.

Boyer, E. L. (1990). *Scholarship reconsidered: Priorities of the professoriate.* Princeton, NJ: The Carnegie Foundation for the Advancement of Teaching.

Boyer, E. L. (1994, March 9). Creating the new American college. *The Chronicle of Higher Education,* A48.

Bronfenbrenner, U., & Morris, P. A. (1998). The ecology of developmental process. In W. Damon (series Ed.) & R. M. Lerner (Ed.), *Theoretical models of human development.* Vol. 1 of *The handbook of child psychology* (5th Vol., pp. 993-1028). Editor in chief: W. Damon. New York: Wiley.

Carnegie Corporation of New York. (1995). *Great transitions: Preparing adolescents for a new century.* New York: Carnegie Corporation of New York.

Chibucos, T., & Lerner, R. M. (Eds.) (1999). *Serving children and families through community-university partnerships: Success stories.* Norwell, MA: Kluwer Academic Publishers.

Cleaver, E. (1967). *Soul on ice.* New York: McGraw Hill.

Damon, W. (1997). *The youth charter: How communities can work together to raise standards for all our children.* New York: The Free Press.

Dryfoos, J. G. (1994). *Full service schools: A revolution in health and social services for children, youth, and families.* San Francisco: Jossey-Bass.

Dryfoos, J. G. (1998). *Safe passage: Making it through adolescence in a risky society.* New York: Oxford University Press.

Fisher, C. B., & Lerner, R. M. (Eds.). (1994). *Applied developmental psychology.* New York: McGraw-Hill.

Flavell, J. H. (1963). *The developmental psychology of Jean Piaget.* New York: Van Nostrand

Hamburg, D. A. (1992). *Today's children: Creating a future for a generation in crisis.* New York: Time Books.

Harkavy, I. (1998). Organizational innovation and the creation of the new American university: The University of Pennsylvania's Center for Community Partnerships as a case study in progress. In R. M. Lerner & L. A. K. Simon (Eds.), *University-community collaborations for the twenty-first century: Outreach scholarship for youth and families* (pp. 275-287). New York: Garland.

Jessor, R., Donovan, J. E., & Costa, F. M. (1991). *Beyond adolescence: Problem behavior and young adult development.* Cambridge, UK: Cambridge University Press.

Kellogg Commission on the Future of State and Land-Grant Colleges. (1999). *Returning to our roots: The engaged institution.* Washington, D.C.: National Association of State Universities and Land-Grant Colleges.

Kennedy, E. M. 1999. University-community partnerships: A mutually beneficial effort to aid community development and improve academic learning opportunities. *Applied Developmental Science, 3* (4), 197-198.

Ketterlinus, R. D., & Lamb, M. E. (Eds.). (1994). *Adolescent problem behaviors: Issues and research.* Hillsdale, NJ: Erlbaum.

Kretzmann, J. P., & McKnight, J. L. (1993). *Building communities from the inside out: A path toward finding and mobilizing a community's assets.* Chicago: ACTA Publications.

Lerner, R. M. (1986). *Concepts and theories of human development.* (2nd ed.). New York: Random House.

Lerner, R. M. (1991). Changing organism-context relations as the basic process of development: A developmental-contextual perspective. *Developmental Psychology, 27,* 27-32.

Lerner, R. M. (1995). *America's youth in crisis: Challenges and options for programs and policies.* Thousand Oaks, CA: Sage.

Lerner, R. M. (1996). Relative plasticity, integration, temporality, and diversity in human development: A developmental, contextual perspective about theory, process, and method. *Developmental Psychology, 32,* 781-786.

Lerner, R. M. (In press). And a child shall lead you. *Kappa Omicron Nu FORUM.*

Lerner, R. M., De Stefanis, I., & Ladd, G. T., Jr. (1998). Promoting positive youth development: Collaborative opportunities for psychology. *Children's Services: Social Policy, Research, & Practice, 1*(2), 83-109.

Lerner, R. M., Fisher, C. B., & Weinberg, R. A. (1997).Editorial: Applied developmental science: Scholarship for our times. *Applied Developmental Science, 1*(1), 2-3.

Lerner, R. M., & Galambos, N. L. (1998).Adolescent development: Challenges and opportunities for research, programs, and policies. In J. T. Spence (Ed.), *Annual Review of Psychology* (Vol. 49, pp. 413-446). Palo Alto, CA: Annual Reviews.

Lerner, R. M., & Lerner, J. V. (1989). Organismic and social contextual bases of development: The sample case of early adolescence. In W. Damon (Ed.), *Child development today and tomorrow* (pp. 69-85). San Francisco: Jossey-Bass.

Lerner, R. M., & Miller, J. R. (1998). Developing multidisciplinary institutes to enhance the lives of individuals and families: Academic potentials and pitfalls. *Journal of Public Service and Outreach*, 3(1), 64-73.

Lerner, R. M., & Simon, L. A. K. (Eds.). (1998a). *University-community collaborations for the twenty-first century: Outreach scholarship for youth and families.* New York: Garland.

Lerner, R. M., & Simon, L. A. K. (1998b). The new American outreach university: Challenges and options. In R. M. Lerner & L. A. K. Simon (Eds.). *University-community collaborations for the twenty-first century: Outreach scholarship for youth and families* (pp. 3-23). New York: Garland.

Lynton, E. A., & Elman, S. E. (1987). *New priorities for the university: Meeting society's needs for applied knowledge and competent individuals.* San Francisco: Jossey-Bass.

Magrath, C. P. (1993). Comments to the Board on Home Economics on November 12, 1993. Washington DC: National Association of State Universities and Land-Grant Colleges.

Magrath, C. P. (1998). Foreword: Creating a new outreach university. In R. M. Lerner & L. A. K. Simon (Eds.), *University-community collaborations for the twenty-first century: Outreach scholarship for youth and families* (pp. xiii-xx). New York: Garland.

McHale, S. M., & Lerner, R. M. (1996). University-community collaborations on behalf of youth. *Journal of Research on Adolescence, 6,* 1-7.

Piaget, J. (1970). Piaget's theory. In P. H. Mussen (Ed.), *Carmichael's manual of child psychology* (3rd ed., Vol. 1, pp. 703-723). New York: Wiley.

Richardson, W. C. (1996). *A new calling for higher education.* The John W. Oswald Lecture, The Pennsylvania State University, University Park.

Scales, P., & Leffert, N. (1999). *Developmental assets: A synthesis of the scientific research on adolescent development.* Minneapolis, MN: Search Institute.

Schorr, L. B. (1997). *Common purpose: Strengthening families and neighborhoods to rebuild America.* New York: Doubleday.

Spanier, G. B. (1997). *Enhancing the quality of life for children, youth, and families.* Unpublished manuscript, The Pennsylvania State University, University Park.

Spanier, G. B. (1999). Enhancing the quality of life: A model for the 21st century land-grant university. *Applied Developmental Science,* 3(4), 199-205.

Votruba, J. C. (1992). Promoting the extension of knowledge in service to society. *Metropolitan Universities,* 3(3), 72-80.

Votruba, J. C. (1996). Strengthening the university's alignment with society: Challenges and strategies. *Journal of Public Service and Outreach, 1*(1), 29-36.

Votruba, J. C. (1999a). Implementing public policy education: The role of the university central administration. In P. Ralston, R. M. Lerner, A. K. Mullis, C. Simerly, & J. Murray (Eds.), *Social change, public policy, and community collaboration: Training human development professionals for the twenty-first century* (117-120). Norwell, MA: Kluwer.

Votruba, J. C. (1999b). Afterward. In P. Ralston, R. M. Lerner, A. K. Mullis, C. Simerly, & J. Murray (Eds.), *Social change, public policy, and community collaboration: Training human development professionals for the twenty-first century*. Norwell, MA: Kluwer.

4 WHAT IS SACRED IN A SECULAR UNIVERSITY?
A Scenario for the Next Century

Severyn Bruyn
Boston College

Alpha Omega University is located on a beautiful campus of rolling green hills and small pine groves in the Midwest. For the past one hundred and fifty years, it has been a successful private university, with a college of arts and sciences, a school of law, and a school of business. Decades ago, a large state university was established near by; in recent years, it has been attracting students away from Alpha Omega. While Commonwealth State University (CSU) has been growing rapidly, building curriculum diversity, an accomplished faculty, and new science and technology laboratories, Alpha Omega has been struggling. The administrative costs at Alpha Omega are high, too high to be competitive with CSU.

Commonwealth State University is in need of local space to grow; for the past few years, it has been forced to reject qualified and promising applicants because they do not have any more space to build new student housing. At the same time, applications are flooding into CSU because of its reputation for funding advanced research, faculty excellence, and low tuition. In light of the declining enrollment and difficult financial situation at Alpha Omega, the president of CSU has proposed a merger to the president of Alpha Omega. CSU offers to purchase a controlling interest in Alpha Omega, pay-off its debts, and seek a middle ground between Alpha Omega's sacred tradition and the public purposes of CSU.

The president of Alpha Omega is pondering the offer. Alpha Omega once had strong religious ties, but its denominational connections and affiliations had been left behind long ago. Alpha Omega has moved with the secular tide in higher learning. It has been competing with the best institutions in terms of academic excellence, including teaching, research, and service. But times have changed at Alpha Omega. With fewer students enrolling at Alpha Omega because tuition costs have grown too high too fast, administrative costs are eating away at the endowment. Alpha Omega may soon face bankruptcy; the president knows that Alpha Omega cannot afford to refuse CSU's offer. And yet, the president thinks to himself, won't Alpha Omega lose the very quality that differentiates it from other schools if it merges with a secular university? Although Alpha Omega has grown beyond its foundation of Christian teachings and traditions, something of the sacred remains. But what is that something?

CSU's offer isn't the president's only headache. He knows as well that a for-profit university is buying land in the region, expecting to compete on its own terms. These new, accredited, degree-granting, for-profit institutions, like the University of Phoenix (with 60,000 students, 4,500 adjunct faculty, $33 million in 1997 profits, a 1999 price/earnings ratio of 50, and a library with no books, only on-line journals and magazines), may soon buy not just small colleges like Alpha Omega but even large state university campuses like CSU. The organizational efficiencies of privatization can lower the cost of producing higher education enough to offer students a better financial deal, more immediate satisfaction, and still make a profit. Whatever is sacred about Alpha Omega, can it possibly be sustained under the organizational rubric of a for-profit university?

In order to preserve the integrity and particular mission of Alpha Omega through the coming period—whether through sale, or merger, or some major income-generating innovation, the president decides that he must discover what is sacred at the University. He must consult with the faculty senate and enlist their aid in this urgent, short-term inquiry. The faculty realize there are fiscal problems and are worried about their jobs and the character of the University. Rather than announcing a merger as a fait accompli, the president decides on the riskier, more anxiety-provoking, but perhaps more creative course. He will interpret the crisis as a dilemma for everyone to think about together, with the aim of reinventing the whole status of Alpha Omega. He will appoint two committees—one starting from the financial end and the other starting from the cultural/intellectual end. Each will keep the other apprised of its progress, and they will work towards making a single recommendation.

We report here only on that portion of his first talk to the faculty senate that addresses the academic side of the problem. He asks for help in marking a difference between Alpha and CSU, if indeed there is any critical difference:

> Alpha Omega has seen many changes. This century has brought with it a wave of secularization that has affected our curriculum and our policies. One hundred years ago, we taught everything from science to literature from a religious perspective. Today, naturalism and humanism are the essential philosophies of our University. Many of us have become Neo Keynesians and postmodernists; we read the latest trade journals and attend three to five conferences a year. And, even though most of us would argue that truth is obviously a relative term, we pursue it as vigorously as

our predecessors once did. Each of you, in your respective fields, operates under the assumption that knowledge is sacred. To imagine a larger sense of the sacred, let us ask this question: How many of us would be able to stand by and watch as books are thrown into a pyre, even if taking action might put us in prison? Not a single one of us. We have dedicated our lives to human knowledge and human truths. But what are these sacred truths?

Many of you are aware of the offer that has been made to us by Commonwealth State University and that a for-profit university is prospecting in this area as well. As you know, we do not seem to be in a position to refuse Commonwealth's offer. And yet, I am certain that none of us, myself included, want to risk losing what has made Alpha Omega a center of learning with an unparalleled commitment to academic and intellectual integrity and to the pursuit of knowledge for the betterment of humankind. This is why I have called this special session and stand before you today. I need your help. I am calling for volunteers to make a study of what is sacred at Alpha Omega. The study team will research schools of thought on "the sacred" and use these definitions to discover what is sacred to us at Alpha Omega. What are the truth-claims our faculty makes? How do we explain the universe to our students, and to ourselves? This is not an easy task, but it is a necessary one.

I propose to you: if we study *what is sacred* at Alpha Omega, we will find a tradition much different from Commonwealth State. I need you to provide us with a new vision for our university, so we can move with wisdom on this critical decision before us. Alpha has a different approach. What is sacred is not found simply in financial rescue by Commonwealth State. We need to deepen our insight into our mission. We need to examine what we teach students, and our own quest for understanding the mystery hidden in our universe.

Those of you interested in volunteering, please stay. Thank you for your support.

We will follow the reports of this academic study team. Appointed by department chairs based on their interest and ability to conduct such a study, the team members are given reduced loads by the president, so that they can devote two full days per week to the inquiry. Here are portions of the first academic team report to the president, after three weeks:

First Study Team Report to the President
Thinkers as far apart in history as Herodotus and Hegel believed that a shared sense of the sacred defines every age. It is the faith, the governing idea, and the ruling belief. G.W.F. Hegel wrote that the sacred is difficult to identify in one's own

time; it can be understood only when the age has passed. Anthropologists agree; many write that it is the idols of an age that reveal what was sacred at that time. Today, certain philosophers claim that Hegel's understanding of the West coincided with its end, that our culture became so rationalized and demythologized that it had lost its poetic power to inspire a future.

A scholar of major religions, Mircea Eliade, writes that the sacred has existed throughout history as "the revelation of the real." Other scholars posit that there are limits to what the human mind is able to discern as "real." For example, Dutch theologian C. A. Van Peursen writes that secularization is the deliverance from what we merely conceive of as sacred.

We have decided that this inquiry into what is sacred at Alpha Omega must include thinking about the relationship between the sacred and religion. But what is religion? Is it the Christian faith? The Muslim faith? Is it the collection of principles that each of us live by? We asked each other: "How can we define religion in a way that offers insight into our quest for what is sacred at our university?"

Some religious scholars have a "substantive definition" of religion (O'Dea, 1968). This definition refers to people's beliefs about a metaphysical (or supernatural) reality. It became clear to us that deeply felt beliefs and intensely held ideas, regardless of their nature, must also constitute the religious, and therefore the sacred.

On the other hand, some religious scholars use a "functional definition" that refers to beliefs that have a deep sense of meaning to people (Bellah, 1968). Functional beliefs are part of everyday life, as in our allegiance to the United States. Allegiance to our nation and its values can be the most vital beliefs by which we live—without assuming any transcendental Divine existence or a Supreme Being.

We realized that the difference in these two types of definitions did not distinguish between the depths, and the intensity of beliefs. We know of atheists, agnostics, and humanists that would sacrifice their life to protect the United States in a defensive war. A very religious person may not be willing to sacrifice his or her life for a religious creed or doctrine. In any case, we decided that deeply felt beliefs or intensely held "meaning systems" should become part of our research.

These perspectives on the sacred (historical, sociological, anthropological, and religious) form the background of our initial inquiry into what is sacred at Alpha Omega. During this inquiry, we have come to realize that the very act we are engaged in is sacred to us: the search for meaning and knowledge in the enhancement of our life. This search, and the pervasive belief in continuing this search at any cost, is the first answer we have found to the question of what is sacred at Alpha Omega.

Second Study Team Report to the President

Following your suggestion, members of our team decided to look for what is sacred in relation to what is secular at Alpha Omega, rather than think of these two ideas as confined to themselves. We did not see these ideas as fixed by sharp definitions or rigid boundaries, or isolated from one another. Indeed, when we first *debated the "sacred," we decided that it was essentially the subject of religion. This subject no longer exists at Alpha Omega. We asked each other: "How can we then define religion in a way that offers insight into our problem of the sacred in our university?"*

We needed to start somewhere. So, we looked for the most prominent ideas that were advanced by our colleagues. We surveyed colleagues' opinions and talked personally with representative faculty. We heard some faculty saying, "There is nothing sacred about what we teach." We decided to investigate this assertion further. We thought this statement might have some complexity.

In our search for what is sacred to our faculty at Alpha, we put aside campus mores and government laws as being in the category of the sacred. Although we know that serious violations of the law could mean prison or the death penalty, that was not our focus. Laws and mores are very serious matters, but we searched instead for our faculty's propensity to create and sustain ideas that seem to be vital and true. We stayed within our own quest for truth and knowledge.

One of us argued that "reason" may not be the "most sacred" at Alpha. Feelings and beliefs are always associated with the sacred and may be no less important to consider. If so, she said, there is something non-rational and sacred in scientific inquiry. When faculty express a deep moral feeling about anything, such as their codes of honesty in research, they hold both a belief and a feeling. Being honest is a very precious belief in our work. And feeling, she said, is never absent from our objective inquiry. It is in the excitement of discovering the last figure in a mathematical formula. Feeling is related to the discovery process itself.

We talked about the meaning of the sacred in terms of very "strong beliefs," "incontrovertible truths," and "a view of the whole." With these attributes in mind, we have begun to interview faculty to assess what carries those attributes. We want to continue our interviewing and to survey our students as well in our search for answers to these questions.

Although the president worries that in this time of enormous pressure to develop a strong direction, the team's first two reports remain at a very high level of abstraction, he is reassured by the team's obvious deep engagement in the task. He asks for a third report in another three weeks that will be delivered to the faculty senate and that will begin to recommend specific actions for the university to take. Here is an excerpt from that report:

After much research and many conversations with various members of the faculty and student body, we have concluded what is in the realm of the sacred at Alpha Omega.

We observe departments in conflict with one other, not only fighting ideological wars, but "doing battle" over space, money, and autonomy. High level administrators refer to our departments as "sacred domains," and "territories of knowledge." Individually, our faculty fight hard to protect and advance their professions as well as the bodies of knowledge they "profess." In fact, we have come to view the very act of being a professor as sacred; it is the act of professing human truths in our quest for knowledge.

Of course, what these truths consist of varies greatly. Faculty members define truth through the framework of their disciplines. We note here one claim a colleague made to us with a sense of final authority: "The whole universe is made of energy and matter." Since this assumption is made in many of our core courses, our study team debated the nature of this truth-claim at length.

Three questions asked by a team member illustrate that these truths are simply claims. This member asked: "What combination of energy and matter is intelligence? What are these questions made of? How close to the essential nature of the universe is intelligence?"

Then, a colleague in the social sciences told us: "Everything is political." We asked ourselves if we could imagine an instance in which the statement "everything is not political" might also be true. We concluded that this opposite claim could also be true.

Many ideas taught by our faculty are accepted as true, although they are based on premises that are not tested. In many cases, the premises that underlie these systems of knowledge cannot possibly be proven or disproved at all. Such is the case with mathematics, a system of knowledge that presupposes so many others, which has been uncertain of its own foundations for the past two hundred years.

Some of us had been alerted to the complexity of this issue long ago in Thomas Kuhn's The Structure of Scientific Revolutions (1962). Kuhn demonstrates how scientific theories attract true believers. Going further than Kuhn, we find students assume physical principles explain the universe, and we (as well as our students) have a faith in them which is almost unshakable. It is as though they are the gospel. Of course, this phenomenon of "accepted paradigms" is not limited to the physical sciences; it is present in the humanities, social sciences, and professional schools of law and business management. We see beliefs buried in all disciplines.

We also discovered that there is a widespread belief among our faculty in reductionism. We defined reductionism as the explanation of one subject, or system of knowledge, in terms of another system of knowledge which commands more authority or carries more "intellectual clout." For example, "consciousness" is explained in terms of the physical brain; the brain, in turn, is explained in the framework of biology and neurology; and in turn, molecular structures explain the "reality" behind neurons, and so forth. We see that students acquire this belief in reductionism without our faculty formally teaching it. It is tacitly learned.

Aside from the way we teach, we also find the sacred in what we emphasize interdepartmentally, in the structure of learning we design for our students: our core curriculum. The courses we choose to include in our core curriculum indicate which ideas and systems of knowledge are most sacred to us. In core courses, faculty members express their beliefs about human nature and the world in which we live. In fact, our core curriculum suggests that we hold a strong belief in segregated departments of knowledge.

We also see something sacred in the total environment of learning on campus. What is most vital and meaningful is generated by our campus way of life. In addition to core teachings and theories, a large body of informal learning occurs through the campus culture: the rules we create for dormitory life, the administrative criteria we use to strengthen certain departments over others, the choice of professional schools to develop on campus, the financial priority to bolster certain subjects, the sort of visitors and lecturers we bring to campus, and student life in local taverns. We found much learning in our football games, sports festivals, banners, colors, and flags. These are all factors that shape what students are learning at Alpha Omega. In this sense, the "sacred" is our whole way of life.

This was a shocking revelation to some members of our team. It led us to think more seriously about how the pattern of life on our campus and how it can become a continuing topic of inquiry and mutual experimentation, rather than of unquestioned habit and prerogative. Some say inquiry is the sacred trust of Alpha, but if so the sacred does not yet penetrate our taken-for-granted daily activities.

In conclusion, the sacred abounds at Alpha Omega; it is what and how we teach, and who we are. But what is truly sacred still remains a mystery. Although a given religion no longer colors the way we understand and teach each subject, something sacred certainly does.

Specific Proposals

We, the study team, propose that Alpha Omega remain distinct as it integrates with Commonwealth State by becoming the Alpha College at Commonwealth and by instituting two new curricular programs in which all Alpha students and faculty will participate. The two new programs enact entirely new inter-disciplines: sacred studies and practical studies.

Sacred studies will not be the same as religious studies. It will question the assumptions behind all fields of academic inquiry, and allow students the space not only to study the sacred, but also to discover what they themselves hold to be sacred. How to integrate the traditional third-person research in the sciences and humanities with the first-person research here called for has been informally explored in classrooms during the past generation. Now for the first time it becomes a central, systematic, explicit, shared research concern.

Practical studies will not be the same as the applied sciences. Practical studies will bring interdisciplinary attention to issues of conflict in our own lives together in the Alpha College at Commonwealth. The aim is to engage in second-person research among the participants in these courses, such that actual ethical, administrative, and cultural dilemmas are resolved in real time, with changes in behavior and school policy. For example, everyone knows vaguely about, but nobody discusses, the enormous divergences in faculty salaries. Should the salary structure be made public? Should it be reviewed and possibly reorganized, and according to what principles? Do we have the dialogue skills and the deliberative institutions to make such a conversation productive, and, if not, can we develop them? Effectual responses to such questions depend as much on an ear for poetry *and a sense of dramatic structure as it may on principles of political philosophy and strategies of organization design. Effectual responses also depend as much on timely actions as on eternal truths.*

After our students complete the normal core curriculum during their first year and a half, they join with the faculty during their remaining years at Alpha Omega, not just as apprentices in the specialized fields of knowledge in which they choose to major, but also as co-participants in courses where faculty may have more to unlearn and as much to learn as the students. Only such a commitment matches the challenge of treating inquiry as sacred at Alpha Omega.

The senate is surprised by the report. Some members are puzzled by the absence of more detailed proposals; some are infuriated by particular statements and wish to quarrel about each; others are shocked at the bluntness of the overall report. Several speakers are thoughtful in their questions of the committee and remind everyone else that their jobs are at stake in the challenge of finding a shared direction soon. The senate recommends that the academic team keep going. Indeed, many more faculty offer to participate with them. The team expands into subcommittees, and now they explore more attributes of "the sacred" in what most faculty see to be a secular university. They are finding what is sacred in what is secular. The two ideas are interpenetrating.

The team reviews teaching and research styles on campus and formulates two new, ideal types of teaching and research to complement lecture/discussion teaching and theoretical/empirical research. These ideal-types concern the way teaching and research lifts *tacit assumptions* and *tacit practices* into the light and encourages validation or disconfirmation, as well as change and transformation.

At this point, with the president's encouragement, the academic and financial teams begin to talk about integrating their work. The finance team verifies the terrible facts about the budget crisis. They say they can find no new source of funding, nor any promising new marketing strategy. They point out that distance-learning technologies permit both for-profit and state universities to compete for revenue with small, elite colleges. For example, Penn State's "World Campus" distance-learning program plans to offer 25 certificate programs to 5,000 students by 2003. They suggest that Alpha Omega consider federating with other small colleges, as small colleges in Pennsylvania recently have done. One of the social scientists on the finance study team points out that "private colleges create power through shared values, not just competition and capital." Hence, it would be consistent with its tradition for Alpha Omega to organize into a federation with other small colleges.

The president considers what has happened lately. Inspired by the suggestions of the academic study team for new types of inquiry and practice that can make Alpha Omega a still more lively version of its historic character, he imagines negotiating a financial relationship with CSU, endowing Alpha's position as a unique program at CSU, emphasizing "the value of inquiry and the practice of values," with a considerable degree of self-governing autonomy.

The president knows the extraordinary difficulties in making such a merger. He remembers how the chair of the faculty assembly at Texas Southern University called for a state takeover to save their institution from bankruptcy because of an enrollment drop, and how he was adamantly denounced publicly by his colleagues. He recalls also how a merger of a state university and a community college in Minnesota had its positive and negative side. Positively, it was designed to make student transfers easier between campuses, reduce program duplication, create new academic programs, reduce costs, and find a new mission for each institution. He remembers the chancellor of the Minnesota system saying, "We've really had to invent everything for ourselves." And he also remembers the head of a faculty group at CSU saying, "By trying to combine two cultures and missions, you wind up with no identity" (Healy, 1996, p. A23).

The president realizes that the time has come for him to move from the sacred studies methodology that he has, in effect, begun practicing with the faculty teams to clarify the assumptions underlying Alpha Omega. He must now move toward a practical studies methodology for taking action in this case. The sacred studies process has been enormously invigorating for the whole campus. A sense of community engagement and pride that has been missing for some years has re-emerged.

Perhaps some joint arrangement between Alpha Omega and CSU can become a model for other private universities facing crises in the next century. The president speaks to the faculty senate with a new eloquence, artfulness, and decisiveness:

> *I trust that you have all had time to review the study team's findings. They indicate that the sacred is like the air we breathe. It is more unconscious than conscious, hidden in the nature of knowing itself, an integral part of our lives and learning. The findings also indicate that our core curriculum is a play of irreducible themes: unity and diversity, sacred and secular, order and transformation, individual freedom and community responsibility, matter and spirit.*
>
> *We must now ask how to put these perennial "oppositions" into practice in our own time. How do they apply to us at Alpha Omega? How do they apply to each of us as we speak and act together? These questions are essential to maintaining the integrity of Alpha Omega as we embark upon the risky process of working with Commonwealth State and as we enter into preliminary discussions with sister institutions about a possible federation of small colleges and universities in this region.*
>
> *We welcome a period of uncertainty and transformation. As we begin this new interaction, we must attend carefully to our day-to-day practices. I want to propose a gesture that will communicate both our respect for what each says and our commitment to listening to one another. This discipline is to pause in silence for*

just two or three seconds after each person speaks in a meeting and scan the assembly to see who is ready to speak next. You will often forget, but whenever members of a meeting remember and enact this practice it will call us back to a dignity too often absent in our meetings. (He pauses three seconds, scanning the room.)

I also want to propose a mythical figure who will remind us of the wisdom, ingenuity, and openness to which we are now called. A folktale in Norway tells about a character named Askeladden who does nothing but improvise. He makes do with whatever haphazard tools he has been given, although he always gets the short end of the stick. Askeladden is given rags and refuse, but rises to each occasion to save the kingdom through improvisation. He celebrates the absurdity of his situation; he sees his way through the fray that was not in the script; and he makes possible those things that no one imagined could happen.

We have already proved that we have the capacity to improvise and innovate during these past stirring months. Let us continue to wear Askeladden's mantel as we face the unexpected together over the next several years.

Let us also remain true to our tradition of academic excellence, intellectual integrity, and spirited inquiry as we build our new programs of sacred and practical studies, and as we talk with Commonwealth State and with our sister small colleges about possible partnerships.

What must become truly sacred to us at Alpha Omega is more than just systems of knowledge and sets of ideas. Not just academic knowledge as we have known it, but the whole of life rests within this pursuit of meaning and truth. Our study of the sacred compels us to know more about who we are as scholars, teachers, researchers, and members of this community. Alpha Omega has a sacred mission. Now our sacred studies and our practical studies will shape who we become in this new partnership. May we close with a moment of silence? Thank you.

REFERENCES

Bellah, R. (1968). Sociology of religion. In D. Sills (Ed.), *International encyclopedia of the social sciences.* New York: Macmillan and Free Press.

Healy, P. (1996). Minnesota tackles the possibilities and problems of a public-college merger. *The Chronicle of Higher Education.*

O'Dea, T. (1968). Sects and cults. In D. Sills (Ed.), *International encyclopedia of the social sciences.* New York: Macmillan and Free Press.

5 TRANSFORMING SOCIAL SCIENCE: Integrating Quantitative, Qualitative, and Action Research

William R. Torbert
Boston College

During the twentieth century, the social sciences have been riven by paradigm controversies—so much so that physical and natural scientists often view this apparent disarray as prima facie evidence that social studies do not deserve the name science. For example, behaviorist and gestalt psychologists argued past one another well into the third quarter of the century; rational choice economists and political scientists, on the one hand, and institutional economists and political theorists, on the other, have tended to turn away from one another; and physical anthropologists and quantitative sociologists can talk to one another more easily than either group can to cultural ethnologists or qualitative sociologists.

At the same time, there is a great strain in the social sciences between research success in the most respected paradigms—Empirical Positivism and Multi-Method Eclecticism (Table 5.1 and the body of the chapter provides specific referents for these terms)—and the kind of outreach research, consulting, and teaching described and endorsed in this volume. During the past half century, faculty who have taken a more socially engaged attitude in their scholarship and teaching have stereotypically been viewed as "softer," as less research-oriented, and as less rigorous and less productive in their publishing.

Today, however, there are signs of new interpretive and participative paradigms that appreciate the ineluctable interweaving of observing, interpreting, and acting in all sciences, but especially in the human sciences. In these approaches, the human sciences are understood as developing knowledge not merely *about* anonymous, generalizable social patterns, but also *for* oneself and others in the midst of real-time social action (Heron, 1996; Reason, 1995; Skolimowski, 1994; Torbert, 1991). From the point of view of these approaches to social science (named Postmodern Interpretivism, Cooperative Ecological Inquiry, and Developmental Action Inquiry in Tables 5.1 and 5.2 and in the descriptions in the body of this chapter), the three main "difficulties" "in the way of" social science are in fact the very starting points of a true social science, rather than blockages to be avoided. These three "difficulties" are that: 1) persons hold different interpretive and action paradigms at any given time; 2) clarifying how subjectivity, intersubjectivity, and (at least relative) objectivity interweave is an ongoing lifetime inquiry project for each person rather than an intellectual puzzle that some can resolve for others; and 3) paradigms transform through some as yet little known alchemy of action and inquiry.

This chapter describes a "paradigm of paradigms" that organizes seven fundamentally different, yet also interweavable, approaches to social science. The chapter ends with an invitation to each reader to join in a Cooperative Inquiry aimed at diagnosing and potentially transforming our own ways of practicing social science. In this way, the chapter highlights the challenge each of us can choose to accept to transform our own research into a bridge between knowledge and practice. Such research need not be "soft," but rather can integrate: 1) "third-person," quantitative rigor with regard to data collected in the past; 2) "second-person," qualitative empathy, disclosure, and confrontation in multiple voices about participants' meaning-making in the present; and 3) our own "first-person" action inquiries that influence future social vision, strategies, performances, and assessments within our sphere of influence.

Today, an increasing number of studies are exploring how to achieve such integration. For example, during the summer of 1998, I witnessed a prize-winning symposium at the Academy of Management that featured completed doctoral dissertations from three different doctoral programs that not only *inform* the reader, but also document the *transform*ation of the researchers themselves, their families, and the organizations they researched (Bradbury, et al., 1998). Also, Fisher and Torbert (1995) describe, in clinical detail and in the multiple first-person voices of different participants, how managers can learn to act more effectively at work using the same theory that guides consultants in the second-person research/practice of catalyzing transformational changes in several organizations. Then, Rooke and Torbert (1998) offer "third-person" psychometric measures of CEOs and consultants in ten different organizations (including the organizations described in Fisher & Torbert, 1995), accompanied by quantitative measures of organizational transformation. The results show that hypotheses based on the same theory achieve statistical significance in predicting which organizations do and don't transform. Taken together, these studies illustrate how a social theory can be validated in first-person, subjective terms (helping managers who use it to become more effective), in second-person, intersubjective terms (helping consultants work with CEOs to change organizations), and in third-person, objective, statistical terms.

The next section offers two cases—one very brief, the other longer—of social scientists applying the seven-paradigm model of science to their own careers. Then, the chapter offers more detail about, and exemplars of, each of the seven paradigms, along with five propositions about the demands to which an adequate, inclusive, and integrative paradigm for the social sciences will respond. As previously stated, the conclusion invites other social scientists such as you, the reader, to join in a Cooperative Inquiry about this matter.

Figure 1. *Similarities and Differences Among Six Social Scientific Paradigms*

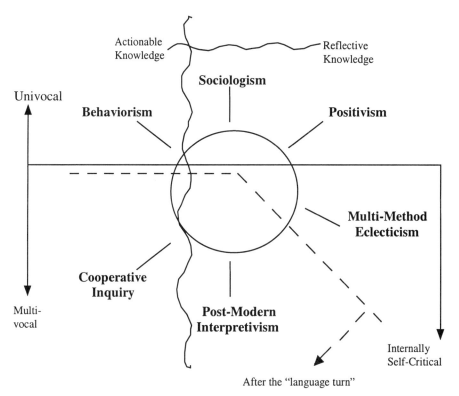

After the "language turn"

1) **Behaviorism, Gestalt Sociologism**, and **Empirical Positivism** are shown as univocal, or one-voiced. The logic of the scientist/protagonist rules all studies conducted under the aegis of these perspectives. By contrast, **Multi-Method Eclecticism, Post-Modern Interpretivism**, and **Cooperative Inquiry**) are each increasingly multi-voiced and increasingly self-critical and self-transforming during the course of a given study.

2) Whereas, **Behaviorism** and **Cooperative Inquiry** are at opposite ends of the spectrum according to the previous division, they are most alike when one divides—by the serpentine line slithering down the page—paradigms that are primarily action oriented from those that contribute primarily to a reflective understanding of the phenomena studied.

3) On the other hand, **Cooperative Inquiry** and **Postmodern Interpretivism** are most like one another in that both appreciate the radical implications of the language turn, the hermeneutical circle, which if followed backwards, upstream, toward origins liberates us from literal-minded enslavement in any paradigmatic assumptions. However, whereas **Postmodern Interpretivism** remains focused on texts, **Cooperative Inquiry** goes beyond the language turn to an "action turn."

Table 5.1 *The Distinctive Aims of Seven Social Scientific Paradigms*[i]

Behaviorism	*Control of the Other*	(through 'operant conditioning')
Gestalt Sociologism	*Understanding of the Other*	(better than that other's self understanding)
Empirical Positivism	*Predictive Certainty*	(valid certainty)
Multi-Method Eclecticism	*Useful Approximation*	(through triangulation)
	(this and foregoing paradigms separate research from practice and focus on third-person research)	
Postmodern Interpretivism	*Re-Presentation of Perspectival Pluralism*	(without privileging the writer's own perspective.)
	(includes first-person, double-loop research/practice)	
Cooperative Ecological Inquiry	*Creating Transformational Communities of Inquiry*	(among multi-perspectived co-committed)
	(includes first-, and second-person, single-, double-, and triple-loop research/practice)	
Developmental Action Inquiry	*Enacting Inquiry & Liberating Disciplines*	(across initially estranged cultures without shared purposes)
	(integrates 1st-, 2nd-, and 3rd person research/practice with all three loops in real-time)	

[i]Each later paradigm dethrones the primacy of the previous aim, reinterprets its meaning, and addresses some of its incompletenesses, by treating it as one strategic variable among others in the service of the new, qualitatively different aim. Each

paradigm after **Empirical Positivism** becomes more inclusive of uncertain realities (rather than counting as reality only that about which one can be certain), and also more inclusive of realities that are transformed by the very act of inquiry into them (e.g., the researchers' own awareness and actions during the study).

THE PARADIGM ADVENTURES OF TWO SOCIAL SCIENTISTS

One way of embodying the bare bones of Figure 5.1 and Table 5.1 is to reflect on one's own career through the lens of the multi-paradigm model. The following pages offer the reflections of Harvard's J. Richard Hackman and Boston College's Dal Fisher on their own scholarly careers after they had read the extended descriptions of each paradigm which are presented after their cases. J. Richard Hackman began his career as an experimental social psychologist in graduate school at the University of Illinois, then worked at Yale for a generation, and has held appointments in both Business and Psychology at Harvard for the past decade:

> I'm pleased that the paradigm descriptions are not hatchet jobs.
> I was clearly in the Empirical Positivist mode in graduate school at Illinois when I ran hundreds of experimental groups for my dissertation, but jumped to the Multi-Method Eclectic approach almost immediately upon arriving at Yale in 1966, influenced by Argyris and Lawler; and that approach characterizes my job enlargement work.
> Later I began to play in the direction of Postmodern Interpretivism, seeking, ambivalently, my clinical voice, taking literature as a genre more seriously, and doing a longitudinal case study at People's Express.
> But I think I've stopped in between those two positions at a place I guess I would call Multi-Conceptual Empiricism. I guess the sociologist in me doesn't see what going all the way to pure subjectivity buys you.

Dalmar Fisher, my colleague at Boston College's Carroll School of Management, offers the following more extensive and typically self-effacing self-portrait based on the model of multiple paradigms:

> The influence that brought me into the field of organizational behavior was that of Charlie Savage. Charlie was a thoroughgoing Gestalt Sociologist, who taught the old Harvard small group cases with quiet wit and puffs of the pipe tobacco that too soon killed him. His book, *Factory in the Andes*, a thick, sensitive, ethnographic description, was impressive to me. I thought, Wow, you can think in terms of imagery when you look at organizations, as when understanding a poem or novel. I was an MBA student at

BC, and had applied to a variety of doctoral programs. I added HBS to the list due to Charlie's influence.

At HBS, I remained ethnographic, doing as my first field project a study of a small sales office, replete with lots of diagrams of the subgroupings, what the norms were, critical incidents, etc. I took a seminar with Fritz Roethlisberger where he retold the Western Electric studies and praised the clinical methods of Piaget and Freud. It was the method he dwelt on. We hardly talked about the theory—though *The Moral Judgment of the Child* planted a seed in me that came to life later when I began working with Bill Torbert on human development.

Questionnaire methods and quantitative data analysis were just beginning to be employed by the HBS Organizational Behavior people at that time. I worked with Dave Moment on a study of managers in a department store. The project was quite thin on theory, had no hypotheses, and we (he) made up the methods as we went along, not a happy formative experience for me as an apprentice researcher, especially one who was in a doctoral program that didn't even have a research methods course. I didn't realize I was lacking something important in this area, and that I should do something about it. The department store project did, however, move me somewhat out of the Gestalt Sociologism paradigm, with now at least a toe into Empirical Positivism, or maybe into Multi-Method Eclecticism, in the sense that we were using two methods, albeit without rigor. Dave wrote a long, rambling manuscript about these data, replete with masses of mainly uninteresting quantitative tables, that was turned down for publication by the HBS Division of Research.

Dave was a great help to me on my thesis, however. I went out interviewing among the product managers and others they worked with in a division of General Foods. I had no plan, no design, no hypotheses, but Dave helped me see in the interviews that the kinds of preferences the product managers' associates had for them were systematically related to where the associates were in the organization. These expectations were incompatible, so we had a role conflict situation. Egged on by Barnes to take a close look at how product managers coped more and less well with this situation, I proceeded to do just that, using ratings of the product managers made by their variously focused associates as the criterion. So I had actually managed to find some structure for this project, at least compared to the black hole of the department store study, and came out of it with a doctorate and a chapter in a book edited by Lorsch and Lawrence on effectiveness in the integrator role. The differences in frames of the product managers' associates and the product managers' success and failure in working with people holding different frames were threads I would pick up much later in working with Bill Torbert on managers' developmental stages.

I mentioned some lacks in my doctoral education, but maybe the biggest was that nobody clued me in that you should extend and exploit your work. I had some really nice results in the thesis study, all built on top of theory, instrumented with measures, and with plenty of hypotheses that could now be stated, but I never followed up on it. I think I was too dependent on someone else to prompt me to do things—not enough of an initiator—as is still true. Looks sickeningly like the diplomat stage to me.

I did follow up in a partial way by joining Bruce Baker and Dave Murphy at BC on a funded study of project management. My inclusion was based on the nature of my thesis work. It was wholly a survey project. I made a few contributions, but didn't really get into it the way I might have if we had been able to look at role sets instead of just individual project managers, and we didn't interview any of our subjects, so we were very removed from "the territory," as Fritz would have termed it.

So I spent a chunk of my life on the project management study, and then a chunk on writing an organizational communication textbook. The textbook might be called Multi-method Eclecticism. It drew on literatures of all sorts. But I never really saw it as research. I didn't feel I was discovering anything new, or that I was trying to say something new with it. If I were re-living my life, I would omit both the project management study and the textbook project and do more work on product managers in their role sets (even if there were an interplanetary law stating that you could not do something different because that might mess up history).

I am grateful that Bill Torbert rescued me from the oblivion I had fallen into. His work based on developmental theory resonated with my interests going back to doctoral study days. My first involvement was with Keith Merron on the in-basket study, a solidly (both feet in) example of Empirical Positivism, a box we might have peeked out of toward Cooperative Inquiry when we gave feedback to the participants, although we did not follow up by exploring what happened when we gave the feedback. At any rate, I felt I was back in the realms of qualitative and quantitative data analysis, new ways of looking at managerial thought and action, and scholarly writing, all in a big way, aided enormously by Bill, not to mention Keith.

Our interview study of Achievers and post-Achievers (Fisher & Torbert, 1991) might possibly be termed a developmental move to Multi-Method Eclecticism. The methods weren't numerous, but interweaving the Washington University psychometric test of ego development with the open ended interview method allowed us to discover a lot more things about Strategists vs. Achievers as managers than could possibly be seen in the in-basket data, and some of these things were unexpected. Although we did again give feedback to our subjects on their developmental positions as measured by the Washington University test, the work cannot really be called Cooperative Inquiry, since the subjects did not participate in the formulation and conduct of the inquiry, and I have still not ventured into that kind of inquiry since that time.

The book I wrote with Bill, *Personal and Organizational Transformations* (1995), actually is in a late stage paradigm, maybe Developmental Action Inquiry. I can't really claim to have adopted that paradigm myself, however, since Bill wrote virtually all the parts of the book that invite the reader to take developmental action. I was beginning to get with this during the writing, but didn't fully. Nor did I even think of the book as "research" until, as some will recall, I was asked by Hilary Bradbury, in one of our Ph.D. seminars, what kind of research it was. I should think of more of what I do as research, e.g., teaching the new Managerial Practice sequence in the MBA program. Also, it didn't really dawn on me until after we completed the book that it could be seen as a new kind of social science writing, wherein the authors establish a dialog with the reader(s). That does look to be Developmental Action Inquiry. Perhaps I will put in a second foot.

FULLER DESCRIPTIONS OF
THE SEVEN SOCIAL SCIENCE PARADIGMS

The following pages offer brief developmental stage portraits of seven types of social science—Behaviorism, Gestalt Sociologism, Empirical Positivism, Multi-Method Eclecticism, Postmodern Interpretivism, and Cooperative Ecological Inquiry. These archetypal portraits have been developed by moving back and forth between a close study of the scientists studied as exemplars of each type and the action-logics characteristic of each personal and organizational stage of development (Table 5.2, below, summarizes the analogies across personal, organizational, and scientific archetypes; and Chapter 13, Table 13.4, offers more detail on each organizational action-logic.)

Table 5.2   *Analogies Among Personal, Organizational, and Social Scientific Developmental Paths*

Personal Dev't	Organizational Dev't	Social Scientific Dev't
I. Birth-Impulsive(0-6yrs)	I. Conception	I. Anarchism (Feyerabend, 1975)

(multiple, distinctive impulses gradually resolve into characteristic approach [e.g., many fantasies into a particular dream for a new organization])

| II. Opportunist(7-12?) | II. Investments | II. Behaviorism |

(dominant task: gain power [e.g., bike riding skill] to have desired effects on outside world)

| **III.** Diplomat$^{(12-?)}$ | **III.** Incorporation | **III.** Gestalt Sociologism |
| | | *(table continued)* |

(looking-glass self: understanding others' culture/expectations and molding own actions to succeed in their [e.g., market] terms)

| **IV.** Technician$^{(16-?)}$ | **IV.** Experiments | **IV.** Empirical Positivism |

(intellectual mastery of outside-self systems such that actions = experiments that confirm or disconfirm hypotheses and lead toward valid certainty)

| **V.** Achiever$^{(20?-?)}$ | **V.** Systematic Productivity | **V.** Multi-Method Eclecticism |

(pragmatic triangulation among plan/theory, operation/implementation, and outcome/evaluation in incompletely pre-defined environment—single-loop feedback unsystematically but regularly acted upon)

| **VI.** Strategist$^{(30?-?)}$ | **VI.** Collaborative Inquiry | **VI.** Postmodern Interpretivism |

(self-conscious mission/philosophy, sense of timing/historicity, invitation to conversation among multiple voices and to reframing of boundaries—hence, double-loop feedback occasionally acted upon)

| **VII.** Magician/Witch$^{(40-?)}$ /Clown of Inquiry | **VII.** Foundational Community of Inquiry | **VII.** Cooperative Inquiry |

(life/science = a mind/matter, love/death/transformation praxis among others, cultivating interplay and reattunement among inquiry, friendship, work, and material goods—continual triple-loop feedback and feedforward is sought, among intent [inquiry], emancipatory strategy [friendship], action [work], and effects [material goods])

| **VIII.** Ironist$^{(50?-?)}$ | **VIII.** Liberating Disciplines | **VIII.** Developmental Action Inquiry |

(full acceptance of multi-paradigmatic nature of human consciousness/reality, including distances/alienations among paradigms, such that few recognize paradigm differences as cause of wars, few seek paradigm disconfirmation and transformation, and few face dilemma/paradox of 'empowering leadership': that it must work indirectly through ironic words, gestures, and event-structures that invite participants gradually to attune themselves to listen for and play with single-, double-, and triple-loop feedback)

IX. Elder?	IX. ?	IX. ?

Behaviorism—Behaviorism emanates from an *assertive, physical quest for reliable, unilateral control* through "operant conditioning" of an unembarrassedly *objectified and atomized external world*. Its preferred method is *laboratory experiments* (maximizing the scientist's unilateral control over variation). Hence, also, its nominalist presumption of isolatable "stimuli" and "responses." Its choice of experimental subjects (rats and pigeons) who are unlikely to interpretively reframe the experiment, or refuse to cooperate, if tangible rewards are offered, masks the limits of the method. This approach has been particularly applicable and successful with populations who share its assumptions about the world and who inhabit total institutions (prisons, asylums, and young children in orphanages).

B. F. Skinner (1953, 1971; Argyris, 1971) can be considered an archetypal behaviorist who unflinchingly made the underlying philosophical assumptions of the Behaviorist worldview explicit. The special brilliance of the greatest lab, experiments—such as the Asch experiments on conformity and the Milgram experiments on obedience to authority—is that they reveal the underlying lateral and hierarchical social pressures, structures, and presumptions through which this paradigm of unilateral control works in the human world, thereby raising the question whether, how, and when the human world works otherwise. Global finance capitalism, with its single, clear, nominalist-type, second-by-second measure of shareholder value in the stock market, is a macro example of this action/research paradigm at work in our everyday world.

In my own field of management and organization studies, Frederick Taylor took an essentially Behaviorist approach to the study of making labor in factories more efficient at the turn of the twentieth century. As is characteristic of Behaviorist studies, Taylor unquestioningly asserted unilateral control over his blue collar subjects (indeed, he chose as subjects those most amenable to such control, Morgan, 1997).

Gestalt Sociologism—Gestalt Sociologism (a neologism intended to remind us of gestalt psychology, qualitative field studies in sociology, ethnography, and the case study tradition in schools of business, education, and law) emanates from an *appreciative, emotional quest to understand wholistically* the *overall pattern* of subjective beliefs, values, and rituals of given "other" cultures. Hence, its preferred method of *non-interventionist, ethnographic field observation*. Hence, also, its essentialist presumption of integrative ideas, norms, and selves (Cooley, 1956; Mead, 1934). And hence, its concentration on ideographic case studies of human groups.

The special brilliance of the greatest such studies—such as Mead's *Coming of Age in Samoa* (1960), or White's *Street Corner Society* (1981)—is that they encourage counter-studies and critiques (Kirk & Miller, 1986), which render them controversial. Then, through the contrast between study styles and between our own culture and the alien culture they depict, they reveal the underlying mechanisms, categories, and presumptions through which our own encultured understanding works. In this way, implicitly if not explicitly, they raise questions over time about the validity of our own cultural assumptions.

In management studies, in the 1920s, Elton Mayo, Fritz Roethlisberger and others at the Harvard Business School engaged in the famous Western Electric studies, taking a Gestalt Sociological approach to understanding the culture of groups of workers at the Hawthorne plant (Roethlisberger, 1977). They also participated in developing the Gestalt Sociological case study method of instruction that lasts to this day at the Harvard Business School, Tuck, Colgate-Darden, and other schools of management.

Empirical Positivism—Empirical Positivism emanates from a *critical* (but not hermeneutically self-critical), *intellectual quest for valid certainty* about *deductively logical, universally generalizable, empirical propositions* (Cook & Campbell, 1979; Hunt, 1994). This paradigm is not necessarily identified with a particular method, but it privileges randomized sample, experimental, hypothesis testing studies, along with computer modeling of intelligence, because of the crisply clear quantitative, binary certainty about distinctions between confirmation and disconfirmation of hypotheses.

The special brilliance of the greatest such studies—such as Herbert Simon's theoretical and empirical demonstrations of the concept of "bounded rationality" in economics and administrative science—is that they show the limits of deductive rationality itself (Hammond & Ritchie; 1993, March & Simon, 1958; Simon, 1947, 1957, 1969, 1989, 1991; Turkle, 1991). The special danger of such work is that it obscures the very possibility of a constitutive, analogical, emancipatory rationality that reaches beyond the inductive, the deductive, and the instrumental. For example, the content of Simon's propositions about rationality may obscure the very type of constitutive rationality that Simon's work itself also is, as well as alternative constitutive rationalities (e.g., those of each of the other developmental stages). The special "cleverness" of work like Simon's is that it uses the Empirical Positivist paradigm, language, and precision to point toward the triangulating, "satisficing" logic of Multi-Method Eclecticism, while simultaneously capturing, in the concept of "bounded rationality," the paradigmatic plight of all the developmentally early paradigms. Such "bounded rationality" is today characteristic not just of children's psychology, but also of over 90% of all adults. (Torbert, 1991).

Simon is himself viewed as a management scholar. As management schools increased their emphasis on research during the 1960s and 1970s, quantitative Empirical Positivism, like Simon's work, increasingly became the dominant paradigm, as indicated, for example, by the very high percentage of quantitative articles in the leading journal of the field, *Administrative Science Quarterly* during that period (Van Maanen, 1998).

Multi-Method Eclecticism—Multi-Method Eclecticism emanates from a *practical quest to increase* validity, understanding, applicability, and *percentage of the variance explained*, along with an aborning suspicion that different methods and measures may yield *incommensurable* results. This approach recommends *triangulation* among quantitative and qualitative methods. It is currently fashionable and in flower in the managerial disciplines (e.g., Bartunek, Bobko, & Venkatramen, 1993; Dyer & Wilkins, 1991; Eisenhardt, 1989).

A brilliant example of Multi-Method Eclecticism is Karl Weick's early work in collaboration with Campbell, Dunnette, and Lawler (Campbell et al., 1970), *Managerial Behavior, Performance, and Effectiveness*, based on a "multitrait-multimethod matrix." "Disagreement between different observers," they say, "should not necessarily be viewed as a mark of unreliability . . . but should instead be viewed as a possibly valid indication that differing aspects of the manager's behavior are being accurately perceived and reported" (p. 115).

Of course, still another possibility in a case of disagreement among observers such as Weick and his colleagues had earlier observed, is that the disagreement may result from differing interpretive schemes of the observers, a possibility that opens toward the next paradigm: Postmodern Interpretivism. As we shall see, Karl Weick is playing a role in legitimizing this paradigm as well, with his 1995 book *Sensemaking*.

Postmodern Interpretivism—Postmodern Interpretivism emanates from a *self-consciousness* encountering the dilemmas of accounting for the radical *subjectivity and fragmentariness of perspective* that embraces every languaged perception and conception. No matter how validly and elegantly the strange, object-ing reality at issue is clothed in the statistical, methodological, and theoretical constructions of the earlier, pre-participative social sciences, the Postmodern Interpretivist (e.g., Denzin & Lincoln, 1994; Macey, 1993) wishes to deconstruct the implicit, presumedly neutral background of the objects foregrounded in any study, as well as the background of the researcher and of the writing, and to foreground multiple interpretive voices about the reality at issue (Fine, 1994, is an excellent brief exemplar, as is Chapter 8 in this book).

The Pfeffer-Van Maanen debate during the early 1990s about the future of management scholarship pits an early, single-frame "Pfeffer-digm" against Van Maanen's Postmodern Interpretivist rhetoric (Frost, Pfeffer, Van Maanen, 1995; Pfeffer, 1993; Van Maanen, 1995). At best, this multi-voiced debate about the future of management and organization studies will open the field to a more significant challenge than either party in the debate identifies—namely, the attempt to delineate and practice a social science that situates all of us as aspiring action inquirers, rather than dividing data collection, reflection, and action from one another.

New types of validity are constructed by Postmodern Interpretivists. For example, Lather (1993) suggests that social scientists commit to developing *reflexive validity, ironic validity, rhizomatic validity,* and *situated validity. Reflexive validity* is raised when a text attempts to challenge its own validity claims. In the case of this text, for example, note the abstract, relatively unillustrated voice of the "description" of this and the other paradigms (as is typical of a great deal of Postmodern Interpretivist writing!). I attempt to correct for this level of abstraction by offering the two cases in the earlier section, as well as by offering examples of research studies based in the Cooperative Inquiry and Developmental Action Inquiry paradigms in Chapters 9 and 13.

Ironic validity is raised by inviting further interpretation by readers. Hopefully, in this text the earlier comments by Hackman and Fisher encourage other readers to apply this seven paradigm model to their own careers (see also Chapter 13 where different voices comment on the original text of that study).

Rhizomatic validity is raised when a text presents multiple voices defining the situation differently. For example, my colleague, Dal Fisher, commented on these paragraphs, prior to the inclusion of these short examples for each of these unfamiliar types of validity: "Can't help on this one, since I don't understand even a fragment of it. I guess I can suggest fewer terms (many fewer) and more illustration of actual works."

Situated validity is raised when a text includes not just a disembodied voice, but an embodied, emotional, reflective voice. For example, one response I have to Fisher's comment and the brief illustrations it has engendered in these paragraphs is "I love Dal's and my differences." Many of the chapters of this book explicitly include the first-person voice of the author.

The reader will note that at present these criteria of validity are stated in nominal terms (a text either does or does not address them). As they become more common, we can expect ordinal criteria of better and worse ways of meeting each validity challenge—indeed, Denzin (1995) and Behar (1997) begin to formulate ways of judging the efficacy of the use of first-person authorial voice and experience in studies.

Postmodern Interpretivism strongly implies the need for a first-person research/practice (e.g., Weick, 1995), but to date this requirement is more often stated in third-person, abstract terminology than practiced in first-person accounts interwoven with second- and third-person research in the midst of ongoing practice. See Bravette (1997) for a striking exception, where she not only includes her own (changing) voice throughout, but also draws her family into a cooperative inquiry.

Cooperative Ecological Inquiry—Cooperative Ecological Inquiry emanates from a *commitment to creating real-time communities of inquiry that bridge subjectivities and differences of perspective and support peaceful, ecologically-sensitive personal and organizational transformation* (Bradbury, 1998; Spretnak, 1991; Torbert, 1976). This kind of cooperative inquiry (Bradbury, 1998; Cooperrider & Srivastva, 1987; Heron, 1996; Reason, 1995) occurs in real time with partners also committed to integrating action and inquiry (to integrating first- and second-person research/practice) and to generating increasing mutuality (the condition for full voice, trust, critique, and transformation). One enters into this kind of "betting-one's-whole-life" exploration with others through the recognition that one does not first learn the truth, then act upon it, but rather that research itself and our lives as wholes are actions. Thus, we act before we deeply care about truth, we act as we seek truth (and as our sense of the truth we seek transforms), and we seek truths that will inform, not just a reflective concept of the world and future plans, but present awareness and action (MacMurray, 1953; Reason, 1995; Torbert, 1981). Social constructivism is an epistemological position consistent with this paradigmatic approach (Gergen, 1994).

The difficult and important questions come to be seen as how—in the midst of participating intersubjectively in specific situations—to listen, experiment, and seek disconfirmation (Argyris, Putnam & Smith, 1985) in a timely fashion (Torbert,

1991). Chapter 9 illustrates this process in great detail. Likewise, the primary question becomes not how to create an off-line community of inquiry among scientific writers and journal editors, but how to create a real-time community of inquiry within one's family, at work, or within voluntary organizations to which one belongs (as Chapter 8 illustrates).

For example, Margaret Mead (1972), Gregory Bateson (1972), and their anthro-philosophico-autobiographical daughter, Mary Catherine Bateson (1984, 1990) have not only been distinctive social scientists in their own right, but have also collaborated with one another as a "family of inquiry" in a variety of ways, including trans-conventional relationships. A scene when the male, paternal Bateson questions in a friendly way whether he and his daughter should violate the incest taboo, and she responds in a friendly but conclusive way that she does not wish to, is a particularly powerful demonstration of the real-time practice of second-person inquiry, mutuality, and disconfirmation.

Developmental Action Inquiry—Developmental Action Inquiry emanates from a growing appreciation that different persons, organizations, and cultures are complex, chaotic interweavings of the six prior paradigms (Alexander & Langer, 1990; Cook-Greuter, 1999; Kegan, 1994; Lavoie & Culbert, 1978; Miller & Cook-Greuter, 1994; Pondy & Mitroff, 1979; Torbert, 1987; Wilber, 1995). No one of these paradigms will win the paradigm-war once and for all. Indeed, this very definition of the situation is illusory: not martial arts and paradigm wars, but the arts of healing and inter-paradigmatic conversation and work become a beckoning and shareable (but not easily shareable) purpose. An interweaving of first-, second-, and third-person research/practice, with single-, double-, and triple-loop feedback (see Table 5.2 and Figure 5.2) makes such inter-paradigmatic conversation and work sustainable.

In third-person research/practice of this kind, Ironist leadership creates Liberating Disciplines (see Figure 5.2, below, as well as Table 13.4) that introduce organizational members to the interplay of first-, second-, and third-person research/practice, such that they can gradually elect to practice in these ways, thereby challenging both themselves and the initial leadership to further voluntary, mutual transformation. In my work with colleagues, we aim to exemplify the Developmental Action Inquiry paradigm (while discovering from study to study how incomplete our sense of it is!). We have long combined experimental laboratory studies (Merron, Fisher & Torbert, 1987; Torbert, 1973), with clinical interview and observation studies (Fisher & Torbert, 1991; Torbert & Rogers, 1972), and with intervention studies (Fisher & Torbert, 1995; Rooke & Torbert, 1998; Torbert, 1991), all in real-time organizations that we are co-constructing with the other research participants.

From the integrative Developmental Action Inquiry perspective, each paradigmatic perspective, when it is taken in recognized complementarity to the other action-logics, is a positively powerful, beneficial, and valid analogue of the preeminent features of a situation at different moments. By contrast, each paradigmatic perspective becomes demonic to the degree that it is asserted as the only legitimate kind of truth in all moments. "An active consciousness holds all ideas lightly" (Marshall, 1995).

Earlier paradigms tend to emphasize their revolutionary dissimilarity from the paradigms prior to them. In contrast, Developmental Action Inquiry highlights the contrapuntal rhythms, cross-scale interruptions, and interventions in developmental movement from one paradigm to another, whether in single conversations or in whole lives (Torbert, 1989). All types of validity testing described in earlier paradigms are accepted as conditionally appropriate, depending upon the degree to which one's current aims correspond with the purpose of truth seeking in that paradigm. Finally, however, in Developmental Action Inquiry, generalization to all moments is recognized as occurring: 1) voluntarily; 2) one person at a time, and 3) "slowly" within that person (i.e., over a lifetime), as she or he practices awareness-expanding action inquiry at more and more moments.

Figure 5.2. *Single-, Double-, and Triple-Loop Enactment*
           and Feedback
           In Personal, Interpersonal, Organizational, and Scientific
           Research/Practice across Four Territories of Experience

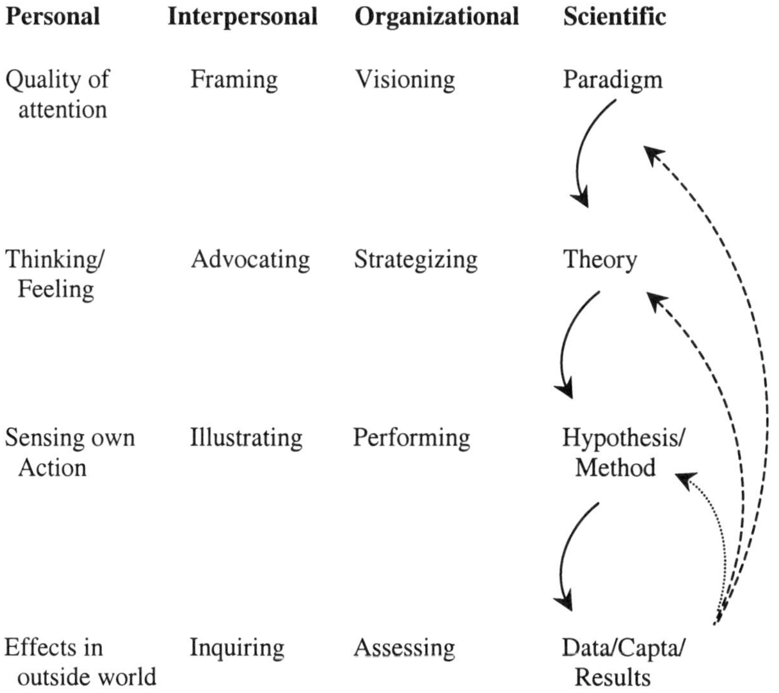

Personal	**Interpersonal**	**Organizational**	**Scientific**
Quality of attention	Framing	Visioning	Paradigm
Thinking/ Feeling	Advocating	Strategizing	Theory
Sensing own Action	Illustrating	Performing	Hypothesis/ Method
Effects in outside world	Inquiring	Assessing	Data/Capta/ Results

FIRST-, SECOND-, AND THIRD-PERSON RESEARCH/PRACTICE

I have been using the unfamiliar terms first-, second-, and third-person research/practice until now without offering any extended description of what I mean, leaving it to the reader's intuition and the context to generate clues. The notion of the relatively unfamiliar later paradigms can come a little clearer through explicating these terms a bit further.

In the most general sense, first-, second-, and third-person research/practice are kinds of research and practice in real time that we adults can potentially conduct in the midst of our daily practices of working, loving, and wondering. Initially, one is likely to regard some actions, such as asking someone a question, as a kind of research, and other actions, such as telling a subordinate what to do, as a kind of practice. Later, one increasingly recognizes how each action is both a practice that influences what happens next and research that leads one to confirm or disconfirm what one knew before. First-person research/practice in general includes all those forms of research/practice that any one of us can do by oneself by dividing and otherwise stretching one's attention (Torbert, 1991) to encompass all four territories of experience shown in Figure 5.2. Second-person research/practice includes all times when we engage in supportive, self-disclosing, and confronting ways with others in shared first-person research/practices and in creating micro-communities of inquiry among those present. (Such inquiry does not go on forever on any given topic because the question of what actions are timely when is itself an ongoing key issue.)

Third-person research/practice can be of two very different sorts. The first sort, which is by far the most common (and is characteristic of the early paradigm types of social science up through Multi-Method Eclecticism), does not really qualify as research/practice at all because it conceptually and operationally segregates research from practice, as well as treating first- and second-person research practice as pre-scientific or unscientific. The second, and much more rare, kind of third-person research/practice, characteristic of Developmental Action Inquiry, also begins by developing impersonal structures (whether survey instruments or an organizational design) for persons initially unknown to the initiators of the organizing process. In all other respects, however, the aims of "true" third-person research/practice differ from bureaucratic organizing and positivist research. First and foremost, the actual tasks defined by true third-person research/practice structures *require* that, over time, participants transform toward engaging in first- and second-person research/practice that tests their personal and interpersonal assumptions, if they are to become increasingly effective participants in the organizing process.

Because the previous paragraphs offer long, abstract of definitions, let us turn to a more concrete illustration of how these ideas relate to one of the institutions that directly touches all of us in one way or another—the health care system (or should we in the U.S. in 1999 call it the "health care chaos"?). A general definition of health-enhancing first-person research/practice may be something like "pro-active, self-chosen exercise—whether mental, emotional, or physical—engaged in with an ongoing sensitivity to the pace that suits oneself." No amount of doctors' care and medicine can keep us healthy for long without this sort of first-person research/practice. We are beginning to learn that a second critical element in making our health and our life as a whole better or worse is the daily character of our second-person research/practice—our associational activities at work, with our family, and during our leisure (Karasek & Theorell, 1991). At present, however, medical schools strongly emphasize third-person research and encourage the best students to become specialists who focus on third-person research, rather than to become managed care generalists who integrate first-, second-, and third-person research/practice and who can lead their clients toward an appreciation of their own daily first- and second-person research/practices (Howe, 1996).

Having offered a brief definition of each type of research/practice and a very brief illustration of how the three tend *not* to interweave in our current health care institutions, let me now offer a slightly fuller description of each.

First-Person Research/Practice—As stated above, first-person research/ practice in general includes all those forms of research/practice that each of us can only do by and for ourselves, by dividing and otherwise stretching our attention. This includes a variety of forms of writing—for example, journal or diary keeping, episodic or comprehensive memoir or autobiographical writing (Alderfer, 1989; Bedeain, 1993; Harrison, 1995; Min, 1993; Raine, 1998; Ramsey, 1995), and the recording of dreams or role plays of future scenarios (and these can all become sources for second-person and third-person research/practice as well; Torbert & Fisher, 1992; Fisher & Torbert, 1995). First-person research/practice also includes the varieties (and there are many) of meditation and prayer, either as distinct activities in a distinctive setting, or in the midst of everyday outer activities (see Schmidt-Wilk, Alexander & Swanson, 1996, for a whole tradition of retrospective, third-person research on the effects of regular first-person meditation). Furthermore, first-person research/practice can include chanting, asking a question of the *I Ching* (the ancient Chinese "Book of Changes"), or Tarot cards, and movement (e.g., t'ai chi, Dervish whirling, Gurdjieffian movements), or otherwise physically exercising in an awareness-widening fashion. It can include craft or artistic work engaged in, not primarily for the sake of the end product, but equally for the experience of awareness-discovery during the activity itself. An occasional, frequent, or continual effort to re-contact the four territories of experience, as represented in Figure 5.2, and to determine from feedback whether we are acting with integrity (saying what we mean, doing as we say, and having the effects we intend) is one way of expressing the aim of first-person research/practice.

Second-Person Research/Practice—Second-person research/practice includes all times when we engage in supportive, self-disclosing, and confronting ways with others in shared first-person research/practices. Another way of putting this is that second-person research/practice includes all conversations where those present share an intent to learn about themselves, about the others present, about a shared activity, and/or about the relationships that are forming, transforming, or dissolving. This can, but in empirical terms only rarely does, happen today, in a therapeutic or consulting relationship; between friends or lovers; among team members at work, at school, or at play; in a theatrical production or improvisation; between a doctor, lawyer, or other professional and the client; and, of course, between a master/teacher and one or more apprentice/pupils. Twelve-step meetings can be said to be intended to be second-person research/practices that support the first-person research/practice of non-addictive behavior. If such conversations are audio- or videotaped, then the resulting tapes can be used in further first-person research/practice, second-person research/practice, or third-person research/practice. (Again, Chapter 9 offers an in-depth illustration of a particular effort at conducting such second-person research/practice.)

Second-person research/practice is characterized by alternations between rehearsal and performance, periodic feedback among the participants about their perceptions of themselves and others present and periodic "feedforward" about what vision and strategies ought to guide continuing action. As first-, second-, and third-person research/practice become increasingly artful, continual, and mutually coordinated, they increasingly generate not only single-loop learning (the loop between Assessing and Performing in Figure 5.2, i.e., how to change performance to achieve a goal more effectively), but also double-loop learning (the loop between Assessing and Strategy, i.e., how to transform one's overall action-logic, whether "one" be person, relationship, or organization), and triple-loop learning (the loop between Assessing and Visioning, i.e., how to transform one's present awareness; Austin, 1996; Bartunek & Moch, 1987; Nielsen, 1993, 1996; Torbert, 1973; Torbert & Fisher, 1992).

At its best, second-person research/practice gradually transforms hierarchical aspects of the relationship toward more peer-like qualities (or else simply concludes the engagement, if it was purely professional). This transformation toward increasing "I-Thou" partnership is the normative direction of second-person research/practice because peers are most empowered to challenge, support, balance, and understand one another, that is, to conduct valid research together (Buber, 1958; Grudin, 1996; Heron, 1996; Jourard, 1968; Kramer, 1995; Rank, 1978; Reason, 1994, 1995; Rogers, 1961; Srivastva & Cooperrider, 1990; Torbert, 1991).

Third-Person Research/Practice—Third-person research/practice develops impersonal structures for persons initially unknown to the initiators of the organizing process. In all other respects, however, the aims of "true" third-person research/practice differ from bureaucratic organizing and positivist research. The actual tasks defined by third-person research/practice structures *require* that participants engage in first- and second-person research/practice (expanding their awareness and exercising increasing creativity and choice), in order to accomplish the goals and help maintain integrity among purpose, strategy, performance and outcome. In short, third-person research/practice organizes not only to achieve outcomes, but also to help organizational participants increasingly develop the capacity to see, confront, and transform incongruities among the four territories of experience at the person, team, and organizational levels. Thus, even though subordinate/participants are initially expected to conform to the pre-defined structures, they are simultaneously encouraged and educated to confront them, if they appear to be incongruous with the organizational mission (which is itself held open to inquiry). In other words, true third-person research/practice structures create dilemmas and choices for participants, not just constraints, based on information about relationships among strategic priorities, actual performances, and outcome assessments. Only such Liberating Disciplines (see Table 13.4 and Torbert, 1998) create the increasing mutuality and peer-likeness that both supports and results from personal, group, organizational, and epistemological transformations. The Ironist leadership alertness and the appropriate vulnerability required to be willing and able to generate such third-person research/practice is, of course, rare and can be generated only through long and continuing experience of first- and second- person research/practice (for example, see Torbert, 1991; Fisher & Torbert, 1995; and Rooke & Torbert, 1998).

FIVE PROPOSITIONS TOWARD AN INTEGRATIVE SOCIAL SCIENCE PARADIGM

By way of summarizing the immense distance between Empirical Positivism and Developmental Action Inquiry, I offer five propositions about central concerns of the Developmental Action Inquiry approach that are simply not treated in Empirical Positivism.

Proposition I *An adequate, inclusive, integrative paradigm for the social sciences will show the relationship among three broad types of social research and knowledge: 1) quantitative forms of research and knowledge; 2) qualitative, interpretive forms of research and knowledge; and 3) action-oriented research and knowledge to be practiced in real-time social living.*

Proposition II *An adequate paradigm for the social sciences will permit those working within it to recognize that different cultures, organizations, and individual persons work within different paradigms (indeed, with close self-observation, any given inquirer will find that she/he bounces back and forth among different paradigms at different moments).* For coherent understanding and work to occur under these circumstances, *inter-paradigmatic communications* and *uncoerced paradigm transformation* are necessary (Benhabib, 1986; Moon, 1991). An adequate paradigm for the social sciences (and for intercultural organizations and executives in a global society) will be a paradigm of paradigms that highlights the possibilities for transformational, liberatory rationality and dialogue, while simultaneously recognizing the current empirical preponderance of merely instrumental and strategic rationality in human discourse (Habermas, 1984, 1987; Johnson, 1991). Such an integrative paradigm will teach its practitioners how to respect the dignity of each paradigmatic approach and voice, how to construct multi-paradigmatic research, and how to invite transformation among researchers, practitioners, and organizations in real-time research and action.

Proposition III *An adequate paradigm for the social sciences will recognize that human beings are active seekers of knowledge in the midst of action, not merely passive consumers of pre-digested knowledge in a reflective mode* (even though, tragically, mainstream science and education obscure this reality, so that many people treat themselves as solely or primarily passive consumers of knowledge). In the active, inquiring mode, persons seek not just knowledge of what is generally true in the world outside ourselves, but also what is uniquely true at the present time about ourselves-in-action-with-others. In the active, inquiring mode, an observant participant will listen for his or her own first-person voices and for others' distinctive second-person voices, exploring how these interweave with third-person knowledge and language. Thus, an adequate paradigm of social science will describe the methods and action competences required for valid scientific inquiry in the midst of action in which one is an observant participant. Such a paradigm will not only cultivate (relatively) valid empirical knowledge and theoretical constructs (as both the social and the natural sciences currently attempt to do). It will also cultivate action inquiry skills such as writing, speaking, event structuring, and listening skills that encourage one's readers or interlocutors to initiate and inquire as well. Most of all, such a paradigm of social science will cultivate primarily, not cognitive schemes that serve as reflective answers, but rather an inquiring awareness in the midst of action.

Proposition IV *The type of theory that will characterize an integrative social science paradigm useful in the midst of action not only seeks* decriptive validity *as generalizable to events of the past, but also seeks two other types of validity:* existential validity *as widening/deepening the action inquirer's awareness in the here-and-now; and* prescriptive validity *as normatively ethical and politically timely for guiding actions intended to shape the future.* To achieve these three apparently divergent aims, one seeks an *analogical theory of timely development toward greater awareness, mutuality, free choice, and accountability.* This analogical theory reminds one to seek a more than thought-bound awareness at any time one remembers it, and applies across self, others, groups, organizations, industries, and nations. (Torbert, 1991).

Table 5.2 and Figure 5.2 are both examples of analogical theories. Figure 5.2 shows a theoretical model of four "territories of experience" (explained in greater detail in Chapter 13) and suggests what analogous qualities manifest each territory at the intra-individual, the interpersonal, the organizational, and the scientific scales. The model has potential descriptive, existential, and prescriptive validity (see Fisher & Torbert, 1995). For example, it is existentially valid in that, at all moments when one remembers it, one can remind oneself to widen one's awareness beyond the thinking territory, to one's present sensation and the outside world, as well as "back" toward the pre-cognitive source of awareness itself (of course, guidance from persons who have been exploring such widened awareness can be useful, see Torbert, 1991). The developmental theory in Table 5.2 shows how persons, organizations, and scientific inquiry can analogically develop the capacity to sustain the kind of four-territory action inquiry envisioned in Figure 5.2. Applying this theory in real-time to oneself and the other persons, groups, or organizations interacting can help one invent and produce timely actions.

Proposition V *An adequate inclusive and integrative paradigm for the social sciences will envision a key role for irony, drama, and fiction in social truth-seeking and truth-telling* (as he fictional future scenario in Chapter 4 illustrates). For, *if* persons, organizations, and cultures in fact operate at a given chronological time at different points in developmental time and therefore within different, relatively incommensurate paradigms *which, for the most part, do not recognize the legitimate existence of alternative paradigms, then* inter-paradigmatic messages will tend initially to be mis-interpreted within the receiving paradigm as wrong or as inadequately formed messages. Only if a message is "sculpted" ironically (see

Lather, 1993, on ironic validity) will it appeal to the receiving paradigm enough for the recipient to work through its apparent inconsistencies until the recipient begins to appreciate that it in fact opens up a new world which includes the recipient's old world within it as a subset. In the meantime, because one's sense of one's life-project as a whole is at stake in paradigm differences, the truth-search between paradigms has a dramatic, passionate quality to it, rather than a bureaucratic, dispassionate quality. Whether or not one explicitly puts it to oneself that one is so doing, to sacrifice one action-logic for the possibility of another is inevitably a risky, scary death-and-rebirth transformation. Reason and data will play crucial roles as they do in contemporary social science, but this will be a warm-blooded and wet-lipped affair, not a cold-blooded, dry one.

All of our points of view, including those that claim to treat nothing as reality except what is empirically verified, are fictions (from the Latin *fictio*—a shaping) that we adopt and fashion. Persons can come to recognize increasingly, through observant participation in their own and others' paradigmatic transformations that they play an active role in constructing the worlds they experience. According to the developmental theory represented in Table 5.2, persons begin to cultivate this recognition intellectually at the Strategist stage and begin to develop the quality of will that can detach from and commit to a given paradigm on a moment-to-moment basis only as they evolve toward still later action-logics (Fisher & Torbert, 1995). Put simply, no journal article following early paradigm logic is going to play a major role in teaching us how to work and love and inquire in new way. But this multi-voiced book, or a good novel that interweaves third-person science, first-person autobiography, and second-person fiction, may. The logic of this argument has brought me personally to the point of committing to write a novel as my next attempt at a significant contribution to our field, despite having to start from scratch in order to learn how to do so. (Several years into the effort, I am finding that the cliché about old dogs learning new tricks applies here; although, in the case of paradigm change, a more apt illustration may be "old caterpillars learning to become new butterflies." And, as I am in my late fifties, I can assure you that the notion of aging and dying is no mere exotic metaphor!)

CONCLUSION

This chapter has described seven patterns of doing social science and illustrated them through the reflections of two social scientists. Then, it has enlarged on the process of interweaving action and inquiry by introducing the notion of first-, second-, and third-person research/practice and by offering five propositions about the characteristics of a social science that can integrate quantitative and qualitative methods into one's own action inquiries amidst one's significant others and the organizations in which one participates.

One might proceed next to analyze how this multi-paradigm vision of our field compares to some other 'synoptic visions.' (For example, one could compare it to Zald's 1993 proposal to reconceptualize the foundations of the management field to include a humanistic, enlightenment model as well as an engineering, causal model or to Mitroff and Kilman's 1978 fourfold, Jungian division of science into Analytical Scientists, Conceptual Theorists, Conceptual Humanists, and Particular Humanists). Or, one might analyze the interwovenness of several of the paradigms in the work of certain social science 'giants' like Simon, Foucault, or Argyris. Another tack might be to explore to what degree the very interesting autobiographical work of a number of scholars in the management field (Alderfer, 1988, 1989; Bedeain, 1993; Berg & Smith, 1988; Sjoberg, 1989) qualifies as first-person research/practice. All of these and other sorts of work suggest themselves on the basis of the multi-paradigmatic, developmental perspective outlined in this paper.

Another way to continue the exploration of these ideas is for the reader to begin testing their relationship to his or her own research/practice. For example, scholars may reflect on their own careers to date and their future aspirations through the lens of the multi-paradigm model, much as Hackman and Fisher illustrate at the outset of this chapter.[1]

Of course, many of the other chapters of this book also offer excellent illustrations of early explorations in personal, interpersonal, organizational and interorganizational research/practice.

ENDNOTES

[1] I will be glad: 1) to receive any such autobiographical reflections and commentaries (torbert@bc.edu); 2) to share my own with you (see my website [www2.bc.edu/~torbert]); and 3) to send you a copy of the psychometric measure of personal developmental stage, get it professionally scored, and send you feedback on the results (I will detail the procedure and cost if you contact me).

REFERENCES

Alderfer, C. (1988). Taking our selves seriously as researchers. In D.Berg & K. Smith (Eds.), *The self in social inquiry*. (pp. 35-70). Beverly Hills, CA: Sage.

Alderfer, C. (1989). Theories reflecting my personal experience and life development. *Journal of Applied Behavioral Science*, 25(4) 351-364.

Alexander, C., & Langer, E. (Eds.). (1990). *Higher stages of human development*. New York: Oxford University Press.

Argyris, C. (1971). Essay review of B. F. Skinner's Beyond freedom and dignity. *Harvard Educational Review*, 41(4), 550-567.

Argyris, C., Putnam, R., & Smith, D. (1985). *Action science: Concepts, methods, and skills for research and intervention*. San Francisco: Jossey-Bass.

Austin, J. (1997). Method for facilitating controversial social change in organizations. *Journal of Applied Behavioral Science* 33: 101-118.

Bartunek, J., & Moch, M. (1987). First-order, second-order, and third-order change and organization development interventions: a cognitive approach. *Journal of Applied Behavioral Science*, 23(3), 483-500.

Bartunek, J., Bobko, P. & Venkatraman, N. (1993). Toward innovation and diversity in management research methods. *The Academy of Management Journal*, 36(6), 1362-1373.

Bateson, G. (1972). "Metalogues" and "Theological categories of learning and communication." In *Steps to an Ecology of Mind*. San Francisco: Chandler.

Bateson, M. C. (1984). *With a daughter's eye: A memoir of Margaret Mead and Gregory Bateson*. New York: HarperCollins.

Bateson, M. C. (1990). *Composing a life*. New York: Plume/Penguin.

Bedeain, A. (1993). *Management laureates: A collection of autobiographical essays*. Greenwich, CT: JAI Press.

Behar, R. (1997). *The vulnerable observer: Anthropology that breaks your heart.* Boston: Beacon Press.

Benhabib, S. (1986). *Critique, norm, and utopia.* New York: Columbia University Press.

Berg, D., & Smith, K. (1988). *The self in social inquiry.* Beverly Hills, CA: Sage.

Bradbury, H.(1998) *Learning with the natural step: Cooperative ecological inquiry through cases, theory, and practice for fustainable development.* Unpublished doctoral dissertation, Chestnut Hill, MA: Boston College.

Bradbury, H. Bravette, G., Ludema, J., Cooperrider, D., Reason, P., & Torbert, W., *Creating a transformational science: Dissertations that transform as well as inform.* San Diego: Academy of Management Symposium, 1998.

Bravette, G. (1997). *Toward bicultural competence: Researching for personal and professional transformation.* Unpublished doctoral dissertation, University of Bath, Bath, England.

Buber, M. (1958). *I and Thou.* New York: Scribners.

Campbell, D., Dunnette, M., Lawler, E., & Weick, K. (1970). *Managerial behavior, performance, and effectiveness.* New York: McGraw-Hill.

Cooley, C. (1956). *Two major works: Social organization,* and *human nature and social order.* Glencoe, IL: Free Press.

Cook, T. & Campbell, D. (1979). *Quasi-experimentation: Design and analysis issues for field settings.* Chicago, IL: Rand McNally.

Cook-Greuter, S. (1999). *Postautonomous ego development: A study of its nature and measurement.* Unpublished doctoral dissertation, Harvard University, Cambridge, MA.

Denzin, N. (1995). *Interpretive Ethnography: Ethnographic Practices for the 21st century.* Thousand Oaks, CA: Sage.

Denzin, N., & Lincoln, Y. (1994). *Handbook of qualitative research.* Thousand Oaks, CA: Sage.

Dyer, W., & Wilkins, A. (1991). Better stories, not better constructs, to generate better theory: a rejoinder to Eisenhardt. *Academy of Management Review,* 16(3), 613-619.

Eisenhardt, K. (1989). Building theories from case study research. *Academy of Management Review,* 14(4), 532-550.

Feyerabend, P. (1975). *Against method.* Thetford, England: Lowe & Brydone.

Fine, M. (1994). Working the hyphens: Reinventing self and other in qualitative research. In Denzin, N. & Lincoln, Y. (Eds.), *Handbook of qualitative research* (pp. 70-82). Thousand Oaks, CA: Sage. 70-82.

Fisher, D. , & Torbert, W. R (1991). Transforming managerial practice: Beyond the achiever stage. In R. W. Woodman, & W. A. Pasmore, (Eds.), *Research in organization change and development, Vol. 5.* (pp. 143-173). Greenwich, CT: JAI Press.

Fisher, D. , & Torbert, W. R. (1995). *Personal and organizational transformation: The true challenge of continual quality improvement.* London: McGraw-Hill.

Frost, P., Pfeffer, J. & Van Maanen, J. (1995). Crossroads. *Organization Science,* 6, 680-692.

Gergen, K. (1994). *Realities and relationships: Soundings in social construction,* Cambridge, MA: Harvard University Press.

Grudin, R. (1996). *On dialogue: An essay in free thought.* Boston, MA: Houghton Mifflin.

Habermas, J. (1984, 1987). *The theory of communicative action, Vol. I & II.* Boston: Beacon.

Hammond, S., & Ritchie, J. (1993). Models of learning, models of life: A review of Herbert A. Simon's autobiography. *Journal of Management Inquiry,* 2(4), 326-330.

Harrison, R. (1995). *Consultant's Journey: A dance of work and spirit.* San Francisco: Bass, 1995.

Hauser, S. (1993). Loevinger's model and measure of ego development: A critical review II. *Psychological Inquiry, 4* 23-30.

Heron, J. (1988). Validity in cooperative inquiry. In P. Reason (Ed.), *Human Inquiry in Action.* (pp. 40-59). London: Sage.

Heron, J. (1991). *Feeling and personhood: Psychology in another key.* London: Sage.

Heron, J. (1996). *Cooperative inquiry: Research into the human condition.* London: Sage.

Howe, P. (1996, September 4). Medical schools faulted on emphasis: Low regard found for primary care. *Boston Globe,* p. A9.

Hunt, S. (1994). On the rhetoric of qualitative methods: toward historically informed argumentation in management inquiry. *Journal of Management Inquiry*, 3(3), 221-234.

Johnson, J. (1991). Habermas on strategic and communicative action. *Political Theory*, 19(2), 181-201.

Jourard, S. (1968). *Disclosing man to himself*. New York: Van Nostrand.

Karasek, R., & Theorell, T. (1991). *Healthy work: Stress, productivity, and the reconstruction of working life*. New York: Basic.

Kegan, R. (1994) *In over our heads: The mental demands of modern life*. Cambridge, MA.: Harvard University Press.

Kirk, J., & Miller, M. (1986). *Reliability and validity in qualitative research*. Thousand Oaks, CA; Sage.

Kramer, R. (1995). The birth of client-centered therapy: Carl Rogers, Otto Rank, and the Beyond. *Journal of Humanistic Psychology*, 35(4), 54-110.

Lather, P. (1993). Fertile obsession: Validity after poststructuralism. *The Sociological Quarterly*, 34(4), 673-693.

Lavoie, D., & Culbert, S. (1978). Stages of organization and development. *Human Relations*, 31(5), 417-438.

MacMurray, J. (1953). *The Self as Agent* and *Persons in Relation*. London: Faber.

Macey, D. (1993). *The lives of Michel Foucault*. New York: Pantheon.

March, J., & Simon, H. (1958). *Organizations*. New York: Wiley.

Mead, G. (1934). *Mind, self, and society from the standpoint of a social behaviorist*. Chicago: University of Chicago Press.

Mead, M. (1960/1928). *Coming of age in Samoa: A psychological study of primitive youth for Western civilization*. New York: Mentor.

Mead, M. (1972). *Blackberry winter: My earlier years*. New York: Morrow.

Merron, K., Fisher, D., & Torbert, W. R. (1987). Meaning making and management action. *Group and Organization Studies*, 12(3), 274-286.

Miller, M. & Cook-Greuter, S. (1994). *Transcendence and mature thought in adulthood: The further reaches of adult development*. Lanham, MD: Rowman & Littlefield.

Min, A. (1993). *Red azalea: Life and love in China*. London: Victor Golancz.

Mitroff, I. & Killman, R. (1978). *Methodological approaches to social science: Integrating divergent concepts and theories*. San Francisco: Jossey-Bass.

Moon, J. (1991). Constrained discourse and public life. *Political Theory*, 19(2), 202-229.

Morgan, G. (1997). *Images of organization*. Thousand Oaks, CA: Sage.

Nielsen, R. (1992). "Woolman's I am We" triple-loop action-learning: Origin and application in organization ethics. *Journal of Applied Behavioral Science*, 29, 117-138

Nielsen, R. (1996). *The politics of ethics*. New York: Oxford University Press.

Pfeffer, J. (1993). Barriers to the advance of organizational science: Paradigm development as a dependent variable. *Academy of Management Review*, 18, 699-620.

Pondy, L., & Mitroff, I. (1979). Beyond open system models of organization. *Research in Organizational Behavior*, 1, 3-39.

Raine, N. (1998). *After silence: Rape & my journey back*. New York: Crown.

Ramsey, M. (1995). *Where I stopped: Remembering rape at thirteen*. New York: Putnam.

Rank, O. (1978). *Will therapy: An analysis of the therapeutic process in terms of relationship*. New York: Norton.

Reason, P. (1994). Three approaches to participative inquiry. In N. Denzin, & Y. Lincoln (Eds.), *Handbook of Qualitative Research*. (pp. 324-330). Thousand Oaks, CA: Sage.

Reason, P. (1995). *Participation in human inquiry*. London: Sage.

Roethlisberger, F. (1977). *The elusive phenomena*. Cambridge, MA: Harvard Business School Division of Research.

Rogers, C. (1961). *On becoming a person*. Boston: Houghton Mifflin.

Rooke, D., & Torbert, W. (1998). Organizational transformation as a function of CEOs' developmental stage. *Organization Development Journal*, 16(1), 11-28.

Schmidt-Wilk, J., Alexander, C. & Swanson, G. (1996). Developing consciousness in organizations: The transcendental meditation program in business. *Journal of Business and Psychology*, 10(4), 429-444.

Simon, H. (1947). *Administrative behavior*. New York: Macmillan.

Simon, H. (1957). *Models of man*. New York: Wiley.

Simon, H. (1969). *The sciences of the artificial*. Cambridge, MA: MIT Press.

Simon, H. (1989). *Models of thought*. New Haven, CT: Yale University Press.

Simon, H. (1991). *Models of my life*. New York: Basic Books.

Sjoberg, G. (Ed.), (1989). (Special issue). *Journal of Applied Behavioral Science* 25(4).

Skinner, B. (1953). *Science and human behavior*. New York: Macmillan.

Skinner, B. (1971). *Beyond freedom and dignity*. New York: Knopf.

Skolimowski, H. (1994). *The participative mind*. London: Arkana.

Spretnak, C. (1991). *States of grace: The recovery of meaning in the postmodern age*. New York: HarperCollins.

Srivastva, S. & Cooperrider, D. (1990). *Appreciative leadership and management*. San Francisco: Jossey-Bass.

Torbert, W. & Rogers, M. (1972). *Being for the most part puppets: Interactions among men's labor, leisure, and politics*. Cambridge, MA: Schenckman.

Torbert, W. (1973). *Learning from experience: Toward consciousness*. New York: Columbia University Press.

Torbert, W. (1976). *Creating a community of inquiry*. London: Wiley.

Torbert, W. (1981a). Why educational research is so uneducational: Toward a new model of social science based on collaborative inquiry. In P. Reason and J. Rowan (Eds.), *Human inquiry: A sourcebook of new paradigm research*. (pp. 141-152) London: Wiley.

Torbert, W. (1981b). Interpersonal competence. In A. Chickering (Eds.) *The modern American college*. (pp. 172-190). San Francisco CA: Jossey-Bass.

Torbert, W. (1987). *Managing the corporate dream: Restructuring for long-term success*. Homewood, IL: Dow Jones-Irwin.

Torbert, W. (1989). Leading organizational transformation. In R. Woodman & W. Pasmore (Eds.), *Research in organizational change and development, Vol. 3*, Greenwich, CT: JAI Press.

Torbert, W. (1991). *The power of balance: Transforming self, society, and scientific inquiry*. (pp. 83-116). Newbury Park, CA: Sage.

Torbert, W. (1998). Developing wisdom and courage in organizing and sciencing. In S. Srivastva & D. Cooperrider (Eds.), *Organizational wisdom and executive courage*. (pp. 222-253). San Francisco, CA: The New Lexington Press.

Torbert, W. R., & Fisher, D. (1992). Autobiographical awareness as a catalyst for managerial and organizational development. *Management education and development, 23*(3), 184-198.

Turkle, S. (1991). And machines with big ideas: A review of H. Simon's *Models of My Life*. *New York Times Book Review*, 1.

Van Maanen, J. (1998). *Qualitative studies of organizations*. Thousand Oaks, CA: Sage.

Van Maanen, J. (1995). *Style as theory*. Organization Science 6, 133-143.

Weick, K. (1995). *Sensemaking in organizations*. Thousand Oaks, CA: Sage.

Whyte, W. (1981). *Street corner society: The social structure of an Italian slum* (3rd ed.). Chicago, IL: University of Chicago Press.

6 SEVEN YEARS OF PARTICIPANT RESEARCH
In A Transforming Community School

Mary E. Walsh
Nora E. Thompson
Kimberly A. Howard
Boston College

Catalina Montes
Gardner Extended Services School

Timothy J. Garvin
Allston-Brighton Family YMCA

In the varied topography of professional practice, there is a high, hard ground overlooking a swamp. On the high ground, manageable problems lend themselves to solution through the application of research-based theory and technique. In the swampy lowland, messy, confusing problems defy technical solution. The irony of this situation is that the problems of the high ground tend to be relatively unimportant to individuals or society at large, however great their technical interest may be, while in the swamp lie the problems of the greatest human concern (Schon, 1987, p.3).

The effort to address "problems of the greatest human concern" has challenged many of the traditional approaches to research and many traditional relationships between universities and communities (Kellogg Commission, 1999). It has required a movement in research away from university-based laboratory research to new ways of joining science with practice, inquiry with action, and university with community. Underlying these new approaches is the assumption that social inquiry will not be effective unless it is combined with social action, and likewise, that social action must be guided by social inquiry. Action gives inquiry a validity that can only come from useful knowledge (Lindblom & Cohen, 1979) and it adds complexity to problems that are otherwise understood to be simplistic. Without this grounding, inquiry is disconnected from the substance it tries to consider and is at risk of becoming a body of ideas that is increasingly self-reflective and self-contained (Gergen, 1985). In parallel fashion, inquiry adds reflection, evaluation, and direction to action. Without guidance from inquiry, action is threatened with becoming ill designed and meaningless, however well intentioned. The combination of social action and social inquiry—action inquiry—results in researchers and participants becoming collaborators, searching for useful knowledge and co-constructing learning (Gergen, 1991).

Efforts to link inquiry and action can result in significant changes in the relationship between universities and their communities. With stronger ties between inquiry and action, the university's traditional posture of remaining distant from, and passing knowledge on to the community, is likely to change toward more direct involvement of the university in the life of the community. Community interaction with the university may no longer remain confined to the university community affairs office; it may begin to occur at the level of individual faculty and student involvement. This different level of involvement brings opportunity for new types of relationships beyond the use of community members for research subjects or student training purposes. For example, as faculty and students are increasingly recognizing their responsibility to make knowledge useful to the community, growing numbers of universities are beginning to invite the community to participate in scholarship and inquiry at levels that were previously reserved for university scholars (Brabeck et al., 1997; Harkavy, 1999; Kellogg Commission, 1999; Lerner & Simon, 1998). Universities and communities are engaging in co-learning. This very different approach to scholarship transforms both the community and the university through the mutual interaction.

The act of partnering involves bridging the distance between the rarified "high ground" of universities and the complex realities of daily life in communities. While many advocate that this distance must be crossed, there is little guidance available for the act of partnering. Though "partnerships" have been repeatedly discussed in the literatures of various professions—education, psychology, medicine, and so forth (Bibace, in press; Harkavy, 1999; Knapp et al., 1998, Sherman, 1998), many of these reports discuss the outcomes of partnerships, few focus on the process of partnering. Many so-called university-community partnerships reflect the asymmetrical relationship evident in our society between so- called "experts" and "consumers." That is, they involve one person, almost always from the university, giving knowledge or information to the community. These one-way relationships cast the university in the more powerful position. More recently, university-community partnerships have begun to move toward more symmetrical arrangements in which the partners are co-learners and share the power of acquired knowledge. While their domains of expertise are different, they are nonetheless complementary (McKenzie & Richmond, 1998).

This chapter will describe a single university-community collaboration and the transformations of each partner in the collaboration (Walsh & Andersson, in press; Walsh, Andersson, & Smyer, 1999). Particular attention will be paid to the process of moving toward a more symmetrical and reciprocal relationship between the university and the community. This narrative account of developing and sustaining the partnership is based on multiple data sources. The data consisted of tape recorded planning meetings, steering committee meeting notes and minutes of these meetings, ongoing presentations at conferences, notes of the presenters, information packets, and videos of site visits. In constructing this narrative, we analyzed data using a qualitative methodology, examining critical points in the process of the development of the partnership and critical issues in the implementation of the project.

THE EVOLUTION OF THE PARTNERSHIP

The process of partnering occurs primarily in conversation among the partners. Conversation presumes dialogue—that is initiating statements by one partner, response to those statements by the other partner, and feedback from both partners. A critical aspect of partnership involves the ability of each partner regardless of their perceived power to initiate the dialogue at various points in the process (Bibace, Dillon, & Dowds, in press).

In developing the university-community partnership described here, two key conversations were critical—one in which the community asked the university for assistance, the other in which the university asked the community for assistance. The community's request to the university occurred on the heels of a large research study that was conducted by a university faculty member at a local school (Walsh, Andersson, & Smyer, 1999). As the faculty member prepared to return to the university to analyze the data and publish the study, the school principal intervened with a plea for the university to remain in the school. The principal recounted how poverty and its related sequelae—for example, homelessness, family violence, substance abuse, and malnutrition—had created barriers to learning that limited the academic achievement of a number of students. The school principal believed that knowledge held across multiple professions and disciplines could impact the school's ability to address the wide range of issues confronting children and families. Her perspective is supported by leaders in various professional fields (Illback, 1994; Illback, Cobb, & Joseph, 1997; Jivanjee & Friesen, 1997; Kaufman & Brooks, 1996; Melaville, 1991; Paavola et al., 1995; Pullin, 1996; Searcy, 1995; Stallings, 1995; Tharinger et al., 1996; Wertlieb, 1999).

The principal's request did not lead to an immediate response from the university. However, it did provide a focus for an existing conversation that had been occurring among faculty from across the university's professional schools (i.e., law, social work, education, psychology, health care, and management). These faculty were struggling to understand how the knowledge bases of their various professions could be brought to bear on problems and questions that concerned the community, particularly those issues confronting children and families living in poverty. In the principal's request for assistance, the faculty recognized a concrete opportunity to work with the community on issues of importance to both community members and university faculty.

The second key conversation emerged from the school principal's request to the university for assistance and resulted in the university making a request to the community. Realizing that complex human problems do not come in "discipline shaped boxes" (Petrie, 1992), the faculty believed that preparation of professionals could no longer be isolated within the boundaries of each of the professions (Brabeck, Walsh, Kenny, & Comilang, 1997). In order to address real world issues confronting children and families, future practitioners must be able to collaborate across professions. This would require that professionals become familiar with the perspectives and relevant knowledge bases of other professions (Corrigan, 1996, 1998; McCroskey & Einbinder, 1998; Mostert, 1996; Walsh, Brabeck, & Howard, 1999). Delineation of those aspects of professional knowledge bases relevant to the work of addressing the needs of children and families required faculty to seek community input. Community-based professionals representing a wide array of disciplines, together with parents and community members, provided formal feedback to faculty about the types of knowledge and training that were important in the "real world." This conversation was critical in bringing the expertise of the community to bear on the work of the university.

In the context of conversations about more effective preparation of future professionals, several important shifts in the relationship between the university and the community began to occur. Community-based professionals and family members provided their expertise to university faculty who had traditionally considered themselves "experts" vis-à-vis the community. University faculty began to identify important research questions based on the concerns posed by the community. As the discussion with the community proceeded, the university and community both came to recognize the strong commitment each had to improving the life chances of children and families. It was evident that they shared the "compelling ethos" necessary to drive and energize any successful community project (Schorr, 1997).

However, despite the commonality in their visions, the university and community differed markedly in the strategies they each thought appropriate for addressing the barriers to learning faced by students in the school. The university faculty assumed that the best way to improve children's learning was to provide a range of services to individual children within the school setting. In response to this suggestion, the school principal pointed out that such an approach presumed that the problem was "in" the children, or, at least, "in" the school. "The problem is not in here," she argued, "but out there." "Out there" referred to the myriad social conditions that impacted the children and their families. From her perspective, whatever interventions were agreed upon would have to incorporate the community outside of the school walls. Over the course of many meetings and extended discussions, both the university and the school came to a negotiated agreement. They concurred that dismantling the barriers to learning could best be accomplished in the context of a partnership between the community agencies, parents, community members, and the school. They also agreed that the university should play a significant role in the partnership. The early stages of a school-community-university partnership were beginning to emerge.

The partnership gained significant momentum when both the university and the community collaborated on developing a school-based program to address barriers to learning. The mechanism for catalyzing a collaboration among them was a Request for Proposals (RFP) from a national foundation interested in school-community-university linkages. The goal of the RFP was to promote educational reform by directly addressing the non-academic barriers to learning that are experienced by a significant number of children and their families. The specific project involved the transformation of a traditional urban elementary school into what is known as an extended services school. This extended services school would address not only the academic development of children, but also their physical, social, and emotional development. The university was invited by the funding agency to apply for a planning grant in which the university would partner with a public school to develop an extended services school, or what is more broadly known as a community school (Denham & Etzioni, 1997; Dryfoos, 1994, 1995). This school, as the funder designated it, would be modeled loosely after the Children's Aid Society Community School in New York City (Coltoff, 1998).

> By one definition, a community school integrates the delivery of quality education with whatever health and social services are required in that community. These institutions draw on both school resources and outside community agencies that come into the schools and join forces to provide "seamless" programs. Community "ownership" is an important aspect of community schools. These school buildings are open extended hours every day—over weekends—over the summer—to respond to the needs of the children and their parents in a neighborhood (Dryfoos, 1998).

The community school goal of providing a "seamless" set of programs that address a wide range of needs—physical, psychological, and social—was thought by the principal to be consistent with her belief that the students in her school experienced a wide array of needs which constituted barriers to learning (Brabeck et al., 1997; Lawson and Briar-Lawson, 1997; Sailor & Skrtic, 1996). The opportunity to develop an extended services school seemed like a good fit with the school's desire to address the many non-academic needs of children as well as the university's desire to bring professionals together to collaborate around the needs of children and families. The school, which was educating 500 children from kindergarten to grade 5, was located in the most culturally and linguistically diverse section of Boston. Over 36 languages were spoken among the faculty and children. Eighty percent of the children were on free or reduced lunch programs and eighty percent were limited English proficient. Lack of adequate housing and employment plagued the families. The opportunity to work together to apply for planning and implementation funding provided a concrete means to ground the partnership.

A core planning team, which included representatives from the school (parents and staff), the university (faculty), and the community (Allston-Brighton Healthy Boston Neighborhood Coalition—an organization that included community members and many school parents), was established. A community agency (the Allston-Brighton Family YMCA) was later invited to join as the official partner or "lead agency" of the extended services school. This core team met weekly during the planning and early implementation phases of the project. The initial movements of the partners, who began as relative strangers to one another, were often awkward and always tentative. As they began to address a wide range of decisions about potential programs for the extended services school, they gradually became more aware and respectful of each other's strengths and struggles. Their negotiations increasingly required them to accommodate to differences as they assimilated new ways of thinking and acting into their traditional manner of operating. For example, parents, community members, the community agency, and the university began to develop an appreciation for the complexities involved in the day-to-day operations of an elementary school. Similarly, all the partners gradually gained insight into the fiscal and staffing constraints of community agencies.

A similar process of "give and take" characterized the larger community-wide meetings that included agency and business representatives, parents, and local citizens. The meetings involved an exchange of information, proposals, opinions and decisions. Bilingual and trilingual group leaders helped to make certain that non-English speakers were involved in the conversation. Many participants in the large group sought more active roles as they became invested in both the process and outcome of the project. Volunteer subcommittees of relative strangers—parents, teachers, university faculty, community agency staff—were established to address specific planning tasks (e.g., "adult programs," "evaluation"). In weekly meetings, these subcommittees hammered out a design for the various aspects of the extended services school. In numerous meetings of both the core group of partner representatives, as well as of the larger community, a partnership was forged that would transform each of the partners in significant ways.

TRANSFORMATIONS

The collaboration of university, school, and community in the process of planning and implementing the extended services school engaged each partner in a process that differed substantially from their usual practices. As they struggled to address the countless concrete and often difficult issues involved in building a community school, the university, school, and community were both challenged and changed. The transformations that they experienced occurred around four key issues: articulating beliefs about change, defining "community," linking scholarship and practice, and sustaining a commitment to the work.

ARTICULATING BELIEFS ABOUT CHANGE

As they began to plan an extended services school, it was clear that the partners were in agreement about their vision—that is, improving the life chances of the children. They also were committed to the same general goal of providing children and families a wide range of necessary services and resources. They envisioned the school as the hub and "point of access" to health, legal, employment, recreational, and social services.

Early in the planning process, the partners faced multiple decisions about the types of prevention and intervention programs that would be included in the extended services school. Coming to consensus on this issue required the partners to engage in a process of negotiating their differing perspectives. For example, despite their agreement about the vision and goal of the project, the partners had considerable differences of opinion about precisely how to ground these abstract concepts in the reality of an extended services school. For example, although all agreed that an after-school program should be a core component of the extended services school, they differed about which activities to include in the after-school program. The school viewed the after-school program as an opportunity to extend learning time and improve children's test scores. For the YMCA, after-school was a time for sports and recreation. The university was interested in operationalizing and evaluating "best practices" in after-school care. The parents viewed the after-school program as much needed high quality child-care. While these differing emphases were not mutually exclusive, it took considerable time and reflection to reach consensus about how they were, in fact, complementary.

It quickly became clear that the resolution of differing ideas would be significantly facilitated if each member could identify their theories of change, that is, the beliefs that each partner held about how children and families develop and change (Schorr, 1997). It seemed obvious that individual beliefs about what helps children be successful constituted the foundation of various proposals for programs that would provide children with opportunities for academic and social success. It was assumed that making these beliefs explicit and working through differences would result in a more cohesive and integrated project.

The process of explicating their individual beliefs about human development and change resulted in the first of a number of transformations in both university and community. The partners approached the task of identifying and sharing their beliefs about development with a clear set of assumptions. Meeting notes suggest that the university was not confident that the community agencies and school had reflected on their beliefs about development and change and, furthermore, probably did not hold any organized beliefs. The university assumed that the community viewed practice as a pragmatic activity that was carried out on the basis of trial and error. If the intervention worked, it was deemed valuable. The university further assumed that if the community made decisions on the basis of some theoretical position, it was probably an overly simplistic or watered down set of principles that did not take the complexity of human development into account.

On the other hand, the community expected that the university would offer well-articulated theories of human development. However, they doubted that the university's pronouncements about how their children grow and change would have much relevance to the realities of children's daily lives. On the basis of their past experience, the university's approach had a "pie in the sky" rather than "down in the trenches" orientation. The community found the university's theories to be intellectually interesting but decidedly impractical in the real work of raising and teaching children. While the community partners were polite, they did not believe that faculty had any real sense of what their children needed.

Although the partners' terminology often differed, their protracted discussions eventually revealed that, at their core, they seemed to hold a common set of underlying assumptions about how children develop. Though expressed in varying ways, each partner implicitly espoused a similar theory of change. They all agreed that children develop, not just in a single context, but rather in a wide array of contexts including family, school, neighborhood, and the wider community (Bronfenbrenner, 1979; Lerner, 1986). While the partners initially differed with respect to which context was the most important (e.g., home, school, neighborhood), they all came to agree that all of these contexts have the potential to impact children in positive and growth enhancing ways.

Furthermore, the partners also agreed that children develop simultaneously across multiple domains—biological, psychological, and social (Lerner, 1978, 1986). While they were inclined to believe that one or another domain was more critical than the rest (e.g., the educators leaned heavily toward the psychological domain while the community based youth serving organization favored the social domain), they eventually concluded that adults involved in children's care could not ignore any of these domains. The community agency no longer understood its work in the narrower framework of recreation and social competence. Rather, it began to promote the development of the "whole child" as a new way to frame and concretize its mission. The school no longer focused exclusively on academic outcomes but began to understand the importance of social competence.

The partners also agreed on the importance of adults in the life of the child (Lerner & Lerner, 1987). While their respective institutions focused primarily on either adults or children, they eventually agreed that child-oriented programs without parents would not be effective. They clearly agreed with the research findings that point to the positive consequences of family involvement in schooling (Carlyon, Carlyon, McCarty, 1998; Shartrand, Weiss, Kreider, & Lopez, 1997).

The final assumption about human development on which they reached agreement was the importance of recognizing and building on strengths as well as addressing deficits exhibited by children and families (Lerner, 1995; Lerner, Walsh, & Howard, 1998; Pittman & Cahill, 1992). They concluded that positive development could be enhanced by the protective factors present in the lives of children and families (e.g., community centers, caring neighbors, and churches). They had an interest in fostering competencies that could lead to the demonstration of resilience in children, youth, and families (Lerner, Walsh, & Howard, 1998; Werner, 1989, 1990). Arriving at agreement on this last principle—the importance of both risk and protective factors—was a difficult process. While all partners agreed in principle that addressing both strengths and deficits was crucial in supporting children's development, they held strong views regarding the most effective point of entry to help children. Some felt it was more efficient to focus first on children's deficits while others were inclined to build on strengths. The funder's emphasis on an asset-based model helped to move the group toward consensus about the initial point of entry in the extended services school. Agreement on this principle was reflected in the choice of a youth serving agency (YMCA) as the "lead agency" partner, in contrast to a more deficit-focused agency (e.g., hospital or mental health agency).

In the process of articulating these beliefs about development and change, it became clear to the university and the community that their fundamental theories about human development were surprisingly consistent with one another. The university's view of change, which emerged from theory and research, converged with the community's view, which emerged from the world of action or practice. Coming to understand the similarities in their assumptions was a transforming experience for both the university and community. The university came to realize that it was not the sole purveyor of knowledge. The community, after all, had arrived at the same set of core beliefs and knowledge on the basis of practice. Similarly, the community came to believe that it need not disregard the knowledge offered by the university. They realized that the university could play a role in understanding and explaining how various interventions could make a difference for children and families. Both realized that their respective core beliefs validated the beliefs of the other—that in the end, research, theory, and practice were all of one piece that offered meaning and validity to each other. As each partner learned to value the position and knowledge of the other, the relationship became more symmetrical and reciprocal.

DEFINITION OF COMMUNITY

The process of defining "the community" is an early and critical task in most university-community partnerships (Einbinder & Sloane, 1998; Kellogg Commission, 1999; Knapp et al., 1998; Tippins, Bell, & Lerner, 1998). The definition of community typically emerges from the goal of the particular project around which the partnership is organized. In the case of the extended services school, the overriding goal was to establish functional linkages between school and community that would give children and their families access to a wide range of services and resources. In essence, the school was redefining itself as a community school. The definition of the community to which the school would be linked was vital.

While the partners initially thought this definition of who and what comprised the community could be arrived at in one or two meetings, analysis of the process notes reveals that this issue was a recurring theme that was revisited over months and years, at increasingly deeper levels. In the initial phases of this process, the school struggled to identify the members of its community. In many newly developed community schools across the country, the definition of community has been fairly straightforward. Typically, the geographical area immediately surrounding the school is defined as the school's community. The school develops linkages with the families, community agencies, and businesses within those geographic boundaries. However, this geography-bound definition of community was not applicable in the context of the proposed extended services school. Court ordered desegregation in the City of Boston had resulted in 60% of the school's students living far outside the school's geographic community. Partnership members were confronted with the task of building a community school that would not be limited to the geographical boundaries of the local community. On the other hand, economics as well as sheer logistics would prevent them from including each of their student's far-flung neighborhoods within the community of the extended services school. One school simply could not have working relationships with every agency in a very large city. In order to determine who would constitute the community, as well as which agencies and businesses would be included, the partners developed criteria for the "boundaries" of their community school.

Even as the discussions about who constituted the community were constrained to some extent by logistical and financial considerations, the partners were clear from the outset that the community school must serve *all* of the children in the school and not be restricted to students living within the local area. After extensive and difficult discussions, the core planning team decided to establish close working relationships with the agencies in the immediate area of the school since these agencies had the greatest potential to deliver services within the school walls. However, while they could not set up inter-institutional contracts with more distant agencies, they committed to work with these agencies around the needs of individual students who lived outside of the school's immediate geographic zone. Some of the local agencies that had branches in other areas of the city (e.g., the YMCA) also saw the possibility of working with those branch agencies to accommodate the needs of individual extended services school students. Finally, the partners agreed that, to the extent financially possible, all members of the local geographic community should have access to services—whether or not they had children attending the school.

The partnership's commitment to include within their definition of community every student in the school and his or her family, from all sections of the city, was a decision in which each partner felt invested. It was also a decision that presented many complications. The committee recognized the massive transportation issues that would result in implementing this definition of community at the level of practice. For example, the committee foresaw the difficulty of running an after school program for children who had no way to return to their distant neighborhoods in the late afternoon. According to central school policy, the schedule of buses which took children home at the end of the regular school day could not be altered to accommodate those who remained for the after school program. This transportation problem, as emphasized by parent members of the partnership, would conceivably place serious limits on children's opportunities to participate in the after-school component of the new extended services school programs. Recognizing this barrier, the partnership members united as a team to advocate with the School District for a solution to the transportation problem. This team lobbied, and continues to lobby, city officials, local politicians, and grant funders for increased transportation for city schoolchildren.

This early commitment to a broad definition of community, as well as the concrete tasks involved in creating the possibility for this definition to be functional, resulted in a second major transformation among the partners. In struggling to solve the problem of transportation, the group stumbled upon a deeper understanding of community. As they sought increased transportation from government officials and politicians, they gradually came to consider themselves as "the community" vis-à-vis the external agencies whom they were petitioning. In acting as a collective in advocating for services and policy, they represented a cohesive voice for the concerns of their community.

This new sense of cohesiveness led to an important transformation in each partner's understanding of who constituted the "community" of the extended services school. Partners who had previously thought of themselves as "other than" the community came to realize that they, too, were "part of" the community. For example, the school, which had traditionally considered itself as distinct from the community, now came to refer to itself as "the community" in its requests to city officials. In contrast to their earlier "we-they" posture vis-à-vis the community, they now spoke of "us." Over the course of these discussions, it became clear to the school personnel that they—teachers, school staff and administrators—were part of the very community they served. A similar transformation of identity occurred in the university faculty. The traditional stance among university faculty, as they spoke about going "out to" the community, had been to see themselves as apart from, rather than part of, the community. As they joined the other partners in seeking transportation for all of the children, the university also came to realize that it could not exclude itself from membership in the community.

Similarly, these shifts in the understanding of community impacted the community agencies. Up until this point, it had been useful in certain ways for agencies and resources to consider both the schools and the university as separate from themselves. Taking on the big institutions such as "the universities" or "the school department" had the potential to become a "cause" for the community agencies who perceived themselves as "Davids" challenging the "Goliaths." Negotiating the design and implementation of the extended services school facilitated the community agencies coming to view these institutions as part of the community, and to see themselves as partners with the university and the school.

Over the years, the team has also broadened its advocacy agenda with political leaders in order to promote a more widespread understanding of linking schools and community resources. Political leaders have now begun to come to relevant meetings of the steering committee. Some steering committee members now participate actively on a state legislative subcommittee on school-linked services.

The joining, or partnering, of these three institutions, as they came to view themselves as part of the larger defined community, was both threatening and empowering to each. Their respective positions vis-a-vis the other were forced to change. Interestingly, each of these institutions had hitherto considered themselves in some ways at the top of the hierarchy. For example, the university clearly assumed, due to the knowledge it had to impart to both the community and the schools, that it stood above the others. Meanwhile, the school assumed that because of its critical role in educating and passing knowledge onto the next generation, it occupied the privileged position. The community agencies and resources, because of their intimate connection to "the people in the trenches" saw themselves in the dominant position.

As the partners' mode of interaction shifted from one of dominance to mutuality, long-standing practices and assumptions began to change. These changes were slow, difficult, and not always welcomed by one partner or another. At times, each partner preferred its former posture. At the same time, these changes were empowering and allowed greater opportunity to learn from one another, to share insights, and to be empathic. When their roles were viewed as complementary, each partner became more open to being changed by the others. Faculty no longer viewed themselves as experts who could give answers to the community, but as co-learners who had a certain set of knowledge and skills. They understood that they clearly did not possess all of the expertise required to address the community's concerns. The school saw itself as a community institution whose resources and buildings belong to the community. The agencies came to view both school and university as resources that could help them bolster their efforts to implement their vision and accomplish their goals. Parents came to see themselves as important contributors in shaping the extended services school. These changes in assumptions about co-learning foreshadowed changes that would take place in both the university's and the community's understanding of the relationship between scholarship and practice.

UNDERSTANDING THE SCHOLARSHIP-PRACTICE
RELATIONSHIP

Both the university and the community approached this project with preconceived and fairly resolute ideas about the relationship between research and practice. While each partner was committed in principle to the necessary connection between research and practice, they often acted as if these two activities were distinct and separate. In the early stages of the partnership, both the university and the community assumed that research was the university's forte; practice was the domain of the community—whether within agencies or schools.

The university faculty adhered to a traditional approach to research. As the faculty who were engaged in the project conceived of it, research entailed identifying specific questions, collecting data from the community to answer these questions, and analyzing and reporting the findings in scholarly journals. They assumed that the results of their studies would not only advance knowledge in an abstract manner but could be applied in practice to the complex problems confronting the human community.

Community members, on the other hand, assumed that while the university was doing some sort of important research, this work probably had little or no relevance to the practical problems that the community was trying to solve on a daily basis. As they made decisions about the types of programs that would be best for their community, they relied more on the pragmatic criteria of cost, word of mouth, and ease of implementation, than they did on research findings about the effectiveness of particular programs. Ordinarily, research did not substantially inform the community's daily decision making. Evidence-driven practice simply did not occur.

However, as the university and the community worked with one another to develop the extended services school, they both came to new understandings about the relationship between research and practice, between inquiry and the concrete world of action. In developing a new model of schooling, a "community school," they needed information that was not readily available, such as community preferences for programs to be housed in new school, priority in which child and family needs should be addressed, or "best practices" in extended services schools across the country. Faculty recognized that addressing this need for new knowledge would require a different kind of research in which the research questions were shaped by the parents, teachers, and community members. Further, the answers to these questions were to be found through working as collaborators within the community rather than remaining isolated in the laboratories of the university. Over time, faculty involved in the extended services school made significant changes in how they conducted research. Jensen, Hoagwood, & Trickett (1999) have recently characterized this shift in advocating for changes in research on effective practices in mental health. They state:

> This new generation of studies must in essence move university investigators and their topics of study out of prestigious ivory

towers and into every day earthen trenches. This new type of research demands new partnership—not with other scientists per se, but with experts of a different type—experts from families, neighborhoods, schools, in communities. Only in these settings and from these experts can we learn what is palatable, feasible, durable, affordable, and sustainable for children and adolescents at risk or in need of mental health services (p. 207).

As university faculty realized that former methods of laboratory research would not be effective in capturing the complex interactions of the world of action, they developed new research methodologies in order to incorporate the rich resource of parents, teachers, and community members. For example, the seemingly straightforward task of assessing the community's preferences and needs for particular extended services school programs presented significant challenges to traditional quantitative survey methodologies. In assessing the concerns of parents who spoke little or no English and who among them spoke multiple languages, the university researchers were pressed to develop a variety of strategies, such as bilingual focus groups and teacher- or parent-led interviews. Analysis of this type of data did not prove to be as straightforward as that of more traditional survey methods.

Just as the university came to new understandings of the relationship between research and the world of action, the community also came to appreciate the ways in which their practice could be impacted by research. As they attempted to choose among several possible programs for their new community school, community members became aware of the potential usefulness of research findings. Confronted with multiple options for new programs, community leaders asked the university faculty to "find out the characteristics of effective programs" across a wide range of areas. Their new appreciation of research based information left them reluctant to set up an after-school program until the university was able to summarize research findings about "best practices" in after school child care. It has now become standard practice in the community agency to request formal evaluation for any new partnership program that it develops with schools and other agencies.

As they became consumers of relevant research, community members began to recognize the importance of methodological rigor in gathering and interpreting data. They became more critical of their community-based strategies for collecting data and evaluating programs. For example, rather than assuming the community needs on the basis of scant and poorly designed surveys, community leaders requested that the university work with them to develop "good," "methodologically sound," surveys. The community recognized that data-driven answers to their questions provided them with a firmer base upon which to make decisions.

Over the course of the project, the new understanding of the research-practice relationship was reflected in the increasing participation of each partner in the work of the other partners. In sharp contrast to earlier days in which the researchers and practitioners engaged in distinct work activities, the university faculty and community members joined one another in some aspects of their primary work. Community members joined the university faculty in reflecting how theory and research contributed to the development of the extended services school. In joining faculty members as they systematized these reflections in university courses, conference presentations, or in scholarly publications, community members came to value the opportunity to reflect upon their practice. These occasions helped them to view their work and struggles against the broad frame works of theory and research, thus providing new meaning to their efforts and a widened perspective on the issues that they faced.

In parallel fashion, university faculty worked side by side with community members in some important aspects of the work of the community. Engaging in the practitioners' world of community meetings, political advocacy, media contact, and relentless daily problem solving, university faculty gained a new perspective on the many ways in which their theories and the research often fell short. Life in the "earthen trenches" continually challenged the faculty to modify their theories in order to incorporate the experiences of their practitioner colleagues. Faculty gained new insight on how to better prepare students for the work of practice. As researchers and practitioners shared in one another's work, they came to a new appreciation of the difficulties involved in grounding the abstractions of theory in the world of action.

Working in a partnership led the university and community to a deepened understanding of the research-practice relationship. New research methodologies developed to address the community's questions enabled the community to participate more actively in the design and execution of more relevant research. The new practices developed by the community enabled the university to better prepare practitioners across a wide range of professions. These new ways of combining research and practice, while bringing many benefits to both university and community, also resulted in another challenge for the partners. These transformations in their understanding of the research-practice relationship could only be truly realized if the partnership existed over time. A short-term partnership would not lead to any long-term changes.

SUSTAINED COMMITMENT

At the outset, each partner saw the new partnership as an opportunity to build a radically different model for enhancing the life chances of children and families. Initially, however, they each approached this partnership anticipating a very traditional type of university-community relationship. They assumed that the type and duration of their relationship would mirror their previous engagements with one another. In the past, the community had been involved with two quite different aspects of the university—the community affairs office and the faculty. Their relationship with the community affairs office, which existed over many years, was the most common way in which the community and university interacted. The community affairs office constituted the "human face" of the university in the community as it provided some material resources to the community (e.g., scholarships, jobs, small grants, and space for community events). Through this relationship, the university was able to share its goods with the community, improve the economic status of the community surrounding the university, and build goodwill for the university. Even though both the university and the community benefited from this type of relationship, the relationship was primarily "one-way" with the university in the position of "giving" and the community "receiving."

In contrast to their relationships with the community affairs office, the community's previous relationships with university faculty had been far more limited. These relationships endured only long enough for the faculty to accomplish a specific, time-limited set of tasks. For example, data collection for a study brought the faculty member to the community only until the data collection was finished. Technical assistance for a specific community project ended when the faculty member had shared his or her expertise around some particular issue. Faculty participation in community field sites in which students interned endured only through the period in which students were on-site. In general, the work of the community assisted, but never became a central or necessary part of, faculty teaching and/or research. Within the university, most of this work was considered "service" rather than "research" or "teaching." While the community derived some benefit from these brief relationships, the community was primarily in the role of "giving" and the university of: "receiving." Based on these experiences, both university faculty and community members expected, at some level, that their new partnership would be a short-term engagement in which the faculty would have an opportunity to bolster their resumes and the community would be able to access funds from the grants which the university would help secure.

These expectations changed significantly as the project developed. As the partners began to interact on a weekly and often daily basis, the importance of a sustained commitment became evident to them in a number of ways. They slowly realized that implementing an extended services school would not be an event, but rather a process. First, the partners had made a public pledge to the community that they would not only plan changes to an extended services school, but would also help to implement these changes. Other data gathered by the partners suggested that institutional change of this magnitude could not be accomplished in a short time. In fact, educational reform literature is replete with examples of change efforts that failed because the time committed to implementing the changes was too short to develop the requisite structures and processes to accomplish and sustain the change. It was clear that, in contrast to many externally funded projects, this project could not be abandoned after the initial implementation grant ran out. This process would require a relationship among the partners that endured over time and that was grounded in a two-way exchange.

Second, as they moved into the work of the project, the partners began to realize that the project would require substantial trust among them—trust that could only be developed over time. The partners would ultimately have to come to believe that, in spite of the many reasons they had to mistrust one another in the past, they would have to build relationships in which they were not guests in each other's buildings but partners in a single task. They would have to learn to disagree, confront, support, and act in terms of the best interest of the project rather than each partner's self interest. Their new relationship would require a continual give and take between the partners that involved negotiated understandings, that is, an assimilation by each partner of the other's beliefs and an accommodation to their needs. In contrast to a one-way arrangement in which one partner was giving and the other taking, the new partnership would have to be reciprocal so that partners could complement the strengths and deficits of each other, and in the process, sustain mutual change. The partners would have to recognize the many and important ways in which each partner was a vital component in the successful development of the other's capacity to work more effectively with children and families. While the interests of each partner had to be accommodated, the dominant focus of the collaboration had to be the common good—enhancing the life chances of children and families. Building this type of trust could not be accomplished in a matter of months. The "hit and run" model of earlier faculty-community engagements would not work for this partnership.

Finally, the partners also realized that a long-term involvement was essential to accommodate the changes in practice that resulted within each institution. These changes necessitated a long-term involvement in the project. At the university, for example, the lessons from this project became integrated into curriculum and teaching. Faculty redirected and shaped their research to address the questions generated by the community. Students became involved in the project and committed themselves to this manner of work. The curriculum utilized to train new professionals changed in significant ways as it incorporated the learning acquired in the community. These changes in university practices impacted the long-term work of the faculty and the preparation of students. These changes clearly could not be temporary.

Similarly, the community agency and school began to change their practices in ways that could not easily be reversed. For example, the local branch of the community agency put the development of extended services schools on the agenda of the larger organization. It changed its funding practices to incorporate a partnership with a school. Likewise, the school changed a significant number of its practices in a non-reversible direction. The school principal and staff integrated many aspects of the extended services school into the school day, for example, coordinating in-school and after-school literacy instruction for individual students by hiring an extended services school coordinator who worked with both day and after-school teachers. These kinds of changes in practice within each partner institution did not lend themselves to brief, time-limited implementation, but rather, required a long-term commitment in order to become standard practice.

In light of the partners' realization that a sustained commitment was necessary for the successful implementation of the project and for the transformation of each institution's practices, the partners made an explicit and repeated commitment to "stay with it over time." To solidify this commitment, they sought the backing of the leadership of each of their institutions. The university president, the citywide director of the agency, and the superintendent of the Boston Public Schools all spoke positively and publicly about the work. Their public pledges led to some concrete acts of support. The university gave an honorary degree to the school principal and supported faculty who worked in the project. The school department committed grant funds to support curriculum development within a school plan that was built on integrating academic and non-academic services. The YMCA committed the time of a grant writer from their development office to help secure further funding.

At the same time, within the membership of each institution, there was not complete agreement about the value of this type of long-term commitment. In the university, many faculty members felt that it was not appropriate for faculty to remain in the community over a long period of time. They believed that faculty should be in the community only long enough to share their expertise and "empower" the community to act on its own behalf. Within the community agency, many individuals wondered if this type of engagement was appropriate for an institution whose primary identity was delivering a focused service. Many school staff were concerned that the school's mission of teaching and learning might become diverted or diluted by the ongoing partnership with "outsiders." Some parents wondered if the time required by this partnership was worth the effort. To varying degrees and in varying ways, the partners recognized the demands as well as the uncertainties of their collaborative enterprise.

However, as they reflected on the various concerns of their respective institutional colleagues, their fears were somewhat tempered. The university faculty who were involved in the project believed that empowering others presumed that someone had power to give to the other—a power that the faculty involved in this project did not believe they ever had. Rather, they viewed sustained collaboration as more likely eventually to empower everyone. The leadership of the community agency believed that a more holistic orientation was an important expansion of its narrower mission. The school staff believed that "the school could not do it alone" but must work with groups external to the school in order to address barriers to learning and enhance the academic success of students. The parents and community members believed that a different model of schooling that might provide opportunities for their children was worth the effort. These on-going and frequent reassessments repeatedly led the partners to conclude that the opportunity to enhance children's chances by changing some key aspects of their own practices was worth the significant cost involved in building the partnership.

Over time, the relationship among the partners evolved to a point of near-permanence. In the midst of difficult negotiations on key aspects of the project, they sometimes remarked to one another, "We are in it so deeply now, there's no turning back." The pledge to a long-term and sustained relationship among the partners constituted a significant transformation for both university and community. In turn, this commitment to "stay in it for the long haul" resulted in two further transformations of past practices related to funding and governance.

While the critical element in initiating the partnership was a common vision, the bottom line in sustaining the venture for the long-term was continued funding. The commitment to develop new sources of funding was a straightforward task in which each of the partners agreed to engage. The more difficult issue, however, was the development of strategies for the management of the funds. In keeping with the funder's specification, the initial planning grant was given to the university. However, the funder specified that the implementation grant, six times larger than the planning grant, would reside in the community agency. Coming to terms with this requirement involved significant trust and sharing of power. In the past, the school, the community agency, and the university had each been accustomed to serving as the "principal investigator" for grants they each had written. In this particular collaborative arrangement, the school and the university had to agree to be full partners in the writing and implementing of the grant even though the grant would not reside in either of their institutions. This arrangement represented a major change in the culture of each of these institutions. The negotiation of this agreement, however, did not solve the funding issues for the project.

While the implementation grant supported the early stages of the extended services school, its long-term survival depended upon raising new funds. The process of securing these funds required continued sharing of responsibility among the partners. Potential sources of funds were available to one or another of the institutions represented by the partners, but typically not to all. For example, certain grants, such as the 21st Century Schools grants, could only be awarded to local educational agencies (LEA's). Other grants had to be located in the community agency or the university. Thus, each partner had to agree to support the fund raising efforts of each other partner, even though with respect to any particular grant or source of funds, there may be "nothing in it for them." This approach was a significant shift for institutions that were accustomed to operating in an isolated manner.

In order to manage the operational aspects of the extended services school, partners also had to agree to develop a joint accounting system. Over time, they had to agree to a common reporting arrangement in which data about all available funds, income, and expenses would be kept in a common accounting system to which all members could have access at any time. This arrangement required a significant transformation of the ordinary practice of each institution. Opening "the books" was a new way of doing business for school, community, and university.

In addition to working out arrangements to secure and manage funds, sustaining the partnership required a mechanism for governance. As details were worked out for implementing the extended services school, the members agreed on a model for governing the partnership through a steering committee. Determining the functioning and structure of this committee constituted one of the most difficult aspects of the entire project. The myriad and sometimes unspoken concerns about trust and co-equal participation in the project became concretized in the design of the steering committee. In the final plan, the partners agreed to two representatives from the community agencies, two representatives from the university, two representatives from the parent group in the school and three representatives from the school staff. The preponderance of school representatives on the so-called steering committee reflected the fact that the school would be the single institution most impacted by its transformation into an extended services school. In agreeing to move toward an extended services model, the greatest number of risks would be assumed by the school. For this reason, it was agreed that the school needed additional representation.

This model of governance transformed the partners in a significant way. Immediately, it necessitated that the university back away from its earlier leadership role in the planning grant and assume the role of participant in the implementation grant. The plan for governance also necessitated that the university, parents, and community agencies recognize the significant change in practice that this form of governance represented for the school. In traditional school governance arrangements, teachers were responsible for their individual classrooms and principals for their individual schools. Parents, community agencies, and universities had typically been considered "guests on school" turf. Participating in a partnership form of governance for the "community school" represented a substantial change for the school. While this transformation is still on going for the school staff and is still in its early stages, it appears to be gaining steady momentum.

As these many concrete issues were discussed, the simple concept of "partnership" became a complicated reality. Making a partnership workable for all the members was a transforming struggle. It could not take place without changes and concessions by each member.

CONCLUSION

The distance between the so-called "high ground" of the university and the "lowland" of the community is not easily traversed. However, newly emerging partnerships between universities and communities appear to be powerful vehicles for bridging that distance. As the example outlined in this chapter illustrates, engagement in these partnerships can result in significant and lasting transformations in both the university and the community. However, while the outcome of partnerships is important to document, the future of partnerships is heavily dependent upon an understanding of the process of partnering. Analysis of these processes can serve to guide and facilitate the development of new partnership arrangements. To understand the way in which partners move toward more symmetrical, reciprocal arrangements, it will be important to examine, across a wide range of partnerships, the essential tasks of partnering—assimilating and accommodating to the diverse ideas and beliefs of "the other." As Valsiner (in press) has cogently argued, partnering is a fundamental human activity that not only transforms the partners in a variety of ways but also is essential to the "humanity of human beings."

REFERENCES

Bibace, R. (in press). Partnerships: What's in a name? In R. Bibace, J. Dillon, & D. Dowds (Eds.), *Partnerships in research, clinical, and educational settings*. New Jersey: Ablex.

Bibace, R., Dillon, J., & Dowds, D. (in press). *Partnerships in research, clinical, and educational settings*. New Jersey: Ablex.

Brabeck, M., Bas-Isaac, E., Blanchette, S., Fowler, R., Higgins, A., Hyde, G.J., Kordesh, R., Lewis, T., McCown, G., Montes, C., Puka, B., Roberts, T., Traaen, T., & Weaver, M. (1997). The community school. In A. Etzioni (Ed.), *Character building for a democratic civil society* (pp. 93-103). Washington, D.C.: The Communitarian Network.

Brabeck, M., Cawthorne, J., Cochran-Smith, M., Gaspard, N., Green, C.H., Kenny, M., Krawczyk, R., Lowery, C., Lykes, M.B., Minuskin, A.D., Mooney, J., Ross, C.J., Savage, J., Soifer, A., Smyer, M., Sparks, E., Tourse, R., Turillo, R.M., Waddock, S., Walsh, M., & Zollers, N. (1998). Changing the culture of the university to engage in outreach scholarship. In R.M. Lerner & L.A.K. Simon (Eds.), *University-community collaborations for the twenty-first century: Outreach scholarship for youth and families* (pp. 335-364). New York: Garland Publishing.

Brabeck, M., Walsh, M., Kenny, M., & Comilang, K. (1997). Interprofessional collaboration for children and families: Opportunities for counseling psychology in the 21st century. *The Counseling Psychologist, 25*(4), 615-636.

Bronfenbrenner, U. (1979). *The ecology of human development*. Cambridge, MA: Harvard University Press.

Carlyon, P., Carlyon, W., & McCarthy, A. R. (1998). Family and community involvement in school health. In E. Marx & F. Wolley (Eds.), *Health is academic: A guide to coordinated school health programs* (pp. 67-95). New York: Teachers College Press.

Coltoff, P. (1998). *Community schools: Education reform and partnership with our nation's social service agencies*. Washington, DC: CWLA Press.

Corrigan, D. (1996). Teacher education and interprofessional collaboration: Creation of family-centered, community-based integrated service systems. In L. Kaplan & R.A. Edelfelt (Eds.), *Teachers for the new millennium: Aligning teacher development, national goals, and high standards for all students* (pp. 142-171). Thousand Oaks, CA: Corwin Press, Inc.

Corrigan, D. (1998). Family-centered systems: Focus of the AACTE panel. *Service bridges: Higher education curricula for integrated service providers*. Monmouth, OR: Teaching Research Division of the Western Oregon University.

Denham, C., & Etzioni, A. (1997). Community schools. In A. Etzioni (Ed.), *Character building for a democratic civil society* (pp. 104-112). Washington, D.C.: The Communitarian Network.

Dryfoos, J.G. (1998, Feb.). A look at community schools in 1998: Occasional paper #2. New York: National Center for Schools & Communities.

Dryfoos, J.G. (1994*). Full service schools: A revolution in health and social services of children, youth and families*. San Francisco: Jossey-Bass.

Dryfoos, J.G. (1995). Full service schools: Revolution or fad? *Journal of Research on Adolescence, 5*(2), 147-172.

Einbinder, S.D., & Sloane, D.C. (1998). Reconceptualizing Mr. Rogers' neighborhood: Competing ideas of community and interprofessional collaboration. In J. McCroskey & S.D. Einbinder (Eds.), *Universities and communities: Remaking professional and interprofessional education for the next century*. Westport, CT: Greenwood.

Gergen, K. (1985). The social constructionist movement in modern psychology. *American Psychologist, 40*, 266-275.

Gergen, K. (1991). *The saturated self: Dilemmas of identity in contemporary life*. New York: HarperCollins.

Harkavy, I. (1999, Fall-Winter). School-community partnerships. *Universities and Community Schools, 6*,1-2. Philadelphia, PA: University of Pennsylvania Press.

Illback, R.J. (1994). Poverty and the crisis in children's services: The need for services integration. *Journal of Clinical Child Psychology*, 23, 413-424.

Illback, R.J., Cobb, C.T., & Joseph, H.M., Jr. (Eds.), (1997). *Integrated services for children and families: Opportunities for psychological practice*. Washington, D.C.: American Psychological Association.

Jensen, P.S., Hoagwood, K., & Trickett, E.J. (1999). Ivory towers or earthen trenches? Community collaboration to foster "real world" research. *Applied Developmental Science*, 3(4), 206-212.

Jivanjee, P.R., & Friesen, B.J. (1997). Shared expertise: Family participation in interprofessional training. *Journal of Emotional and Behavioral Disorders*, 5(2), 205-211.

Kaufman, D., & Brooks, J.G. (1996). Interdisciplinary collaboration in teacher education: A constructivist approach. *TESOL Quarterly*, 30(2), 231-251.

Kellogg Commission on the Future of State and Land Grant Universities. (1999, Feb.). *Returning to our roots: The engaged institution*. Washington, D.C.: National Association of State Universities and Land-Grant Colleges.

Knapp, M., Barnard, K., Bell, M., Brandon, R., Gehrke, N., Lerner, S., Rabkin, J., Smith, A., Teather, E., & Tippins, P. (1998). *Paths to partnership: University and community as learners in interprofessional education*. New York: Rowman & Littlefield.

Lawson, H., & Briar-Lawson, K. (1997). *Connecting the dots: Progress toward the integration of school reform, school-linked services, parent involvement and community schools*. Oxford, OH: The Danforth Foundation and the Institute for Educational Renewal.

Lerner, R.M. (1978). Nature, nurture, and dynamic interactionism. *Human Development*, 21, 1-20.

Lerner, R.M. (1984). *On the nature of human plasticity*. New York: Cambridge University.

Lerner, R.M. (1986). *Concepts and theories of human development* (2nd ed.). New York: Random House.

Lerner, R.M., De Stefanis, I., & Ladd, G.T., Jr. (1998). Promoting positive youth development: Collaborative opportunities for psychology. *Children's Services: Social Policy, Research, and Practice*, 1(2), 83-109.

Lerner, R.M., Hess, L.E., & Nitz, K. (1990). A developmental perspective on psychopathology. In M. Hersen & C.G. Last (Eds.), *Handbook of child and adult psychopathology: A longitudinal perspective* (pp. 9-32). New York: Pergamon Books.

Lerner, R.M., & Lerner, J.V. (1987). Children in their contexts: A goodness of fit model. In J.B. Lancaster, J. Altoona, A.S. Rossi, & L.R. Sherrod (Eds.), *Parenting across the lifespan: Biosocial dimensions* (pp. 377-404). Chicago: Aldine.

Lerner, R.M., & Simon, L.A.K. (Eds.). (1998). *University-community collaborations for the twenty-first century: Outreach scholarship for youth and families*. New York: Garland Publishing.

Lerner, R.M., Walsh, M.E., & Howard, K.A. (1998). Developmental-contextual considerations: Person-context relations as the bases for risk and resiliency in child and adolescent development. In T. Ollendick (Ed.), *Comprehensive clinical psychology*. Vol. 5: Children and adolescents: Clinical formulation and treatment (pp. 1-24). New York: Elsevier Science Publishers.

Lindblom, C.E.. & Cohen, D.K. (1979) *Usable knowledge: Social science and problem-solving*. London: Yale University Press.

McCroskey, J., & Einbinder, S.D. (Eds.). (1998). *Universities and communities: Remaking professional and interprofessional education for the next century*. New York: Praeger.

McKenzie, F.D. & Richmond, J.B. (1998). Linking health and learning: An overview of coordinated school health programs. In E. Marx & S.F. Woole (Eds.), *Health is academic: A guide to coordinated school health programs*. (pp.1-14). New York: Teachers College Press.

Mostert, M.P. (1996). Interprofessional collaboration in schools: Benefits and barriers in practice. *Preventing School Failure*, 40(3), 135-138.

Paavola, J.C., Cobb, C., Illback, R.J., Joseph, H.M., Torruellaa, A., & Talley, R.C. (1995). *Comprehensive and coordinated psychological services for children: A call for service integration*. Washington, D.C.: American Psychological Association.

Payzant, T.M. (1992). New beginnings in San Diego: Developing a strategy for interagency collaboration. *Phi Delta Kappan*, 74(2), 139-146.

Petrie, H.G. (1992). Interdisciplinary education: Are we faced with insurmountable opportunities? Review of Research in Education, 18, 299-333.

Pittman, K.J., & Cahill, M. (1992). *Pushing the boundaries of education: The implications of a youth development approach to education policies, structures and collaborations*. Washington, D.C.: Academy for Educational Development.

Pullin, D. (1996, April). Reading between the lines: Shared knowledge bases as the essence of interprofessional education and integrated service delivery for children. Symposium conducted at the annual meeting of the American Educational Research Association, New York.

Sailor, W., & Skrtic, T.W. (1996). School/community partnerships and educational reform: Introduction to the topical issue. *Remedial and Special Education*, 17(5), 267-270, 283.

Schorr, L.B. (1997). *Common purpose*. New York: Anchor Books.

Schon, D. (1987). *Educating the reflective practitioner*. San Francisco, CA: Jossey-Bass.

Searcy, J.A. (1995). *Higher education curricula for integrated services providers: Private foundations, public and private colleges and universities, funded programs, and projects in interprofessional training and development and integrated services*. Monmouth, OR: Western Oregon State College Teaching Research Division.

Shartrand, A.M., Weiss, H.B., Kreider, H.M., & Lopez, M.E. (1997). *New skills for new schools: Preparing teachers in family involvement*. Cambridge, MA: Harvard University Graduate School of Education, Harvard Family Research Project.

Sherman, F. (1998, June). Leadership and lawyering: Learning new ways to see juvenile justice. Paper presented at the Meeting of the Law and Society Association, Aspen, CO.

Stallings, J.A. (1995). Ensuring teaching and learning in the 21st century. *Educational Researcher*, 24(6), 4-8.

Tharinger, D.J., Bricklin, P.M., Johnson, N.F., Paster, V.S., Lambert, N.M., Feshbach, N., Oakland, T.D., & Sanchez, W. (1996). Education reform: Challenges for psychology and psychologists. *Professional Psychology: Research and Practice*, 27(1), 24-33.

Tippins, P., Bell, M., & Lerner, S. (1998). Building relationships between university and community. In M. Knapp (Ed.), *Paths to partnership: University and community as learners in interprofessional education* (pp. 165-192). New York: Rowman & Littlefield.

Valsiner, J. (in press). Partnership in the social world: Opportunities for science and practice. In R. Bibace, J. Dillon, & D. Dowds (Eds.), *Partnerships in research, clinical, and educational settings* New Jersey: Ablex.

Walsh, M.E., & Andersson, D.G. (in press). University-school-community partnerships. In R. Bibace, J. Dillon, & D. Dowds (Eds.), *Partnerships in research, clinical, and educational settings.*

Walsh, M.E., Andersson, D.G., & Smyer, M. (1999). A school-community-university partnership. In T. Chibucos & R. Lerner (Eds.), *Serving children and families through community university partnerships: Success stories* (pp. 181-187). Norwell, MA: Kluwer Academic.

Walsh, M.E., Brabeck, M.M., & Howard, K.A. (1999). Interprofessional collaboration in children's services: Toward a theoretical perspective. *Children's Services: Social Policy, Research, and Practice, 2*(4), 183-208.

Werner, E.E. (1989, April). Children of the garden island. *Scientific American*, Volume 106-111.

Werner, E.E. (1990). Protective factors and individual resilience. In S.J. Meisels & M. Shonkoff (Eds.), *Handbook of early intervention* (pp. 97-116). New York: Cambridge University Press.

Werner, H. (1957). The concept of development from a comparative and organismic point of view. In D.B. Harris (Ed.), *The concept of development* (pp. 125-148). Minneapolis: University of Minnesota.

Wertlieb, D. (1999). Society of pediatric psychology presidential address-1997: Calling all collaborators, advancing pediatric psychology. *Journal of Pediatric Psychology, 24*(1), 77-83.

7 DEVELOPING INTERPROFESSIONAL COMMUNITY IN COLLABORATIVE SETTINGS: Understanding and Refining the Lawyer's Role

Judith A. McMorrow
Boston College Law School

Law is now infused into every aspect of our lives, making the input of lawyers often a necessity. Whether in business, social service, educational or nonprofit settings, the legal perspective may be necessary to understand the legal dimensions of an issue, to maneuver the web of government regulation that may apply, or to avoid claims by or against others that may arise. The converse is also true; lawyers increasingly need non-legal perspectives to resolve issues that arise in a legal setting. Eviction is not just a legal problem, but often requires an array of social services to keep a family intact in a home. Divorce has implications beyond the severing of a legal relationship. Some suggest that this contextualization of practice is a return to an earlier style of lawyering (Kerper, 1998). Whether an old or new movement, lawyers in the 1990s increasingly recognize that problems are not just "legal" or "political" or "social" or "personal," but are the result of a range of forces that require a range of responses. As a result of this interdependency, lawyers and nonlawyers increasingly share the work of resolving issues with legal dimensions.

Legal practice is transforming in response to this interdisciplinary trend. Law firms provide consulting services on organizational issues, tax and financial advice, trust management, and legislative, government relations and lobbying services (Goldberg, 1992; Weidlich, 1992). Lawyers now affiliate with economists, engineers and other professionals (Abel, 1989). We market ourselves as mediators and fact-finders and neutrals (Martindale-Hubbell, 1997). Legal aid lawyers often find themselves acting as part social worker, community activist, and lobbyist. (Peters,

1986; Lubin, 1988) Lawyers seem to welcome this expanding definition of the practice of law, which allows them not only to tackle the deeper roots of problems, but also provides a mechanism to absorb the increasing number of lawyers entering the legal profession (Abel, 1989).

It is not as clear that non-lawyers welcome the incursion of a legal perspective, or lawyers, into the daily lives of other professions. Lawyers often bring to the table insights that inform the ultimate decision. But particularly in collaborative settings, lawyers are too often perceived as a necessary nuisance. Whether seen as too narrowly focused, too rights oriented, too adversarial, to unwilling to share relevant information, risk adverse or negative, lawyers are often cast in the "yes, but" role (Patry, Wexler, Stolle & Tomkins, 1998). Some of the criticisms of the lawyer's role in collaborative settings stem from very legitimate concerns about the style of lawyer interaction. But some critiques stem from a fundamental disagreement about how the lawyer perceives his or her role in representing the client.

This article explores some of the sources of the tension between lawyers and non-lawyers in collaborative settings. The increasingly collaborative nature of legal practice is placing pressure on the adversarial, partisan representation paradigm that has traditionally described a lawyer's duties and responsibilities. The adversary system of dispute resolution is the dominant model in our legal system. Though there is legitimate question whether there is a better alternative available in our pluralistic society, this model is deeply embedded in our constitutional system and is unlikely to be rejected in the near future (Luban, 1988). However, those who question the utility of the adversarial, rights-based model of dispute resolution should not despair. There is significant play both in how one defines an adversarial, partisan duty and how it is implemented in particular situations. A rich definition of the lawyer's role offers significant opportunities for more effective interdisciplinary dispute resolution. Models of comprehensive lawyering, captured in movements such as "holistic lawyering," "therapeutic jurisprudence," and "creative problem solving" search for ways to enlarge the adversarial model to capture the context of the underlying problem (Kerper, 1998; Wexler, 1994). For issues that are likely to be resolved in the shadow of an adversarial process, however, a broader definition of the lawyer's role must arise from, rather than substitute for, a partisanship model. To understand why lawyers do not blithely abandon a partisanship model, one needs to have a fuller understanding of how lawyers define both their role and the underlying values behind the role. From this understanding we can better identify the positive and important function that lawyers can play in interdisciplinary collaborations. Those who yearn for more radical change can take some solace in a few structural experiments that move away from the adversarial paradigm altogether. In these circumstances lawyers must also reconsider the adversarial premise of their traditional role.

UNDERSTANDING THE DUTY OF PARTISANSHIP:
THE ADVERSARIAL PARADIGM

Loyalty and Zeal

The dominant model of lawyering in the United States asserts that the lawyer is an advocate of the client and is ethically bound to pursue the client's interests zealously within the bounds of the law. In *Lawyers and Justice*, David Luban describes this as rooted in the principle of partisanship—that a lawyer must, within the constraints of professional advocacy, maximize the likelihood the client's objectives will be met (Luban, 1988). In the most strongly stated version, this duty of partisanship means that "lawyers are expected to give near-total primacy to their clients' interests— without regard to their social utility, without regard to the relative ability of those adversely affected to protect themselves, without regard to the advocate's own personal beliefs or human reactions" (Lesick, 1992). This strongest version of partisanship is both "widely defended, although also strongly questioned" (Lesick, 1992).

Pronouncements by most bar groups and virtually every state's rules of professional responsibility reflect these concepts, at least in some form. In the last 90 years the legal profession has articulated three influential codes and all incorporate this concept of zeal and loyalty (Canons, 1908; Model Code, 1969; Model Rules, 1981). The 1969 Model Code of Professional Responsibility captured this advocacy theme in Canon 7's pronouncement that "a Lawyer should represent a client zealously within the bounds of the law." The 1983 Model Rules of Professional Conduct, which now are used in some form in the majority of states, does not expressly adopt the concept of zeal in the text of the Rules but captures the underlying value of loyalty and devotion to the client throughout its requirements. In requiring "reasonable diligence and promptness in representing a client," the comments to the Rules gives an expansive definition to these words.

> A lawyer should pursue a matter on behalf of a client despite opposition, obstruction or personal inconvenience to the lawyer, and may take whatever lawful or ethical measures are required to vindicate a client's cause or endeavor. A lawyer should act with commitment and dedication to the interests of the client and with zeal in advocacy upon the client's behalf (Model Rule 1.3, 1998, comment [1]).

This notion of zealous representation, of partisanship, is inculcated in prospective lawyers throughout our culture. Television and movie portrayals typically show lawyers as the zealous fighter for the underdog in heroic terms, and as zealous tools of the powerful in a derogatory fashion. This captures our social ambivalence of the lawyer's role and hints at the underlying value of a partisanship model.

The most prominent justification for this partisan role of the lawyer is embedded in the adversary system. The phrase "adversary system" is most commonly used to describe court procedures: neutral judge and advocates for plaintiff and defendant. The notion that courts can, in theory at least, present a level playing field is a strongly cherished belief. Facts, especially those that will result in the loss of liberty, should not be tested in a charged atmosphere of public opinion, which can too quickly judge the marginalized members of society. Rather, if each side has an advocate who can put forth the best version of the facts, the neutral decision-maker can make a more measured, informed and fair decision. The structural justification for partisanship is that a devoted advocate is essential for a valid adversarial process: the lawyer should not also serve as judge because another has already been assigned that role. Another way to describe this function is to place the lawyer in the role of a facilitator of first class citizenship, in which the lawyer's role promotes the autonomy of the client and assists in implementing concepts of equality (Pepper, 1986). Yet others have described this lawyer-client relationship as one of a "special friend" (Fried, 1976).

In the context of an adversary system, in which the lawyer has been cast in the role of advocate, other values emerge to sustain this role. The principle of partisanship says that a lawyer owes a client a degree of devotion and loyalty. This promise is either explicitly made or implicit in the societal role of the lawyer. Given the social expectations, the lawyer would have an obligation to express clearly his or her decision not to comply with that common expectation in order to avoid deceiving the client and causing detrimental reliance.

The Model Rules contain several important caveats to soften the "client is everything" model and provide a richer model of advocacy. The comments to Model Rule 1.3, quoted above, state that "a lawyer is not bound to press for every advantage that might be realized for a client. A lawyer has professional discretion in determining the means by which a matter should be pursued." This means-end distinction is one crack in the facade of zealous representation. Of greater significance are corresponding duties to counsel clients fully.

Fully Informed Client

The attorney-client relationship is grounded in a notion of respect for the autonomy of the client. In that context, clients need to be fully informed before making decisions. This imposes on the lawyer a duty to give "information reasonably sufficient to permit the client to appreciate the significance of the matter in question" (Model Rules, 1998, Terminology [2]). The Rules and Model Code expressly provide that the lawyer is allowed, and even encouraged (in theory at least) to present non-legal considerations, many of which may be more important to the client than legal concerns (Model Rule 2.1, 1998, Comment [2]; Model Code, 1981, EC 7-8). For example, a misdemeanor conviction may be less important to a teacher than the possibility of losing one's job.

This counseling role provides a promising avenue for a richer vision of representation. In this counseling role the lawyer needs to understand fully not just the immediate goals of the client (for example, a child's desire to "stay in current household") but the underlying interests that shape that goal (desire to be with family, friends, stay with a teacher, desire to protect a weaker sibling, etc.) By understanding the interests at stake of both the client and of the other actors (such as other family members, classroom teacher, and so forth) the lawyer can think more creatively about solutions with the client. In addition, part of that counseling also includes an obligation to deliver bad news to the client—including your professional assessment that the client's goals are unlikely to be successful or persuasive as articulated. Through conversation the client's expectations may change through the persuasion of the lawyer.

In the course of this counseling, the lawyer can ask—and even urge—the client to forego an imprudent or unjust goal (Model Code, 1981, EC 7-9) or can limit the scope of the representation to "exclude objectives or means that the lawyer regards as repugnant or imprudent" (Model Rules, 1998, 1.2, Comment [4]). Lawyers can provide their own moral views to the clients "whether or not the clients have requested such enlightenment" (Ellman, 1990). This last phrase hints at why lawyers—and most professionals—hesitate to go to the language of ethics and morality in counseling clients. Like so many of us, lawyers wonder whether they have the full range of insight to make such judgments of others in a professional context. But even with that caveat, a great many lawyers raise ethical or moral concerns dressed up in the language of law. For example, a lawyer might try to reach a client who seems to be quite rough—bordering on abuse—with the children through a description of how the conduct might be perceived by outsiders as abuse and the legal exposure that yields. Lawyers can be a voice of reality for clients who appear to deny their situation. A lawyer representing a client who has been charged with drunk driving may directly tell the client that she has a drinking problem and needs to get help.

Lawyering Outside the Courtroom

One critical challenge to this partisanship model is that much of law functions outside the traditional adversarial setting of a courtroom. The decision-maker might not be neutral, some interested parties may not be at the table, and some interested parties may not have advocates. This different forum may change the method by which the lawyer tries to articulate the client's point of view, but most lawyers would embrace a duty to continue to press the client's point of view in a technically non-adversarial setting because the adversarial system will likely be the forum to determine any unresolved issues. For example, determining the right educational program for a special needs child who has been involved with the criminal justice system involves considering at least three different "shadows" cast by law: duties to provide special education services, the juvenile justice system, and the child welfare system. Actions taken in this seemingly non-adversarial setting can profoundly affect the rights and liabilities of the child if the child ends up in a legal dispute that is to be settled by a judge.

Perhaps because the adversary system typically steps in if the parties cannot resolve their dispute, there is a tendency to adopt an adversarial approach in non-legal settings. Whether the legal system, and lawyers as its agents, are the cause or the effect of this approach is a subject of some debate (Glendon, 1991). But whatever its source, many—including lawyers—decry the general tendency to bring a competitive or adversarial approach to problem solving. As discussed below, a lawyer will be a much better advocate by taking advantage of the non-adversarial setting to identify the larger interests and goals and to craft a creative solution.

Non-Accountability

The principle of non-accountability is a natural corollary to the principle of partisanship: if the lawyer must represent the client zealously, and hold the client's goals as primary, then the lawyer should not be legally, professionally or morally accountable for the means used or the ends achieved, as long as those means or ends are within the bounds of the law (Luban, 1988). Advocating what you do not believe in is, under this construction, "ethically neutral" (Curtis, 1951). For example, Model Rule 1.2(b) provides that "A lawyer's representation of a client, including representation by appointment, does not constitute an endorsement of the client's political, economic, social or moral views or activities." This is implemented, as a practical matter, by imposing upon the lawyer the obligation to "abide by the client's decisions concerning the objectives of representation."[1]

This notion of non-accountability is also supported by the long-recognized value that unpopular clients and unpopular causes may not get full representation unless we see value in the lawyer's work independent of the client's cause. A classic question every lawyer faces is "how can a lawyer represent a client you know is guilty." The classic response is, again, the systemic justification. Power, especially power of the state, can be used wrongly. We therefore have a constitutional value to require the state to prove guilt beyond a reasonable doubt. To make an exception for someone one "knows" is guilty sets up the public for manipulation and railroading of potentially innocent individuals. To great public scorn Daniel Webster represented the British soldiers in the Boston Tea Party and northern lawyers represented black defendants in the Scottsboro rape trials. Under the adversarial justification, "[i]t is particularly important that it be made as easy as possible for a lawyer to take a case that other people regard as bad" . . . for "[i]n a way the practice of law is like free speech. It defends what we hate as well as what we most love" (Curtis, 1951).

Consistent with the notion of non-accountability, the lawyer codes urge lawyers to make legal representation available, including to unpopular clients. The Model Code urges that lawyers should not "lightly decline proffered employment" because of the "objective of the bar to make legal services fully available," and exhorts that "[t]he fulfillment of this objective requires acceptance by a lawyer of his share of tendered employment which may be unattractive both to him and the bar generally" (Model Code, 1981, EC 2-26). Drawing on a model of honorable lawyering to support the downtrodden, the Model Code gives noble imagery:

> History is replete with instances of distinguished and sacrificial services by lawyers who have represented unpopular clients and causes. Regardless of his personal feelings, a lawyer should not decline representation because a client or a cause is unpopular or community reaction is adverse.[2]

Lawyers must be honest in recognizing that the principle of non-accountability has been a handy tool to absolve lawyers of any duty of thoughtful reflection on the social consequences of one's acts. It leaves lawyers vulnerable to the "cynicism and greed" that many see now pervades the profession (Livingston, 1995; Kronman, 1993).

A great many lawyers are concerned about clients engaging in conduct that is technically legal but morally questionable. Lawyers often will raise these concerns when counseling the client. Many lawyers will continue to represent a client with whom they disagree because of larger social values (need to check government or market power, empowering the traditionally unempowered, and so forth). But lawyers do have an "out." If the lawyer feels that he or she does not want to be associated with the client's ends, the lawyer's option is to withdraw (Ellman, 1990; Luban, 1988). This ability to withdraw is a recognition that lawyers are providing a personal service. In some cases the lawyer's disagreement may prevent the lawyer from effectively representing the client (Model Code, 1981, EC 2-30). But many lawyers avoid certain clients because they do not wish to be associated with the client's goals, just as other lawyers embrace clients because they wish to foster the client's goals (civil rights, pro and anti-abortion, and so forth.) Consequently, the notion of non-accountability is more complex than it appears on the surface. To completely abandon non-accountability would leave the unpopular people and causes potentially unrepresented, which could encourage governmental tyranny. But to embrace non-accountability unconditionally strips the lawyer of any duty to consider the consequences of one's actions, a position that is fundamentally immoral. Most lawyers appear to embrace non-accountability when they perceive that others are articulating alternative perspectives. But where serious harm will flow from potentially immoral client conduct, as discussed below most lawyers will search for an avenue that prevents the harm. The initial premise, however, is that client autonomy should be respected.

The duty of partisanship, and the concomitant principle of nonaccountability, help explain why lawyers often come to the table with an "attitude." That attitude is a sense of duty and loyalty to the goals of the client—which helps give the client full voice for the client's lawful ends. As long as the lawyer is functioning as a representative and fiduciary of an identified client, lawyers are unlikely to abandon a sense of loyalty. The principle of non-accountability explains why lawyers do not typically see ethical issues in choosing to give a client representation because representation enhances the full explication of the client's point of view.

But to acknowledge the social value of representation does not end the inquiry. Both lawyers and non-lawyers occasionally assume that "partisanship" is synonymous with obstructionist, noncommunicative activity. Both lawyers and non-lawyers often assume that serving as a client's "hired gun" means that the lawyer must adopt the client's definition of the problem without question. And legal training often encourages lawyers to compartmentalize the problem so that they see only the technical legal issue and miss the larger social, psychological and political issues also raised by the problem at hand. Debunking these erroneous assumptions provides a much richer model of advocacy, especially when the lawyer is functioning in a collaborative setting.

BEYOND PARTISANSHIP:
DEVELOPING RICHER MODELS OF REPRESENTATION

We can quickly and easily reject a model of advocacy that suggests that lawyers must adopt a *style* that is bombastic, arrogant, loud or insulting. A lawyer can be firm, assertive and disagree without being personally disagreeable. A loud, or offensive style is not confined to lawyers, for any other member of an interdisciplinary team might have those attributes. But lawyers must acknowledge that the adversary system does not structurally discourage people with tendencies toward being loud and bombastic from asserting those tendencies. There is some evidence that characteristics often associated with lawyers—such as a tendency toward dominance and competition—are personality attributes more often exhibited by law students than other professional students, indicating that law attracts people with this personality type (Daicoff, 1997). Lawyers often need to tone it down and turn it off.

The more common problem is lawyers who define the issues presented to them in too narrow a fashion, seeing only (or primarily) the legal dimensions. Lawyers tend to focus on "objective, rational analysis of rules and codification of rights" more than the general population (Daicoff, 1997). This tendency is exacerbated by legal education, which is dominated by a case method in which law students focus on the "legally relevant" facts and often are not told—or told it is "unlawyerly" to focus on—non-legal facts that do not have an apparent direct impact on the outcome of the case (Kerper, 1998). Increasingly lawyers are rejecting a too narrow or premature legal diagnosis. For example, the most prominent text on legal interviewing and counseling emphasizes a client-centered approach to counseling that encourages open communication of underlying values and concerns, active listening, and identification of non-legal consequences (Binder, Berman & Price, 1991). A rich literature has emerged to help lawyers develop the skills for engaging in "creative problem solving" and "therapeutic jurisprudence" in which they anticipate the psychological consequences of the legal choices available (the "psychological soft spots") and think creatively about how the law can most therapeutically be applied (Patry, et al., 1998).

These movements (if one can give such a grandiose claim to a style of lawyering that some lawyers have practiced without a formal "name") are ideally suited to interdisciplinary collaboration. They start with a premise that lawyers must be proactive in identifying the larger social and psychological contexts of legal problems and crafting solutions to those larger problems (if possible). Lawyers in this setting will be active listeners, will seek to identify underlying values and concerns of all parties, and will practice with the humility that every professional must bring to the table in interdisciplinary collaboration. As a proponent of "creative problem solving" explains, "[w]e must endeavor to find better ways of listening, not just faster and more effective ways of talking" (Cooper, 1998).

This collaboration will take place under the shadow of the larger duty to continue to act for the client's best interest. As much as participants in the interdisciplinary collaboration may wish to suspend the adversary system, in all likelihood the life of the individual who is the subject of the collaboration—for example, a child—will be judged by the rules of our legal system. The tensions and challenges become clearer as we examine the lawyer's duties in particular settings.

POSSIBLE ROLE TENSIONS IN IMPLEMENTING LOYALTY AND ZEAL

Zeal, loyalty, devotion to the client, even when practiced in a therapeutic or holistic model, are implemented through a series of express obligations. Three over-arching duties shape how a lawyer functions in collaborative settings. First, a lawyer may not undertake conflicting interests. Second, a lawyer has a duty to maintain the confidences and secrets of the client. Third, as described above a lawyer has a duty to fully inform the client and allow the client to make decisions about the client's interests and goals. These obligations are embodied in the professional codes, so that lawyers are subject to professional discipline for violating these obligations. Of greater practical significance, lawyers are subject to malpractice claims if they do not keep clear the path of client loyalty. The source of the interprofessional tensions becomes clear as we implement in collaborative settings the duties to avoid conflicting interests and to maintain confidences.

Conflicts of Interest

Lawyers are forbidden from undertaking a representation that will be directly adverse to another client [Model Rules, 1998, 1.7(a)]. For example, a lawyer cannot represent both a husband and wife in a child custody dispute since a positive resolution for one client often means a negative outcome for the other. Most lawyers recognize and avoid direct conflicts.

The more common source of problems are situations in which the representation of the client may be "materially limited" by the lawyer's responsibilities to another client, a third person, or to the lawyer's own interests [Model Rules, 1998, 1.7(b)]. As long as the conflict is merely potential, and the lawyer reasonably believes she can adequate represent each client (or the individual client), and the client consents after consultation, representation can go forward [Model Rules, 1998, 1.7(b)].

These rather dry rules become clearer if we examine them in a collaborative setting. Consider a lawyer who takes part in an evaluation meeting at a junior high school to assess the appropriate placement of a special needs child, whose learning disability manifests itself in aggressive behavior, including an act of property vandalism (breaking windows of an abandoned house) that resulted in criminal prosecution. Working with a special team comprised of the principal, classroom teacher, and social worker, the group agrees that the shared goal is the optimum educational experience for the child. In implementing that goal, however, members of the team are likely to have different needs and concerns, which result in different assessments of what is "optimal." The classroom teacher may place a higher value on order and minimizing disruption to other students and urge removal of the child. The social worker may conclude that the best interest of the child means that the child should be removed to another district, where the other parent lives, despite the child's wishes. The lawyer, through confidential interviews with the child, knows that the child desperately wants to remain in the custody of the parent within the school district and does not want to be removed from the school, due to a complex range of factors, including a desire to stay with an older sibling and near friends despite the cold emotional environment offered by the custodial parent. The child often is not allowed to be part of this meeting, where others are deciding her fate. The lawyer may speak strongly, passionately, even to the point of annoyance to others, about the critical importance of keeping the child in the classroom. The other members of the team may begin to feel frustrated that the lawyer is not giving sufficient weight to competing values: what is in the school district's interest and what is in the child's "real" interests based on the adults' judgments. The lawyer is likely motivated by the lurking question of who will speak passionately for the child, making sure that *her* point of view gets a full and fair hearing by the decision-makers, if not the lawyer. In other words, absent an indication that the child is unable to understand and reach conclusions about his or her own well-being (Model Rules, 1998, 1.14, Comment [1]) and absent a statutory duty that conflicts, the majority of lawyers will represent the child's *expressed* interests (Buss, 1999). The lawyer will likely counsel the child-client with special care to encourage the child to consider and embrace other alternatives that, in the lawyer's view, may better meet the child's goals. But generally the child's expressed goals, fully discussed in the lawyer-client counseling, will guide the lawyer.

The most effective lawyer in this setting will recognize that the most likely path to success is to explore the underlying needs and interests of each party and seek a resolution that satisfies these underlying needs. But a lawyer is not likely to abandon the client's needs in this process. In addition, this whole meeting will occur "under the shadow of the law" (Mnookin & Kornhaser, 1979). The lawyer will likely be constrained from making arguments that have no chance of prevailing in court should the issue get that far. The lawyer is likely also to be constrained in making arguments that are unlikely to persuade the decision-maker at all, such as a claim that this child's interests should be given greater priority than any other child's interests. These constraints, however, do not flow from a lawyer's conflicting obligations as a representative of these other interests, but from a rational conclusion about what constitutes effective advocacy. The lawyer is likely to push hard to persuade the group that the other interests should not take precedence over this child's express interests.

In the duty to provide a full voice for the client, some lawyers are fairly criticized for expressing the client's point of view in a disagreeable or rude form and failing to respect and hear alternate points of view (Daicoff, 1997). This is often a function of poor lawyering style since in collaborative settings respectful persuasion is generally more successful than browbeating. But often the complaints about lawyer involvement take a more subtle form: the lawyer should appreciate the school's point of view and acquiesce, or acquiesce sooner. But it is not clear that lawyers should be expected to subsume readily the interests of the child for the interests of the school system. If the school system feels that exclusion of the child is an appropriate decision, that decision should be made with the best possible presentation by the child's point of view.

Confidentiality

Conflict of interest concerns are often inextricably intertwined with confidentiality obligations. The lawyer has a duty not to reveal confidences and secrets unless the client consents or revelation is impliedly authorized (Model Rules, 1998, 1.6; Model Code, 1981, DR 4-101). This duty of confidentiality has deep roots within the legal profession, tracing back to Roman law (Wolfram, 1986). The value behind this duty of confidentiality parallels the value behind the similar duty in other professions. We take as a given that individuals should have access to legal counsel, and that effective legal counsel requires the client to give full information to the lawyer (*Upjohn Co.* v. *United States*, 449 U.S. 383 (1981). We wish to respect the autonomy and dignity of the individual and, even more important for purposes of an enforceable duty of confidentiality, we wish to encourage full disclosure by clients. The duty has such strong weight within the courts that every state recognizes an attorney-client privilege, which prevents the other party in litigation from compelling disclosure of attorney-client confidences except in very limited circumstances (Wolfram, 1986).

Most other professionals have similar duties of confidentiality. Lawyers, however, are unique in the narrow range of exceptions to this duty. The classic version set out in the Model Rules states that the lawyer "*may* reveal such information to the extent the lawyer reasonably believes necessary . . . to prevent the client from committing a criminal act that the lawyer believes is likely to result in imminent death or substantial bodily harm" (Model Rules, 1998, 1.6(b)(1)).[3]

In addition, the attorney-client privilege, the rule of evidence that protects communication from disclosure in a courtroom, can be waived if the lawyer discloses information to third persons. One creative scholar has urged the extension of an attorney-client privilege to interdisciplinary teams, but no jurisdiction to date has adopted that suggestion (Wydra, 1994). Consequently, lawyers often feel that they cannot share relevant, but potentially harmful, information with the interdisciplinary group without compromising the client's rights to have communications protected as confidential.

Other professionals often express surprise at the scope of the attorney's duty of confidentiality. Consider the client who expresses what appears to the untrained lawyer to be suicidal statements, the juvenile who is on the run from a placement facility and contacts the lawyer, the elderly client facing eviction who appears to be in danger of accidentally starting a fire, or the child who reveals abuse by a parent. Each client has developed a relationship of relative trust with the lawyer. Each has revealed information in an unguarded moment. In each case the lawyer will give very strong weight to the obligation to maintain confidences and will likely struggle with whether the values behind the duty of confidentiality will be impaired by disclosure, whether the rules provide a basis to disclose, and whether—even if the rules do not allow disclosure—the lawyer should violate the rules and disclose nonetheless.

Whether to disclose child sexual abuse highlights the particular tension. Professionals who come in contact with children, such as teachers, social workers, psychologists, physicians and nurses, have all been given the duty to report child abuse. Every state has a mandatory reporting statute that compels disclosure of suspected child abuse by those listed in the statute (Rosencrantz, 1995). The duty to report typically is triggered by the professional's reasonable belief that abuse has occurred and statutes typically impose criminal sanctions for failure to disclose that information (Rosencrantz, 1995). To encourage disclosure, all states give immunity to the reporter for reports made in good faith. The value behind such statutes is evident: protect vulnerable and usually voiceless children by giving the state information necessary to determine whether to intervene in the parent-child (or custodian-child) relationship.

Despite the well documented seriousness of child abuse, only Mississippi and Guam include lawyers as mandatory reporters of child abuse (Rosencrantz, 1995). Many states expressly exempt attorney communications from mandatory reporting. Other states imply an exception for attorney-client communications. At best lawyers fall into the category of discretionary reporters, who have no *duty* to report under the statute. In these circumstances, the lawyer's general duty of confidentiality would presumably operate.

This general exception for attorneys to the duty to report child abuse may derive in part from the multiple ways in which lawyers may learn of the abuse. If a criminal defendant charged with abuse confesses some inappropriate behavior to his lawyer, the duty of confidentiality would trump. In that case the state already has information and presumably has stepped in. The criminal sanction machinery is now at work and criminal justice values of the right to counsel would attach.

The harder cases occur when the lawyer learns in a civil proceeding, such as representing a spouse in a divorce, that abuse is taking place. This information may occur through "confession," but in all likelihood the information will come through more indirect sources: veiled references, expressions of self-remorse, observations of behavior that leave a question in the lawyer's mind. Certainly a thoughtful lawyer is completely justified—and compelled—to counsel the client about the implications of this behavior. While we acknowledge that it is very harmful for the child to be abused, it is also not in the client's interest to be engaging in abuse. It is wrong—and it exposes the client to tremendous legal risk. The lawyer would explore with the client avenues to get help. Assuming full and open counseling has taken place, many lawyers will hesitate to take the next step to report their suspicion to authorities.

In this context, most lawyers will feel the weight of the underlying value of confidentiality of attorney-client communications. Most lawyers see taking acts that are not otherwise compelled by law, which affirmatively expose the client to greater legal sanctions as a direct assault on the attorney-client relationship. However flawed the client, the client has given the lawyer trust and disclosure is a breach of that trust. If the lawyer reports that suspicion, the client will see this act as disloyal. It is unlikely that the client will trust the lawyer with any other confidential information, even though the information may be needed for effective representation.

Yet there is a vulnerable child exposed to possible abuse. Unlike social workers or health care professionals, most lawyers have not been trained to recognize abuse. They will wonder if their suspicion rises to the level of certitude that would justify reporting such a serious claim. In all likelihood, most lawyers will look for ways both to protect the attorney-client relationship while still protecting a vulnerable child. They will struggle to find other professionals who are mandatory reporters to see if they have been exposed to the underlying information. Most lawyers will desperately look for an avenue that would offer protection to the child without having the lawyer's hand expose the client to the serious legal liabilities and other consequences that could flow from reporting the client to the social services authority within the jurisdiction.

Other professionals may look aghast at the lawyer's anguish given the compelling interest of protecting a vulnerable child. Most lawyers will not see this as an easy call. For most lawyers the decision to report is likely to be determined at a level of conscience, with the rules of confidentiality as only one small part of the analysis.

The scenario becomes even more complicated if we presume an instance in which our junior high school client above discloses—in an unusual moment of candor—that her father has been beating her, sometimes so seriously that it leaves welts. She does not like the abuse, but she is confident about her ability to protect herself from her father. "He only beats me when he's drunk, and it isn't *that* often."

She desperately does not want to go live with her mother, who may not beat her but who is highly critical. She knows from the experience of her friends what happens when kids get put into foster care: they often get moved away from local schools and friends and lose contact with families. I anticipate that a great many lawyers would respect the decision of the client. It is tragic that in that in our flawed legal and social service scheme a 13, 14 or 15 year old should be confronted with this choice. But unless the lawyer or another professional in this situation can arrange a resolution that will protect her underlying interests, her decision is very rational. It may not be the decision that others would make on her behalf, but a lawyer is likely to say that her autonomy—one of the underlying values protected in an attorney-client relationship—should be respected where possible. At least one bar association has expressly adopted this view, concluding that lawyers who represent minor children 12 and over must preserve confidences and secrets about abuse unless the client consents, disclosure is required by law, or if necessary to prevent death or maiming (Assoc. of the Bar of the City of NY, Ethics Op. 1997-2).

The situation grows quickly more complex as the lawyer becomes less comfortable with the ability of the client to make rational and autonomous decisions, especially if the choice is not the one the lawyer would make. For example, suppose the juvenile client wishes to stay with an abusive boyfriend. As evidence of some sort of incapacity or impaired judgment increases, the lawyer is more likely to move from a model of representing the client's expressed interest to a model of representing the client's best interest—the model typically associated with social work. The legal ethics rules acknowledge the murky nature of this problem and essential urge the lawyer to proceed "as far as reasonably possible" to maintain a normal client-lawyer relationship with the client (Model Rules, 1998, 1.14). Excellent literature has developed to help guide lawyers in this complex problem (Margulies, 1996; Peters, 1996; Tremblay, 1994; 1987). Again, however, the starting presumption is typically of autonomy, with a move away from that model only in compelling circumstances.

TOWARD A NEW PARADIGM OF LAWYERING

When stripped of the rhetoric, many of the challenges to lawyers' conduct are challenges to our structural approaches to problem solving. Our legal system uses a rights-based language scheme and implements these rights in an adversarial setting (Glendon, 1991). That rights-based language operates even outside of the purely adversarial context. The rights-based approach is mirrored in the social and legal responses to deviance. When confronted with deviant behavior, even in the case of children, our society is increasingly moving to a punitive model. If we have set up a punitive structure in which negative information will almost inevitably lead to punishment, we have a scheme that discourages disclosure of information and consideration of the interests of third persons. While a richer vision of client counseling gives thoughtful lawyers an opportunity to raise the interests of third parties, lawyers also have to be honest about the risks to a client.

As long as the problem solving continues in a rights-based model, lawyers will continue to serve as advocates in the traditional sense. The problem is not cured if you simply demand that lawyers abandon the rights-based approach or stop being so "adversarial." The many actors who operate under the shadow of the legal system understand that it will come down hard and swift with a rights-based sanction scheme. Shooting the lawyer for delivering that message is not the cure to the problem.

The full potential of interdisciplinary service may not be achieved unless we move away from the rights-based approach to problem solving. Interesting models have emerged, often driven by an interdisciplinary perspective, that offer some new paradigms of problem solving. The development of mediation and movements embracing "restorative justice" provide exciting opportunities for a richer vision of "partisanship" (Wexler, 1994). While these emerging systems operate under a rights-based scheme, courts often are willing to give official sanction and protection to outcomes under these schemes, which makes them a viable alternative to the current system.

Structural changes, such as restorative justice systems, provide one small example of a new paradigm for problem solving. Restorative justice understands crime as a harm done not just to the victim, but also to the community and the offender herself (Van Ness, 1993). The offense is a rupture of the community fabric, which is healed by involving the victim and the offender and other community members in a jointly designed plan to undo the damage (Basemore & Umbreit, 1995). Restorative justice envisions the wrongdoing as an injury to be healed rather than a crime to be punished. Restorative justice programs include victim-offender mediation and community peacemaking circles which encourage active participation by affected individuals and allows the participants to focus not just on material losses, but also on emotional and other consequences that flow from wrongful behavior (Van Ness & Nolan, 1998).

A lawyer's role in a restorative justice system is different from the typical adversarial role. The lawyer for a defendant is likely to be very involved in the initial counseling to explain the consequences of entering a restorative justice scheme rather than staying in the traditional adversarial or criminal law system (assuming the defendant has a choice.) Defendants in restorative justice systems may end up agreeing to sanctions that a court would not be authorized to award (specific forms of community services, apology, and so forth) Such systems, however, may offer a healing process, and avoid long-term criminal justice system involvement. Once the client has entered into a restorative justice system, a lawyer should make clear the redefined role that will likely emerge. The client is agreeing to work toward consensus and compromise, so that both the client and the lawyer have this shared understanding. A lawyer in this system is likely to feel even more willing to articulate actively the voice of others to the client and to push the client to see these alternate points of view. The lawyer is less likely to serve as a voice for the client, and more likely to move toward a secondary role of advisor. Even in this role, however, lawyers have that ongoing duty to inform the client of the legal consequences of any agreement that the client might make. Lawyers and clients should know that under some schemes the client's statements to victims or third persons may not be protected by any confidentiality obligations. But presumably the client can achieve other goals, such as repentance, that may not be satisfied in a traditional system.

CONCLUSION

Interprofessional collaborations offer the promise to move us out of the old and artificial boxes that have unduly constrained our creative problem solving. As professionals, however, we do not operate on a clean slate. Each profession has certain values that will be carried forward in collaborative schemes. Indeed, sharing and understanding other professional values can help us enrich our own professional paradigms. Lawyers can be better and more effective advocates in collaborative settings by understanding the constraints that other professionals bring to the table. Lawyers can be more effective advocates by presenting their clients' points of view in a way that is most likely to be heard and understood by skeptics. Lawyers can be more effective advocates by making sure that they have engaged in full and rich counseling to help identify their clients' underlying interests and help shape realistic client expectations. But lawyers are still going to be advocates—giving a voice to a point of view—in these settings. It is who we are.

ENDNOTES

[1] Model Rule 1.2(a) and (c) (lawyer "may limit the objectives of the representation *if* the client consents after consultation" (emphasis added). See also DR 7-101(A)(1) ("A lawyer shall not intentionally: Fail to seek the lawful objectives of his client through reasonably available means"). The 1969 Model Code of Professional Responsibility also reflects this principle, with slightly different language. An advocate "may urge any permissible construction of the law favorable to his client, without regard to his professional opinion as to the likelihood that the construction will ultimately prevail." Model Code, EC 7-4. It also exhorts lawyers to "always remember that the decision whether to forego legally available objectives or methods because of non-legal factors is ultimately for the client" and not the lawyer. Model Code, EC 7-8. But see DR 7-102(A)(1) ("In his representation of a client, a lawyer may where permissible, exercise his professional judgment to waive or fail to assert a right or position of his client").

[2] The Model Code recognized the danger that this conceptualization, and the principle of zealous advocacy when coupled with non-accountability, could lead to a conclusion that lawyers must always speak the words that would be in the client's best interests. The Model Code envisioned limits: the obligation of loyalty "implies no obligation to adopt a personal viewpoint favorable to the interests or desires of his client. While a lawyer must act always with circumspection in order that his conduct will not adversely affect the rights of a client in a matter he is then handling, he may take positions on public issues and espouse legal reforms he favors without regard to the individual views of his client." Model Code, 1991, Ethical Consideration 7-17.

[3] Lawyers are allowed to disclose information as a claim or defense in actions by or against the lawyering concerning the representation [Model Rules, 1998, 1.6(b)(2)]. The dissonance of this exception is beyond the scope of this chapter.

REFERENCES

Abel, R. (1989). *American lawyers*. New York: Oxford University Press.

Association of the Bar of the City of New York Committee on Professional and Judicial Ethics, Opinion 1997-2, 8/21/97. FRAN

Bazemore, G. & Umbreit, M. (1995). Rethinking the sanctioning function in juvenile court: Retributive or restorative responses to youth crime. *Crime and Delinquency* 41, pp. 296-316.

Binder, D.A., Bergman, P. & Price, S. (1991). *Lawyers as counselors: A client-centered approach*. St. Paul, MN: West Publishing Company.

Buss, Emily (1999). Confronting developmental barriers to the empowerment of child clients. *Cornell Law Review*, 84, 895-966.

Curtis, C.P. (1951). The ethics of advocacy. *Stanford Law Review,* 4, 1-18.

Cooper, J.M. (1998). Toward a new architecture: Creative problem solving and the evolution of law. *California Western Law Review,* 34, 297-323.

Daicoff, S., (1997). Lawyer, know thyself: A review of empirical research on attorney attributes bearing on professionalism. *American University Law Review*, 46, 1337-1427.

Fried, C. (1976). The lawyer as friend: The moral foundations of the lawyer-client relation. *Yale Law Journal*, 85, 1060-1089.

Ellmann, S. (1990). Lawyering for justice in a flawed democracy. *Columbia Law Review*, 90, 116-190.

Glendon, M. A. (1991). *Rights talk: The impoverishment of political discourse*. New York: Free Press.

Golberg, S. (1992). More than the law: Ancillary business growth continues. *American Bar Association Journal*, 54-57.

Kerper, J. (1998). Creative problem solving vs. the case method: A marvelous adventure in which Winnie-the-Pooh meets Mrs. Palsgraf. *California Western Law Review*, 34, 351-374.

Kaufman, A. (1986). A commentary on Peppers "The lawyer's amoral ethical role." *American Bar Foundation Research Journal*, 651-655.

Kronman, A. (1993). *The lost lawyer: Failing ideals of the legal profession*. Cambridge, MA: Harvard University Press.

Lesick, H. (1992). *Being a lawyer: Individual choice and responsibility in the practice of law*. Minneapolis, MN: West Publishing Company.

Livingston, M. (1995). Confessions of an economist killer: A reply to Kronman's "lost lawyer." *North Western University Law Review,* 89, 1592-1621.

Luban, D. (1988). *Lawyers and justice: An ethical study*. Princeton, NJ: Princeton University Press.

Margulies, P. (1996). The lawyer as care giver: Child client's competence in context. *Fordam Law Review*, 64, 1473-1504.

Martindale-Hubbell (in cooperation with the American Arbitration Association) (1996). *Dispute resolution directory*. New Jersey: Martindale-Hubbell.

Mnookin, R. H. & Kornhaser, L. (1979). Bargaining in the shadow of the law: The case of divorce. *Yale Law Journal*, 88, 950-997.

Model Code of Professional Responsibility (1969; as amended through 1981).

Model Rules of Professional Conduct (1983, as amended through 1998).

Patry, M. W., Wexler, D.B., Stolle, D. P., Tomkins, A. J., (1998), Better legal counseling through empirical research: Identifying psychological soft spots and strategies. *California Western Law Review*, 34, 439-455.

Pepper, S. (1986). The lawyer's amoral ethical role: A defense, a problem, and some possibilities. *American Bar Foundation Research Journal*, 613-635.

Peters, J. K. (1996). The roles and context of best interests in client directed lawyering for children in child protective proceedings. *Fordum Law Review*, 64, 1507-1570.

Rosencrantz, R.H. (1995). Rejecting "Hear no evil speak no evil": Expanding the attorney's role in child abuse reporting. *Georgetown Journal Legal Ethics*, 8, 327-365.

Tremblay, P.R. (1994). Impromptu lawyering and de facto guardians. *Fordham Law Review*, 62, 1429-1445.

Tremblay, P.R. (1987). On persuasion and paternalism: Lawyer decisionmaking and the questionably competent client. *Utah Law Review*, Vol. 1, 515-584.

Upjohn Co. v. United States, 449 U.S. 383, 389, 101 S.Ct. 677, 682, 66 L. Ed.2d 584 (1981).

Van Ness, D.W. (1993). New wine and old wineskins: Four challenges of restorative justice. *Criminal Law Forum*, 4, 251-276.

Van Ness, D.W. & Nolan, P. (1998). Legislating for restorative justice. *Regent University Law Review*, 10, :53-110.

Weidlich, T. (1992) Ancillary businesses prospering quietly. *National Law Journal*.

Wexler, D.B., (1994). An orientation to therapeutic jurisprudence. *New England Journal on Criminal & Civil Confinement*, 20, 259-264.

Wilkins, D. (1990). Legal realism for lawyers. *Harvard Law Review*, 104, 468-524.

Wolfram, C.H. (1986). *Modern legal ethics* §6.1. Minneapolis, MN: West Publishing Company.

Wydra, H.A. (1994). Keeping secrets within the team: Maintaining client confidences while offering interdisciplinary services to the elderly client. *Fordham Law Review*, 62, 1517-1545.

ACKNOWLEDGMENTS

I very much appreciate the insights from Francine Sherman, and Jackie Gardina, and Linda Maloney. Information on the lawyer's duty to report child sexual abuse was greatly aided by student papers from Jennifer Kaiser, Sara Passaretti, and Joanna Wrobel. Information on restorative justice was developed by Rudy Perkins and Sally Jameson.

8 SEEKING SOCIAL JUSTICE:
A Teacher Education Faculty's Self Study[1]

Marilyn Cochran-Smith
Lillie Albert
Philip Dimattia
Sara Freedman
Richard Jackson
Jean Mooney
Otherine Neisler
Alec Peck
Nancy Zollers
Boston College

As is now well documented, the numbers of children of color, poor children, and children with identified disabilities are on the rise in the United States, and in some places "minority" groups are now the majority of the school population (National Education Goals Panel, 1997). At the same time there is mounting evidence that the present educational system is failing to serve disproportionately large numbers of children who are not part of the mainstream (Christensen & Dorn, 1997; Darling-Hammond, 1995; Kozol, 1991). In response, there have been many calls for reform of public schooling and of teacher education (Banks, 1997; Dilworth, 1998; Rice-Jordan, 1995). A number of scholars have argued that we need teachers (and teacher educators) who enter and remain in the teaching force not to carry on business as usual but to work for social change and social justice (Ayers, Hunt & Quinn, 1998; Cochran-Smith, 1995, 1998; Oakes & Lipton, 1999; Skrtic & Sailor, 1996).

Embracing a general—but at the time largely unexamined—commitment to social justice, the nine co-authors of this paper, all faculty members of the relatively large and complex teacher education department, embarked upon a multi-year collaborative research and professional development project. The project, which came to be known as "Seeking Social Justice," was designed with several purposes:

1) to allow us to examine our own biases and understandings of equity, diversity, access, power, and social justice as part of the process of helping our students do the same; 2) to enhance the research mission of the university; and, 3) to encourage our students to work for social change as part of responding to the increasing diversity of the K-12 school population. In this article we discuss the framework for this project, analyze the first two years of collaborative work, and then describe efforts currently underway.

We suggest that our work together provides a "proof of possibility" for faculty groups attempting to emphasize or infuse social justice into preservice teacher education despite profound differences in politics, disciplines, and perspectives. Part of what made this possible was a commitment to extended and repeated conversation that evolved over time into a culture of careful listening and cautious openness to new perspectives. We began the project with the somewhat ambiguous intention of developing "shared understandings" of teaching and teacher education for social justice. What emerged over time, however, was not "shared understanding" in the sense of consensus. Rather, as we struggled to put our individual ways of knowing together, what developed were deeper and richer understandings of our own biases as well as where our colleagues were coming from on particular issues and how each of us differently constructed the issues. We argue here that it was these deeper understandings, and not consensus, that allowed us to take action–designing and implementing new administrative policies and practices, establishing social justice as the centerpiece of the curriculum, and beginning to look critically and publicly at our own pedagogy as teacher educators.

TEACHING AND TEACHER EDUCATION FOR SOCIAL JUSTICE: RELATED LITERATURE

We did not begin this project, as we might have, by common reading of major theoretical works on social justice teaching or by establishing explicit and unanimous criteria for defining the concept. Rather because all of us stated at the outset that we were already generally committed to the idea, we began by trying to uncover and understand the range and variation of the individual meaning perspectives we brought to the table.[2] Over time we discovered that various members of the group had widely differing views of social justice, of the sources of *in*justice in school and society, and of educators' obligations to alter unjust systems (Zollers, Albert, & Cochran-Smith, in press).

Much later in the project some of us concluded that had we begun by locating our individual perspectives within particular schools of thought or by characterizing them in explicit political, religious, paradigmatic, or ideological terms, we might well have splintered the group irreparably and thus halted the project almost before it began. We are all teacher education faculty members at Boston College—a Catholic and Jesuit institution with a long-standing commitment to social justice as part of its historical mission. However, as we came to realize, the nine individuals who were part of this project for its first two years make up a quite diverse group with different commitments, different disciplinary and research backgrounds, and very different life experiences. We are men and women, tenured and untenured faculty, African American and White European American. We are disabled and able-bodied, Catholic, Protestant, and Jewish. We have concentrated our professional energies on research and writing, and we have concentrated on the practice of teacher education. Each of us locates the roots of our ideas about teaching for social justice within highly idiosyncratic configurations of personal and professional experience and in relationship—more or less—to an array of theoretical frameworks, politics, histories, and religious commitments.

In the section that follows we elaborate on these multiple roots by listing some of the social, intellectual, and educational movements that have influenced us. We want to make it clear, however, that no single member of our group affiliates with all of the movements listed below, that some members of the group explicitly reject some of these perspectives, and that a few of us do not affiliate strongly with any of them. This project was not intended to foreclose differences in meanings but to deepen understandings. Over time we realized that each of the movements listed below at times implicitly informed many of our discussions about teaching and teacher education for social justice.

- *The liberatory education movement* in Latin America, particularly the literacy work of Paulo Freire (Freire, 1970; Freire & Macedo, 1987);
- *European critical educational theory*, particularly the influence of Antonio Gramsci and Karl Marx as well as the Frankfurt School's economic and social critique of western society and schooling based on hegemonic class relationships;
- *The American civil rights movement*, particularly the struggle for equal educational opportunity regardless of race or disability and the subsequent development of critical multicultural and inclusive pedagogies as well as radically inclusive school arrangements (e.g., Banks, 1997; Banks & Banks, 1993; Skrtic, 1995; Sleeter & Grant, 1987; Ladson-Billings, 1995; Tatum, 1992);
- *The social teachings of the Catholic Church*, including the idea that individuals must grapple with the *in*justices of their local and larger communities (Hollenbach, 1995; Land, 1972), particularly Jesuit educational traditions and the social justice mission derived from Ignatian ideals (Meirose, 1994);
- *North American critical educational theory*, particularly its call for critical curriculum analyses and pedagogy openly committed to interrupting historical systems of oppression in order to forge a more just and democratic society (e.g., Apple, 1995; Anyon, 1994; Aronowitz, 1988; Giroux, 1983; McLaren, 1994; McCarthy, 1993);
- *Feminist critical theory/pedagogy* that theorizes the previously marginalized issues of gender (Lather, 1992; Gore, 1993; Luke, 1992) and race (hooks, 1994; Collins, 1991; Gordon, 1995) and problematizes voice, authority, and positionality in educational contexts (e.g., Fine, 1992; Ellsworth, 1989; Lather, 1992);
- *Inclusive curriculum design/pedagogy* that addresses the need to mediate learning experiences through strategic instructional approaches that enhance understanding and make curriculum accessible to all students regardless of ability/disability (Brown, et al., 1991; Deshler & Schumaker, 1988; Ellis & Lenz, 1990).

Clearly these ideas are different from one another. Despite their differences, however, each promotes critique of educational systems in terms of access, power, and privilege based on race, culture, gender, language background, ability, and/or socioeconomic position. And each acknowledges that the structural inequities embedded in schooling help to perpetuate unequal access to learning opportunities for various segments of the school population. As importantly, each constructs the role of educator as agent for change in school and classroom contexts as well as in larger movements for a more just and democratic society. Over the course of our project, many of these ideas and the ways they interacted with our personal and professional experiences were the sub-texts, spoken or unspoken, of agreements as well as disagreements.

A number of educators have argued that teaching for social change and social justice should not be supplements to teacher education, but should instead be a fundamentally different way of doing the daily work of teacher education (Cochran-Smith, 1995, 1998; Irvine, 1992; Ladson-Billings, 1995; Larkin, 1995; Zeichner, 1993). Most college faculty who are attempting to teach for and about social justice, however, have not had professional development that specifically prepares them to do so (Bell, Washington, Weinstein, & Love, 1997). Hence many teacher educators need opportunities to develop self knowledge regarding their own social identities, to confront their own biases, to learn how to respond to the biased comments that may emerge in their classrooms, and to gain familiarity with the risks and dangers of participating in such a discourse.

There have been several efforts by teacher educators to engage in self-examination of this kind and to reinvent curriculum and pedagogy in keeping with the goals of social justice. For example, some teacher educators have engaged in self-studies or in practitioner research projects to rethink their own assumptions (Hamilton & Pinnegar, 1998; Cole & Knowles, 1998), their teaching strategies (Rosenberg, 1997; Sleeter, 1995; McIntyre A., 1997), and, in some cases, their missed opportunities to clarify or connect with students (Cochran-Smith, 1995; Zeichner, 1998). Although a few of the reported self-studies are collaborative, most have been conducted by individual teacher educators within the contexts of their own courses or in projects or programs controlled largely by individuals or small groups. The literature seems to suggest that it will take more than individual efforts to integrate social justice into the fabric of the preservice curriculum. Research on K-12 professional development suggests that learning communities may be among the most promising contexts for this kind of work–for constructing meaningful local knowledge, challenging assumptions, posing problems, studying students' learning, and reconstructing curriculum (Cochran-Smith & Lytle, in press; Lieberman, 1992). The hallmark of these inquiry communities is joint participation as co-learners and co-researchers (Reason, 1998; see Waddock & Spangler, Chapter 11; Walsh, Chapter 6; Sherman, Chapter 12) by those who are differently positioned from one another and who bring different kinds of knowledge and experience to bear on the collective enterprise.

SEEKING SOCIAL JUSTICE

It is not surprising that all the faculty in our program were comfortable with the general concept of social justice as an educational goal. This is an emphasis of the core curriculum for all students at Boston College and has been part of its institutional mission since inception. Informed by Ignatian pedagogy, this mission is based on respect for the "freedom, right, and power of individuals and communities to create a different life for themselves" (Meirose, 1994, p. 2). Further, faculty are enjoined to advance research that will "both enrich culture and address important societal needs" (Boston College University Academic Planning Council, 1996, pp. 2-3). Along these lines, "social justice" was identified by School of Education faculty in the early 1990s as one of four sub-themes that unified curriculum across accredited education programs.

PROJECT DESIGN

Despite the fact that social justice had long been a mission of the university, it was readily apparent when this project began that there was not a clear definition of the concept of teaching and teacher education for social justice that was known or shared by all. In addition, in the five or so years preceding the project, a large number of newcomers had joined the faculty, and many major curricular and organizational changes had occurred. This situation coupled with the desire to engage in collective research related to teacher education prompted a group of faculty members[3] to come together in the summer of 1996 to plan a collaborative research and professional development project that focused on social justice. The project centered on three major questions:

1)   What happens when a diverse teacher education faculty meets over time to try to develop shared understandings about teaching for social justice, particularly what are their common and divergent constructions of the concept?
2)   How are relatively abstract understandings of social justice put into practice (or not) in the day-to-day business of teacher education, including curriculum development, course instruction, and assessment of students' learning as well as student/faculty recruitment, retention, advising, and mentoring?
3)   What issues, related to research, emerge from collaborative self-study; especially what are the ethical and methodological issues related to data collection/analysis, confidentiality, power relationships, and voice?

When the academic year began, the summer group proposed to all who participated in regular teacher education program meetings (i.e., 16 Teacher Education faculty members and three administrators who worked closely with the programs) that attention to issues of social justice become a regular part of the ongoing business of the group and that the smaller summer group, which came to be known as "the research group," document and analyze the process.[4]

In many ways this project can be thought of as "self study," a term used to describe "new" kinds of practitioner inquiry primarily at the higher education level and primarily in teacher education (Cole & Knowles, 1998; Zeichner, 1998). As Hamilton and Pinnegar (1998) describe it, "those involved in self study systematically collect evidence from their practice, allowing them to rethink and potentially open themselves to new interpretations and to create different strategies" (pp. 1-2). Most of these "new" self studies have been conducted by individuals or pairs of teacher educators exploring aspects of their own teaching or professional development work and/or their own assumptions and beliefs. (See, for instance, the collection of pieces in Hamilton and Pinnegar, 1998, or the examples cited in Zeichner, 1998). Department-wide or school-wide teacher education evaluations are also broadly referred to as "self studies," particularly those prompted by the National Council for Accreditation in Teacher Education (NCATE) or other state level or national accreditation or re-accreditation reviews. Projects of this kind, although self studies in the sense that they evaluate practices and policies internal to given programs, are almost always intended to demonstrate adherence to explicit standards rather than explore multiple interpretations.

Our project was intended to be a self study in the first sense above but was also intended to be a collaboration among a relatively large group of people, requiring engagement by each participant in design and analysis. In this sense, the project may be closer to what Heron (1996) calls "cooperative inquiry" or what Reason (1998) calls "participative inquiry" wherein "all those involved in the research are both co-researchers, whose thinking and decision making contribute to generating ideas, designing and managing the project, and drawing conclusions from experience, and also co-subjects, participating in the activity being researched" (p. 264). In this project the line between being researchers and being researched subjects was always blurry and at times nonexistent as was the line between studying the work and doing the work of teacher education (see Lykes & Haney, Chapter 14). This ambiguity coupled with the issues of exposure, voice, and influence that are inherent in any long-term collaboration among differently positioned people, allowed for powerful insights—even transformations—at the same time that it created misunderstandings, coercion, and exclusion. (These issues are discussed in more detail in a later section of this chapter.)

The time-consuming nature of collaborative decision-making immediately became apparent as the group debated the ground rules for documentation–when audio taping would occur, who could turn the recorder on and off, who owned the data, and what procedures would govern use of the data for presentations and publications. These discussions as well as questions raised by the school's human subjects review committee focused primarily on scrutinizing the risks of participation, especially to untenured faculty, and on protecting the identities of participants, a task made more difficult by public presentations and publications. Over time the struggle had the effect of pulling group members together and reinforcing our commitment to the work.

Table 8.1 lists some characteristics of the larger teacher education group that participated in social justice conversations and of the research group, a subset of the first, that documented the project.

Table 8.1
Participants in the Social Justice Conversations
and in the Research Group

	Social Justice Conversations	Research Sub-Group
Tenured Senior Faculty	9	5
Untenured Junior Faculty	5	4
Adjunct Faculty	1	1
Administrator	3	0
Male	7	3
Female	11	7
General Education Faculty	9	5
Special Education Faculty	6	5
European American	16	8
African American	2	2

The research group met bi-weekly to design the project, first to develop research questions and plan data collection strategies, then later to analyze data and prepare dissemination reports and presentations. The research group also planned for and reflected on the discussions of the larger group. Inevitably their discussions exposed additional attitudes and questions about social justice. Hence the smaller group's discussions were also considered a major data source for the project.

Over a two-year period, seven two-to-three hour discussions occurred around the topic of social justice. These were interspersed with meetings that focused on ongoing administrative and curricular issues. The seven large-group discussions as well as the research group meetings were audiotaped and transcribed. The research group also collected agendas, meeting notes prepared by assigned note takers, email messages, transcriptions of flipchart notes from large and small discussions, materials from regular teacher education meetings that related to social justice, curriculum materials, notes from personal conversations with colleagues when the social justice discussions spilled over into regular professional conversations, as well as notes of other school meetings, memos, and decisions that related to social justice issues. The primary data base was annotated transcriptions of small and large group discussions based on audio recordings, field notes, and documents related to the sessions. During the second year of the project, the research group also documented how and to what degree the understandings of social justice explored during the first year was instantiated in the day-to-day business of teacher education. This was based on analysis of meeting agendas, notes, and handouts as well as notes and multiple drafts of policies, practices, and other documents representing the program. The research group engaged in multi-layered collaborative data analysis in pairs, small groups, and whole group as well as multi-staged collaborative writing and preparation for presentations. (See Neisler, 1998, for further comment on collaborative research methods and methodological issues.)

TALKING ABOUT SOCIAL JUSTICE

As we began this project, we had some sense that we held different views about the meanings of social justice and how to achieve it. We realized early on that trying to establish a consensual and explicit definition of social justice would not only be a lesson in futility but, more importantly, would prevent us from achieving our most important goal–building a teacher education program committed to social justice. The paradox, of course, was trying to do the latter without doing the former.

We therefore developed a series of structured conversations to explore our differences and develop greater understandings of each other's points of view as well as how we came to hold these perspectives and how they changed over time. Each session included some combination of individual writing, break-out discussion groups, small group reports, individual sharing of experiences with the large group, presentations and question/answer sessions with guest speakers, pre-reading followed by discussion of printed materials, whole group discussions, and analyses of case studies. Table 8.2 provides an overview of the seven conversations by topic, format, and date.

Table 8.2
Seven Conversations of the Social Justice Research Project

Date	Topic	Format
10/10/96	What does social justice mean to you?	• Individual Writing • Small Group Sharing • Large Group Discussion
10/24/96	If our teacher education program *were* committed to social justice, what would it look like?	• Individual Writing • Small Group Sharing • Large Group Discussion

(table continued)

Date	Topic	Format
11/21/96	What are the implications of social justice issues for the ways we conduct the everyday business of teacher education, particularly faculty collaboration, mentoring of new faculty, promotion and tenure issues?	• Large Group Discussion
01/30/97	What does social justice have to do with issues of disability and of students with special needs, particularly with issues of inclusion in general education classrooms?	• Pre-reading of cases related to inclusion in classrooms • Facilitator-led whole group discussion
03/20/97	What are the experiences of gay and lesbian young people in school and community contexts? What does this have to do with social justice and our work as educators?	• Presentation by speakers followed by brief question and answer session
04/10/97	What are our own experiences and memories of racial awareness, racism, and identity? How do these influence our work as educators?	• Facilitator presentation • Facilitator-led individual sharing and whole group discussion *(table continued)*

Date	Topic	Format
02/10/98	What are our experiences as educators in relation to the cycles of oppression that operate in our society and in our schooling institutions? What should our roles be as educators committed to social justice?	• Facilitator presentation • Small group tasks/discussion • Whole group processing/discussion

As Table 8.2 indicates, our first session, which was designed to uncover autobiographical and ideological underpinnings of our views of social justice (Bullough & Gitlin, 1995; Florio-Ruane, 1994), addressed the original research question directly and broadly. Each participant responded in writing to the question: "What does social justice mean to you?" which was then discussed in small and large groups. Next we narrowed the focus to the relationship between the understandings voiced in the first discussion and how they might—hypothetically—affect practice in teacher education. Individuals and small groups were asked to respond to the question, "If our teacher education program *were* committed to social justice, what would it look like?" Again each small group reported back to the large one, and key ideas were compared and contrasted. During the third session, we shifted from hypothetical to actual situations by considering the implications of social justice issues for the ways we conduct the everyday business of teacher education, particularly in relation to faculty collaboration and relationships, evaluation of faculty contributions to teaching and research for tenure and other decisions, and mentoring of new faculty. These three sessions revealed that participants constructed "social justice" differently based on at least three key issues: conceptions of fairness and equity, the roles and responsibilities of institutions versus those of individuals regarding social justice and injustice, and the importance of individual versus collective beliefs and actions in advocating for social justice (Zollers, Albert, & Cochran-Smith, in press).

For the next four sessions, we explored several topics with the help of outside facilitators: meeting the special needs of students through various inclusion programs, the school experiences of gay and lesbian youth, and the impact of race and racism on teaching, learning, and schooling. To explore issues of disability and diversity, we used case studies of classrooms; these quickly exposed our ideological differences as we debated the "fairness" of differential treatments of students within the same classrooms and considered issues of grading, special accommodations, classroom aides, curriculum design, and interprofessional collaboration. Consultants available through a state grant led a session on issues facing gay and lesbian youth in public high schools, which was informative for all of us but, disappointingly, allowed for very little interaction.

Beverly Tatum, well known for her work with prospective and experienced teachers struggling to explore issues of race and construct anti-racist curriculum (Tatum, 1992; Lawrence & Tatum, 1997) led our group in two discussions about race and racism. These were especially important to the development of the group and were often referred back to over the months that followed. Tatum began by reflecting on some of her own childhood memories related to race and racial identity and then invited us to do the same. We learned a great deal about each other that day. We had glimpses of the children each of us had been, and we had insights into how our childhood experiences were interwoven into the fabrics of our current personal and professional identities in terms of race and ethnicity. Some members of the group told stories of how they had been the targets of oppression in a racist society. Others recounted memories of discrimination based on immigrant cultures and/or minority religious affiliations. Some talked about their own school experiences at times of intense racial tension and violence. Our stories were powerful and in many cases disturbing; they were laced with memories of embarrassment, fear, anger, rage, loneliness, suicide, and powerlessness. We questioned aloud how early negative feelings affected our abilities to speak and act comfortably in the present time.

Ten months later, again led by Beverly Tatum, we drew on those prior images of who we had been and delved deeper into our current sociopolitical attitudes. In small and then large groups, we focused on how we participate in what Tatum (1992) calls the "cycle of oppression." Our examples linked oppression with racism, sexism, and classism. Many stories were painful for both tellers and listeners; we asked some hard questions and made some unsettling discoveries. A few men could not think of one incident in the course of a lifetime when they had experienced discrimination or oppression. Some of us asked questions about how to break the cycle. Others asked whether it was possible that those who were targets of oppression could also be perpetuators of the cycle. We learned that some of us lived in neighborhoods where others were afraid to travel. One member of the group expressed what many of us felt:

> I was thinking how important it is to have conversations like these because of collusion. I know I struggle with these issues of racism within myself . . . at the unconscious level. And trying to get that ugly stuff out is difficult unless you're in a group of people who can raise a question and help you critically examine some of the assumptions on which you base your behavior.

This session was the last in the series of seven departmental conversations convened explicitly to talk about issues related to social justice. But this was decidedly not the last time the topic was considered. To the contrary, by the time of the last structured social justice conversation, the concept had become a major theme in all of our certification programs and an ongoing consideration in our work as a department.

THE IMPACT OF TALK

Integrating extensive discussions about social justice into the business of the department over two years influenced individual beliefs and perspectives and made possible new insights into the perspectives of others, as the following section points out. Talking about social justice also influenced who we were as a department and how we carried out the daily work of teacher education–negotiating policies, establishing practices, developing curriculum, and working with students.

At The Individual Level

Sharing our personal journeys and our early experiences with racial and ethnic issues as well as our personal constructions of social justice have influenced how we understand each other as well as the work we do individually. As we mention in the first conversation our individual notions of social justice were wide ranging. On the one hand there were what might be thought of as micro-conceptions of social justice focused on the individual's responsibility to create a just society. For example, one member of the group wrote:

> Social Justice for me is social change. Because we do not currently have a just society, seeking social justice requires activism. Therefore, I try to be "just" in my own activities and interactions as mother, teacher, colleague, daughter, neighbor, wife, citizen and friend. [I try to] make my search for justice an active part of my life.

On the other hand, there were more macro, critical perspectives on social justice that emphasized the socioeconomic forces that shape daily life in society and the need to radically change the infrastructure if equitable learning and living opportunities are to be available for all. In one of the early discussions, another individual wrote:

> Social Justice has to do with working toward a more just society and a more democratic life. To me, social justice requires altering the status quo—the way resources, privileges, and opportunities are distributed and passed along from generation to generation.

Part of our work involved conducting our own interrogations and confronting our own deficiencies. This process is very personal. But having other people along on that journey made it what Westerhoff (1987) describes as a pilgrimage rather than an odyssey. Certainly, the search for meaning within ourselves began to have implications for our ability to act as resources for other people's learning. One member of the group wrote:

> In my work with student teachers, I am much more aware of how our students of color struggle to carve out a place for themselves at BC. And I am more painfully aware of many of our 'privileged' white students who also struggle to understand and cope with the

increasingly diverse students in our schools. Many of them come to their placements in Boston with a fear that is grounded in ignorance. My personal goal is to foster our students' growth in learning to find a place for themselves in the schools—to contribute in meaningful ways to their 'coming of age' as teachers in diverse settings.

The process of self-study gave us the opportunity to confront our own worldviews and to discover how they differ from others'. During the conversation wherein we tried to imagine what our teacher education program would look like if it were based on social justice, one member of the group raised a fundamental issue related to communication and community:

One aspect in communication is facial expressions–body language. [These] are as important as words. How do we respond when someone treats another in a disagreeable way? How do facial expression, body language, and tone of voice in conversations impact what is being said in a community?

Comments like this turned the issue of social justice inward, forcing us to recognize that questions of justice are not simply played out on a grand scale in social and political movements but also have to do with the ways we treat each other on a daily basis.

Subtle messages are also conveyed by choice of words, spoken as well as written. Growing sensitivity to language in written expression is becoming evident. One individual shared the following insight:

I have become more aware of language in texts and more conscious of the way I write. For example I [had written on my syllabus] "the way we handle students," [now I've] changed it to 'the way we work with students'.

We are also coming to recognize that language can convey meanings that are not intended. Taking for granted that all listeners understand our individual perspectives can lead to misunderstanding and unintended messages. For example, one member of the group wrote:

I hadn't realized the degree to which some faculty believe that race motivates what others say to them. I'm still not convinced that race is the motivation in many cases, but I am now aware that it is perceived to be the motivation. That has led me to try to evaluate whether race is unconsciously motivating any of the statements I'm making to colleagues.

Trying to sort out not only the meanings behind our own words but also the ways those words are likely to be perceived by others whose experiences and beliefs are different from our own is difficult and sometimes almost paralyzing work.

But the real value of collaborative self-study about social justice is determined by the degree of impact not simply on what we say, but on what we believe and what we do. Over the course of time, many members of the group altered or broadened their beliefs: some began to include disability within their understandings of diversity, some linked their own analyses of the inequities in the current educational system to larger critical social and economic theories, some shifted the focus of their attention from individual to societal causes and remedies for injustices, and some began to see connections across what had previously seemed extremely disparate agendas for social justice. Dunn (1987) suggests that there is an ontological link between personal beliefs and public behaviors. Perhaps the true test of the connection between personal understandings and individual and/or collective public responsibility, then, is the degree to which any of the talk we engaged in about social justice prompted us to a different kind of activism.

Several members of the group began to use Tatum's idea of "disrupting the cycle of oppression" as a measure of their own efforts to change. Some began to move toward other kinds of deliberative action. After one of our sessions, for example, one member of the group reflected on the cycle of oppression and its relevance to her own developing understanding of the role teachers play in the lives of gay and lesbian students. She wrote:

> A few years ago there was a real confrontation of the alliance of gay and lesbian students and the administration that had not yet recognized the group as a legitimate student organization. In . . . a faculty meeting, a motion was introduced to support the position of the students. I raised my hand like everybody else and then didn't really think about it again until the . . . workshop on homosexuality. It finally got through to me that all teachers, even those in early childhood classrooms, need to project positive attitudes towards various sexual orientations. When I began to think of the issues in terms of child development, it all made sense . . . Now I realize a need to design a more substantive module on sexual identity and the needs of students who are gay or lesbian to include in the diversity course I teach . . . I am finally understanding that I need to be pro-active and not just reactive.

In a very real sense, building into the daily work of teacher education opportunities for extended and repeated discourse about social justice provided a unique opportunity for individual and collective professional growth. Typically, professional development in higher education is a matter of personal choice. Faculty members work alone or within small groups of like-minded people to improve teaching and learning in a particular area or to develop research strategies around a particular problem. In this instance, however, all the members of a department made a commitment to participate in and support a collaborative research and professional development project with a unified agenda identified by the participants themselves. In this sense the project has been what Kember and Gow (1992) call "practical action research" in that it uses facilitators and focused conversations to study the issues of social justice in the work of teacher education.

As we revise our curriculum and establish new policies by making value judgments about what is and is not important, we have an opportunity to achieve emancipatory action research "in which the practitioner group takes responsibility for the development of practice through democratic decision-making. It implies that the group becomes concerned with the social or power sphere which influences the actions it desires to take" (Kember & Gow, 1992, p. 307). To achieve this level of commitment to social justice, some individual members of the group may move toward more emancipatory and critical conceptions of the educational enterprise (Webb, 1992). At this point, we have no way to measure each individual's commitment to discourse that is genuinely open or to a personal stance that is more critical. Personal transformation was not a goal at the outset of the project. Rather the goal was the design of a coherent program in teacher education grounded in principles of social justice. The degree to which individual professional development is a by-product and/or a prerequisite of the project is not yet clear.

Beyond The Individual Level

Talking about social justice had an impact beyond the level of individual intellectual perspectives. It also influenced how we identified ourselves as a group of professionals, how we socialized newcomers into our community, how we established and implemented departmental policy and practice, and how we constructed curriculum and pedagogy. About a year into this project, the various pieces of general teacher education, special education, and curriculum and instruction actually became a department rather than a collection of multiple and loosely connected certification programs. Although departmental status was primarily the result of a major administrative reorganization following appointment of a new dean, it was also made possible by a growing sense of collaboration across teacher education programs and a certain degree of intellectual unity about social justice as a central tenet. As a group, we were coming to see that teacher education itself could and ought to be regarded as an act of social justice.

The day-to-day work of a teacher education department that serves some 1200 undergraduate and master's level students is complex. Whether there was a direct or causal relationship between two years of conversations about social justice, on the one hand, and radical alterations in the work of the department, on the other, is impossible to say. What we can say, however, is that as we struggled over certain departmental decisions, social justice became a central concept in the debates. Undoubtedly individuals continued to construct social justice differently, but the concept—along with its various meanings—was continuously brought into the deliberations and used as a way of contesting or forwarding competing agendas.

Along these lines, social justice became a unifying theme in how we described our work and in our identity as a group that worked together to tackle difficult issues. This was evident in the ways we began to present ourselves to prospective students and faculty and in the ways we socialized newcomers into the department.

In addition, as part of preparations for re-accreditation, faculty reconsidered the themes that had been constructed six years earlier in preparation for a prior review. When faculty reconsidered the themes, it was obvious to nearly everyone that the overarching theme across programs in Teacher Education (TE) had become teaching for social justice. We also added a new theme that emphasized school-community and school-university collaboration to account for and honor the views of all stakeholders in the educational process, particularly those of traditionally marginalized groups. Reprioritizing and refining teacher education themes suggests that social justice had become paramount and had become a way to unify and conjoin our other program themes.

As we continue the process of curriculum review, we have begun to ask whether our personal and departmental commitments to social justice are clear to students. Does the concept of teaching for social justice really influence instruction and the nature of students' field experiences? Are students aware of how the subject matter knowledge they learn in various courses relates to the idea of social justice? There is some scattered evidence that this is the case. For example, in a letter supporting one faculty member as recipient of an award for teaching, a student commented that the faculty member had helped her promote social justice. Evidence of a more systematic impact, however, is departmental agreement to use a basic template for all syllabi in teacher education that begins with an explicit statement of common themes. As we experiment with the template and adjust it to accommodate our unique courses, faculty members are wrestling with how their individual courses, complete with long-standing assignments and favorite readings, actually construct the issues related to social justice and help students make sense of them. Rethinking the format and emphasis of each course is an important step as we begin to shift away from the idea that teaching for social change and social justice is a supplement or add-on to the curriculum and toward the idea that it is a fundamentally different way of doing teacher education (Larkin, 1995; Zeichner, 1993).

Policies and practices around graduate admissions were also influenced by our focus on social justice. Traditionally individual program coordinators made autonomous and more or less idiosyncratic decisions that were later approved by two levels of administrators. A new admissions policy established a collaborative decision-making process featuring multiple readings of each application within whole group meetings of department members. In addition to academic record, test scores, and writing samples, criteria for the evaluation of candidates explicitly included school experience, work with children in diverse contexts, and contribution of candidates to the diversity of the student population. Processes were created for handling inconsistent evaluations and for arguing for exceptions to the normal academic standards. What was most important about this new process was not only that it made issues of diversity an explicit part of the admissions process but also that it took faculty differences in values, beliefs, and experiences—usually left unspoken in admissions decisions—and made them explicit and public, thus also opening them to critique and question by others.

The process used to search for new faculty was also influenced by departmental emphasis on social justice. Partly as an outcome of our social justice conversations, we saw simultaneous openings for four faculty members in teacher education as a dramatic opportunity for change and for making our commitment to diversifying the faculty a priority. As a department, we proposed to search for all four positions at once, with areas of expertise broadly stated and not tied to specific ranks, a strategy in keeping with successful faculty diversification programs in higher education (Blackwell, 1990; Ruffins, 1997). Newly worded advertisements emphasized teaching and teacher education for social justice as well as scholarship that linked theory, policy, and practice. The decision to use this strategy was not an easy one for us, nor was it ever completely unanimous among members of the department. Diversifying the faculty, replacing existing positions, strengthening programmatic emphasis on social justice, and securing the most outstanding professionals in the field were agendas perceived by some as competing and possibly mutually exclusive and by others as dovetailing and possibly mutually enhancing. Ultimately, the strategy was used and was largely, if not completely, successful.

This project has also allowed us to link with concurrent efforts of other university units. For example, representatives of our group have participated with faculty from other schools at the university in an interdisciplinary dialogue around the role of the university in fostering a civil society. Finally this project has been of considerable interest to other educators beyond the immediate context. Presentations have been made at the American Educational Research Association and other national conferences (Albert, et al., 1997, 1998; Cochran-Smith, et al., 1999; Neisler, 1998), and several articles in addition to this one have been published or are in preparation (Zollers, Albert & Cochran-Smith, in press).

Tensions, Contradictions, And Risks

Although we initially expected that creating a forum for conversation would lead to eventual agreement of some kind, we found instead that there was considerable disagreement around almost every aspect of social justice. Over time we discovered that an inevitable result of seeking social justice was not only increased opportunity for understanding but also increased tension around self exposure and self knowledge, orientations to social justice and research, and issues of community building.

Self-Exposure/Self-Knowledge

Extended and repeated conversations about social justice changed the boundaries of what could be included in the discourse of teacher education and took us outside the safe space of our own expertise as professionals (Hayning, 1997; McIntyre, D., 1997). This had positive effects—it allowed us to be more honest and forth coming and prompted new insights into the viewpoints of others. At times this was affirming for the group, and we were gratified that we were "actually getting at some real issues." But honest talk is complicated. Our individual past experiences and socially constructed subjectivities meant that some of us talked more than others about certain issues, some of us talked far more personally, and almost all of us said some things we feared would expose our ignorance, prejudice, or suppressed anger, even rage. In addition, members of the group were differently positioned, entangled with each other in multiple professional and personal relationships. Issues of rank and job security clearly influenced who felt free to speak on what topics and under what circumstances as well as who felt silenced at certain times.

It is important to note, of course, that the setting for this "honest talk" was a university, an institution traditionally characterized by hierarchy, secrecy, and privilege. As the talk of our group became more honest, some of us felt more vulnerable—unclear about whether it would be safer to be silent, non-committal, or completely unsensational in all of our comments. Although some of us categorically affirmed that we felt safe in every one of the social justice conversations, others believed that there were serious vulnerabilities and risks involved in the situation. There were also a few moments when members of the group shared what most people would consider deeply troubling experiences. In at least one of these instances, the group was silent, a response the speaker interpreted as indifference. There may have been other such instances that were not caught on tape and hence are not part of the permanent record but are indeed part of some individual's internal reckoning. In addition, for some individuals, being part of the social justice group exacerbated personal issues with others and fed into tensions about status and role. The most personal of these issues are of course those that are impossible to write about in a collaborative article and/or inappropriate to reveal in a public context. Part of what this project pointed out, then, is that the considerable tension between a commitment to collaboration, on the one hand, and genuine critique of others' ideas and positions, on the other, is a tension that is always operating in this kind of group inquiry—sometimes just beneath the surface of conversations, at other times bubbling up and breaking through the surface, and in a few instances erupting into confrontations or withdrawals from the group.

Research Orientation/Social Justice Orientation

This project has also generated tension between the conventions and imperatives of the research process, on the one hand, and the conventions and imperatives of talking about and acting on social justice, on the other. We wonder, for example, whether carefully documenting our conversations (a good research practice) created greater potential for self-censure (a not-so-good practice in exploring assumptions and biases). These concerns are compounded by the fact that everything we said became part of a record that is permanent as well as public, at least in the sense that it is available to the teacher education faculty and used as a data source for public presentations and written dissemination. This raises more questions: Is it actually possible to conduct research on social justice and, at the same time, hold honest, open, useful discussions about it? Would anyone really admit that he or she did not feel safe to talk about certain things? What paradigm of thought and action becomes dominant in this kind of situation, especially within the context of a research university: a research paradigm where issues of thorough documentation and analysis take priority over all others, or a paradigm of critical discussion and action wherein self-examination and sometimes radical imagining and reinvention are paramount. Or, is there a kind of third space created in this kind of work–is it possible that some new paradigm of social inquiry and social action emerges from this kind of work? We believe that the latter may be true.

Presenting the work of the group in public presentations and in journal articles such as this one where the reputation and profile of the teacher education faculty of Boston College are on display generates another set of tensions. In the preparations for each presentation and the writing of each piece, new tensions emerge. Whose voice is heard in public presentations and published works? Is it possible to recognize and authentically present different interpretations of social justice using one voice, or does this in and of itself mean that we have reached shared understanding at the expense of honoring differences? Is it possible to represent multiple voices and individual contributions and still produce a coherent representation of the group's work? Our group worked hard to develop a way of writing and planning public presentations and papers that was genuinely collaborative. We resisted the temptation–often used in collaborative writing– wherein one member takes the largest share of responsibility for drafting an article and then others respond or add. Instead we co-planned and co-wrote drafts of every section of every document, producing multiple drafts with various portions written and edited by pairs, small groups, as well as the whole group. Still the tensions of publicly engaging in critical discussion and the struggle to preserve ones individual voice within a relatively large group remain.

Constructing Community/Deconstructing Community

Before this project began, we had already begun to work more collaboratively on a number of departmental decisions and policies. As we began the social justice conversations, some of us worried that changing the boundaries of the discourse could jeopardize the sense of community that was emerging. On the other hand, some worried that *not* having conversations that got at difficult issues would be worse–allowing us to stand still in our thinking instead of moving forward.

It is important to point out that even though we struggled with many issues, we did not engage in some of the deepest and most difficult talk about issues related to diversity that sometimes occurs in groups that are mixed in terms of race, class, gender, ethnicity, and position. For the most part, we deliberately stayed away from rage and from some of the hardest confrontations about issues. We avoided intentionally exposing anyone or relentlessly pushing others to change their minds and shift to more "enlightened" perspectives. And we did work hard at listening carefully and wholeheartedly–albeit sometimes silently–to perspectives that were dramatically opposed to our own. In this sense, our conversations often reaffirmed our individualness rather than our adherence to a collective set of values of beliefs. On the other hand, we told stories about our very different lived experiences, we described our different paths as teacher educators and researchers, and we worked to respect others' integrity and commitments. For some of us, the process of telling stories was healing, creating boundaries that brought resolution to unsettling events.

In the course of all this, we also spent a considerable amount of time together, debating at length what sometimes seemed the trivial details of process rather than substance, but were later realized as efforts to move forward while also validating different perspectives, conclusions, and intuitions as well as respecting each others' rights to hold them. The format of extended and repeated conversations gave us the breathing space we had sought at the beginning of the project to explore our understandings of each others' perspectives as well as our own. Josselsen, et al., (1997) suggest that these are among the most important features of co-operative inquiry where the emphasis is on collective ways of knowing about ourselves and others, or, legitimizing "scholars working together, despite diversity, to collectively explore understanding" (p. vii). In the final analysis, then, this is perhaps what explains the paradox we posed earlier in this article–how to build a teacher education program committed to social justice without first stating explicitly and unanimously what social justice is. Instead of laboring to hammer out an explicit definition, which we realized early on would be futile as well as counterproductive, we built a community that talked about and validated multiple perspectives and accommodated inconsistencies across and within definitions, beliefs, and values. This culture of shared understanding allowed us actually to do the hard work of reinventing department policies and rethinking our daily work as teacher educators.

Perhaps this means that hard talk is not necessary–and is even to be avoided–in conversations about social justice among faculty members who have to live and work with each other on a close daily basis. But finding a momentary answer to one puzzling question often creates another. Does avoiding the hardest talk mean that we do not and cannot uncover the most important and even most dangerous assumptions we hold as individuals, let alone develop a process whereby we examine and challenge them collectively? Does this mean that what we do uncover are the safest and most innocuous of our assumptions? We do not know the extent to which our conversations affirmed or confronted assumptions. Nor do we know the extent to which our public conversations remained safe while inner turmoil forced deeply held beliefs to the forefront of our consciousness to be dealt with in a more private arena. These questions are unfolding and ultimately unanswerable. They are and will always be part of work of this kind. Over time our group has struggled to recognize that aspect of this work.

As we continue with the project, however, there are other questions: Will we be able to continue moving from conversation to policy decisions to concrete and sustained action? A critical mass of the teacher education faculty now uses similar terms of analysis and articulated positions within a shared framework of social justice, even if we do not speak in one voice and do not all agree. If we continue our conversations and develop new frameworks, will we gain in understanding among each other while further differentiating ourselves from those outside the conversation, including newcomers to our own department? How will the work and standing of the teacher education faculty as a whole, as well as each of us as individual faculty members within the larger school, be affected by these conversations?

CONCLUSIONS/WAYS FORWARD

As of this writing, the "Seeking Social Justice" project is midway through its third year. The work is exciting and rewarding in many ways. As we have made clear, we are diverse in our experiences, perspectives, professions and disciplines. We also differ in race, gender, age, position, and disability status. Yet, we have found a certain kind of connectedness in building a teacher education community committed to understanding different perspectives and constructing a program with the goal of social justice. The research group has always been open to any teacher education member who was interested. As the third year of the project began, all three new faculty members as well as two other members of the department and the directors of the practicum office joined the group. This means that the research sub-group now includes fifteen of the nineteen people who regularly attend teacher education meetings. Thus there has been a substantial increase in the proportion of faculty and administrators who have chosen to be active participants on the "researcher" side of collaborative self-study as well as increased diversity in the group in terms of age, gender, race, academic rank, school experience, and scholarly interest.

As we have said throughout this article, the first two years of the project were devoted to exploring concepts of social justice and how those concepts were (or were not) played out in the business of teacher education. As we began the third year, we launched two complementary efforts building on the previous work–one to explore the ways individual teacher educators and their students understand social justice issues in relation to the content of specific course and fieldwork experiences, and the other to examine how the curriculum review process occasioned by preparation for NCATE re-accreditation is influenced by the understandings of social justice we have built over the last two years.

With the first project, the initial task for members of the research group was to interrogate their own understandings of social justice vis-à-vis the content of the courses or practicum experiences they are responsible for. Each individual then identified a particular course component (e.g., an activity or set of activities, a particular assignment, a set of readings on a given topic, a series of small and large group discussions, a course project that evolves over time) that could function as a strategic research site for exploring how students make sense of the ideas presented in class or the situations they experience in K-12 school placements in relation to the issues of social justice. As of this writing, our research group conversations are taken up with sharing course activities and engaging in collaborative analyses of how we link the concept of social justice to particular subject matters or fieldwork experiences–secondary history methods, curriculum theory, or instructional strategies for students with special learning needs, for example, as well as initial classroom observations, functioning as teacher aides and assistants, or working as full-time student teachers. As a group, then, we are beginning to look publicly and critically at our own individual pedagogies and at the kinds of learning opportunities we construct with students across and among courses and practica in our program. This process has required us to wrestle collectively with a whole new set of issues: the tension between equity and excellence; the possible negative impact of the increasingly powerful standards movement on educators' efforts for social justice; and the tension between inviting our students to try out and take on new perspectives, on the one hand, and indoctrinating them into our own viewpoints, on the other.

The second focus of this year's project is to explore program revisions prompted by preparation for an upcoming NCATE review in light of the social justice understandings we explored over the last two years. It has been argued persuasively that if teacher education programs are to encourage prospective and experienced teachers to critically analyze their own developing pedagogies, then the political nature of teacher education will have to be assumed (Ginsburg & Lindsay, 1995), and, as teacher educators, "our lives, our work, must be an example" (hooks, 1994, p. 54) for our students, our colleagues, and ourselves. This means that teacher educators must not only develop and critique their understandings of social justice but also instantiate these into all aspects of their professional work. Whatever else might be said about the routine and cyclical activity of preparing for NCATE reaccreditation, the process does provide institutions, programs, and individual faculty members with opportunities for serious self-examination. As a faculty seeking social justice, it became clear that we needed to examine how our individual and collective understandings played out in the major decisions we were making regarding curriculum, instruction, fieldwork arrangements, and program policies. Thus our second project has taken us well beyond the normal NCATE required documentation of faculty meetings and course changes. Instead, we are attempting to focus on whether or not and to what extent social justice functions as the operational (and not simply rhetorical) centerpiece of the curriculum by examining how it is implicated in difficult decisions, in our prioritizing of the professional knowledge needs of prospective teachers, and in the ways we construct, face, and solve problems as individuals and as members of a collective.

Collaborative efforts to seek social justice in teaching and teacher education will always involve tensions and contradictions. Some of this tension is necessary for growth and change. Other tensions are worth trying to resolve. As collaborative researchers and active teacher educators who are also the subjects of our own scrutiny, nearly all of us have chosen to stay with the project over the long haul. We have chosen to stay in the group and continue to work collaboratively even though it is sometimes frustrating, sometimes painfully slow, and often difficult. And we have chosen to stay with a commitment to constructing a culture of careful listening in support of our pursuit of social justice in teaching, in teacher education, and in the work in which we and our students are engaged in schools and school districts in the Boston area and beyond.

ENDNOTES

[1] This chapter first appeared in the International Journal of Leadership in Education, Volume 2: No. 3, July-September 1999, pp. 229-253. It is reprinted here wth permission of Taylo & Francis, Ltd., London, UK.

[2] Although this approach was developed collaboratively by the participants in this project, it is similar in intention to processes developed by Patricia Carini and colleagues at the Prospect School in that the goal was to foster a deepening of individual understandings and at the same time contribute to a larger community of understandings that might not be shared by all the members of a group.

[3] Participation in the project was open at all times to all teacher education faculty. In response to the initial invitation, ten faculty members came together. At the end of the first year, one of these moved to another university.

[4] One faculty member, who had a secondary appointment in teacher education, opted not to attend those meetings that featured discussions about social justice.

REFERENCES

Albert, L., Cochran-Smith, M., DiMattia, P., Freedman, S., Jackson, R., Mooney, J., Neisler, O., Peck, A., & Zollers, N. (1998). *Seeking social justice: A teacher education faculty's self study, Year II.* Paper presented at the Annual Meeting of the American Educational Research Association, San Diego, CA.

Albert, L. R., Cochran-Smith, M., DiMattia, P., Freedman, S., Jackson, R., Mooney, J., Neisler, O., Peck, A., & Zollers, N. P. (1997). *Seeking social justice: A teacher education faculty's self study, Year I.* Paper presented at the Annual Meeting of the American Educational Research Association, Chicago, IL.

Anyon, J. (1994). Teacher development and reform in an inner-city school. *Teachers College Record, 96*(1), 14-34.

Apple, M. (1995). *Education and power.* New York, NY: Rutledge.

Aronowitz, S. (1988). *Science as power: Discourse and ideology in modern society.* Minneapolis, MN: University of Minnesota Press.

Ayers, W., Hunt, J. A., & Quinn, T. (Eds.). (1998). *Teaching for social justice. A democracy and education reader.* New York, NY: The New Press, Teachers College Press.

Banks, J. A. (1997). *Educating citizens in a multicultural society.* New York, NY: Teachers College Press.

Banks, J. A., & Banks, C. A. M. (Eds.). (1993). *Multicultural education: Issues and perspectives.* Boston, MA: Allyn and Bacon.

Bell, L. A., Washington, S., Weinstein, G., & Love, B. (1997). Knowing ourselves as instructors. In M. Adams, L. A. Bell, & P. Griffin (Eds.), *Teaching for diversity and social justice* (pp. 299-310). New York, NY: Routledge.

Blackwell, J. E. (1990, June). Operationalizing faculty diversity. *American Association of Higher Education Bulletin,* 8-9.

Boston College University Academic Planning Council. (1996, May). *Advancing the Legacy.* Chestnut Hill, MA.

Brown, L., Schwarz, P., Udvari-Solner, A., Kampshroer, E. F., Johnson, F., Jorgensen, J., & Gruenwald, L. (1991). How much time should students with severe intellectual disabilities spend in regular education classrooms and elsewhere? *The Journal of the Association for Persons with Severe Handicaps, 16*(1), 39-47.

Bullough, R. V., & Gitlin, A. (1995). *Becoming a student of teaching: Methodologies for exploring self and school context.* New York, NY: Garland Publishing, Inc.

Carini, P. (1986) Prospect's Documentary Processes, Bennington, VT, Prospect's School Center.

Christensen, C. A., & Dorn, S. (1997). Competing notions of social justice and contradictions in special education reform. *The Journal of Special Education, 31*(2), 181-198.

Cochran-Smith, M. (1995). Uncertain allies: Understanding the boundaries of race and teaching. *Harvard Educational Review, 65,* 541-570.

Cochran-Smith, M. (1998). Teaching for social change: Toward a grounded theory of teacher education. In A. Hargreaves, A. Lieberman, M. Fullan, & D. Hopkins (Eds.), *The International Handbook of Educational Change* (pp. 895-951). The Netherlands: Kluwer Academic Publications.

Cochran-Smith, M., & Lytle, S. (1999). Relationship of knowledge and practice: Teacher learning in communities. In A. Iran-Nejad & C. D. Pearson (Eds.), *Review of research in education* (Vol. 24) (pp. 251-177). Washington, DC: American Educational Research Association.

Cochran-Smith, M., Dimattia, P., Dudley-Marling, C., Freedman, S., Friedman, A., Jackson, J., Jackson, R., Loftus, F., Mooney, J., Neisler, O., Peck, A., Pelletier, C., Pine, G., Scanlon, D., & Zollers, N. (1999, March). *Seeking social justice: A teacher education faculty's self study, Year III.* Paper presented at the Annual Meeting of the American Educational Research Association, Montreal, Canada.

Cole, A. L., & Knowles, J. G. (1998). The self-study of teacher education practices and the reform of teacher education. In M. L Hamilton (Ed.), *Reconceptualizing teaching practice: Self-study in teacher education* (pp. 224-234). London: Falmer Press.

Collins, P. (1991). *Black feminist thought.* New York, NY: Routledge.

Darling-Hammond, L. (1995). Inequality and access to knowledge. In J. A. Banks & C. A. M. Banks (Eds.), *Handbook of research on multicultural education* (pp. 465-483). New York, NY: Macmillan.

Deshler, D. D., & Schumaker, J. B. (1988). An instructional model for teaching students how to learn. In J. L. Graden, J. E. Zins, & M. J. Curtis (Eds.), *Alternative educational delivery systems: Enhancing instructional options for all students* (pp. 391-411). Washington, DC: NASP.

Dilworth, M. E. (1998). *Being responsive to cultural differences. How teachers learn.* Thousand Oaks, CA: Corwin Press, Inc.

Dunn, J. M. (1987). Personal belief and public policy. In F. S. Bolin & J. M. Falk (Eds.), *Teacher renewal: Professional issues, personal choices* . New York, NY: Teachers College Press.

Ellis, E., & Lenz, K. (1990). Techniques for mediating content-area learning: Issues and research. *Focus on Exceptional Children, 22*(9) (pp. 1-16).

Ellsworth, E. (1989). Why doesn't this feel empowering? Working through the repressive myths of critical pedagogy. *Harvard Educational Review, 59*, 297-324.

Fine, M. (1992). *Chartering urban school reform: Reflections on pubic high schools in the midst of change.* New York, NY: Teachers College Press.

Florio-Ruane, S. (1994). Future teachers' autobiography club: Preparing educators to support literacy learning in culturally diverse classrooms. *English Education, 26*(1), 52-66.

Freire, P. (1970). *Pedagogy of the oppressed* (Ramos, M. B., Translator). New York, NY: Seabury Press.

Freire, P., & Macedo, D. (1987). *Literacy: Reading the word and the world.* South Hadley, MA: Bergin and Garvey.

Ginsberg, M., & Lindsay, B. (1995). *Comparative perspectives on policy formation, socialization, and society.* Philadelphia, PA: Falmer.

Giroux, H. (1983). *Theory and resistance in education.* South Hadley, MA: Bergin & Garvey.

Gordon, B. (1995). Knowledge construction, competing critical theories, and education. In J. Banks (Ed.), *Handbook of research on multicultural education* (pp. 184-199). New York, NY: Macmillan.

Gore, J. (1993). *The struggle for pedagogies: Critical and feminist discourses as regimes of truth.* New York, NY: Routledge.

Hamilton, M. L., & Pinnegar, S. (1998). The value and the promise of self-study. In M. L. Hamilton (Ed.), *Reconceptualizing teaching practice: Self-study in teacher education* (pp. 235-246). London: Falmer Press.

Hayning, K. (1997, March). *Professionalism and reform in teacher curriculum: An archeology of postsecondary education.* Paper presented at the Annual Meeting of the American Educational Research Association, Chicago, IL.

Heron, J. (1996). *Co-operative inquiry: Research into the human condition.* Thousand Oaks, CA: SAGE.

Hollenbach, D. (1995). The Catholic university and the common good. *Current Issues in Catholic Higher Education, 16*(1), 3-15.

Hooks, b. (1994). *Teaching to transgress: Education as the practice of freedom.* New York, NY: Routledge.

Irvine, J. J. (1992). Making teacher education culturally responsive. In M. E. Dilworth (Ed.), *Diversity in teacher education* (pp. 79-92). San Francisco, CA: Jossey-Bass.

Josselson, R., Lieblich, A., Sharbany, R., & Wiseman, H. (1997). *Conversation as method: Analyzing a relational world of people who were raised communally.* Thousand Oaks, CA: Sage.

Kember, D., & Gow, L. (1992). Action research as a form of staff development in higher education. *Journal of Higher Education, 23*(5), 528-554.

Kozol, J. (1991). *Savage inequalities: Children in America's schools.* New York, NY: Harper

Ladson-Billings, G. (1995). Toward a theory of culturally relevant pedagogy. *American Educational Research Journal, 32*(3), 465-491.

Land, P. (Ed.). (1972). *Justice in the world: An overview.* Vatican City: Pontifical Commission of Justice and Peace.

Larkin, J. M. (1995). Current theories and issues in multicultural teacher education programs. In J. M. Larkin & C. E. Sleeter (Eds.), *Developing multicultural teacher education curricula.* Albany, NY: SUNY Press.

Larkin, J. M., & Sleeter, C. E. (1995). *Developing multicultural teacher education curricula* (pp. 1-16). Albany, NY: SUNY Press.

Lather, P. (1992). Critical frames in educational research: Feminist post-structural perspectives. *Theory into Practice, 31*(2), 87-89.

Lawrence, S. M., & Tatum, B. D. (1997). White elephants as allies: Moving from awareness to action. In M. Fine, L. Weis, L.C. Powell, & L. M. Wong (Eds.), *Off white: Readings on race, power, and society.* New York, NY: Routledge.

Lieberman, A. (1992). The meaning of scholarly activity and the building of community. *Educational Researcher, 21*(6), 5-12.

Luke, C. (1992). Feminist politics in radical pedagogy. In C. Luke & J. Gore (Eds.), *Feminism and critical pedagogy* (pp. 25-53). New York, NY: Routledge.

McIntyre, A. (1997). *Making meaning of whiteness: Exploring racial identity with white teachers.* Albany, NY: State University of New York Press.

McIntyre, D. (1997, April). The profession of educational research. *British Educational Research Journal, 23*(2), 127-140.

McCarthy, C. (1993). Multicultural approaches to racial inequality in the United States. In L. A Castenell & W. F. Pinar (Eds.), *Understanding curriculum as racial text* (pp. 225-246). Albany, NY: SUNY Press.

McLaren, P. (1994). *Life in schools.* New York, NY: Longman.

Meirose, C. E. (1994). *Foundations.* Washington, DC: Jesuit Secondary Education Association.

National Education Goals Panel. (1997). *National education goals report.* Washington, DC: Author.

Neisler, O. (1998, January). *In search of social justice: A faculty self-study.* Paper presented at the Annual Meeting of Qualitative Inquiry, Athens, GA.

Oakes, J., & Lipton, M. (1999). *Teaching to change the world.* Boston, MA: McGraw-Hill College.

Reason, P. (1998). Three approaches to participative inquiry. In N. Denzin & Y. Lincoln (Eds.), *Strategies for qualitative inquiry* (pp. 324-339). Thousand Oaks, CA: Sage Publications.

Rice-Jordan, M. L. (1995). Reflections on the challenges, possibilities, and perplexities of preparing pre-service teachers for culturally diverse classrooms. *Journal of Teacher Education, 46*(5), 369-374.

Rios, F. A., & Gonzales, G. M. (1995). Psychology and developmental perspectives in a multicultural framework: Exploring some possibilities. In J. M. Larkin & C. E. Sleeter (Eds.), *Developing multicultural teacher education curricula* (pp. 79-104). Albany, NY: SUNY Press.

Rosenberg, P. (1997). Underground discourses: Exploring whiteness in teacher education. In M. Fine, L. Weis, L. Powell, & L. Wong (Eds.), *Off-white, readings on race and power in society* (pp. 79-86). New York, NY: Routledge.

Ruffins, P. (1997, October 16). The shelter of tenure is eroding ad for faculty of color gaining membership may be tougher than ever. *Black Issues in Higher Education, 14*(17), 20-26.

Sleeter, C. (1995). An analysis of the critiques of multicultural education. In J. A. Banks & C.A. Banks (Eds.), *Handbook of research on multicultural education* (pp. 81-96). New York, NY: Macmillan.

Sleeter, C. E., & Grant, C. (1987). An analysis of multicultural education in the United States. *Harvard Educational Review, 57*(4), 421-444.

Skrtic, T. M. (1995). *Disability and democracy: Reconstructing [special] education for postmodernity.* New York, NY: Teachers College.

Skrtic, T. M., & Sailor, W. (1996). School-linked service integration: Crisis and opportunity in the transition to postmodern society. *Remedial and Special Education, 17*(5), 271-283.

Tatum, B. (1992). Talking about race, learning about racism. The applications of racial identity development theory. *Harvard Educational Review, 62*(1), 1-24.

Webb, G. (1992). On pretexts for higher education development activities. *Higher Education, 24,* 351-361.

Westerhoff, J. H. (1987). The teacher as pilgrim. In F. S. Bolin & J. M. Falk (Eds.), *Teacher renewal.* New York, NY: Teachers College Press.

Zeichner, K. M. (1993). *Educating teachers for cultural diversity.* North East Lansing, MI: Michigan State University.

Zeichner, K. M. (1998, April). *The new scholarship in teacher education.* Paper presented at the Annual Meeting of the American Educational Research Association, Vice Presidential Address for Division K, San Diego, CA.

Zollers, N. J., Albert, L. R., & Cochran-Smith, M. (In press). In pursuit of social justice: Collaborative research and practice in teacher education. *Action in Teacher Education.*

9 THE CHALLENGE OF CREATING A COMMUNITY OF INQUIRY
Among Scholar-Consultants Critiquing One Another's Theories-In-Practice

William R. Torbert
Boston College

This chapter offers a "blow-by-blow" account of a small group of scholar/consultants that referred to itself as a "Community of Inquiry" (Torbert, 1976; 1991). The general model of a "Community of Inquiry" can potentially be recreated in a variety of settings—businesses, schools, or government agencies—where the aim is to improve the congruity among mission, strategy, members' practices, and outcomes (and to question what each of these terms means). Argyris, Putnam and Smith (1985) propose the creation of "communities of inquiry within communities of social practice" as a social change process, and we see a variety of illustrations of this approach in this book, particularly in Chapters 4, 8, and 11.

A "Community of Inquiry" is a real-time, second-person research/practice—a dialogue in which participants are engaged in an inquiry together that pertains to the practice of the current conversation as well as to practice in other settings (Alexy, 1990; Argyris, Putnam, & Smith, 1985; Evered & Tannenbaum, 1992). In this particular yearlong series of monthly, taped sessions, the members test together: (1) whether they are helpful to clients? (2) how they can be more helpful? (3) how they can help one another right now? (4) how can one tell what helps? (5) is "the proof in the pudding" in the sense that helpful action is assessed by later results the colleague or the colleague's clients achieve? (6) is "the proof in the pudding" in the sense that some actions are intrinsically helpful, whereas others are not? 7) is there, indeed, a pudding at all in the case of social action, let alone a proof? 8) how does a given theory help and how does it limit a helper's helpfulness?

In the service of these questions, each monthly meeting of this group during

1990-91 was based on a draft paper or other materials describing the practice of a given group member, and each meeting was taped for educational and scientific purposes. This chapter presents parts of a dialogue that took place in one such meeting. The dialogue was later transcribed and another meeting was dedicated to discussing what each individual wished to learn next, after having reviewed his or her part in the first dialogue. Parts of this meeting are also described.

The participants in the dialogue believe there is a profound need for cultivating a dialogic action science (Argyris, Putnam & Smith, 1985; Schon, 1983; Torbert, 1976; 1998) given that the assumptions, theories, and findings of the physical and social sciences are constantly applied in action, sometimes with nightmarish results, and rarely with any careful study. Such a dialogic action science encourages its practitioners to test *in real-time*: 1) the effectiveness of their actions; 2) the power, the justice, the openness, and the validity of their theories; 3) the alignment of practitioners' theories and actions; 4) the aesthetic assumptions and limits of their paradigms. However, as the ensuing dialogue itself illustrates, there are profound dilemmas on the path toward such an action science, even for those committed to and learned in its early practice.

In particular, as we engage in action (even action which is, for the most part, reflective speaking), each next comment can only be a partial explication of the speaker's vision/frame, strategy/advocacy, performance/illustration, and assessment/inquiry (see Figure 5.2, Chapter 5). Therefore, the next speaker is invariably engaged in attributions, interpretations, and assessments of prior comments (and how they relate to each other), only some of which can possibly be tested for validity at that moment (and, of course, most of us engage in such validity testing only rarely).

Moreover, there are at least two different ways in which we may take our own attributions and interpretations for granted, "re-truing" them rather than successfully testing their validity. The first way—Level I—is that we may altogether fail to test, or test in such a biased way that the test is likely to yield invalid data (e.g., "Isn't my new hairdo great?"). The second way—Level II—is that, even though we have a carefully designed validity-testing system, the validity-testing system as a whole may generate a systemic bias over time simply by virtue of ignoring certain variables. For example, Empirical Positivism in third-person science (see Torbert, Chapter 5) is one validity-testing system. The seven guidelines of action science (Argyris, Putnam & Smith, 1985, p. 258ff) are another validity-testing system. By assuming that a scientist must be a pure observer because a participant in action disturbs the setting and perceives data from an interested rather than a disinterested perspective, Empirical Positivism ignores the question of how one can do validity testing in action. By contrast, action science takes on the challenge of getting participants in real-time action to test the validity, efficacy, and emancipatory power of their actions. However, it ignores issues of trans-cognitive awareness, timing, and of how to balance validity testing with other life concerns. We will return to this theoretical and practical issue of how to test and increase the timeliness and whole-life-validity of a validity testing system when we analyze the dialogue presented below.

THE PARTICULAR "PLAYERS" AND THE "PLAY"

The seven participants present for this meeting are here named Cy, Greg, Gwen, John, Pat, Susan, and Terry[1]. All members of each meeting are conversant with both developmental theory (Kegan; 1982, 1994; Loevinger, 1978; Kegan & Lahey, 1984; Pascual-Leone, 1990; Souvaine, 1985; Souvaine, Kegan & Lahey, 1990; Torbert, 1987) and the theory-of-action perspective (Argyris, 1994; Argyris, & Schon, 1974; Argyris, Putnam & Smith, 1985; Torbert, 1991). Indeed, five of the ten authors just referenced were among the seven participants at the meeting.

In the first meeting, Susan presents her case. Shortly into the meeting, John suggests that certain of Susan's actions, guided by the interpretive emphasis of developmental theory, may "over-protect" clients, preventing them from learning from negative feedback and the effects of their actions. As the dialogue continues, John enlarges upon this issue, eventually citing additional evidence from the present dialogue that suggests to him that Susan acts in ways that do not test her theory of intervention but instead "re-true" it.

This meeting was recorded, transcribed, and summarized, and it was decided that it would be the subject of a later meeting. What follows is a summary of the first half of the first meeting, followed by actual dialogue from the second half of the meeting, interspersed with analysis and theoretical discussion. In conclusion, events from the follow-up meeting are summarized and questions critical to the ongoing development of second-person research/practice are raised.

IS THERE A PROOF IN THIS PUDDING?

The meeting began with administrative comments and proceeded to high merriment, including champagne, with a celebration, with champagne, of the approval of Greg's thesis. The new doctor offered a benediction from Karl Popper on this section of the meeting: "We differ in the bits of knowledge we possess; but in our infinite ignorance we are all equal."

Then the group turned to discussion of the case Susan had sent of a group of 14 school system members that she and another developmentally-oriented colleague had worked with over a period of 13 weekly sessions. Participation was voluntary, with the opportunity to leave after the first meeting (as two people did), and no one reported directly to other meeting participants. The purpose was to discuss work issues and lessons to be learned from them. Over the weeks, each member of the group worked through each of five steps on a particular problem: 1) identifying assumptions they were making about the situation; 2) exploring how they knew their assumptions were true; 3) evaluating whether the original basis for holding the assumption was still operative; 4) testing for the degree to which the person had been "re-truing" the assumption, rather than truly testing its validity; and 5) designing experiments to try alternative behaviors.

Greg asked how their developmental approach was different from the theory-of-action approach he had illustrated the month before. Cy pointed to some differences he saw, such as the lack of direct testing of attributions, including the "laughable" assumption Sarah made in her case. She believed the principal must not value her teaching because he did not specifically praise her, in a comment she *overheard* him making in which he praised another teacher and said nothing whatsoever about her. Cy said one probably shouldn't laugh (since such untested attributions are common), but John asked why not? It struck him that the developmental approach tended to be over-protective of its clients. Susan emphasized that in their approach, they let each client choose which issues they wish to address so that they will feel safe.

Pat raised the question whether persons at different developmental stages responded differently. Susan said yes, in theory, and said they discovered later that all but one of this group were at stage 4 [2] with some self-reflective ability, which is where she and her colleague believe people must be developmentally for this approach to work. She also said that one person was closer to stage 3 and that this was the person with whom they had the most difficulty. This person would continually jump in saying things like "That's ridiculous" and would also externalize problems as caused by others. Pat wondered how one would work with organizations, such as his, in which numerous people are at such earlier stages.

John challenged whether Susan was willing to test the assumption that persons have to be at a certain developmental stage before they can engage in self-reflective learning. She clarified that this in fact constituted such a test because they had *tested* persons' developmental stages before the class, but had not *scored* the tests until after all the sessions. Hence, they were not reacting to the person later scored at level 3 based on knowledge of that fact.

Cy asked how she and her colleague actually responded when this man intervened in apparently inappropriate ways. John commented that her response was a recipe for telling people to lay off one another, and Susan agreed. John said she didn't have a universalizable rule because she herself wasn't "laying off" the man. She agreed, but said that the exception is when someone is hurting someone else. John said this was another example of over-protectiveness.

Gwen suggested that the rule was really more complicated. Here there was a verbal tussle between John and Gwen, each seeking to control the sequence of the dialogue, with laughter from others. John won, talking over Gwen several times. Susan asked what John's preferred rule would be, and he offered one that included seeking disconfirmation. By contrast, he saw Susan "re-truing" her theory rather than seeking disconfirmation.

For this first part of the meeting from Susan's introduction of her paper, relative participation, in terms of sheer number of comments, was as follows: Susan: 27;

John: 30; Gwen: 17; Cy: 11; Greg: 6; Terry: 5; Pat: 4. (Since these happen to add up to 100, the numbers also represent percentages.) These proportions remain quite consistent throughout the session, Greg's increasing some and Gwen's falling, so that at the end of the session, of 303 total comments, the percentages were as follows: Susan: 24%; John: 31%; Gwen: 12%; Cy: 12%; Greg: 11%; Terry: 6%; Pat: 3%.

"RE-TRUING" VS. VALIDITY TESTING

At this point, Susan said she would like to hear more examples of how she may be "re-truing." Gwen and John tussled again about where the examples should come from, Gwen wanting to address the paper, John wanting to address issues raised in this conversation. And this is where we join the actual transcript:

> Gwen: I was stating a preference for seeing illustrations from her paper about their work. 1

> John: The reason my preference is for illustrations that are directly or indirectly connected to our behavior here is that they are richer data. I don't want to find myself arguing a position that is only illustratable through Susan's summary, without a transcript, because the inferences I am making come out nicer in those examples than they otherwise may. But we can try both. 2

> Greg: Could I try to recreate the data that I think we're talking about? We had Sarah saying that she assumes that not being talked about when talk is favorable means that she is not seen favorably. Cy said something like "I'd laugh," or "That seems ridiculous." Now, I'm making a leap here . . . 3

> John: He also said, "Perhaps I shouldn't say that."4

> Greg: Right. 5

> John: And I said, "Perhaps you *should* . . . 6

> Greg: OK, and now I'm making the following leap, that I think is shared, that this guy that you saw as problematic in the group did just this kind of thing. 7

> Susan: That's right. 8

Greg: OK, and when he did it, you and your colleague, one or the other, said in effect, "We designed a rule that we'd like to establish as a norm in this group . . . "Well . . . maybe it's better for you to say it at this point. What is the thing that you'd say to this person who laughed and said that it's ridiculous? 9

Susan: Basically, "On behalf of creating an opportunity for Sarah to learn at her own pace the things that she wants to learn about, we're asking people to hold their evaluations of what they think about—certainly the silliness of what someone else is saying—to themselves." 10

John: There was more. Let me add something and see if you agree. It was more like saying to this person, "You know, be patient, because there's validity to what people are doing. They're not just—Sarah's not just—everyone strives to grow, and they have their own way of growing, and let's see if we can create a culture in which we can facilitate that." 11

Susan: No, I wouldn't say that. I'd say that everybody has a right to think the things they do, and she's not silly for thinking that. 12

John: That's what I heard, yeah, I like that, OK. 13

Greg: OK. So, if I were the recipient of that on your part, I think the meaning I would get that would lead me to shut up is that I should not express comments that communicate that someone is silly. 14

Susan: Yes. 15

Greg: That's one thing the leader is saying to me and that is "lay off." Now, is the next step for you, John, to show how that is an illustration of "re-truing"? 16

John: Well, I don't know. Let me try. I asked then the question, "How do you know that the laughter in Cy's case would not facilitate the goal that Susan just said. And you'll have to help me, but the only answer I could get was an answer within her own logic. 17

Greg: Gee, I don't remember an answer at all, actually. 18

Gwen: *I* gave an answer. 19

John: No, no. You gave a clarification—you gave her the more complicated rule. 20

Gwen: But I also said that I don't think you do know. 21

John: Pardon me? 22

Gwen: "I don't think you do know." 23

John: I think that's a different issue. I think that what Greg is trying to get at is, "What is the deal with this? What did I say and how did Susan deal with it? How is it re-truing? How do you, John . . ." 24

Susan: How *is* it re-truing by my saying . . . 25

Greg: Let me now try. I think I see a way in which it is re-truing. That if you tell the guy who says, "Sarah, that's ridiculous"—if you give the speech you just gave—the meaning then is "Greg, you shouldn't say things like 'That's ridiculous'." Then you act in the group in ways that prevent you from learning that 'disrespectful actions' like laughing at her silliness might in fact be growthful. 26

Susan: Yeah. 27

Greg: In that sense, you would re-true your view of what are helpful comments and unhelpful comments in the group. 28

Susan: Yes. 29

John: Fair enough. 30

Susan: I feel like . . . I'm willing to re-true here on behalf of a belief I have—based on experiences which may well be self-selected on the basis of my having this belief to begin with—that being laughed at, people experience as hurtful, leading them to draw in. Which is not to say that they're not going to learn from it, because down the line they may learn something from the hurt of being laughed at—it's quite possible. But it leads the person to withdraw from the group and not have the opportunity to play around with any of the things we're trying to learn during our 14 weeks together. 31

John: And I think that is another example of re-truing. I don't remember if you were in this class: remember, there was a woman who made a point and the class went around being supportive, and I said—these are no longer the same words, but they sure convey my meaning—"What you're saying is fuzzy, inconsistent, and I would never hire you," and she either burst into tears or welled into tears, and some members of the group supported her in the sense of being cared for. She was hurt, deeply hurt. And I had several people in the class who said, "That went too far." The next session she said to the whole group, "There's only one person I really care for and that's John because what he said a lot of other people have been saying to me, and I've not listened to them. Instead, I listened to the support I got from you. Now it shows me how weak I was if that's what you think I need." When you see someone hurt and therefore back off, there's another theory that says, "When the person is hurt, hang in there." All I'm saying is, "I don't know which is right, but unless you find a way of finding that out, you are re-truing." 32

Susan: This is the same thing as learning about whether someone's laughing can be a source of learning for someone else. 33

John: And whether someone's crying is a sign that you can legitimately ask people to back off. Because you asked us all to back off before Sarah might have gotten near the point of being upset. 34

Gwen: It just seems to me that you can take this the reverse way too. You chose, when you said what she did that was fuzzy "and I wouldn't hire you," you chose a particular action, I assume out of a particular belief you have about what is helpful learning. And it seems to me that someone could just the same way ask you, "How do you know that it wouldn't be helpful learning for this person if you had instead supported her?" 35

John: I think I just said that I don't know *which* is right. All I'm presenting is data. See, I'm not taking the position that mine is right. I'm taking the position that she at that point is doing re-truing, and that is all I'm saying. For example, I didn't know what she was going to do the next session. What if she came in and said, "John, I just want you to know that I didn't sleep, I didn't learn" and so on. Then the question would be to watch my behavior, how am I learning? Because she at that point is attacking me in the way she thought I attacked her. What if I were able to learn from her? That begins to give some data about whether some people can learn from those kinds of attacks and others can't. Is that sort of developmentally caused, or is it because they haven't had enough practice in learning under conditions in which they are normally uncomfortable? 36

Cy: There's another angle to this whole thing. So far, there seems to be a bi-polar assumption that either you ask somebody to back off when they do this 'inappropriate' behavior, or else you let them do it. But it seems to me that you don't have to choose either of those poles. You can start testing with him or her what the effect of that statement is. You might set up a situation in which he ends up learning not to say "That's ridiculous" then and there rather than just being told not to say it. Or she may in fact say she is learning from his comment, so you learn that stopping him would have been overprotective. 37

Susan: Right. 38

Cy: There are all kinds of possibilities. 39

Gwen: But I see something else going on: because you (John) have a different rule, you don't find out what happens when you do it this (Susan's) way. That's all I'm saying. I'm interested in what goes on if you do it this way. 40

Let us review this part of the dialogue with our earlier distinction between Level I and Level II re-truing in mind. In a sense, the entire dialog is explicitly concerned with, and an illustration of, the dilemma of effective validity testing in action. Susan and her colleague have created an educational process for their school system clients which is intended to help these administrators and teachers identify the assumptions framing their prior behavior, test their validity while explicitly attempting to avoid re-truing, and design alternative, more effective actions. John raises the creative and provocative question whether her approach, which he identifies more generally as the "developmental" approach, may be "over-protective" of her clients and herself, and whether her responses to his challenges may be re-truing rather than true validity testing (see John's comment #32). At different points, Cy, Greg and Gwen all challenge John about whether his actions may also have the character of re-truing rather than true validity testing (see Gwen's comment #35). Let us examine Comments #31 through #36 more closely to see if we can ferret out who, if anyone, is re-truing and how.

We find that, in Comment #31, Susan acknowledges re-truing and explains her willingness to continue doing so in this sort of instance, even though she recognizes that her entire justification for doing so may itself be another instance of re-truing (" . . . I'm willing to re-true here on behalf of a belief I have—based on experiences which may well be self-selected on the basis of my having this belief to begin with . . ."). Her openness about her re-truing can suggest that she is available to be confronted if anyone should have an illustration of how her re-truing is harmful.

In his following comment (#32), John confronts Susan as again re-truing, as though he is showing her something new and as though she has not just acknowledged that she may be re-truing right now in her justification for feeling comfortable re-truing on a different occasion. He then gives an illustration of how a woman he confronted strongly in another situation was deeply hurt, but came back a week later to say she had learned from the hurt. He offers his theory for how to act in such cases, and then steps outside his own theory to say that the fundamental issue is how to find out which actions are truly helpful ("unless you find a way of finding out, you are re-truing").

After two more brief comments back and forth between Susan and John, Gwen confronts John (#35) about whether his type of behavior ("hanging in there") doesn't have the same systemic possibility as Susan's of blinding him to alternative ways of helping someone learn. John's response (# 36) deflects the question by at first seeming to agree that he too may be re-truing, but then emphasizing again that Susan is re-truing. He continues by giving a hypothetical example of how someone could determine whether he re-trues ("Then the question would be to watch my behavior, how am I learning?").

If one watches John's behavior closely in *these* exchanges, he does not appear to be paying attention to what Susan says in Comment #31, or to seriously consider what Gwen is saying in Comment #35. Instead, he seems more focused on (a) making his case and (b) elaborating a complex systemic view of how effective action and validity testing are interrelated in general, with little or no awareness that there may be times, such as this, when his general point is not timely. But notice how subtle this is: nothing he says is overtly inaccurate or defensive. Indeed, his illustration of the woman weeping under his confrontation is riveting, self-disclosing, and on-point in two different senses. It is on point in the sense that it illustrates someone learning close to the time when she is hurt, contrary to Susan's just-stated belief. It is also on point in a prescient sense, since a parallel scene unfolds as this conversation continues. (At the same time, John is asking the present group to take his description of this other event on faith, just the sort of move he resisted making with regard to discussing other details of Susan's written case.)

After Gwen confronts John about whether his validity-testing system isn't susceptible to the same Level II re-truing dilemma as Susan's system (#35), he dodges the issue she raises by claiming he doesn't know "*which* is right. All I'm presenting is data." Then he returns to the there-and-then situation, and becomes hypothetical about that. In the final comment so far presented (#40), Gwen returns to her earlier point (#35). Let us see how John responds this time:

> John: Well, let me tell you the worry I have. I think I can find out and you've been in plenty of sessions with me where I've behaved in ways that people find intimidating and so on . . . But when you said "I want to learn what she (Susan) learns from her approach . . ." 41

> Gwen: Right. 42

> John: Let me tell you the worry I have. I can't be against learning. What worries me is learning independent of responsibility for action. She's selling a pill, and I'm selling a pill—as a metaphor—and she'd be in jail this moment if we ever applied the rules of pill making. Some of the things she has on tape and your kind of comment. Just imagine being in front of a jury and saying "Yes, sir, that is what we did, but we were trying to find out what would happen." So, if I understand your question, I have an issue of ethics here, of research that separates inquiry from action and that doesn't couple them intimately. 43

> Greg: . . . later on the page you say "we ask Sarah to watch for other instances of this assumption operating. We ask her not to change anything that she does . . ." Then I start to pull in some things I know about paradoxical family therapy, right? If you tell someone in therapy "Now, that's good, that's great; now, don't change that problematic behavior" (laughter) . . . It's a different way of motivating change. I don't know if the right word is 'indirect,' or 'judo'—this kind of a thing. 44

> Cy: Paradoxical. 45

> Greg: And the last thing I saw in that domain is, you ask her to consider the risks and to consider, "Is the worst case outcome bearable?" And now I may be reading too much in, but in your concern that people remain safe, that they don't go too far, are you sure you're ready to take the risk, is the sort of thing that in paradoxical family therapy can get people to say (loudly) "For God's sake, I'm ready to move!" So, my construction of those cues was that—with what degree of intentionality I don't know—here is an alternative of dealing with the common problem of, how do you help people unfreeze deeply held, automatic, taken-for-granted re-truing of their assumptions? Do you challenge them and reveal the

illogic of their assumptions in a more forthright, let me say, way; or here's an alternative approach. I'd like to hear your reaction to that. 46

Susan: Well, my first reaction is, I think, the proof has to be in the pudding. If Sarah or someone who takes this safe route actually does have more options opened to them, or can unfreeze some way that they have been looking at something, perhaps it is—and I think it's likely to be a less "important" issue—but if they do unfreeze, it suggests to me that this can work. Now I don't know exactly what the features are of what we do that lead that to happen. But I do know that in Sarah's case she was willing to do something different than she was in the beginning. A lot of the people in the group did something different. A lot of them had to do with evaluation. Someone confronted a principal on an evaluation she had received, which she earlier never would have conceived herself capable of doing. I would like to hear from people whether that is reasonable thing to be focusing on because that kind of outcome has been what has fueled my sense that it makes sense to try to see what are the things that contribute to that happening. 47

Cy: One thing that I would like to have both in the case of confronting the principle and in this case is more data on the outcome and the feelings surrounding the outcome. All the last two paragraphs I want to know more about what she actually did in front of the mirror and more about what she actually did in the classroom and whether she felt that it worked even though she felt awkward—more of a sense of that, because right now it's hard for me to tell whether it's something she's going to carry one step beyond the support she's getting from you and your colleague. 48

Susan: Yeah . . . 49

Terry: I'm having—I don't know if anyone else is having this—I feel that Greg asked a really big question and I don't feel like it was answered. And maybe I . . . 50

Greg: No, I was just musing about that—that either I wasn't clear about it, or else it just missed in terms of Susan's interpretive system, but then Cy also . . . 51

Many voices. 52

Terry: Let me say what I think wasn't answered. I heard Greg say something about paradoxical family therapy theory, and how some of the actions that you took, some of the instructions you gave here, could either be interpreted as direct requests to just observe, don't change, or they could have been intended to create the opposite effect. I didn't hear you answer whether your intention was a direct request, or to have an opposite effect. I would like to know that. And I thought I heard you say "the proof is in the pudding"; to me, that translated to "the ends justify the means" and "if the outcome is that Sarah is exploring more options, then it doesn't matter how I got there really." So, I would like to hear you speak more about that. 53

Susan: OK 54

Terry: Did you answer that? 55

Susan: Well, my answer to whether the instruction was paradoxical is that it could have had that effect, but 56

Cy: But it wasn't intentional—you weren't consciously working . . . 57

Susan: No, it was really with the intent of—it all ties together with this safety—with creating a safe pace—that a person keeps their own pace . . . 58

Cy: It's more Rogerian, in a sense? 59

Susan: Yes, it's client centered. 60

John: And I go back and think "You are the one who is creating a safe place for *you*" and I see much less concern about Sarah. If you couple your answer "I can't know" with "the proof is in the pudding"—if you can't know, then how can you get to the second? What's the scientific, the research-oriented reasoning that says "I can't know, but the proof is in the pudding." Look, that's defensive reasoning. If you can't know . . . 61

Susan: I guess I don't see how I can know which of the features—I mean we're not controlling for each one of the interventions we're making, to know which of all the things that we're doing allows somebody ultimately to play around and have a different relationship . . . 62

John: But that doesn't mean you can't get a little better data—maybe you have it—can't get a little more differentiated answer than you gave Greg . . . 63

Susan: Right. Give me a for—instance because I see the problem . . . 64

John: Well, I thought I heard the confrontation was that he said to you it could have been the following: it could have been paradoxical. I would have thought you could tell him "(a) I really can't tell you in some ultimate sense, but here are the things we do to test whether our intentions are experienced by Sarah the way we wanted. So, here is what Sarah said and it is from this kind of data that we believe it wasn't paradoxical (but that doesn't mean it wasn't; it just means it's the best we can do)." I heard you not even care about doing what I just suggested: "The only thing I can tell you is 'the proof is in the pudding.'" 65

Terry: I think "not caring" is strong. I got the sense that Susan hadn't thought about that. 66

Greg: I understand the 'proof is in the pudding' comment differently. I understand that to mean, "If we've achieved what appears to be a valuable change, and I think we have, I take that as an indication that we should go forward, so we can have future work tease out what it is that had the good impact." 67

Susan: That's right. 68

John: How is that different from mine? Because it's exactly what you said that just bothered the hell out of me, if she goes along with it. If she said, "If it's right" as you said, "If it is a positive thing, then we're encouraged." 69

Greg: Right. 70

Cy: "(encouraged) *to do further testing.*" 71

John: Yeah . . . Wait a minute! I'm saying that the statement "If it's positive . . ." is equivalent to a pill maker who says, "Well, if people felt better, we're going to continue our further testing." 72

Terry: It's as if the evaluation happens at the end and there isn't a check, for example of "observe but don't change your behavior." "Did your behavior change or not?"—that would be a way of testing. 73

Susan: Well, sure, I mean each one of these steps was a step unto itself. So that, is identifying an assumption somebody makes really helpful? We can't really know that until we go further down the line. As far as I can see, there isn't much we can know about the usefulness of that until we know about next steps. One of the sessions beyond that there was an occasion for each person to talk about what any of it meant to them. 74

John: Let me quote to you from p6 now: "From there, we ask, 'How do you know that your assumption is true?'" How do *you* know that people have to go through the first to get to the second to get to the third. In other words, I'm doing to you what you did to Sarah. How do you know your assumption is true? 75

Susan: I don't know that they have to start at #1 to go to #2. 76

John: Well, I thought—maybe I misunderstood you—that that's what your answer was. You said you had to do one at a time. 77

Susan: What I was responding to was "Is there a way I can know about the usefulness or helpfulness of any one of these steps?" And my answer was that the first one is not something we can learn something about its usefulness unto itself. 78

John: I thought I heard your (Terry's) question was something like "Gee, Susan, I thought you waited until the end. Isn't there anything you could have done between the beginning and the end which would provide some data—more than what you provided. I didn't hear her say for each step there *has* to be a test. But if she did, I wouldn't. I don't think you have to have a test each step. But I do think there ought to be more than "these are the things we did, and she did the following." And "we believe the proof is in the pudding." 79

Cy: Well, it seems like, to me, Susan has broken down the general statement about 'the proof is in the pudding' into six little statements still based on the same model: 'the proof of the pudding' of step 1 is what happens in step 2, and 'the proof of the pudding' of step 2 is what happens in step 3. That's what I heard you saying: "There's lots of little proofs along the way." But it still has the same—*maybe* it still has the same—basic set-up to it that you're always looking for after-the-fact evidence, rather than 'during-the-fact' evidence. I don't know if that's what the essential issue is, perhaps, here right now? And the question is, could you *also* use 'during-the-fact' methodologies? Because after-the-fact is certainly used all the time in social science and has some value, but what's been raised is whether there's a whole additional methodology of 'during-the-fact' evidence that seems as though it hasn't been your style so much. 80

John: The abstraction of the evidence is pretty high level. There's relatively little directly observable data, so that we can make up our own minds as to what do you do; what does Sarah actually say. So we're caught in your description. It would have been helpful even to take just one or two steps—getting back to your (Cy's) previous comment—giving us some quotes so that we can make up our own mind—we're not just caught up. So, it's partly the level of data (said quietly). 81

(fairly long pause)

Terry: This is a group that Susan and her colleague were working with; I don't know to what extent your and your colleague's skills are oriented in this direction. Still, it would be difficult to do all this testing with 13 people, in my imagination. So, I can see that you might have been constrained by the numbers. Even with that, it may be very helpful for my learning. 82

In these comments, we hear two distinct streams of concern and tones of confrontation. One stream of concern focuses on the degree to which Susan in her theory-in-practice actually seeks out Level I disconfirming data. Cy's most recent comment (#80) poses the issue in what may be its most elegant form. He in effect argues that Empirical Positivism and modern science in general only generate "after-the-fact" disconfirming data, at best, whereas the kind of second-person, real-time research/practice this group is currently engaged in can go further and generate "during-the-act" disconfirming data that can potentially influence action in real-time. The critical issue about the quality of such data is the degree to which the actual behavior is characterized concretely (#44, 48, 63, 81), so that different participants can test whether they make the same inferences about it.

The second stream of concern focuses on the degree to which Susan's theory-of-practice seeks out Level II disconfirming data. Remember that the first comment (#41/43) is John's response to Gwen's confrontation (#35, 40) about whether *his* approach isn't just as likely as Susan's to "re-true" itself at Level II. Instead of responding about *his* approach, John ups the ante in his confrontation of *Susan's* approach: he uses a very strong and emotional analogy ("She's selling a pill . . . and she'd be in jail this moment if we ever applied the rules of pill making"). Greg and others return the focus to a more concrete level (#44-60), but then John re-enters the conversation (#61), confronting Susan's whole approach as "defensive reasoning" ("You are the one who is creating a safe place for *you* and I see much less concern about Sarah").

John may or may not be right about Susan's tendency to re-true at Level II; but when we remember that all this strong confrontation has the effect of deflecting attention from Gwen's two invitations to John to consider whether his approach may also re-true at Level II, the concrete data from this dialogue seem to support Gwen's contention more clearly than John's, even though the power of John's rhetoric makes it hard for this view to surface. Indeed, even John's use of concrete data (#61 "If you couple your answer 'I can't know' with 'the proof is in the pudding'—if you can't know, then how can you get to the second?") is confusing because it is he who is coupling and interpreting otherwise disconnected phrases.

By contrast, Susan repeatedly indicates her openness to learning (#64) and that her "can't know" comment was not can't-know-in-principle, but rather can't-know-from-the-current-study because they simply did not collect some of the data that this group is suggesting to her would be useful (#67 and 68). John, however, hears her differently (#65—" . . . I heard you not even care about doing what I just suggested" and #69). Cy tries to clarify for John (#71) and John momentarily agrees (#72—"Yeah"), but then for some reason (because he realizes that his agreement deflates his argument?) he jumps back strongly ("Wait a minute!") to his inquisition of Susan. Susan suggests that she and her colleague do have data about what the sessions meant to participants (#74), but rather than inquiring about that, John stays with his agenda, returning to the abstract issue of whether she is re-truing her assumptions (#75).

As we return to the transcript, we now find Greg attempting to raise the issue of John's overall theory-in-practice:

> Greg: I've thought of a way to say this, which is to preface it by saying, I don't know to what degree it's my defensiveness or protectiveness, but I've been feeling just in the past 10 minutes a kind of unfairness in the critique of Susan—particularly in what you've been saying, John. I'm sure there is a chunk of my defensiveness hooked in, but I just want to say, substantively, how come? Because it seems to me they've got a theory-based intervention, based on developmental theory. So they didn't just pull it out of a hat. They've got theories we can disagree with and so on. They find what appear to

be positive results: some teachers are trying some things they haven't tried before. In my work with these people, I imagine that if a person designed an experiment and tried to carry it out, I'd say "Hmm, that's quite a success." Now when Susan says, "I can't know what impact particular interventions have," I have some trouble with that because I would like to engage more on what your thinking was about this particular one where you ask her not to change anything. But it seems a reasonable thing to bring into this group; this description comes up with seemingly useful results; and then she says, "Now if you agree these are interesting results, we think it's worth pursuing how are we creating them." It's true there's relatively little directly observable data and that frustrated me too; but by the time you got to that point, I think my juices were flowing a little bit, and I was defending that by saying she wrote that for us—for this group. Let me stop there and get reactions. I need help. 83

John: Before you get reactions, I still haven't heard what's unfair. 84

Greg: OK 85

John: I'd ask you to be a lot more clear about what's unfair about *my* behavior. 86

Greg: The discussion about 'the proof is in the pudding'—I'm going to need help in reconstructing. I think you made an attribution about Susan that, in saying 'the proof is in the pudding' and in saying 'I don't know what the impact of particular interventions was' that was an illustration of a highly defensive response. 87

John: Yes, she says she *can't* know. I want to know what's unfair about that? 88

Greg (astonished): You took it seriously! ("*can't* know") 89
laughter

John: Yes, I *do* take it seriously. 90

Greg: You're right. And, you see, I discounted that. She said, "I can't know." I didn't believe that. I thought she meant, "I don't know looking back with Sarah which one of those things had an effect." 91

John: That I buy. She couldn't know from this description. 92

Susan: I don't mean by that, just to clarify, "there's no *way* to know." What I mean is . . . 93

John: Is there any way for *you* to know? 94

Susan (perplexed): "Is there any way for *me* to know?" 95

John: Yes. 96

Susan: In this situation with Sarah . . . 97

John: Yes. 98

Susan: I can't know which of the particular things . . . 99

John: *I didn't ask you that* (strongly). I asked you to say something about other than "'the proof is in the pudding' is the only answer." I haven't asked you—in fact I think if you listen to the tape I said 'if she was saying 1, 2, 3, 4 . . .' I just want to know if there's something between the first and the last. So I'm still going to hang in there. I want to know what is unfair. I think she said, "I can't know." 100

Greg: Well that's right. And my assumption in her saying "I can't know" is that it means "in looking back at Sarah, I don't know, but looking forward there are ways for me to learn." I attribute all those meanings to her. 101

John: From this report, what data are there—from what you know are the criteria of learning—regardless of any theory—what evidence is there that she can learn in the future? from this report? from the way she presented it? from the way she crafted it? 102

Gwen: Boy, I'd be surprised if she couldn't learn something . . . 103

John: That's a different issue. He's talking about my unfairness and I just want to find out; but you may be dead right. 104

Greg: I see this report as including a number of things which make it possible to engage in a learning discussion. For example, the steps they go through at an intermediate level of abstraction; and the reaction of what the other person did, again at an intermediate level. So, for us to engage her in more testing, we have to dig into episodes, as we have done. Again, I'm attracted to this notion that what was unfair is that you took *seriously*—and by that I mean *literally*—"I can't know"; or, in the case of the report, the analogous thing is—the way I give leeway that I think you're tougher—I say "She produced this in a short period of time just for this group. There's plenty of material for this group to talk about." So, to say that this report does not supply the level of directly observable data that would allow us to make independent judgments is accurate, yet I thought it was unfair under the circumstances. 105

Cy: It doesn't *prove* that she's not willing to learn . . . 106

John: I'm not questioning her motivation to learn. I'm asking, "Could it be that their theory is overprotective?" So, I'm not questioning about her motive. If that were true, I wouldn't be here. I think everyone here is interested. What interested me is you (Greg) discounted something for which there was directly observable data . . . . I don't know anybody who's written a book like you have that has as much directly observable data, right? 107

Greg: Right. 108

Cy: I don't think it's fair to call it "discounted." You mean . . . 109

John: He said it. 110

Cy: Well, he may have said that, but I think you (Greg) were unfair to yourself because you came back later and defended yourself and I think your defense made sense. He didn't *discount* it; he interpreted it not-literally. He made some inferences about what she meant . . . 111

John: Oh no, I'm not talking about that. I'm talking about discounting—after all, we're not talking about 'beginning students.' He (Greg) made the choice at some point in his life . . . (to) do a fine-grained analysis . . . because he had some criteria of how does he learn and how do you help other people to learn in such a way that they can confront him on his theory. And I say I don't know anyone who's focused as much as Greg on the fine-grained analysis. I don't know if Susan wants to use the hours as a reason, but she could have taken the same amount of time to say, "I'm just going to give you one or two of these and work it in detail." 112

Greg: So, that's the choice, and the time did require to pick between those . . . (inaudible) 113

Cy: And I think our whole discussion could conceivably persuade her to go out and *do* a fine-grained analysis. So, she can't know from what she did, maybe; she can't know because she didn't collect that kind of data and make those type of interventions. But that doesn't mean she can't know in principle and may not know next time . . . 114

John: I don't think his concept of unfairness was an attribution that I said she can't learn in principle. I was saying she was giving an answer—put it in my words— "Given my theory, and given how I studied this, I can't answer your question other than 'the proof is in the pudding.'" I'm saying, "I need to know what's unfair." Because that is the kind of thinking that, if it goes on in the real world, can get people into trouble. Look at how many managers say, "I don't know what the hell did it, but look at what happened." It's the same thing. And that just makes me as anxious as hell. 115

Greg: Right. 116

Cy: How do you understand this, Susan? Can I ask? I mean the conversation that's going on now and the level of John's attribution about your defensive reasoning and so forth? 117

Susan: Well, what I'm focusing on now is to really get with what John means by the problem with saying "the proof is in the pudding" as some way of learning. The choice that I made in writing this up was to present a picture that was close enough to what my colleague and I were doing that I was hoping it would in an overall way provide data or material for people to make judgments about the usefulness or non-usefulness of this. To the extent that you need to have what people are calling a fine-grained analysis in order to know that—is not something that I considered. So, I don't know whether that, unto itself, was a form of protecting myself. But, given that's not the way I did this, I've heard a lot about how this doesn't meet the standard, from John. And then I've heard, from Greg and Gwen more so, sort of take this broad brush stroke and say what they saw at that level. So, I guess I'm somewhere in between those and not knowing what to make of it . . . 118

Gwen: Is there something that would be helpful to you at this point for us to talk about to help make sense . . . 119

(pause)

Susan: What's going on for me is . . . 120

(pause)

John: I'll try—is there a question you would have hoped would have been answered that hasn't been answered in this discussion? Would that be a way of getting at . . . so that you would feel more like *you* got something out of this? 121

Susan: Oh no. I feel . . . 122

John: I don't see you deprecating what you've learned, but I just wanted to add to and be supportive of, if there's a question the group could focus on - that would be of real interest to me. 123

Cy: But I'm seeing Susan somehow working quite actively they're (looking at her face and throat moving) somehow to try to say . . . 124

John: I may have moved in too fast . . . 125

Susan (weeping): I am upset . . . (pause) I feel . . . what I'm doing is making very strong either/or kinds of conclusions . . . (long pause) When I focus on . . . Well, so I'm taking these general things from what people are saying and thinking this is an unfair and unhealthy thing for me to be doing . . . feeling like there's something in this that makes sense to pursue along with a far more active learning about the things that are helpful to me about what John has said to me tonight about the ways I can be protective of other people. I think I feel . . . 126

(pause) . . . (end of tape) (meeting ended shortly after)

Through this period of the dialogue, Greg is evidently experiencing John's style as not maximally helpful, for he says (#83) that he feels a kind of unfairness in John's critique. He does not describe (and may not have fully known) what was unfair about John's behavior, and John asks him to do so. Greg refers back to comment #61, and John defends himself by re-quoting Susan's "can't know" comment with the emphasis on the in-principle *"can't,"* even though Susan has already clarified that she did *not* mean it in principle. Again, John appears to be listening more closely to his conceptual scheme than to the conversation. Greg, however, is buffaloed (#91), though Susan follows by once again clarifying that she did not mean it in principle. John interrupts her to ask a question, the purpose of which is unclear, but the effect of which is to give him control (#94). He interrupts her twice more in quick succession (#98, 100) with anger in his voice the second time. Horror of horrors: she is evidently not playing this game the way he wants to see it played! And he wants to know what is unfair about his behavior! (Or does he?)

John's interruptions of other participants continue (#104, 107, 110). Despite repeated refutations of his interpretation of Susan's "can't know" comment, he now (#107) "describes" Greg as "having discounted something for which there was directly observable behavior." Finally, someone gives John a concrete illustration of what is being heard as unfair in his behavior, when Cy (#109 and 111) disputes John's "description." John, however, interrupts both times ("Oh no, I'm not talking about that . . ."), evidently not *too* interested in knowing what's unfair about his behavior—at least, not as interested as in what *he is talking about*.

On another point, John's phrase "directly observable behavior" suggests that there is such a thing as uninterpreted direct observation which serves as irrefutable data and to which John has access. This whole exchange suggests, to the contrary, that there is no such thing as uninterpreted data, and that John's difficulty in hearing others' interpretations of what Susan's comment meant to them is reinforced by his belief that he has access to irrefutable data. This is a particularly dysfunctional twist in the conversation, not only because it keeps the conversation cycling rather than proceeding, but, even more importantly, because it potentially serves to discredit the notion of using illustrations from current behavior to test persons' inferences. Yet this procedure is one of the most powerful that action science offers for making people aware, precisely, of their interpretations. In *Action Science,* Argyris, Putnam, and Smith carefully speak of "*relatively* directly observable data" (emphasis added). Without this emphasis, this validity-testing procedure can veil a speaker's Level II re-truing process, as it appears to this reader to do in this instance.

The session ends, just as in John's earlier story about another incident, with a woman weeping.

HOW HAPPILY THEY LIVED EVER AFTER

Pat discontinued participation in the meetings after the foregoing session, on the grounds that neither he himself nor other members of his organization could learn to reconsider their overall approaches under conditions as tense, competitive, and harsh as this meeting generated.

All of the other members continued. The later meeting when the transcript was reviewed was also marked with tension. But other meetings, such as the very next meeting after this dialogue when Terry presented, were not as tense. So, the session presented above is *not* representative of all "community of inquiry" meetings in this respect.

The assignment for the second meeting was to review the summary and the transcript, with each participant asking how she or he might act differently in retrospect. At the outset, Greg said that his central concern was to explore what John had done that he called "unfair" in the first meeting and whether his own reaction was over-protective of Susan. Gwen said that her central question is what she was trying to do early in the first session, why she gave up, and how she might have addressed John about the unfairness she too was experiencing. Susan said that she reviewed the transcript trying to find out how she came to feel as thoroughly incompetent, unethical, and stupid as she did at the end and what she learned from this experience. She identified John's use of highly charged analogies ("She's selling a pill . . . and she'd be in jail this moment if we ever applied the rules of pill making") as one of the factors. John said that he liked all those topics and hadn't developed any introductory comments of his own. Cy said that he wondered how he could have been more competent at influencing John in the first meeting, but that he found his attention straying all the time to the shape and power of John's interventions, which irritated him and unfocused him from his own question.

As the second session continued, Greg suggested that Susan may have been hurt by the confrontations during the first meeting and then responded by polarizing and magnifying the issue beyond what was said. He tested with her whether his attribution was correct. He also reminded the group of occasions when John said he was *not* altogether dismissing the developmental approach, when he used specific, concrete evidence from the dialogue, and when he asked questions that invited others to disconfirm his point of view. Cy said he experienced Susan as open to learning and as actively struggling to learn during the first meeting. By contrast, he experienced John's overall manner—including the number and length of his comments (John made the most comments at each meeting, 31% each time) and his pace—as indicating an unwillingness to look at the question of whether he has something to learn about his whole style. John, Gwen, and Greg told Cy that he had become too prosecutorial in this second session, moved too quickly among issues, and did not use sufficiently concrete data from the dialogue to be maximally helpful. Cy told John, "I am trying to mirror yourself to you."

Later in the second session, John said that he experienced the other members at the first meeting as defending Susan and as "anything from mildly to very pissed off at me . . . What I heard was, 'If you would just shut up, John, we could learn.' And I wasn't about to be shut off." Still later, he said to Gwen, "Let me ask you, because if you're right, first I've really screwed it up, and second it would have been very helpful for you and your colleagues to say, 'Wait a minute.'" Gwen began to offer an illustration of how she did so, but was interrupted by John.

At the end, someone suggested that the group would never have explored this issue of how to help so intensively had it not been for John's strong insistence on his points during the first meeting, and that John himself did not indicate an openness to possible negative effects of his approach until late in the second meeting, after Cy had insisted with comparable strength on questions about John's approach.

Two years later, Susan described instances in her consulting work when she had been helped by remembering the issue raised so vividly in the foregoing dialogue. She now asks herself, as she works, "In talking with clients about how to deal with conflict, am I myself toning down conflict (and thus not modeling what I am advocating)?" However, she also says that the provocative analogies, the "heat," and the pace of this session were *not* useful to her.[3]

FINAL REFLECTIONS

The analysis of John's actions during the first meeting has taken on a prosecutorial tone similar to that with which Cy was charged at the second meeting, so it probably comes as no surprise to most readers that Cy is the pseudonym for the author of this chapter. The suggestion, at the end of the second meeting, that the dogged confrontativeness of both John at the first meeting and Cy at the second meeting may have been the "prime movers" of major learning leaves me with an ongoing conundrum about how to act in my efforts to participate in the creation of communities of inquiry. Since I felt primarily critical, especially late in the first meeting, about John's "frozen" perspective, and since I achieved a similar degree of combativeness only as a desperate ploy to mirror John to himself, what should this experience teach me about my efforts to play a constructive role in helping my family, my academic department (see Chapter 13), and other settings evolve toward transforming communities of inquiry?

I think it tells me that those of us who deeply pursue the discipline of second-person research/practice must not only develop a system, like the seven guidelines of action science, for testing validity in dialogue and avoiding Level I re-truing, but must also be alert at a trans-cognitive level for occasions when the validity-testing system itself may generate dysfunctional Level II re-truing and when true learning will be heightened by stepping beyond the system. In my case, this may mean stepping beyond my "constructive, diplomatic" personality at times.

To cite a much more all-encompassing example, the most serious and systematic effort to avoid re-truing in modern times has been the development of mainstream scientific method. However, since mainstream scientific method is based on treating the scientist as a pure observer, detaching him or her as completely as possible from the observed action, it cannot validly test, but only re-true, the proposition that a participant in action cannot, finally, know objective truth about the current situation as it unfolds. This accords with our ordinary experience of wiser and cooler thought after the fact. Centuries ago, Adam Smith, in *The Theory of Moral Sentiments* (1759/1969) eloquently expressed the dilemma so:

> When the action is over . . . and the passions which prompted it
> have subsided, we can enter more coolly into the sentiments of the
> indifferent spectator. . . . But our judgments now are often of little

importance in comparison of what they were before, and can frequently produce nothing but vain regret and unavailing repentance, without always securing us from like errors in time to come. It is seldom, however, that (we) are quite candid even in this case. . . . He is a bold surgeon they say, whose hand does not tremble when he performs an operation on his own person; and he is often equally bold who does not hesitate to pull off the mysterious veil of self-delusion which covers from his view the deformities of his own conduct (p. 262).

Yes, pulling off the veil of self-delusion in the midst of action is certainly difficult. But then, so too is learning and practicing mainstream scientific method as we now know it. The questions that mainstream science dismisses because of its systematic assumptions, without really addressing, remain. *Is there a kind of scientific inquiry that participants in action can conduct at the time of action? And, more particularly still, is there a kind of scientific inquiry participants in the action can conduct at the time of action without necessarily falling prey to the systemic re-truing of assumptions that occurs in modern science?*

This chapter illustrates how difficult it is to accomplish this aim, yet argues that the answer to both questions is "Yes." In *Action Science* (Argyris et al., 1985), seven rules are offered for testing validity in the midst of action (p. 258ff), and the first two are clearly guidelines that can help a practitioner do Level I validity testing. They are "*Rule 1:* Combine advocacy with inquiry . . . (and) *Rule 2:* Illustrate your inferences with relatively directly observable data." However, as we have already seen in our protracted illustration, Level II validity testing—testing the validity of our theory-in-practice system as a whole—is profoundly more difficult because: 1) a true validity test at Level I may mask re-truing at Level II and 2) a lot of re-truing at Level II is functional (no system can test its own systemic validity at every move), so the real questions at Level II are whether a system *ever* truly tests Level II validity and whether it does so in a *timely* way.

Two of the seven *Action Science* rules pertain to such systemic validity testing, and the reader will see that they are inherently more complex than the Level I rules mentioned above. The two rules are: "*Rule 3:* Make your reasoning explicit and publicly test for agreement at each inferential step . . . (and) *Rule 7:* Design ongoing experiments to test competing views . . ." These two rules are very complex to implement as stated (even with the elaborations provided in *Action Science*). Yet they do not address the questions of when and how they should be followed and how to interpret the results. Nor do they raise or address the question of whether these very rules, as a system, re-true themselves.

As stated near the outset of this chapter before there was a context to make it meaningful to the reader, the Argyrisian version of action science ignores issues of trans-cognitive awareness, of timing, and of how to balance validity-testing with other life concerns. Whereas systematic thought—even systematic thought about an action science—operates within assumptions that inevitably frame it and are inaccessible to it, a Level III trans-cognitive awareness that can hold lightly all one's changing thinking, acting, and inquiring perceptions thereby transforms assumptions into potential variables (see Figure 5.2, Chapter 5; also, Torbert, 1973, 1994, 1999). Just as a systematic Level II approach to validity testing in action, like action science, is necessary in order to reduce Level I re-truing, the Developmental Action Inquiry paradigm introduced in Chapter 5 proposes that a Level III, triple-loop learning process is necessary in order to actively reduce dysfunctional Level II re-truing. Intellectually, this means holding more lightly one's theoretical orientation and one's systemic, Level II validity testing process. This, in turn, permits one to tolerate, appreciate, and truly invite Level II questions, challenges, and modifications unlike John who raised such questions of others, but warded them off when addressed to him.

When persons feel—no matter how sophisticated their theory and their practice—that their ability both to know what is occurring at the moment and to act lovingly moment-to-moment is radically incomplete, they embark upon a transformative journey toward Level III conscious awareness, often seeking help from awareness-transforming spiritual practices (Alexander et al., 1990; Heron, 1998; Pascual-Leone, 1990; Wilber, 1998). To make this effort is to do the task which Adam Smith characterized as *pulling off the mysterious veil of self-delusion* in the midst of action. Mainstream science forswears this task, and Argyrisian action science addresses it only incompletely. Each person initiates and sustains this effort voluntarily. But this effort is required to cross the theory/practice divide successfully in universities and communities where individuals and groups begin from highly divergent models of inquiry and action.

ENDNOTES

[1] These participants had all agreed to the taping of meetings and to the use of the tapes by any members who so chose for research purposes, with the qualification that the other members would be invited to offer feedback on drafts of any articles or chapters, as they have been in this case. Two drafts of this article have been reviewed by the five most active participants, and they have made numerous comments resulting in changes. The participants chose to be represented by pseudonyms in this article, with the additional suggested precaution of altering the gender-identity of one or more members.

[2] In developmental theory, Stages 3 and 4 are called, respectively, "Conformist" and "Conscientious" (Loevinger, 1978), "Diplomat" and "Achiever" (Torbert, 1987), or "Interpersonal" and "Institutional" (Kegan, 1982).

[3] See footnote 1. Although analogical consistency between espoused theory and current practice is a primary value in action science, the question of how to determine the validity of analogies between a there-and-then situation and the current situation has yet to be addressed. (Abbott [1991] addresses the related issue of the validity of stories and analogies used in political theorizing.)

REFERENCES

Abbott, P. (1991). Story-telling and political theory. *Soundings:* 74, (3-4), 369-398.

Alexander, C., Davies, J., Dixon, C., Dilibeck, M., Drucker, S., Oetzel, R., Muehiman, J., & Orme-Johnson, D. 1990. Growth of higher stages of consciousness: Maharishi's Vedic psychology of human development. In Alexander, C., & Langer, E. (Eds.), *Higher Stages of Human Development* New York, NY: Oxford University Press.

Alexy, R. (1990). A theory of practical discourse. In S. Benhabib & F. Dallmayr (Eds.), *The communicative ethics controversy*. Cambridge, MA: MIT Press.

Argyris, C. (1994). *Knowledge for Action*. San Francisco, CA: Jossey-Bass.

Argyris, C., and Schon, D. (1974). *Theory in practice: increasing professional effectiveness*. San Francisco, CA: Jossey-Bass.

Argyris, C., Putnam, R., & Smith, D. (1985). *Action Science: Concepts, Methods and Skills for Research and Intervention*. San Francisco, CA: Jossey-Bass.

Evered, R. & Tannenbaum, B. (1992). A dialog on dialog. *Journal of Management Inquiry*, 1, 43-55.

Heron, J. (1998). *Spiritual Science: Person-Centered Study of the Spiritual and the Subtle*. Ross-on-Wye, UK: PCCS Books.

Kegan, R. (1982). *The Evolving Self* Cambridge, MA. Harvard University Press.

Kegan, R. (1994). *In Over Our Heads: The Mental Demands of Modern Life*. Cambridge, MA: Harvard University Press.

Kegan, R., & Lahey, L. (1984). Adult leadership and adult development: a constructivist view. In Kellerman, B. (Eds.), *Leadership: Multidisciplinary Perspectives*. Englewood Cliffs, NJ: Prentice-Hall.

Lovinger, J. (1978). *Measuring Ego Development, Vol. 1 & 2*. San Francisco, CA: Jossey-Bass.

Pascual-Leone, J. (1990). Reflections on life-span intelligence, consciousness, and ego development. In Alexander, C. & Langer, E. (Eds.), *Higher Stages of Human Development*. New York, NY: Oxford University Press.

Schon, D. (1983). *The Reflective Practitioner*. New York, NY: Basic.

Souvaine, E. (1985). Creating contexts for effective action and the development of meaning-making. *Qualifying Paper*. Cambridge, MA: Harvard Graduate School of Education.

Souvaine, E., Lahey, L. & Kegan, R. (1990). Life after formal operations: implications for a psychology of the self. In Alexander, C. & Langer, E. (Eds.), *Higher Stages of Human Development* New York, NY: Oxford University Press.

Smith, A. 1759/1969. *The Theory of Moral Sentiments*. Indianapolis, IN: Liberty Classics.

Torbert, W. (1973). *Leaning from Experience: Toward Consciousness*. New York, NY: Columbia University Press.

Torbert, W. (1976). *Creating a Community of Inquiry: Conflict, Collaboration, Transformation*. London: Wiley.

Torbert, W. (1991). *The Power of Balance: Transforming self, society, and scientific inquiry*. Newbury Park, CA: Sage.

Torbert, W. (1994). Cultivating post-formal development: Higher stages and contrasting interventions. In M. Miller & S. Cook-Greuter (Eds.), *Transcendence and Mature Thought in Adulthood*. Lanham, MD: Rowman & Littlefield.

Torbert, W. (1998). Developing wisdom and courage in organizing and sciencing. In S. Srivastva & D. Cooperrider (Eds.), *Organizational Wisdom and Executive Courage*. San Francisco, CA: The New Lexington Press.

Torbert, W. (1999). The distinctive questions developmental action inquiry asks. *Journal of Management Learning*. 30, (2), 189-206.

Wilber, K. (1998). The marriage of sense and soul: Integrating science and religion. New York, NY: Random .

10 SERVICE-LEARNING
As a Vehicle in Training Psychologists for Revised Professional Roles

Maureen E. Kenny
Laura A. Gallagher
Boston College

With an awareness of the many challenges facing children, youth, and families, the Boston College Counseling Psychology program strives to strengthen student commitment to social justice and work with diverse populations in underserved areas (Brabeck, Walsh, Kenny, & Comilang, 1997). Given the severity and complexity of the problems facing children and families, the program also seeks to prepare scientist-practitioners to design, deliver, and evaluate comprehensive corrective and preventive interventions in collaboration with other professionals and community partners (Knitzer, 1993; Lerner, 1995). The goals of training students for interprofessional collaboration and for comprehensive and socially active roles in the delivery and evaluation of services has led us to examine and gradually revise our methods of teaching and training. New methods of professional training are being considered by other professions, as well. Sherman, for example, in Chapter 12 illustrates how clinical legal education can be conducted to address new roles for lawyers.

Service-learning is a pedagogical approach with the potential to provide a foundational understanding of systemic issues and to transform professional training for socially active and collaborative professional roles. Altman (1996) and McCall (1996) recommend service-learning as a method for renewing university responsibility and commitment to societal needs. Within the academic discipline of psychology specifically, but across higher education generally, service-learning has been heralded as an approach for linking the traditional domains of foundational knowledge (e.g., concepts, theories, history, and methodology of a discipline) and professional knowledge (e.g., practitioner skills and content), with a new emphasis on socially responsive knowledge (e.g., knowledge, skills, and experiences to understand and act on social problems) (Altman, 1996). Despite the obvious potential of service-learning, guided by outreach scholarship, for transforming social inquiry and linking the classroom and the world of practice, such programs are difficult to implement successfully (Hondagneu-Sotelo & Raskoff, 1996). Unless faculty and administrative directors of service-learning programs carefully attend to complex systemic issues, service-learning can contribute to the exploitation, rather than to the empowerment of, community partners (Harkavy, 1996; Maybach, 1996).

This chapter examines service-learning as a vehicle for transforming social inquiry and social action in graduate education in psychology and the problems that can limit that realization. We begin by identifying the limitations of traditional practica/internship training experiences in psychology as a mechanism for social change and preparation for expanded, innovative roles as psychologists. We will then examine the goals of service-learning and seek to identify best practices to guide the development of socially responsive and pedagogically effective service-learning courses. We will discuss how service-learning can enhance student training in preparation for expanded moral and activist roles in outreach scholarship, prevention, program evaluation, and interprofessional collaboration. Finally, we also reflect on our current efforts in developing service-learning experiences in the Counseling Psychology program at Boston College.

PROFESSIONAL TRAINING IN PSYCHOLOGY

Traditional training of mental health counselors and psychologists, similar to other types of professional training, includes field-based components, known as practica and internship. These aspects of professional preparation typically involve placement in established training sites, where students carry out specific professional responsibilities under the supervision of credentialled psychologists. During these experiences, students must meet program and state requirements regarding hours of supervision and number and types of services provided in order to be eligible for future licensure. Although opportunities for exposure to new professional roles are sometimes possible through formal practica and internship, these experiences often reflect well established, rather than innovative, practice. Students typically seek sites with a strong reputation for the delivery of mental health services and the training of students in individual counseling/therapy and assessment skills. Given the variety of professional roles that mental health professionals can be expected to fulfill in the future, a solid mastery of traditional competencies provides an important and strong foundation for future innovation in professional roles. Yet, this training can limit the vision and skills of future professionals who seek to work with schools, families, and communities in ways that go beyond traditional professional boundaries. Traditional psychology training focuses on individual adjustment to social realities with minimal attention to effecting social change or to the moral obligations or community responsibilities of either psychologist or client (Doherty, 1995).

THE VARIED AGENDAS OF SERVICE-LEARNING

In comparison with traditional practica/internship training in psychology which focuses on professional socialization and the development of clinical skills, service-learning seeks to promote moral sensibilities (Noddings, 1984), foster the appreciation of diversity and pluralism (LeSourd, 1997), enhance social and civic responsibility, increase awareness of societal structures that contribute to social problems and solutions, and empower participants to solve social problems (Brevard Community College, 1994; Wutzdorff & Giles, 1997). In addition to this long list of student goals, service-learning is also intended to meet authentic needs of the community (American Association of Higher Education, 1992) and foster lifelong connections between students, their communities, and the world beyond the classroom (Crews, 1997). Service-learning has also been identified as a vehicle for urban revitalization (Harkavy & Puckett, 1994; McCall, 1996). (See Table 10.1 for a comparison of service-learning and traditional psychology training goals.)

Table 10.1 *Comparison of How Practica/Internship Training and Service-learning Differentially Meet the Counseling Psychology Program Model Goals*

Counseling Psychology	Traditional Practica/Internship	Service-learning
Scientist-Practitioner model	Clinical training in individual/ group assessment skills; theoretical conceptualization emphasized in BC university seminar; little focus on program evaluation or PAR	Integrates theory, research, and applied therapy and knowledge through service and academic components; critical examination of theory; opportunities for program evaluation and PAR
Strengths/Assets-focused	Focus on client problems	Focus on community strengths
Developmental orientation	Depends on field site; BC university seminar includes developmental orientation	Considers developmental level in type of service; assessments, program development, and evaluation.
Multicultural training	Emphasis on culturally sensitive practices with individual clients	Culturally sensitive practices with individual clients, as well as emphasis on broader contextual understanding of race and culture
Social justice	Individual needs addressed; little focus on moral and community responsibility	Focus on community needs and social change

(table continued)

Preventive	Traditional focus on problem remediation and symptom relief	Focus on developing prevention programs and brief interventions in the community
Interprofessional collaboration/ Integrated services	Collaboration typically limited to other professionals at site; little community and interdisciplinary partnerships	Extends collaboration to professionals and other partnerships in the community in efforts to integrate services

Service-learning pedagogy has been embraced by educators who strive to link social inquiry and social action, relating classroom learning to relevant social, economic, and environmental problems, while also considering the moral and ethical consequences of social action. The basic pedagogical premise of service-learning is derived from Dewey's notion that "[L]earning starts with a problem and continues with the application of increasingly complex ideas and increasingly sophisticated skills to increasingly complicated problems" (Ehrlich, 1996, pp. xii). By connecting theory and practice, service-learning is intended to provide a context for understanding abstract principles and an opportunity for testing and refining existing theories and developing new theories (Brevard Community College, 1994). It is worthwhile to note that a commitment to public service and the application of scholarship to improve life is not shared by all academics. Within the traditional field of academic psychology, for example, an emphasis on scientific, theory-driven basic research has contributed to a devaluation of applied and practical scholarship (McCall, 1996).

WHERE SERVICE-LEARNING FAILS

In light of the multiplicity of agendas linked to service-learning programs, including educational reform, student learning and community partnership, many programs fall short in achieving all of their goals, especially in the realm of community benefit. Harkavy (1993) notes that traditional service-learning focuses on improving teaching and fostering civic consciousness, with less focus on devising solutions to core civic problems. Maybach (1996) similarly criticizes traditional service-learning projects for directing almost exclusive attention to the growth of the student and minimal attention to the needs of those being served or the impact of the service efforts on the community. Maybach laments, furthermore, that existing practices contribute to the oppression of the needy as persons who need to be cared for, despite the good intentions of the service providers. In addition, Harkavy (1996) asserts that universities often conduct a form of exploitative community-based research to enhance faculty research and publications, neglecting the potential value of student and faculty research as community service. This pattern is illustrated in the history of the community described by Fairfax in Chapter 2.

SOLUTIONS: NEW MODELS

With increasing awareness of the exploitive effects of well-intentioned traditional service-learning programs, alternative models are emerging. Maybach (1996) recommends a model that invites community members to define their own needs, enhances student awareness of the historical and social context of poverty, and teaches students how to be involved in mutually empowering relationships with diverse groups of people in ways that address the root causes of their needs, as well as the symptoms.

The Haas Center for Public Service at Stanford University (1998), describes a field research model of service-learning in which students serve as knowledge brokers for community agencies. This type of service is based upon the premise that knowledge is the most fundamental resource that a university can offer. The service provided is not hours of direct service to the needy (e.g., preparing and serving meals to the homeless), but work with community members and agency personnel to determine the kinds of knowledge and information that are needed to enhance their organization and to alleviate pressing problems. The resources of the university are used to provide needed knowledge and information. Providing program evaluation services is an example of this type of service.

Participant observation and participatory action research (PAR) provide additional alternative models. Participant observers do not provide a direct service to others, but provide an opportunity for reflection on academic issues through participation and action in the community setting. A course offered at Georgetown University on prison literature, in which students and prison inmates reflect on and critique selections of literature about the imprisoned, is an example of participant observation (Brown University, 1998). Harkavy (1996) identified (PAR) as a fruitful service vehicle for "strategic academically-based community service," which is based upon the commitment to use the broad range of university resources to alleviate social problems and contribute to community well being. PAR requires collaboration between academics and nonacademics through all stages of the research process, as academics strive to learn with and from members of the community in the process of solving significant community problems and significant theoretical/intellectual problems (Harkavy, 1993). A doctoral dissertation completed by a student at the Annenberg School of Communication, University of Pennsylvania, examined newsmaking as a strategy for self-determination among African American high school students. The interaction between the researcher and the high school students led them to publish a school-based community newspaper in West Philadelphia. This type of study exemplifies the PAR approach (Harkavy, 1993), and is also an illustration of what Torbert means by second-person research/practice in Chapters 5, 9, and 13.

We next examine existing literature for an overview of recognized best practices that would provide specific guidelines for establishing service-learning programs. We do so because of the espoused potential of service-learning pedagogy as a means for transforming social inquiry and social action and for linking classroom and community. We also do so with an awareness of the difficulty in trying to enhance student academic, cultural, and moral learning while simultaneously effecting meaningful and socially responsive community change. Above all, we are seeking guidelines to help any of us who engage in service-learning to avoid the pitfalls of community exploitation in program development and implementation.

SOLUTIONS: WORDS OF WISDOM FROM THE FIELD

Guidelines for exemplary service-learning programs attend to factors that foster student learning, as well as to factors that contribute to mutually beneficial university-community partnerships. Although some proponents of service-learning have identified community improvement as the primary goal (Harkavy, 1996), and others maintain a primary focus on the educational agenda of higher education (Barber & Battistoni, 1993), it is evident that both sets of needs must be met if mutually beneficial university-community partnerships are to be achieved and sustained. Thus, we sought to identify guidelines that attend to both sets of concerns, while being attentive to ways in which the agendas of the university and the community can best be integrated.

A number of best practice guidelines relate to the structure and organization of service-learning courses. It is clear from our perusal of outstanding programs that successful service-learning courses should be academically rigorous and require thorough preparation and careful planning, with a clear and comprehensive structure and clear objectives set for skills to be learned (Howard, 1993). While these criteria appear to be applicable for any good university course, it is critically important that the justification, relevance, and goals of the service experience be clear, and articulated for both university and community partners. Service assignments need to meet actual community needs, with all parties involved in defining these needs (Ward, 1997).

An ongoing process of evaluation is needed to match available resources and community needs for the reciprocal benefit of the students, university, and community partners (Bradley, 1997; Crews, 1997). Careful evaluation of process, as well as outcome goals, from the perspective of all stakeholders is necessary to determine whether the program is simultaneously meeting specific student learning goals and community needs (Bradley, 1997). Traditional, objective scientific methods of inquiry may not be adequate for these purposes. A holistic assessment approach has been recommended (Serow, 1997), which utilizes both quantitative and qualitative techniques, examines community as well as individual level data, considers the needs and interests of academic and practitioner audiences, and examines changes among all participants within the context of their broader life circumstances and community contexts.

Success in being responsive to community needs requires considerable faculty effort and preparation. The professor should have knowledge of the cooperating agency or community organization and ideally should volunteer in the agency along with or prior to students in order to be aware of the mission of the agency, know how to best enter the system, and be aware of possible antagonisms towards outsiders (Porter & Schwartz, 1993). Student training, supervision, monitoring, support, and evaluation need to be coordinated by the faculty and cooperative agency (Crews, 1997). Time to organize projects, to provide coordination with on-site supervisors, to communicate with on-site supervisors concerning course objectives, to train students, and to process the emotional reaction of students to their service experiences requires a substantial faculty commitment (Porter & Schwartz, 1993). If the university tenure system does not reward public service, or applied, collaborative and interdisciplinary research (McCall, 1996), the cost for junior faculty who engage in service-learning may be extraordinarily high, and faculty may lose interest or feel obligated to abandon this type of work. Therefore, institutional and university commitments are necessary in order to promote and ensure the success of integrating service into the academic curriculum. Planners need to anticipate potential pitfalls and take the time to build a base of support for the curriculum among administrators, faculty, and the community at large (Schine, 1997).

For service-learning courses to be successful, commitment and preparation by agency personnel are also essential. The agency or other community partner needs to be willing to devote ample human resources to organize tasks and projects, to provide coordination and supervise students, and to be aware of student learning objectives. Efforts to facilitate the connection between the university and community agency often include a visit to class by an agency representative, who can help to prepare students for entry into the community.

Student preparation should include consideration of legal and ethical issues, such as confidentiality and the rights of clients, guidelines for student safety, a clear definition of the types of tasks that are being requested by the agency, and their fit with student skills, expectations, and learning goals (Porter & Schwartz, 1993). Student reflection on their basis for entering the community as an equal with community participants is also vital. Students often lack an adequate understanding of their own background of privilege and enter the community with a bias of elitism, viewing community members as objects of curiosity, rather than as persons from whom they can learn. Ward (1997) notes that middle-class students often enter low-income, ethnic minority communities to perform service from a "deficit" model, expecting that those they serve should be grateful for the charity they receive. Although students may come away from that experience feeling good about themselves, "it is worrisome that they may gain a sense of superiority through the process of making incorrect or inappropriate assumptions about the social groups and the nature of the help provided" (Ward, 1997, p. 144). According to Ward, classes with a service-learning component must help students change from a "charity" orientation to a "change" orientation in which skills of advocacy and political action augment their basic altruistic intentions. The effective service-learning curriculum should examine the imbalance of power that exists in a service relationship in which expert or helper has access to knowledge, resources, or services that are needed by community members (Ward, 1997).

Barber and Battistoni (1993) similarly propose to teach students a "civic" view of service, which emphasizes mutual responsibility, enlightened self-interest, and the interdependence of rights and responsibility, in contrast with the "philanthropic" view of service, which emphasizes altruism and charity for the less advantaged. According to the civic approach, service is integral to civil responsibility and is grounded in democracy. Without mutual responsibility and acceptance of obligations that accompany rights, free democratic communities cannot prevail. Community is understood as the common group to which we all belong, and not as the group outside of the university, which is in need of university help.

Student training in sensitivity to issues of race and class is also considered to be vital (Ward, 1997). When larger issues of class, ethnicity, and race are not considered, the potential for student condescension increases, and the impact on both the student and the community served can be more negative than positive. Diversity principles of good practice in combining service and learning include classroom dialogue about cultural differences in defining and interpreting such concepts as "responsibility," "action," and "common good" (Cruz, 1996). The concept of "need" should be discussed, with an awareness that those who have suffered the costs of colonialism, slavery, patriarchy, and other forms of oppression, may not define themselves as in "need."

Although service-learning is intended to increase empathy, reduce stereotypes, and contribute to more structurally sophisticated views of social problems and solutions (Wutzdorff & Giles, 1997), service experiences may also reinforce culture and class stereotypes if students are not properly prepared (Ward, 1997). Sheckley and Keeton (1997) provide a theoretical model for conceptualizing the processes through which service-learning challenges pre-existing stereotypes. Cultural norms, individual values, and personal expectations impact what we attend to and remember from our experiences and the meaning we give to them. We are most likely to attend to, and make sense of, situations in ways that confirm our existing beliefs and expectations. Disconfirming experiences that challenge our existing beliefs can also be derived from service experiences. Assistance from instructors in processing ongoing experience (as opposed to brief efforts) in the service setting can enable students to observe information that is discrepant with prior beliefs and to incorporate new information in revising the set of images, values, expectations, and concepts that are used to understand the world. Information from instructors in the absence of real life experience is also likely to be ineffective in transforming beliefs in a lasting way (Sheckley & Keeton, 1997).

Ward (1997) notes that ethnic and cultural beliefs are particularly difficult to change as they are often unconscious and are shaped by cultural values, roles, and priorities. She provides some examples, however, of educational strategies that can aid students in becoming more culturally competent and effective service providers. Course readings and discussion should include in-depth analyses of specific social problems from multidisciplinary perspectives. Social policies that serve to remedy or exacerbate these problems should be critically examined. Self-examination of one's personal biases, values, and interests is critical in enhancing self-awareness and sensitivity toward other cultural groups. According to Ward, these instructional components can contribute to the development of "change" oriented, rather than "charity" oriented service providers.

The university must also consider its basis for entering into a service partnership. Reciprocal relationships between universities and their surrounding communities are not the norm, given the typical discrepancies in power, wealth, and status. The university, however, needs to recognize that its welfare is intertwined with that of the community (Brown & Harkavy, 1995). Advances in theory and research occur through partnerships with the community in solving real-world focused problems. "Practitioner-based and community-based knowledge . . . is a necessary complement to expert knowledge, resulting in better theory and practice" (Brown & Harkavy, 1995, p. 66). Ward (1997) notes that students and faculty often attempt to establish service-learning ventures without a good understanding of the history of school-community partnerships. Resentments stemming from prior failed promises, and unethical and culturally insensitive practices, have left some communities reluctant or unwilling to participate in new university partnerships. Students and faculty who wish to collaborate with community partners must be aware of the influence of past history on current efforts, and must involve community representatives in the discussion of issues and in setting priorities (Ward, 1997).

Our discussion has attributed much of the blame for failure of service-learning programs on weaknesses in the university partnership. The university and faculty implementing these programs have tended to focus more on the goals of student learning and/or faculty scholarship as the priority for the university, instead of placing equal value on community needs and in preparing students for entrance into partnership with the community. The challenge is to integrate the two seemingly disparate goals of student learning and community benefit. However, these goals should not be mutually exclusive if best practice guidelines are carefully considered. By recognizing how the service-learning paradigm fits with the goals and mission of Counseling Psychology training programs, we propose an innovative and socially responsive means to bridge the gap between applied, professional, academic, and service-learning.

HOW SERVICE-LEARNING FITS WITH
COUNSELING PSYCHOLOGY

We believe that service-learning can enhance professional training in psychology in a number of ways. Involvement in service-learning prior to professional practica and internship can provide the student with an expanded conceptual and experiential framework through which personal and societal assumptions, expectations, and biases can be examined. Service-learning can enhance multicultural training by examining social policy, the definition of "need," the role of power in the helping relationship, and the complex role of structural and contextual factors in human development. Students can clarify for themselves and affirm their commitment to social justice by assessing what they mean by "responsibility," "action," and "the common good." Integrating service-learning into the curriculum in new and innovative ways can promote caring, moral responsibility, and a commitment to community concerns traditionally lacking in psychology training (Doherty, 1995).

Service-learning should not only extend the psychologist-in-training's intellectual understanding of systemic/contextual and cultural factors that impact human development, but should also provide opportunities for developing skills that support systemic, rather than individual intervention. Counseling Psychology students can learn how to develop true partnerships, not just with other professionals, but also with community members and organizations. Such experiences can focus on the development of skills in community consultation and collaboration, identifying the strengths that each partner brings, being aware of what they can contribute as well as their own limitations, and seeking to identify and change systemic causes of oppression.

Furthermore, service-learning advances training in scientist-practitioner attitudes and skills by providing opportunities to discuss and challenge theory encountered in class readings with experience gained in the field (Byrne, 1995). Students collect data and observations in the field, and, through discussion with peers and faculty, actively connect questions of human concern with knowledge from theory and research. Analysis of social problems on a macro and micro level can help students to think more expansively and creatively about social problems, going beyond and challenging current knowledge, and can be helpful in exploring social policies that have implications for the development of preventive interventions.

Service-learning experiences can also be developed as a means for masters' and doctoral level students to work collaboratively with other professionals and community partners and to acquire skills in designing, implementing, and evaluating programs intended to promote positive youth development. Students can work with community partners in the completion of community analyses or assessment of needs and in collaborative program evaluation. Students can gain experience in contextual models of program evaluation, which combine multiple (quantitative and qualitative) types of data and which assess the goals and perspectives of all stakeholders in both process and outcome evaluation (Ostrom, Lerner, & Freel, 1995). Skills in grant writing can also be practiced as external funds may be needed to enhance community resources. Training in program evaluation and grantsmanship do not play a central role in traditional field-based practica and internships, but are becoming increasingly relevant to the professional roles of doctoral level psychologists in community, as well as academic settings.

INTEGRATING SERVICE-LEARNING
AND COUNSELING PSYCHOLOGY TRAINING

The Counseling Psychology program at Boston College espouses a scientist-practitioner model of training, a developmental orientation, an adherence to culturally sensitive practices, and a commitment to enhancing social justice. Our program, which reflects the above goals, provides an academic foundation for service experiences, as well as opportunities for reflection on theory/practice links. Coursework in normal and abnormal developmental processes, in a developmental contextualist (Lerner, 1995) orientation to the understanding of human behavior, conceptually supports the science and practice of prevention and intervention. A master's level course in Multicultural Issues and doctoral seminar in Culture and Psychology seek to enhance student sensitivity to multicultural issues and provide a structural/systemic understanding of contemporary racism. Our doctoral research core has been revised, and course offerings in Participatory Action Research, Program Evaluation, and Qualitative Methods add to students traditional preparation in Quantitative Methods, increasing the range of skills they may apply in holistic program evaluation and action-oriented inquiry. A seminar in Outreach Scholarship has been added to our department course offerings and has included graduate students from multiple disciplines who have grappled with issues involved in collaborative community research, including the design and evaluation of preventive programs to promote positive youth development.

Service-learning is highly compatible with the training model in Counseling Psychology that we have set forth at Boston College. Our program commitment to promoting social justice is consistent with the mission of the Jesuit university of which we are part. Traditionally, Jesuit education has sought to foster learning as a tool for achieving social justice, emphasizing not only the acquisition of knowledge, but also the constructive and responsible use of that knowledge in service to others. The mission of Boston College provides a context of institutional support for our program goals and for the extension of university service-learning. The Boston College Center for Child, Family, and Community Partnerships provides an important resource for the development of service-learning programs. (Lerner, Chapter 3) The focus of the Center on collaboration with community members to determine priorities, to build on community strengths in order to effect positive change, and to engage in a co-learning relationship that will ensure that "needs are real, solutions are feasible and measurable, and long-term results are sustainable" (Walsh & Thompson, Chapter 6, Lerner, 1997, p. 6) is highly consistent with the models of Counseling Psychology and service-learning that we have been describing. The Center supports student and faculty research that provides a service to the community as advocated by Harkavy (1996) and has similarities with the university as knowledge-broker model provided by the Haas Center (Stanford University, 1998).

Our current efforts to extend service-learning experiences build upon and integrate initiatives that have been in place for several years as part of our efforts to train Counseling Psychology students in interprofessional collaboration and prevention (Brabeck et al., 1997; Kenny & Comilang, 1997; Walsh, Kenny, & Andersson, 1998; Walsh, Kenny, & Brabeck, 1998). As we discuss several of these service experiences, we will describe how each is intended to contribute to training for revised professional roles, how it reflects lessons learned from our review of best practices, and how it exemplifies the complexities of implementing service-learning experiences.

For over four years, first-year pre-internship masters' students in Counseling Psychology have been providing service in a group prevention program at an urban elementary school. Our doctoral students have contributed to the design and implementation of a developmentally based prevention program and have been involved in the supervision of the masters' students who have carried out the preventive intervention. Over time our involvement with the elementary school has evolved into a more broad-based partnership, leading to the transformation of the school into an Extended Services School (see Chapter 6). This transformation has provided increased opportunities for doctoral student training for revised professional roles. Linking knowledge of theory, research, and psychology practice, students gain experience in supervision, interprofessional collaboration, and the design and evaluation of prevention programs.

As part of the Extended Services School, Boston College undergraduates have become involved in a service-learning program that provides services in the after-school program. An advanced doctoral student in Counseling Psychology is training and supervising a master's level student, who in turn is supervising the undergraduates who serve as tutors in the after-school program. In reflecting upon her experiences, the doctoral student explains how she is incorporating what she learned academically in her doctoral coursework in supervision as she supervises the master's student and teaches the master's student how to supervise undergraduates. Although her coursework emphasized the importance of considering the developmental level of the supervisee, this lesson only gained meaning as she was faced with the different levels of personal and professional development of the masters' students, the undergraduates, and the elementary school students with whom they are working. Recognition of the developmental levels of her supervisees has been especially important as the doctoral student has considered the ethnic and cultural belief systems of her supervisees and was to prepare them and undergraduate students for effective collaboration in a complex urban school. Efforts to increase her supervisees' understanding of complex systemic and structural issues deepens her understanding of these factors, and becomes critical as the undergraduates are struggling with the tensions between their idealistic motivations and the complexities of effecting change amidst the crises of daily life in an urban school. The doctoral student supervisor strives to incorporate the lessons of Ward (1997) and Scheckley and Keeton (1997) in hopes that the master's and undergraduate students will not experience disillusionment or reinforce prior stereotypes, but rather emerge from the service experience with a more sophisticated understanding of social problems. In addition to gaining experience in supervision and the design of preventive intervention, the doctoral student is learning first-hand about program evaluation. Following the suggestions of Bradley (1997) for ongoing evaluation, the doctoral student has been striving to obtain regular feedback from all participants (e.g., masters' students, undergraduate tutors, teachers) in the after school tutoring program for purposes of modifying the program and processes to meet the needs of all participants. This advanced doctoral student is carrying out a complex set of responsibilities under the supervision of our program faculty. Although this experience is appropriate only for a more advanced student, her account illustrates clearly the complex skills she has gained through this experience. Her skills in supervision and her sensitivity to systemic, developmental, and evaluation issues facilitate the complex coordination of the learning needs of the university and the needs of the urban elementary school.

Through the initiative of another Counseling Psychology faculty member, the Educational Advocacy Program was initiated at an urban public high school (Sparks, 1998). The program grew out of an identified need to provide additional services for high school students who are at-risk for academic failure and who are potential risks for dropping out. Boston College master's students in Counseling and Developmental Psychology serve as volunteer educational advocates, who work with high school students, parents, teachers, and social service providers to address students' educational and psychosocial needs. Two of our doctoral students have supervised master's student advocates, and have participated in the training of staff and teachers concerning the program. In contrast with traditional practica (see Table 10.1), this project involves doctoral students in the development of a prevention program that focuses on the strengths of adolescents and enhances the understanding of contextual and systemic factors that limit youth achievement. These students also grapple with issues ranging from the practical matters that impact the day-to-day activities of the project, such as finding physical space to meet with students, how to become an integral part of the school, to more challenging systemic issues including the effort to effect change in an established institution (system), and the challenges of true collaboration.

Despite these varied initiatives, all of our students have not been involved in service activities and, thus, we are striving to more extensively integrate service experiences within our formal curriculum. Consistent with this perspective, one faculty member arranged for students in his doctoral Counseling Theories Seminar to participate in weekly treatment team meetings at an urban community mental health center, providing an opportunity for students, faculty, and mental health practitioners to discuss their understanding of theory and its relevance to the realities of community mental health. Students are asked to keep a journal of reflections on treatment team discussions and relate these to class readings and discussion. Because class members attend several different treatment team meetings, they are also responsible for bringing back one case presentation from the community mental health center for discussion in the university seminar. The community mental health center views this collaboration as a way of engaging the intellectual resources of the university in solving the complex challenges encountered in community mental health. For doctoral students, this provides an opportunity to integrate what they are learning in class with a broader contextual and systemic understanding of community mental health centers and the lives of the clients they serve. This form of community-based learning is similar to the participant observation model of service-learning that we described. According to one doctoral student beginning this experience, his initial challenges are to establish collaborative relationships with the community mental health team, as students initially are uncertain of their contribution, and to coordinate the tight schedules of their student lives with the unpredictable realities of scheduling in community mental health.

We have also developed consultation and service experiences for first-year doctoral students to enhance their understanding of interprofessional, systemic, and multicultural issues. Two doctoral students, for example, are currently involved in the Juvenile Rights Advocacy Project (see Chapter 12). This experience contributes to student skill development in interprofessional collaboration and increases understanding of the legal system as a social structure, as well as awareness of community resources available for serving youth (see Table 10.1). As an interdisciplinary training opportunity, the students are assigned to collaborate with a law student in work on a specific case in addition to attending a weekly seminar with law students. Our students have learned that counseling, advocacy, confidentiality, and professional boundaries have different meanings across professions. Although both law and psychology are intended to serve the interests of the client, they do so from different perspectives and through different means. One of our students explained it this way; "Lawyers stress being the voice of the client, and the counselor seeks to understand the client first." The counseling approach focuses on establishing rapport and working with clients over time to identify options and make choices. The goal of a legal interview may focus on clarifying the client's immediate goal, such as staying out of jail. This difference in perspectives was exemplified, for example, when the psychology and law students collaborated in an interview with a developmentally delayed client. The psychology student began the interview with some general questions to assess the client's level of understanding. The supervising attorney was not familiar with the goals of the psychologist and expressed an eagerness to move ahead in discussing the client's housing options. Later in the interview, the psychologist felt that the client was not understanding what had been said and made a statement that the information was confusing, hoping to provide an opportunity for the client to admit her misunderstanding and seek clarification. The lawyer did not recognize the psychology student's intent and suggested that they talk about this later. These collaborative experiences are viewed as very valuable by the psychology students who believe the "best interests" of the child will be fully served through improved interprofessional understanding, communication, and coordination.

Two additional doctoral students have been involved in the development of a preventive intervention in an urban high school to increase school engagement among urban youth. Like the Educational Advocacy Project, this effort focuses on the strengths of adolescents, empowering them to define their needs, which will serve as a basis for later intervention. The doctoral students gain experience in needs assessment and interprofessional collaboration with school personnel, and reflect upon the contextual factors that impinge upon the lives of these youth. These experiences are providing students with the opportunities to work with a diverse, underserved population that may not have been available in traditional training settings. Additionally, these experiences provide students with a vision of social change, in conjunction with an understanding of the difficulties in achieving consensus on goals when universities seek to collaborate with public school and community partners. Faculty members from across departments play an important role as mentors to our students, providing them with unique opportunities for collaboration and learning new skills, including grant writing and program development. The triumphs and the frustrations of the process provide students with valuable practical lessons in collaboration and consultation. Because collaborations take time to develop, all partners need support in evaluating the results of their efforts. Students need to understand how their efforts are situated in a larger project and in a myriad of complex systemic and structural factors that they can appreciate. Community and school partners need to identify results that are significant enough to sustain their commitment over time.

At the master's level, a course in Clinical Child Psychology, which is required for students in School Counseling and an elective for students in Mental Health Counseling, emphasizes prevention and the interplay of family, school, community, and societal factors in contributing to positive and maladaptive youth development. A service component to the course provides students with an opportunity to reflect on the interplay of individual and systemic factors contributing to risk and resilience in the lives of these youth and the implications for intervention. This course follows the traditional model of service-learning in which students are required to relate their experiences to the academic learning of the course through a journal, class discussion, and an integrative research paper. Course readings emphasize cultural diversity and structural/systemic bases for poverty and ongoing instructor input is provided through an e-mail list-serve and on student reflection papers. As predicted by the literature, instructor time requirements in structuring the class and reading weekly student journals have exceeded typical teaching demands, with benefits experienced by students have also been consistent with those exemplified in the literature. One student, for example, reflects upon how linking the class readings and field experience have enhanced critical thinking, "Integrating readings and field experience have helped me work through confusions, challenged former beliefs, and created a greater awareness for asking more questions in the future." Another student reflects upon the link between theory and practice, "I was able to critically analyze my practical experience in relation to the theoretical ideas in the reading . . . the reading and research gave a backbone to my practical work with kids and their families." Other students noted how the class strengthened the contextual, systemic, and developmental understanding of youth, "This class has helped me view my clients from all angles, as I reflect on how all domains, familial, biological, cultural, etc., may determine who a client is." The student continued, "The reading, class discussions and my practical field experience have given me greater insight into developmental hurdles that adolescents face. The combination of theory and practice enables me to contextualize that which I witness first hand."

CONCLUSION

Although graduate training in professional psychology has historically included practica and internships that link classroom learning and practice in the field, we do not believe that these experiences typically prepare psychologists for revised professional roles in community and interprofessional collaboration, program design and evaluation, prevention, and societal change. Individual counseling and assessment focus on individual adaptation or adjustment, with little attention to changing macro-system factors that sustain the social conditions, that are at the root of many of the psychological symptoms that our clients present. We believe that service-learning experiences are instructional mechanisms that can instill a sense of moral responsibility and community commitment in graduate psychology students, enhance multicultural training, and provide opportunities to practice skills in collaboration, community needs assessment, program design, program evaluation, and participatory action research, while also mutually benefiting community partners.

Service experiences can be linked with classroom learning in ways that enhance student preparation for revised professional roles. Faculty outreach scholarship can be readily linked to student placements and coursework. The stated mission of our university, and the presence of the Boston College Center for Child, Family, and Community Partnerships, provide necessary institutional supports at our university that can enhance this instructional mission and pedagogy. For example, in Chapter 11, Waddock offers another illustration of a service-learning orientation. Yet, we are aware that good intentions can fail and that service-learning courses can contribute to the problem, rather than to the solution. The many lessons that have been gleaned from existing literature provide some guidelines for our efforts. It is clear from our own experiences and the accounts of our masters' and doctoral students that service-learning collaboration is complex. Facilitating communication and the identification of common goals among numerous partners whose ideas and daily priorities are shaped by different life experiences, professional training processes, contextual demands, and urgencies in time schedules is a challenge, but one that is critical to the establishment of service-learning partnerships that meet student learning, faculty scholarship, and community/social agency needs. We hope to contribute to the literature of best practices as we evaluate and document the successes and failures of our service-learning efforts and determine how service-learning can enhance the training of Counseling Psychologists for revised professional roles.

REFERENCES

Altman, I. (1996). Higher education and psychology in the millennium *American Psychologist, 51*, 371-378.

American Association for Higher Education Assessment Forum. (1992). *Principles of good practice for assessing student learning.* Washington, DC: American Association of Higher Education.

Barber, B. R., & Battistoni, R. (1993). A season of service: Introducing service-learning into the liberal arts curriculum *PS: Political Science, 26*, 235-262.

Brabeck, M. Walsh, M. E., Kenny, M. E., & Comilang, K. (1997). Interprofessional collaboration for children and families: Opportunities for counseling psychology in the 21st century. *The Counseling Psychologist, 25*, 615-636.

Bradley, L. R. (1997). Evaluating service-learning: Toward a new paradigm. In A. Waterman (Ed.), *Service-learning: Applications from the research* (pp. 151-171). Mahwah, NJ: Lawrence Erlbaum Associates.

Brevard Community College (1994, July). *The power.* Cocoa, FL: Brevard Community College.

Brown, G., & Harkavy, I. (1995). Making the connection: A relationship based on trust. In M. Smith (Ed.), *Service counts: Lessons from the field of service and higher education.* Campus Compact.

Brown University. (1998). *For lives of purpose: A guide to service-learning.* Howard R. Swearer Center for Public Service. Providence, R.I.: Brown University.

Byrne, P. (1995). Paradigms of justice and love. *Conversations: On Jesuit higher education, 7*, 5-17.

Crews, R. J. (1997). *The University of Colorado at Boulder service-learning faculty handbook, 2nd edition.* Boulder, CO: The University of Colorado Office of the Director of Service-Learning.

Cruz, N. (1996). Proposed diversity principles of good practice in combining service and learning. In B. Jacoby (Ed.), *Service-learning in higher education: Concepts and practices.* San Francisco, CA: Jossey-Bass.

Doherty, W. J. (1995). *Soul searching.* New York: Basic Books.

Ehrlich, T. (1996). Foreword. In B. Jacoby (Ed.), *Service-learning in higher education: Concepts and practices.* San Francisco, CA: Jossey-Bass.

Harkavy, I. (1993). University-community partnerships: The University of Pennsylvania and West Philadelphia as a case study. In T. Y. Kupiec (Ed.), *Rethinking tradition: Integrating service with academic study on college campuses* (pp. 121-128). Denver: Education Commission of the States.

Harkavy, I. (1996, August). *Service-learning as a vehicle for revitalization of education institutions and urban communities.* Paper presented to the Education Directorate Miniconvention on Urban Initiatives: In Partnership with Education. American Psychological Association Annual Meeting, Toronto, Canada.

Harkavy, I., & Puckett, J. L. (1994). Lessons from the Hull House for the contemporary urban university. *Social Service Review, 68*, 299-321.

Hondagneu-Sotelo, P., & Raskoff, S. (1994). Community service-learning: Promises and problems. *Teaching Sociology, 22*, 248-254.

Howard, J. (1993). Community service-learning in the curriculum. In J. Howard (Ed.), *Praxis I: A faculty casebook on community service-learning* (pp. 3-12). Ann Arbor, MI: Office of Community Service Learning Press.

Kenny, M. E., & Comilang, K. (1997, August). Training for interprofessional collaboration. In M. Walsh & M. E. Kenny (Chairs), *Opportunities for counseling psychology: Interprofessional collaboration for children and families.* Symposium conducted at the 105th annual convention of the American Psychological Association, Chicago, IL.

Knitzer, J. (1993). Children's mental health policy: Challenging the future. *Journal of Emotional and Behavioral Disorders, 1*, 8-16.

Lerner, R. M. (1995). *America's youth in crisis: Challenges and options for programs and policies.* Thousand Oaks, CA: Sage.

Lerner, R. M. (1997). *Strategic plan.* Chestnut Hill, MA: Boston College. Center for Child, Family, and Community Partnerships.

Lerner R. M., Ostrom, C. W., Miller, J. R., Votruba, J. C., von Eye, A., Hoopfer, L. C., Terry, P. A., Taylor, C. S., Villarruel, F. A., & McKinney, M. H. (1996). Training applied developmental scientists for community outreach: The Michigan State University model of integrating science and outreach for children, youth, and families. In C. B. Fisher, J. P. Murray, & I. E. Sigel (Eds.), *Applied developmental science: Graduate training for diverse disciplines and educational settings.* (pp. 163-188). Norwood, NJ: Ablex Publishing Corporation.

LeSourd, S. J. (1997). Community service in a multicultural nation. *Theory into Practice, 36,* 157-163.

McCall, R. B. (1996). The concept and practice of education, research, and public service in university psychology departments. *American Psychologist, 51,* 379-388.

Maybach, C. W. (1996). Investigating urban community needs: Service-learning from a social justice perspective. *Education and Urban Society, 28,* 224-236.

Noddings, N. (1984). *Caring: A feminine approach to ethics and moral education.* Berkeley: University of California Press.

Ostrom, C. W., Lerner, R, M., & Freel, M. A. (1995). Building the capacity of youth and families through university-community collaborations: The development-in-context evaluation (DICE) model. *Journal of Adolescent Research, 10,* 427-448.

Porter, J. R., & Schwartz, L. B. (1993). Experiential service-based learning: An integrated HIV/AIDS education model for college campuses. *Teaching Sociology, 21,* 409-415.

Rude, S. S., Weissberg, M., & Gazda, G. M. (1988). Looking to the future: Themes from the third national conference for counseling psychology. *The Counseling Psychologist, 16,* 423-430.

Sheckley, B. G., & Keeton, M. T. (1997). Service-learning: A theoretical model. In J. Schine (Ed.), *Service-learning: Ninety-sixth yearbook of the national society for the study of education* (pp. 32-55). Chicago, IL: The University of Chicago Press.

Schine, J. (1997). Looking ahead: Issues and challenges. In J. Schine (Ed.), *Service-learning: Ninety-sixth yearbook of the national society for the study of education* (pp. 186-199). Chicago, IL: The University of Chicago Press.

Serow, R. C. (1997). Research and evaluation on service-learning: The case for holistic assessment. In A. Waterman (Ed.), *Service-learning: Applications from the research* (pp. 13-24). Mahwah, NJ: Lawrence Erlbaum Associates.

Sparks, E. (1998). *Description: Educational Advocacy Program at Brighton High School.* Unpublished manuscript, Boston College.

Stanford University. Haas Center for Public Service. (1998). *About the Haas Center: Mission statement.*

Walsh, M. E., B. Kenny, M. E., & Andersson D. (1998, August). Prevention training in a public setting. In M. Waldo (Chair), *Prevention in counseling psychology.* Symposium conducted at the 106th annual convention of the American Psychological Association, San Francisco, CA.

Walsh, M., Kenny, M. E., & Brabeck, M. M. (1998, August). Preparing counseling psychologists with a focus on prevention. In J. L. Romano & M. Waldo (Chairs), *Prevention training in counseling psychology programs: Preventing violence, racism, and neglect.* Symposium conducted at the 106th annual convention of the American Psychological Association, San Francisco, CA.

Ward, J. V. (1997). Encouraging cultural competence in service-learning practice. In J. Schine (Ed.), *Service-learning: Ninety-sixth yearbook of the National Society for the Study of Education* (pp. 136-148). Chicago, IL: The University of Chicago Press.

Waterman, A. S. (1997). An overview of service-learning and the role of research and evaluation in service-learning programs. In A. Waterman (Ed.), *Service-learning: Applications from the research* (pp. 1-12). Mahwah, NJ: Lawrence Erlbaum Associates.

Wutzdorff, A. J., & Giles Jr., D. E. (1997). Service-learning in higher education. In J. Schine (Ed.), *Service-learning: Ninety-sixth yearbook of the national society for the study of education* (pp. 105-117). Chicago, IL: The University of Chicago Press.

11 ACTION LEARNING IN LEADERSHIP FOR CHANGE: Partnership, Pedagogy, and Projects for Responsible Management Development

Sandra A. Waddock
Eve Spangler
Boston College

"What we have to learn to do, we learn by doing."
Aristotle, *Nichomachean Ethics*
"If you want to *know* this, you must *do* this."
Ken Wilber, *The Eye of Spirit*, p. 90

A number of years ago several sociology and management faculty at Boston College came together to develop a joint executive education program with two main objectives: to promote social responsibility in business and to employ an action-learning pedagogy appropriate to adult, work-based learning. The integration of these two objectives occurred primarily through major projects undertaken by participants within their employing organizations. These projects had to define (when necessary), develop, and implement business practices that optimized both conventional economic returns and social returns for at least one of the sponsoring organization's many stakeholders: employees, customers, suppliers, neighbors, or the environment. The program was initially called Leadership for the Common Good and later re-named Leadership for Change (LC).

Leadership for Change represents a radically new approach to management development. For example:

- LC differs from conventional university-based programs in requiring extensive action learning projects as the primary learning methodology.

- LC differs from workshop formats in continuing over an 11 month cycle, structuring alternating periods of new learning, application, reflection-debriefing, interlaced with employment-based practice and reflection.

- LC differs from conventional leadership development programs in requiring the creation of partnerships at many different levels that inform the pedagogical practice in the classroom and in the workplace.

- Perhaps most importantly, it differs from conventional social change management programs in advocating for a very particular kind of social change, namely a move toward a more socially responsible form of business practice, what we term multiple bottom lines (i.e., financial and social), or, alternatively, stakeholder (rather than shareholder) capitalism.

In its design and implementation, LC's approach constitutes a form of outreach to business enterprises. The university context becomes a place to design, develop, assess, and strengthen innovative business initiatives. Further, the business community and academics become partners in program design, development, and implementation.

This chapter describes the history of Leadership for Change along three primary dimensions: partnership, pedagogy, and projects. These dimensions capture the ways in which the LC program differs from both traditional management education and management development programs. We also highlight the ways in which the LC can be considered a form of outreach scholarship that is focused on developing action-oriented managers promoting responsible business behavior.

BACKGROUND

The word "manage" derives from the Latin *mano*, to handle, an inherently active concept. In contrast to disciplines that primarily use a lecture format to convey information, management education offers students an array of more active pedagogies. These pedagogies can include, for example, business case studies (pioneered by the Harvard Business School), designed to present "real world" problems to students. Other popular teaching techniques include simulations, experiential exercises, and group projects as well as lectures. Many of these activities can typically be found in at least some courses in a conventional management curriculum.

Despite this array of pedagogical techniques, the International Association for Management Education (formerly the American Assembly of Collegiate Schools of

Business), which is the accrediting body for management schools, recently strongly criticized management faculty for lack of effective pedagogies, particularly focused on real-world business contact. AACSB called for less resistance to change, combined with faster adoption of new technologies and teaching methodologies, and more cross-disciplinary integration in place of a narrow and linear disciplinary focus (AACSB, 1996). LC's multi-disciplinary, partnership-based emphasis on action learning and reflective practice for responsible business behavior represents one effort to overcome these criticisms.

The Leadership for Change Program (which began approximately at the same time as—albeit independently of—other outreach scholarship efforts at Boston College described elsewhere in this volume) is a unique blend of management development and management education. Offered jointly by faculty in the Carroll School of Management and Sociology Department, LC grants twelve graduate-level credits to participants upon successful completion. Blending the hands-on and action-oriented approach necessary to engage adult learners (Knowles, 1983) with action learning even in the classroom (Raelin, 1997), LC operates through a sequence of six Friday-Saturday modules, monthly facilitated learning groups, methodological workshops, and an intensive action-learning project.

Given the "outreach" character of the LC program, it is no accident that three of the LC faculty became members of the Faculty Advisory Committee (FAC) at the Center for Child, Family, and Community Partnerships (CCFCP) (see Lerner, Chapter 3; Kenny, Chapter 10) early on in its existence. To some degree, these linkages reflect areas of substantive overlap, for example, as in the case of school-to-work projects promoted both by local schools and by area employers. More importantly, however, these linkages also represent an attempt by faculty committed to outreach scholarship to work together to create not only a mosaic of individual projects but also a university-wide recognition of and commitment to outreach scholarship (Kenny, Chapter 10).

Outreach scholarship in the LC program is characterized by the development of research and action programs that are of immediate service to some group of end users in the community, that *at the same time* are of substantial intellectual interest, and that also provide significant opportunities for participants to learn, particularly in the realm of linking theory with practice. In the past, universities have been clear about rewarding research that demonstrates qualities of intellectual reach and training opportunities, but less consistent in rewarding research that is of service to the community. Through an examination of our experiences in LC, we will explore below the reasons why outreach scholarship—and outreach in general—rests somewhat uneasily in its university home.

A brief description of the LC program will help set the context. Even in its origin, LC differs from traditional management development activities. About five years prior to this writing, a creative and entrepreneurial graduate student armed with a vision of social change for business organizations drew together a group of sociologists and management faculty. This group began a series of discussions about their shared interests in understanding the broad role that change agents play in business as it relates to society. The program originated in the context of a joint

MBA/Ph.D. in sociology program that had been in marginalized existence in a traditionally discipline-based academic institution. Faculty typically communicated with each other collegially but seldom intellectually across disciplinary lines.

Conceived as a multi-dimensional partnership in which program participants would engage in employer-sponsored action learning projects, LC is a modular program. LC meets on a once monthly Friday-Saturday schedule for five months, with a sixth module reserved for project presentations at the end of the eleven-month sequence (and, more recently, a number of shorter workshops during the project period). Additionally, LC organizes participants into six or seven member Facilitated Learning Groups that meet monthly with faculty facilitators to discuss readings, assignments, work-related issues relevant to course materials, and, particularly, action learning projects developed by participants during the second half of the program. The action learning projects are work-based change efforts (Revans, 1983; Raelin, 1997) that attempt to integrate both bottom-line gains to the employer with some sort of social (or common good) benefit. Such projects have explicit, work-related consequences for participants, who put themselves at risk in undertaking sometimes-significant projects frequently outside their traditional domain of responsibility.

BOTH/AND LOGIC FOR POSITIVE SOCIAL OUTCOMES

Faculty began the LC program with recognition that neither business, organizational, community, family, nor individual problems come packaged neatly in disciplinary boxes (see Sherman, Chapter 12; Walsh, Chapter 6). We also had a belief that it was possible, indeed necessary, for companies to focus not only on the bottom line in a financial sense, but also on other types of impacts related to stakeholders. In taking this perspective, we believed we could produce a program that focused on the both/and of profitability and beneficial results from operating responsibly with respect to key stakeholders (Freeman, 1984), without necessarily imposing "our" values on participants.

The LC program's rationale is also partly based on an effort to overcome what one observer has called the "Cartesian split" (Overton, 1998) and others have termed an either/or logic (Collins and Porras, 1995). This logic tends to cause us to separate problems, issues, and situations into their smallest logical components, generating a process of atomization that results in a fragmented approach to problem solving, disciplinary specialization that grows ever stronger, and problems communicating across disciplinary lines (Capra, 1997, 1984; Stacey, 1991, 1992). In this rather narrow either/or framing, doing well (financially) seems at odds with doing "good" in the social sense.

This atomized approach is also highly evident in the specialization of disciplines, in the lack of cross-fertilization of disciplines across organizations and society, and in what re-engineering gurus Hammer and Champy (1993) termed the "stovepipes" by which organizations are structured. It is particularly reflected in the "common wisdom" that one must either serve the bottom line (maximizing shareholder wealth, in the economist's terminology) *or* the needs of stakeholders and society. Indeed, the prevalence of this atomization is the very reason why numerous initiatives to integrate organizations across functions have emerged in recent years.

Specialization in professions today resembles all the king's horses and all the king's men tackling the puzzle created by the fragments of Humpty Dumpty's broken body. Professionals, be they managers, management consultants, health care providers, teachers, social workers, or lawyers, are tackling problems, such as improving or reforming schools, making communities healthy, or creating models of sustainable business development, with only some of the knowledge needed to solve the problems. In business organizations, despite some movement toward project-based teams and cross-functional integration, units are still predominantly specialized into professional groupings, such as marketing, sales, production, accounting, finance, and operations.

Despite the fragmentation into professional specialties, professionals and managers are expected to somehow put their—and only their—pieces of Humpty Dumpty back together again. Further, they are to accomplish this task without really understanding what Humpty looked like in the first place, or what the other professions can do to make him whole again. Clearly, this model does not work. In addition to their traditional areas of expertise, professionals must be able to see society holistically, through lenses capable of integrating multiple perspectives simultaneously. And, by extension, this new holistic approach must begin in professional education programs.

Despite the need for cross-disciplinary integration, the particular and unique insights of each discipline also need to be maintained if adequate problem solving is to take place. In the conundrum of the need for both specialization *and* holistic approaches (Senge, 1990), however, lies an opportunity to develop new forms of management education. This new approach involves working across disciplines, on multiple levels of analysis, on holistic participant-generated projects that benefit both the employing organization and the communities in which businesses operate (what program faculty call the common good). LC is an attempt to build just such a program.

Our project can be understood as one of numerous attempts by management practitioners, consultants, and scholars to re-integrate disciplines in a range of ways over the past decade. Ironically, these approaches also re-integrate a values-basis into management thinking almost without recognizing what is happening. Such efforts include re-engineering models (Hammer & Champy, 1993); total quality improvement initiatives (e.g., Deming, 1982; Fisher & Torbert, 1995); learning organizations (Senge, 1990); and numerous approaches to strategic management and visionary organizations (e.g., Collins & Porras, 1995; Hamel & Prahalad, 1994; c.f., Mintzberg, 1994; see also Senge, 1990). Liedtka (1998) demonstrates the common values on which such initiatives are based. These management techniques are generally aimed at realigning organizations so that they can deal more holistically with problems and processes toward a common end. What is striking about these recent integrative efforts is that they incorporate a "both/and" logic by exploring ways in which organizations can simultaneously do well and do good (e.g., Anderson, 1997; Liedtka, 1998; Raiborn & Payne, 1996; Waddock & Graves, 1997a, b). LC also attempted this integration in the partnerships that developed and sustained it, in the pedagogy that is at its core, and in the practice that is fosters.

But LC also creates a conundrum. Though program faculty believe it to be a good idea, actually launching the program and sustaining it, never mind replicating it, have proved difficult at best. The answer to this conundrum may lie in the complexities of integrating multiple partners, a pedagogy that links theory and practice, and working and reflecting on real-life projects as primary learning vehicles. As we discuss each of the distinctive features of the LC program below, we will therefore also be discussing the immense obstacles and on-going issues encountered by a project that can be described accurately as one dedicated to producing win-win scenarios for all.

PARTNERSHIP

One way to conceive of LC is as a series of partnerships operating at multiple levels of action.

Management-Sociology

As noted above, the program began as a collaboration between two units within the university: the Carroll School of Management and the Sociology Department. Although faculty in the university are friendly and collegial, there is rarely opportunity for interaction on program or research activities. The particular possibility of LC grew out of a joint MBA/Ph.D. in Sociology program that had been developed and led a marginal existence within the university for about ten years prior to the arrival of a graduate student with a vision. The graduate student in this joint program drew together faculty from both units into a series of meetings to discuss ways of working together. Initially intrigued by the possibilities, faculty members began discussing common interests and possible forms of collaboration. Many of the early conversations seemingly led nowhere, although they did play an important role in helping faculty get to know each other's perspectives. Eventually, after many meetings, the group hit upon an idea that seemed feasible: to create an interdisciplinary management development program that would incorporate both a "multiple bottom lines" approach and an action learning pedagogy. The idea was that business organizations could be *both* profitable and simultaneously socially responsible, in the sense that they treated all stakeholders well. One fundamental goal of the program became to develop an approach that would engage practicing managers in change efforts to incorporate this "both/and" logic into their day-to-day activities.

Despite differences in disciplinary orientation, rank and status within their respective fields, and perspectives (i.e., the sociology faculty tended toward Marxist analysis while the management faculty tended to favor capitalism, albeit with a significant social orientation), the group moved forward in a trusting and reasonably open communication process to develop the program's structure. Because most of the sociologists in the group were both left of center and politically engaged in a variety of community- and union-based projects, they were drawn to LC as an experiment in making progressive social changes from *within* corporations. For business faculty with an active consulting and scholarly life inside corporations, LC offered the possibility of capturing whole organizations in the context of a larger effort to create a socially responsible economy. The program was thus grounded in the combined passions of the founding faculty, rather than in market demand for such a program, and this history, in turn, was significant in shaping the program's on-going struggles to attract students. The developmental process and the program itself also served as a definite source of community for faculty hungry for colleagues with shared passions and interests.

Originally called Leadership for the Common Good, the program continues to reflect the faculty's general concerns with both leadership development and the need to move businesses toward more positive societal outcomes and stakeholder relationships. Leadership for Change was thus focused on the frontier between the business community and the university. Traditionally, this frontier is heavily trafficked in the area of product development, but is much less frequented on issues of corporate social responsibility. In the domain of outreach scholarship, Leadership for Change is also distinctive, because it focuses less on issues of distribution or access to social services than it does on re-organizing production along more socially responsible lines.

LC came into being about two and a half years after initial conversations with a small cohort of middle-level managers. Now renamed Leadership for Change (LC) to reflect the "market's" apparent inability to relate to the term "common good," the program clearly broke many of the university's traditional written and unwritten rules. To succeed, this project required on-going collaboration between sociology and management faculty whose disciplines have very different measures of success. Sociology is a "book" discipline, while management faculty were more likely to be rewarded for writing a series of articles. Arts and sciences faculty are paid on a much lower scale than management faculty in a university where the sharing of pay information is vigorously discouraged.

Program and University

Two major divisions of the university—the College of Arts and Sciences and the Carroll School of Management—were visionary enough to welcome the cross-school program into the offerings of the university. Major obstacles were dispatched with varying degrees of difficulty. For example, the Educational Policy Committee of the Carroll School of Management proved willing to grant 12 graduate level course credits to the program as presented once all departments had been visited and apprised of the nature and content of the program.

However, in many ways, large and small, the LC program was "out of sync" with its university host. For example, in a fairly hierarchical and authoritarian university with no faculty senate and no sustained representation of faculty in university governance, the LC program is governed by the community as whole (through monthly "heart and soul" meetings). Faculty, business partners (see below), and staff all have an equal voice in program development in these meetings (see Walsh, Chapter 6). Even in small ways, the program faced initial difficulties in fitting into the university. For example, during the first two years of classes, the program began in January, putting its calendar totally out of line with the University's fiscal year and creating seemingly endless bureaucratic problems. Similarly, operations began during a period when the University was systematizing its computer based operations (for payroll, material acquisition, student billing, and so forth) and "glitches" in computer operations created overwhelming problems for the part-time administrative staff.

Faculty-Business Partners

Recognizing that business interests needed significant representation in both the design and delivery of the program (as well as in meeting some of the AACSB's criticisms of management education), faculty collaborated extensively with a number of business partners from the program's inception. Business partners, most of who are consultants with extensive experience, are truly *partners*, not just advisors as is more typical in such program development. Business partners play crucial roles in developing and delivering curriculum, program orientation, marketing and strategic focus. They also teach rather extensively in the program. Business partners are fully represented in the heart and soul committee, which provides program oversight.

As operating practice for university programs, it is quite unusual to have such involvement by individuals who would be considered "outsiders" in most universities. The business partners' involvement represents a determined effort to ensure that real business needs and interests are present in the program. Potential differences of opinions, values, and styles between faculty and business partners have remained muted partly because many of the business partners have extensive university teaching and because interests in the program content are shared. Further, and importantly, the business partners were interested in the program primarily for its own sake and not as a marketing tool for their practices as consultants. Had any of these factors been otherwise, it is likely that the collaboration between the university faculty and the business partners would have been much harder to achieve.

Faculty-Participant

The LC program also operates as a partnership between participants (which is what they are called, mainly because they are working adults with their own relatively extensive experience and working backgrounds) and faculty/business partners. Together, faculty[1] and participants actively involve themselves with the work-related dilemmas of participants as they attempt to engage in organizational change efforts for their projects, during in-class exercises, in facilitated learning groups, and through mentoring/coaching processes built into the program.

Although the program grants graduate credit (applicable in both management and sociology), which means there are significant written and project-based assignments, participants need to be treated not as students but rather as adult learners (see Torbert, Chapter 5; Cochran-Smith, et al., Chapter 8). Participants average 35-38 years of age and generally hold middle-level management positions in a wide range of organizations. Program designers recognized that such individuals bring a great deal of knowledge and capability with them into the program, which needs to be tapped not only in class-based experiences, but also as the primary basis for their project. Co-learning, between participants and faculty (including business partners) is common in sessions where participants work in small groups struggling to understand the relevance of readings and theories to specific work based issues. In this model, faculty frequently find themselves learning almost as much as the participants.

Nevertheless, tensions remain both within the program and between the faculty and participants. These tensions tend to focus on the extent to which traditional academic requirements (extensive reading, and long narrative papers about project development and implementation) should be a part of the program's demands and expectations.

Program-Employer Partnership

There is a deliberate effort to create a program-employer (sponsor) partnership as well. Each participant is required to have a sponsor within his/her employing organization who approves and supports the action learning project. Sponsors are invited to attend part of the orientation session as well as final project presentations. Occasional networking events, which present new and emerging ideas, attempt to engage and re-inspire sponsors, participants, and program alumni alike. The generosity of sponsors towards their staff has proven to be both a great boon and a source of weakness. Many sponsors encourage their staff to participate without being much engaged in the process of project selection and development. Occasionally, sponsors attempt to exert too much "business" influence on projects, without as much regard for the "social bottom line" as is needed to satisfy faculty concerns that the both/and thinking be incorporated into the project. In the five-year history of classes, only three sponsors have deliberately used the program as a management development tool, picking participants who were being groomed for promotion. Many participants have, however, received promotions at least partially as a result of their participation in the LC program.

Participant-Participant-Faculty Partnership

Each participant joins a facilitated learning team consisting of six or seven other participants and a faculty/partner facilitator. The learning team meets monthly throughout the 11-month program. In these learning teams participants discuss issues of project development and implementation, application of readings and theories to work situations, and intellectual issues related to course content. Most team members come to rely upon each other for support and encouragement, not only for course-related issues, but also for issues relating to work and even personal life, thus creating peer-networks of like-minded individuals working on similar problems of leadership and change.

Partnership as A Way of Program Development

Most academics are quite unused to working collaboratively with outsiders to develop and deliver programs. Taking the advice of individuals without the same background and academic status comes hard, but is necessary to meet the AACSB's criticism that faculty are out of touch with issues in the real world. Being collaborators requires not always being the expert and not always having the faculty's views dominate the conversation. Indeed, there is significant evidence within the program of business partners' influence on curriculum content. Additionally, changes are made to scheduling, program content, and design, as a result of extensive feedback from participants. It turns out that such mutual engagement with outside business partners, sponsors, and participants, is a rewarding and stimulating way to structure rigorous learning in a setting that does not assume that the faculty are experts with all the answers, as will be discussed in the next section on pedagogy.

PEDAGOGY

Partnership at the multiple levels described above makes action learning possible. Only with a rather dramatic shift away from lecture and even case-based pedagogy does the type of co-learning embodied in the LC program become feasible. Kolb and Fry (1975) suggest that a complete learning cycle requires processes of experience, feedback, reflection, and active experimentation. Knowles (1980) suggests that adult learning (which he terms androgogy) works best when it is learner-designed and directed, that is, self-directed. In a recent advance, Raelin (1997) suggests that work-based learning, the core of the LC program, has both explicit and tacit dimensions

(Nonaka, 1994) and requires theory-based conceptualization and experimentation, and practice-based results and experience.

The following sections will illustrate the ways in which the LC program exemplifies this work-based learning model and creates a forum for outreach scholarship in management education. LC accomplishes this task by shifting pedagogy away from lecture and memorization toward more androgogical techniques. Action-learning is consistent with both action inquiry (Fisher & Torbert, 1995) and the co-learning, problem-driven, reflective and active orientation of outreach scholarship described elsewhere in this volume. After a brief description of the action-learning orientation of the LC program, Raelin's four-part model will be used to frame the discussion.

Action Learning for Outreach

Action that is both ethical (doing the right thing) and efficient (productive for the organization—or doing things right) is at the heart of leading change as we define it. As the quote from Aristotle at the outset of this article highlights, we believe that action, *doing* in the real world, is a sound basis for the development of effective managerial leadership skills (see also Bilimoria, 1998). But ethical and efficient action is not only a matter of activity, that is calories burned and a pro-active stance announced. As Raelin (1997) points out, conceptualization, reflection, experimentation and experience must shape action if it is to be both ethical and efficient. The program provides extensive opportunities to experience all four aspects of learning and to simultaneously develop a decided spirit of community among participants.

Specifically, participants undertake a major action-learning project at the workplace, but typically outside their current area of responsibility, where substantial risks and responsibilities are present in real time. Action learning projects are also expected to combine both bottom-line benefits to the employer and some sort of social "good" to reflect the common good program orientation. For example, projects have involved a recycling initiative designed to enhance revenues while also improving environmental concerns, or a welfare-to-work program aimed at enhancing employee retention while providing jobs to the disadvantaged.

Conceptualization: Linking Theory and Practice

An old saying goes, "there is nothing as useful as a good theory." In the LC program, theory and conceptualization is a critical basis for leadership practice. Much to the chagrin of some participants, the program (partly because it is offered for graduate credit) requires relatively extensive prior reading and preparation for each of the first five modules, development of a project proposal, and significant writing assignments after each module. All of this work is in addition to the action learning project, which is captured in an extensive written report and presented formally at the end of the program.

In the readings, participants are exposed to ideas and theories at each of the four levels of analysis with which the program deals (individual, group, organizational, and societal). As Raelin (1997) points out, readings provide a common language, common analytic tools and principles, and new approaches to problems. Further, participants keep journals in which they reflect on their readings, develop their insights, and share (mostly with themselves) their concerns. During in-class sessions, readings are discussed in small group and plenary formats, and again in the facilitated learning groups, which meet between the learning modules. Arguably, however, these reflections would bear little fruit in terms of leadership or change agent development if they were not directly linked to experimentation and experience.

Thus, the heart of conceptualization as it applies to the LC program is the strenuous effort to link theory and practice, through experimentation both at work and through the many in-class exercises, role plays, and activities that generate "in the moment" reflection on actions and words. Not only do such exercises create situations in which the ideas from the readings are put to immediate use and drawn upon during de-briefings, but participants are also expected to share their vulnerabilities and concerns about moving their ideas forward into action in their work settings. As they come to know each other, they also learn how others think, and, as well, are better able to recognize the need for the common language that theory provides for a deeper understanding of their experiences, both in the classroom and at work, more richly (see Torbert, Chapter 9 for discussion of similar communities of practice).

Experimentation

Raelin (1997) argues that experimentation is generally a tacit form of learning. When experiments in class can be linked to concepts read and used to highlight the power of the concepts and illuminate what might otherwise be considered intractable problems at one of the levels, participants gain insights they might not otherwise gain. For example, during the organizational module, they read a good deal about the importance of organizational vision; during the module itself, they engage in a visioning exercise that involves "articulating" what an ideal organization would be (in small groups) by doing a "creative drawing." Not only does this mini-experiment help make explicit values and ideas that might otherwise be tacit (especially when they explain their drawings to the whole class), but it also shows the power of integrating the concepts into practices that they can adopt with their own work groups after class. Following an adult learning pedagogy, most class sessions of LC are active and experimental in nature. Although some cases and discussions are used, in many sessions participants are divided into small groups (differing in composition depending on the purpose of the exercise or experiment) to apply theory readings or class discussion to themselves, their work situation, or their organization. Then they report discussions back to the class for further reflection on what was learned.

For instance, one theory that is used extensively in the program is action inquiry, a way of generating action through framing, advocating, illustrating, and inquiring (e.g., Fisher & Torbert, 1995). During class sessions, participants frequently experiment with techniques of action inquiry as a way of gaining practice with these techniques so they can bring them into their work settings successfully. Additionally, this intensive work combining small groups and the plenary helps to create a sense of community among participants and faculty, a growing shared vision and experience, and a common focus for the class as a whole. Similar experiments take place in the facilitated learning groups, with mentors/coaches, and on the job, as the participants gain confidence in their own use of learned concepts. It is the link to the work setting, especially through the action learning project, where experience is engaged.

Experience

Experience is generally considered to be the best of all teachers. The LC program philosophy, however, suggests that learning from experiences can be improved when such experiences are flanked by theorizing and conceptualizing beforehand, and by reflection afterward. As discussed above, in-class experiments provide an opportunity to practice new ideas and behaviors in relatively risk-free settings. The action learning project, as well as actual on-the-job experiences that are illuminated by current readings provide experiences that reinforce the value of reflective action, in settings that carry more risk because of their potential job-related consequences (Raelin, 1997).

Action learning projects are developed by the participant with the input and help of the sponsor at work, the facilitated learning group, and various program faculty. Rather than being traditional research papers, the projects require participants to begin some new activity, action, facilitation, or process in the work environment. Because the action learning project is based in the work setting, it has characteristics that make it important to the participant's job, to his or her development as a leader and, therefore, to his or her status within the employing organization. Ethical dilemmas, political realities, organizational obstacles, personality conflicts, not to mention power differentials, among other organizational facts of life are encountered along the way and must be worked through in a successful project implementation.[2]

Such projects thus have consequences (sometimes significant) for participant and organization, particularly because many participants find themselves taking on projects for which they have no official organizational authority. Instead, most participants initiate an idea that gets buy-in from superiors and, through their actions and reflections, push the idea forward. Further, many projects are quite incomplete when they are formally presented at the time of the program's end. For example, one participant designed a project to foster better understanding of organizational competencies in the context of clarifying and implementing an organizational mission statement. This project not only resulted in a significant promotion for her, but also is still expanding three years after its initial phase. Another project began as an idea that employee training programs should be expanded throughout a credit union operation and has now exploded into an extensive, employee-directed, company-wide program offering more than 50 courses per year (and a promotion to vice president for the participant).

Reflection

Reflection on what has occurred in the classroom, on readings, on observations at work (and other settings), in learning groups, and through the action learning projects is an essential element of LC. Numerous opportunities are provided for reflective practice (Schön, 1983). These opportunities help participants overcome and understand the barriers they face in their organizations (c.f., Argyris, 1993). Reflection occurs through journalizing, class-based activities in which participants share various experiences, discussions in learning groups, and in papers associated with each of the modules as well as the project. Each participant is also associated with one faculty member, business partner, or staff member in a coaching or mentoring relationship to provide both support for the activities and learning, and an additional opportunity for reflection.

Raelin (1997) defines reflection as "the ability to uncover and make explicit to oneself what one has planned, observed, or achieved in practice." Thus, reflection explicitly captures what worked and what did not about the participant's changing behavior or actions in the organization. Reflection occurs in class and with coaches, through dialogue in the learning groups, and by writing and thinking about what has happened. A particularly important task is highlighting the assumptions behind specific actions or reasoning (Argyris, 1993; Senge, 1990). Since one dominant assumption of LC is that reflection *is* essential to learning (Raelin, 1997, citing Bandura, 1986), instilling *habits* of reflection into participants is a key component of the program.

Practice: Participants Roles

It must now be clear from the foregoing that learning in the LC program is interactive, problem-driven, and critical in its reflection on the system. Learning outcomes, especially the project, are open-ended, dialogic, and on going, rather than finite. Additionally, the role of the faculty member (and the business partner acting as a faculty colleague) shifts dramatically away from lecturer in this model toward a model of co-learner, facilitator and guide, and problem clarifier or questioner. This role contrasts sharply with that of the expert who drives learning through maintaining the stance that the academic knows best and can ask (and answer) all the appropriate questions. To be successful in this model of learning, however, participants need to actively exercise their own "voice" rather than assuming the role of passive recipient of knowledge (see Sherman, Chapter 12).

INTERACTION: FACULTY AS LEARNERS

The processes of collaborative learning are valuable in their own right. Through the work of dialogue, interaction, and the design of solutions, as well as the longer-term processes involved in implementing jointly constructed solutions, a community of practice is created in which innovation, risk, and cooperation can flourish. Working through problems, which are frequently as new to the faculty member as they are to participants, and doing so *with* "students" calls for faculty who can let go of the expert model and become co-learners. The faculty member has to be open to learning from participants as well as from practiced professionals working in the field. The faculty member cannot assume that he or she has all the answers, but rather has to be embedded to some extent in the action of the moment, learning and dialoguing with, both students and community members. A sense of mutuality and a willingness to let go of status and power differentials is essential to this form of teaching. This type of learning is less focused, more complex, messier, more applied than book learning. Significantly, it does much more closely mirror what goes on in real-world practice than does the typical classroom experience.

As LC participants, working in their organizations, define a work-related project meaningful to that individual's job, they begin to explicitly apply what has been learned in the classroom. This learning process is supported throughout in many ways: peer advisement through a regularly-scheduled learning group meeting; facilitation at the group meetings; irregularly scheduled conversations with faculty member or business partners serving in the capacity of learning coach, counselor, and consultant; and informal interactions with alumni when needed. In these interactions, faculty members frequently learn as much as the participant/students do, particularly when glitches are encountered or new ways of approaching the situation need to be developed on the spot.

Co-Learning

The approach of faculty in the university shifts with the collaborative model of LC. Designs for curriculum, teaching approaches, field assignments, and research, in this model, are multiple-sided polygons, with input, decision-making capacity, and voice received iteratively from many sources. LC does not provide the square-boxed and regular solutions that might otherwise be provided by faculty experts. The faculty expert model suggests that the answers can be designed by the expert sitting at a desk in the university, no matter what the challenge: a learning experience, a field assignment like the action learning project, curriculum content, or a work-based project. This design can then be "placed" appropriately, in the classroom, in the field, or in the community, with little or no input from anyone but the faculty. Co-learning requires a very different model. No longer the sole experts with all the knowledge, faculty working in the co-learning mode discuss the needs and interests, ideas and input of participants, their sponsoring organizations, as well as other faculty and business partners.

This co-learning model is inherently interdisciplinary in nature, with a fundamental premise that one discipline alone cannot resolve problems of the whole and that input is needed from others whose specialties may be different. Thus, co-learning models move away from individual problem solving towards a model of bringing together a team of individuals who bring different expertise to bear (see Sherman, Chapter 12, Table 12.1).

Community Spirit

Faculty and business partners walk a tightrope in the LC classroom, where they must model the very behaviors of reflective practice they hope to generate among participants. Giving and receiving feedback is built into the program and into many of the exercises and simulations. Additionally, the sharing that occurs through the experimentation, both from the faculty/business partners and participants, further helps to generate the spirit of community, trust, and even (secular) spirituality that pervades the program.

Evidence of this spirit, generated by creating a "safe space" for participants to be vulnerable and to share what they might not otherwise be able to share about their work, about balancing work and family, and about themselves, exists throughout the program. It is particularly poignant during the fifth content-oriented module, held as participants begin their projects and experience a gap of several months before meeting again. Invariably, there is a session in which participants share what participation in the program has meant to them and equally invariably, there is a surprising amount of emotion expressed, as participants recognize their feelings of loss and separation as they go on to projects. Although they will continue to meet in learning groups, as in the early days of the program, they would not be together as a plenary until the final presentations. Recognizing the importance of the community and depth of this feeling of loss, new shorter sessions have gradually been added during the intervening months, while the projects are under way that brings the whole community together again.

Another aspect of community is almost as important as that created in the classroom. As alluded to briefly above, for many faculty who joined the initiative, LC represented a safe space in which to share ideas about what the common good meant, to explore new and interactive pedagogies, to work closely with other faculty on a long-term common project. In short, the LC program represented a home within the larger institution where reasonably like-minded individuals could work toward what they (we) viewed as a common, and perhaps "higher," purpose that had some potential to make a real difference in the world. Particularly for faculty who were somewhat alienated from the current model of management within the institution (as was one of the authors), LC represented a source of community and inspiration that provided fertile ground for personal growth and development.

This strong sense of community internal to the program also makes "entry" for new faculty, as the other author of this paper experienced, lengthy at best. Community norms developed around program development, and time commitment. Intensive knowledge of program spirit and norms are needed, the "heart and soul" community agrees, before someone can (or should be) allowed to teach in the program. Thus in an ironic way, joining the community requires an up-front commitment to learn about the program before any other type of reward (e.g., payment for teaching) can be garnered.

Reflection on the System

Critically important, co-learning with students requires significant reflection (e.g., Schön, 1983; Raelin, 1997) on the part of not only the participant, but also the faculty member and partners teaching in the program. Memorization of textbook theory simply is insufficient in complex settings where there is an on-going and iterative dialogic process that defines learning as well as practice, where faculty, participants, business partners, and sponsors *together* in many respects define the learning and action plans. In a more traditional model, students and faculty do reflect on what they are learning and how to make their learning and their practice better. This reflection, however, generally occurs within the context of classroom and what is appropriate knowledge as it is defined by the faculty member serving as expert.

Participants and faculty in LC occasionally find themselves questioning not only whether they are doing well (the traditional "efficiency" and "efficacy" questions), but also whether they are, in fact, doing the right thing (the ethics question). Exploration of the fundamental assumptions about the system under study: What is being done? Why is it being done? How can it be done differently? Why are conditions as they are? What should be we be doing? . . . all are appropriate and recurring questions that are raised in reflective practice. Thus the reflective practice of LC fundamentally questions the system that currently exists, placing participants and faculty in the role of critics working for change from within the system.

PROBLEM-DRIVEN PROJECTS

Projects are at the core of the LC learning experience. Rather than being designed from theory and based on the interests of faculty as they are expressed through assigned readings, projects in the LC program are generated by the problems that participants face in their daily work lives. This means that projects tend to be unstructured, messy, and without particular shape, especially at the outset, making it imperative that the participant develops a coherent plan around the project. Often participants undertake projects for which they have no official authority (although their sponsors are aware of the nature of their projects) and, almost always, these projects result in significant new visibility and recognition for participants. Developing these projects in a co-learning model requires time management, trust building, conflict resolution, and listening skills for participants with other members of their employing organization as well as with faculty and peers in the program.

Especially for faculty, significant changes are needed to operate in this type of enterprise. For example, faculty participating with active business *partners* at meetings to discuss the development of curriculum, outreach, and program structure may find themselves listening more than speaking and becoming deeply entwined in what we have termed *co-learning* with the business partners. No one perspective provides all the answers in such conversations; each person learns from the others and the end product may be something quite different from anything any one individual envisioned at the start of the conversation. To get to co-learning, however, requires that jargon terms be understood, perspectives shared, assumptions unearthed and examined, and time given over to dialogue and real learning within the meeting so that a "rich" solution can be reached. Making sure that all voices are heard is an important part of the processes associated with ventures where co-learning is occurring.

In one area, however, the faculty does reserve the right to set the agenda. Projects undertaken by the participants must be addressed to some form of dual bottom line. That is, each project has to demonstrate that financial returns to the employer can be enhanced by virtue of acting with an enhanced sense of social responsibility toward other stakeholders: employees, community neighbors, customers, suppliers or the environment. Put differently, projects cannot only be platforms for participants to demonstrate their abilities to enhance corporate performance in conventional economic terms. Every project must have a multiple (at least dual) bottom line as evidenced in the following bottom line characteristic examples of projects addressed to the interests of different stakeholders.

Employees

Perhaps the majority of projects undertaken in the first four years of Leadership for Change are designed to enhance the "bottom line" by making the workplace better for employees and therefore making employees more loyal and productive. The preference for employee/stakeholder projects is easily understood since our participants are themselves employees and can usually secure easy access to other employees in the company.

Several successful projects have been devoted to increasing the educational options available to employees, thereby enhancing their effectiveness at work. One participant, a relatively new sales representative, found that her department had its peak period in October and had never found a satisfactory solution to surges in their workload. Overloading employees did not work and neither did the hiring of office temps, who took too long to train. A neighboring department, however, had a peak workload in December and a lot of down time in October. The participant designed and implemented a cross-training program. She had to face issues of conscience (Was she engaged in a speed-up?) and effectiveness (Were the newer, more flexibly cross-trained employees going to be suitably rewarded?), issues of documentation (Could she document the gains that one might, commonsensically, expect to flow from her project?), issues of research and curriculum development (she prepared much of the cross-training material herself), issues of advocacy (some older employees were doubtful about the project).

Another project focused on the retraining of employees whose jobs were being eliminated during a major company wide re-evaluation and re-organization of staff positions. This project is on-going at this writing but we already know that it will require the participant to confront the enormous fears that spread through any organization undertaking a restructuring effort.

Three participants have developed self-directed learning programs in their organizations, allowing employees to define not only their learning needs, but also to develop and deliver the courses that are called forth from the needs assessment project. The most ambitious of these three projects also involved supervisor/sponsors for each learning project or course so that the real benefits of additional training could be captured by the employer. Again, to meet the dual bottom line requirements, these projects must address issues of enhanced rewards for workers in return for enhanced work from them.

Education and retraining have not been the only topics of employee-focused projects. Many of our participants have been caught up in the major mergers occurring in health care and banking institutions in the Boston area. Several projects have focused on clarifying questions of institutional mission and institutional governance following mergers. One sought to expand representation on newly formed clinical boards of directors in a health care agency. Another restructured the whole communications process that was used to announce a post-merger company-wide job redefinition, informing all affected employees within a two-day period rather than going first to the shareholders and the press.

Community Neighbors

Several projects have sought to meet business needs by making the corporation a better community citizen. Included among these projects are several school-to-work projects that simultaneously enhance the apprenticeship opportunities available to students and the labor supply available to corporations. One project, a welfare-to-work project at a bank, garnered a great deal of region-wide media coverage and is now running its third training cycle. Still other projects have provided insurance company support for small business initiatives in the community.

Clients and Customers

Some projects have sought to cement customer loyalties by providing additional and innovative services to customers. For example, two participants developed a program that allows an insurance company to provide educational and training services to non-profit customers. Specifically, United Cerebral Palsy (UCP) found that it was faced with sharply declining government support and had very little in-house fund raising expertise. Two participants in a team, working for the health insurance provider for UCP, developed a training program to bring UCP staff up to speed on fund-raising skills. A number of other projects among health care providers have expanded services available to patients: for example, providing weekend and evening hours of operation at a clinic, and adding acupuncture, chiropracty and massage to the menu of services available to subscribers.

Environment

Two notably successful projects were in the area of environmental protection. In one, our participant took it as his mission to get his manufacturing company to sign on to the Coalition for Environmentally Responsible Economical principles, with all the internal self-scrutiny and change that is required. He was so dedicated to this project that he changed jobs twice during our yearlong program to seek out an employer who would welcome this process. We have also had participants from the public sector doing projects designed to enhance interagency cooperation (between Environmental Protection Agency and municipalities and among the various departments within municipal governments) throughout the New England region.

CONCLUSION

Projects that link theory with practice, habits of active reflection, sustained partnership, and responsible business innovation are the hallmarks of the program. It is clear from the foregoing that developing and participating in the program involves engaging the messy complexities and ambiguities associated with collaboration and co-learning, as well as countering traditional mindsets. The greatest unresolved challenge to date is the fact that the projects our participants so painstakingly build are more often ignored than resisted. Many of our participants have won promotions on the strength of leadership qualities they demonstrate while doing their projects. Yet few of the projects that seem to be so well received are lastingly institutionalized once their creators are promoted.

Nevertheless, the rewards are well worth while. The spirit of the program and its participants, created by the experience- and reflection-based activities, by the sharing and vulnerabilities, linger in the sense of community and belonging that engage the participants and the faculty/business partners so intensely during the program. We know at a rather deep level that we are engaged in a common enterprise. That enterprise has to do with the very purpose of the program: creating the common good and simultaneously assuring organizational and individual success in all the traditionally measured ways.

ENDNOTES

[1] When we refer to faculty in the comments below, we include business partners who teach in the program as well.

[2] A successful project implementation, in our definition, shows that real learning has taken place and does not necessarily mean that the project itself is *necessarily* a rousing success in the organization.

REFERENCES

Anderson, Carl (1997). Values-based management. *Academy of Management Executive*, 11(4): 25-46.

Argyris, Chris (1993). *Knowledge for action: A guide to overcoming barriers to organizational change.* San Francisco: Jossey-Bass.

Bilimoria, Diana (1998). From classroom learning to real-world learning: A diasporic shift in management education. *Journal of Management Education*, 22(3), June, 265-268.

Deming, W. E. (1982). *Out of the Crisis.* Cambridge, MA: MIT Center for Advanced Engineering Study.

Evians, R. W. (1983). The validation of action learning programmes. *Management Education and Development*, 14, 208-211.

Fisher, D., & Torbert, W.R. (1995). *Personal and Organizational Transformations: The True Challenge of Continual Quality Improvement.* London: McGraw Hill.

Hamel, G. & Prahalad, C.K. (1994). *Competing for the Future.* Boston: Harvard Business School Press.

Hammer, M. & Champy, J. (1993). *Re-Engineering the Corporation: A Manifesto for Business Revolution.* New York: Harper Business.

Knowles, M. S. (1980). *The modern practice of adult education: From pedagogy to androgogy.* Chicago: Association Press.

Kolb, D. & Fry, R. (1975). Towards an applied theory of experiential learning. In C. L. Cooper (Ed.), *Theories of Group Process* (pp.33-57). New York: Wiley.

Liedtka, (1998). Constructing an ethic for business practice: competing effectively and doing good. *Business and Society*, 37(3), September, 254-280.

Mintzberg, H. (1994). *The rise and fall of strategic planning.* New York: Free Press.

Nonaka, I.(1994). A dynamic theory of organizational knowledge creation. *Organization Science*, February, 5(1),14-37.

Raiborn, C. & Payne, D. (1996). TQM: just what the ethicist ordered. *Journal of Business Ethics*, 15, 963-972.

Raelin, Joseph A. (1997). A model of work-based learning. *Organization Science*, 8(6), Nov.-Dec., 563-577.

Schön, Donald (1983). *The reflective practitioner: How professionals think in action.* New York: Basic Books.

Senge, P.M. *The fifth discipline: The art and practice of the learning organization.* New York: Doubleday, 1991.

Stacey, R. D. (1991). *The chaos frontier: Creative strategic control for business.* Oxford: Butterworth-Heinemann.

Stacey, R.D. (1992). *Managing the unknowable: Strategic boundaries between order and chaos in organizations*. San Francisco: Jossey-Bass.

Waddock, S. A. & Graves, S.B. (1997a). The corporate social performance-financial performance link. *Strategic Management Journal*, 18 (4), 303-319.

Waddock, S. A. & Graves, S.B. (1997b). Quality of management and quality of stakeholder relations: Are they synonymous? *Business and Society*, 36(3), 250-279.

Wilbur, K.. (1998). *The eye of spirit: An integral vision for a world gone slightly mad*. Boston: Shambala.

12 LEADERSHIP AND LAWYERING:
Learning New Ways to See Juvenile Justice

Francine T. Sherman
Boston College Law School

Launched in the Fall of 1996 at Boston College, the Juvenile Rights Advocacy Project's Girls' Initiative (JRAP) uses critical lawyering to serve traditional legal needs of delinquent girls, engage their needs across disciplines, and support their voices in policy and program development. This chapter begins by describing the historical context within which critical juvenile rights lawyering is developing. Next, it draws on the girls' voices heard in discussion groups held in 1996 and 1998 to demonstrate the connection between individual client goals and system goals on behalf of clients. The chapter then follows one girl's situation through a single issue approach to legal representation, a fully collaborative, cross-categorical approach to individual representation, and finally a political approach aimed at system reform. That case examination is followed by an initial discussion of the sort of thinking required of critical lawyers and the pedagogy appropriate in a law school clinic designed toward critical lawyering for delinquent youth.

In a 1995 report assessing access to counsel and quality of representation in delinquency proceedings, the American Bar Association concluded that lawyers for children are often poorly trained in the legal, developmental, and social services issues that confront their clients (Puritz, 1995). Due to this inadequate training, high case loads, and court cultures that do not value zealous representation for children, few delinquency attorneys or attorneys for children provide comprehensive advocacy for their clients (e.g., Humes, 1996).

Reflection on the nature and quality of representation in delinquency proceedings (and other children's cases) is not new (e.g., Dohrn, B. & Green, B. A., 1996). Historically, attorneys viewed their role as advocating for the child's best interests. Yet, as due process protections in the juvenile justice system increased, attorneys have increasingly come to see themselves as advocates for the child client's expressed wishes, just as one would for the adult client. Regardless, attorneys for children must be educated in child development, education, and the social and cultural issues relevant to their clients. Moreover, because children involved with the state so often present multiple educational, developmental, health, and social issues, lawyers for children ought to be educated in the range of legal issues that cross a child's life. Representing children is complex—requiring lawyers to develop relationships with clients over time and fully understand the context of the client's life.

However contextual it may be, individual representation rarely addresses the system issues that make it so difficult to achieve client goals (e.g., Matthews, 1996). Nor does individual representation address the political issues felt by kids in the system. Beyond questions of the appropriate model of individual lawyering in delinquency cases (and other children's cases), delinquency lawyers should use their skills to facilitate system reform essential to their clients' futures. The delinquency clients need both short-term legal strategies designed to protect their rights as well as long-term strategies aimed at the whole child. Because the system is so disempowering and programmatic options are so restricted, delinquency lawyers must use their access to political systems to advocate for laws supporting rehabilitation for youth, progressive programs that provide the best chance at rehabilitation for juvenile offenders, and procedures that are not disempowering.

"Critical lawyering" provides a model for this representation, which promotes the client's voice through collaboration with the attorney and empowers clients by mobilizing them toward reform strategies (Alfieri, 1988; Brustin, 1993; Buchanan & Trubeck, 1992; Johnson, 1991; Lopez, 1992; Trubeck, 1991; White, 1988, 1994). Critical lawyering projects cross subject areas and vary in their emphasis on two overall themes: 1) developing client voice through attorney/client collaboration, and 2) mobilizing clients toward long term social reform (Trembly, 1992). In recent articles developing the model, Louise Trubek has set out its broad contours as follows:

> Humanize: resist reduction of client stories to legal categories; frame issues in human terms.
> Politicize: Use critical legal theory to provide insight into the contingent nature of client disempowerment; apply feminist and anti-racist analysis to help resist marginalization of clients' voices.
> Collaborate: encourage participation of clients and client groups in practice decisions; attempt to dismantle the lawyer/client hierarchy.
> Strategize: seek to access client experiences regarding strategies for struggle and resistance; develop a healthy skepticism regarding traditional advocacy arenas; continually re-evaluate advocacy effectiveness from a client perspective.

Organize: encourage organization and collective efforts by clients; work with existing social movements and client groups. (Buchannan & Trubeck, 1992, p. 691; Trubeck & Kransberger, 1998, p. 204)

By supporting client voice in representation through fuller attorney/client collaboration, critical lawyering answers the tendency of traditional lawyering for children to foster client dependence. Moreover, critical lawyering is consistent with delinquency clients' increasing recognition of the politicization of delinquency. The race, gender, and age politics which juveniles see surrounding delinquency, contributes to the overwhelmingly disempowering experience of the juvenile justice system. Thus, it addresses the need of young people in the juvenile justice system to exercise some control by recognizing the political nature of the juvenile justice system and promoting their voices. Overall, the critical lawyering movement corresponds to, and illustrates, the scholarly paradigm that Torbert in Chapter 5 calls Postmodern Interpretivism.

The historical moment for juvenile justice in the United States is right for critical approaches to delinquency representation. Juvenile justice is being driven by politics as society re-evaluates its legal and social relationships to children. Recent state and federal legislation have legitimized a view of children as less worthy of society's protection and care (Smith, 1995). This dynamic of diminished expectations justifying diminished compassion is a driving force in juvenile justice reforms based on a redefinition of teenagers as "superpredators." With this shift in attitude about juvenile justice has been a shift in resources. More in protection, less in prevention. More in law enforcement, less in social services. Our juvenile justice system has become less forgiving, removing the second chances that were once the hallmark of rehabilitative juvenile justice (e.g., Bishop, Frazier, Lanza-Kaduce & Winner, 1996).

FRAMING IMMEDIATE NEEDS IN POLITICAL TERMS— GROUP DISCUSSIONS WITH GIRLS IN THE JUVENILE JUSTICE SYSTEM

In the fall of 1996 and the winter of 1998 students and faculty from the JRAP engaged in group discussions with girls in juvenile justice facilities in Massachusetts. The first series of discussions took place over eight weeks and was intended to identify issues that would inform the mission and content of the JRAP's Girls' Initiative. In the winter of 1998 the discussions were more tightly structured and focused on what the girls considered quality legal representation.

These girls closely associated their individual concerns with political and system issues. Both individual and system issues were informed by their pervasive sense of lack of power. The girls felt disempowered by unfair administrative processes that determine length of incarceration, court processes that relied on legal representation which was less than zealous, and treatment that relied on case workers who did not listen to the girls' points of view. At the system level they identified gender bias as a cause of inadequate resources for girls and extended incarceration often imposed on girls for running away. They saw racial bias in their caseworkers' conclusions about their conduct, and age bias in the system's attempts to prevent behavior typical of teenagers.

In one 1996 session three girls were asked to role-play lawyer for a friend, whose case had just been presented to the Department of Youth Services classification panel to determine her term in a hardware-secure delinquency facility.[1] The girls were in a detention facility awaiting the final dispositions of their delinquency cases in court and the Department of Youth Services' final determination of disposition. Their arguments on behalf of their friend reflected the close connections between individual case goals and the system issues that both drive and constrain their cases. Their arguments reflected awareness of the need for treatment as well as the lack of adequate treatment options for girls; a sense of disempowerment they bring to a system that continues to give them no voice; and an ability to see one another's strengths and form connections in a system that moves them around and undercuts long-term relationships.

> *Girl #1: I feel that my client should not [be given secure treatment] because she has kept her level over 1 1/2 months and now you know with the structure of this program it is very hard for these females to keep level that long. My client has been doing seven months dead time and we should all sit here and look at how good she has done, she knows it was dead time and she could of acted out, she could of done anything just because it is dead time and it's not gonna count against her, but no my client chose to do different. She chose to work with the program and get out of it what she could. Now she has maintained her focus on herself, on the little things she can work on here, cause she does not have a lot of therapy she can get here, they don't have a lot of those things available for her.*
>
> *She has maintained her focus for seven months dead time, can we just sit here and look at that, can you imagine being surrounded by girls who do worse crimes and see them moving on to less secure places, while you are being detained doing dead time. My client has never flipped out, I have not heard of my client flipping out, I have not heard of my client throwing chairs or nothing like that. I have heard of my client at times being verbal but every teenager gets verbal, let's face this fact.*
>
> *So I also feel that my client is very independent, my client goes to school, she does her work, I have no complaints from the teachers, she's one of the top rated girls in the school. She is very smart, she has also taught some of the other girls how to do their work, things that the teacher should be doing. I feel that my client*

needs to mature and yes maybe she needs therapy treatment, but secure treatment, I think that's a little overboard. Thank you. [Sherman, F. T., Discussion Group, Old Colony YMCA Girls Secure Detention Unit, Brockton, MA (Nov. 20, 1996).]

Feelings of powerlessness cut across the girls' observations of their individual situations as well as the system's treatment of girls generally. This powerlessness contributes to their sense of unfair treatment by caseworkers, lawyers, judges, and therapists—becoming both an individual and system issue.

My caseworker says, Oh, we can be friends or we can be enemies. What would make you like her? If she'd like listen to what I have to say. Like I said, she's never even met me before.

You've never seen her face?

No.

They talk a lot of jive.

I don't understand how they can put a person that really doesn't know nothing about you and try to be like . . . I mean even if I say something, that's not what's going to happen anyways, because they made a decision about what's going to already happen. I don't understand how they can have a person doing it that doesn't know nothing about you.

I mean I told my case worker you can come here and look at all the girls and you won't be able to pick me out. She was like yeah I got your mug shot, so I know who you are. I was like I don't know who you are, I don't think it's fair to pick up somebody that don't even know me and try to run my life—tell me where I'm going to go, what I'm gonna do, who I can talk to even, who I can write letters to. It's so stupid.

They're out of control.

They have the say. Basically, you listen to what they have to say and you're locked up. And if you don't like what's happening that goes against you.

You can't speak your opinion.

You know what I'm saying? They want us to behave like adults then they should treat us like one [Sherman, F. T., Discussion Group, Old Colony YMCA Girls Secure Detention Unit, Brockton, MA. (Oct. 16, 1996)].

I hate authority. Sometimes I have a problem with authority, but the only time I have a real problem with authority is when that authority knows, you know what I'm saying, well I'm head honcho and I can tell you what to do and still get away with it. And they always throw in your face well I'm getting paid for it so it doesn't matter what you say and do. You know what I'm saying.

But that's true, it's only what we do that's gonna help us. But I hate when they throw it in your face that they're God and do what they want to you. They think they can talk to you in any way they want to, that's not true, cause my mother taught me, you know she raised me if someone disrespects, don't let no one disrespect you regardless of who they are [Sherman, F. T., Discussion Group, Old Colony YMCA Girls Secure Detention Unit, Brockton, MA. (Nov. 1, 1996)].

The girls identified policy issues, which have been identified by juvenile justice researchers and feminist scholars. Girls were quick to note strands of gender bias in the juvenile justice and social services systems and again drew on their sense of powerlessness for explanations.

The boys here play basketball outside, go on trips everyday, go everywhere. Boys get much more. You know girls can sit here and rot. They [boys] get phone calls, like every day, two times a day.

Why do you think [boys] get more privileges?

I don't know. They say that girls are worse than boys but I don't know how because when they made all these lock-ups most of them were made on boys and they just started with the girls. So I don't see how we are worse than boys [Sherman, F. T., Discussion Group, Old Colony YMCA Girls Secure Detention Unit, Brockton, MA. (Oct. 1, 1996)].

When boys get locked up they only get locked up for three months, but when they lock girls up because they don't want them to get pregnant, they keep them in there for like years, it ain't fair that they lock us girls longer than boys [Sherman, F. T., Discussion Group, Old Colony YMCA Girls Secure Detention Unit, Brockton, MA. (Nov. 1, 1996)].

The girls identified the impact of running away in their own experiences and described the cycle of running away that leads to longer sentences and more running. They identified the continuum that begins with the child protection or status offender system and moves girls into the juvenile justice system.

I can say that the system is probably screwed up because my sister was locked up before she was twelve. She was locked up for running away, but her uncle raped her. I can understand her running away, but they didn't even send her back home, they sent her to a foster home . . . She wanted to be home, she wanted to be with her mother. She was twelve years old. [Sherman, F. T., Discussion Group, Old Colony YMCA Girls Secure Detention Unit, Brockton, MA. (Oct. 1, 1996)].

The first time I was in court I was about ten years old, for running away and for being a stubborn child and not going to school. Just for running away they put me in a foster home for three months but I ran away from every foster home . . . That's part of the reason why I'm here today because I ran away a lot. [Sherman, F. T., Discussion Group, Old Colony YMCA Girls Secure Detention Unit, Brockton, MA. (Oct. 1, 1996)].

Most of us, I can say the majority of DYS girls, they come in here for problems that happen at home. It don't even have to be their moms. It can just be something that they do or something that happened to them in life that made them act up. Because people don't just sit there and act up for no reason, but most of us we have something we've had to deal with all our lives.

Everybody does something for a reason. We're not in touch with it, we don't know how to handle it. No.

That's why I'm saying we should have groups here. They should have groups so we can talk about it, ya know. On with it, the girls should be able to talk anyway. [Sherman, F. T., Discussion Group, Old Colony YMCA Girls Secure Detention Unit, Brockton, MA. (Oct. 1, 1996)].

The girls' observations demonstrate the close connection between individual advocacy and system-wide "policy issues" in juvenile justice. The most brilliant individual advocacy for a delinquent girl with a child of her own will be ineffective if there is no adequate program available. If a girl is unable to return to her home or does not want to return to her home, traditional lawyering can never solve her problem without a long-term resource tailored to her individual needs. The absence of these resources for girls is a system-wide problem with complex origins.

Lawyers often approach a client interview prepared to identify legal issues within the client's representation along legal categories that are comfortable to the lawyer and that organize the legal landscape. Critical lawyering attempts to give the client a greater voice in her representation by asking the lawyer to approach a client's problem as a human problem and to be receptive to the client's judgment about issues and strategies although they may not be traditionally legal and are likely to cross legal and disciplinary categories (Alfieri, 1991; White, 1990). Here, we can see a similarity in direction between critical lawyering and the orientation toward interdisciplinary dispute resolution that McMorrow recommends in Chapter 7.

Our 1996 discussions with girls in the Massachusetts juvenile justice system directed us toward a model of lawyering that would advance short-term as well as long-term client interests—emphasizing the human dimensions of cases and promoting cross-categorical representation. To do this, cases were taken in through detention centers for girls after clients had been found delinquent and committed to the Massachusetts Department of Youth Services. That access point both gave students the time they needed to assess the cases and develop strategies, and emphasized the breadth of issues confronting clients. The project sought cases in which girls were involved with multiple systems and presented complex issues, and agreed to provide representation until the client aged out of the juvenile justice system. Representation incorporated psychology, education, and social work through the Boston College Center for Child, Family and Community Partners.[2]

The girls' discussion group suggested system issues that constrained individual representation and were the source of client disempowerment. Girls wanted the system to provide programming in a fair manner that was individualized and responsive to the range of needs and desires they presented (e.g., Ansley & Gaventa, 1997). Consistent with critical lawyering, the JRAP took an outreach or participatory approach to the long-term system wide issues, taking cues from the girls in the system and striving to incorporate their voices into policy advocacy.

Angela: Concentric Circles of Lawyering Over Time

Traditional lawyering artificially categorizes human problems into convenient legal issues, fragmenting the clients' lives. This approach is inconsistent with the complex lives of girls in the juvenile justice system. However, critical lawyering fits well with delinquency representation in encouraging cross categorical thinking about human problems. The following case study demonstrates that juvenile clients' issues cross disciplines, legal categories, and state systems.

Angela's case study demonstrates the power of individual, single-issue lawyering for solving pressing client problems and building the lawyer/client relationship. However, it also demonstrates the need in delinquency cases for cross-categorical individual lawyering based on lawyer/client collaboration over time. Finally, Angela's case study raises the potential for the lawyer and client to collaborate to reform policy, though how that might be accomplished is less clear. These three types of lawyering are concentric circles—the single-issue lawyering is nested within the collaborative, cross-categorical lawyering which, in turn, nests in the political approaches aimed at system reform. Each builds the lawyer/client collaboration and successive forms of representation depend on prior representation.

1. Single-Issue Individual Lawyering

Angela was referred to the JRAP by the most secure girls' treatment facility contracting with the Massachusetts Department of Youth Services. When the referral was made I remembered her from the girls' discussion group held the previous fall. In that group Angela was articulate and opinionated, offering a political perspective on juvenile justice. The contracting agency that referred Angela said that she had a baby in foster care and was not given regular visits.

In our initial meeting, Angela was clear and extremely well organized. She said that she had been promised weekly visits with her son by the Department of Youth Services' case worker who was present when she entered her plea agreement. She related the judge's comments from the bench to the same effect and her feeling that she entered the agreement because the officials present were promising her visitation. She walked into our meeting with a calendar on which she had recorded the visits she was promised and whether or not they had occurred, and a file folder containing formal documents regarding her son, her delinquency case, as well as additional notes she had taken of conversations with case workers and others in control of her visitation.

Identifying Angela's immediate legal need and an initial strategy was relatively straightforward. Angela clearly stated that she wanted a lawyer to help her obtain more visitations with her son. After further discussion with Angela and investigation of the matter with her trial attorney, the JRAP student lawyer decided to move for enforcement of Angela's plea agreement. While the plea agreement did not provide explicitly for visitation, the surrounding circumstances supported our argument that more frequent visits were part of the bargain.

The chosen strategy required technical lawyering in the juvenile court, a traditional legal forum. The outcome was positive for Angela, giving her an enforceable order that increased visitation with her son. She felt fairly treated—the system heard her concerns and supported her relationship with her son. This short-term issue was also critical in developing the relationship between Angela and her

JRAP lawyer. Angela came to JRAP with a specific problem and, in collaboration with her, traditional lawyering achieved the result she wanted (e.g., Trembly, 1992). While the traditional lawyer might have ended the representation at this point, critical lawyering might see this juncture as an opportunity to develop the lawyer/client relationship, and identify legal and extra-legal issues that the lawyer might be able to address with Angela in an effort to resolve her more intractable problems.

2. Lawyer/Client Collaboration Across Categories

An inter-system view of Angela's case raises issues that go well beyond the short term need for increased visitation with her son, to future reunification with her son and, ultimately, a productive life beyond the juvenile justice and social services systems. To assist our thinking about Angela's case, JRAP students "mapped" her pathway through the state systems from birth until 1998. Predictably, the map demonstrates issues that cross categories and disciplines, require multiple advocacy strategies and close attorney/client collaboration.[3]

The stage was set for Angela's involvement in the delinquency system when she was a young child. She had a history of neglect, sexual abuse and disrupted relationships, including her mother's inability to care for her, assault by a foster parent, her mother's death, and her father's incarceration. As a young teenager Angela became involved in prostitution, running away, drug use, and, finally, a violent crime. The state's treatment of Angela seems to have done little to prevent her declining behavior. Between the ages of six and fourteen she was placed in eleven different foster homes, making it difficult for her to establish any lasting relationships. When her behavioral problems became more severe, she was placed in a series of four residential settings. Just as she escalates through the social services system, she escalates through the special education system, each time receiving education designations requiring increasing support and intervention.

Within the juvenile justice system, Angela makes a huge leap from disorderly conduct and shoplifting to armed robbery and assault and battery with a dangerous weapon. As soon as she committed a violent crime she was indicted as a youthful offender.[4] Though her crime was serious, it was committed as part of a group, including her boyfriend at the time. She was not a leader in the criminal activity and does not fit the profile of a chronic violent offender. On the whole her behavior poses more of a threat to herself than it does to society.

Angela's case illustrates the way in which girls escalate through fragmented state systems. Her case is virtually passed from the social services agency to the juvenile justice agency and then, when she has a child, back to the social services agency. There is no coordination between these two agencies and no coordination with the school systems responsible for educating her.

Angela and JRAP student attorneys spent many hours determining a long-term advocacy agenda. Though crises arose and diverted attention from that agenda, it is steadily being accomplished in collaboration with Angela. Angela's long-term agenda includes negotiation of a reunification plan for her and her son, locating foster care where she can live with her son following her incarceration, organizing funding sources for her, and advocating through the special education maze to provide her with an appropriate education plan and resource. Each of these tasks have legal elements and require expertise from allied fields such as social work, education, and psychology. Each of these tasks is based in client directed individual representation but implicates a system wide issue. Negotiating a reunification plan, foster placement, and funding streams directly relates to the need for greater integration of state systems serving children as well as the lack of resources for girls and particularly for girls with children. Advocating for an appropriate educational plan relates both to Angela's individual right to an appropriate education and the bureaucracies surrounding three state systems, each of which is somewhat but not completely responsible for her education.

Critical lawyering based on lawyer/client collaboration that develops over time and addresses long-term as well as short term client needs, fits well with the complex issues Angela's case presents. Moreover, Angela experienced the process of lawyer/client collaboration as non-judgmental and empowering, two essential features for a girl whose life has been controlled by multiple state systems. Nonetheless, the system wide problems that contributed to Angela's current situation and inhibit solutions, remain despite long term individual advocacy. Extending the critical lawyering model toward system reform strategies is a logical next step in the lawyer/client collaboration, consistent with Angela's articulated goals and her needs for empowerment and growth.

3. Critical Lawyering and System Reform

> *I'm sorry but I have different views on things and sometimes I will say what ____ cause that's how I feel the government is run by white folks . . . O.K. I just had to tell you, you know how white folks think in the system, I told the same thing to her, we're just money in their pockets, that what we are.*
> Angela, 1996

Lawyers for children, and particularly delinquency lawyers are an increasing presence in policy forums. At the Juvenile Defense Leadership Summits sponsored by the American Bar Association in October, 1997 and 1998, sessions focused on building coalitions and working toward system reform in legislative and administrative arenas. In part, this is a response to the ongoing federal assault on juvenile delinquents. It is also a recognition that many of the rights afforded juvenile delinquents are hollow in practice and most programming for juveniles fails to live up to the promise of rehabilitation.

Individual lawyering toward Angela's short and long-term goals and the evolving lawyer/client relationship sets the stage to mobilize Angela (and other girls) toward system reform strategies. Without the increased visitation achieved through traditional legal mechanisms, Angela's long-term prospects with her son would be reduced. Moreover, without attention to Angela's placement and education, work at system reform would do little to improve Angela's life. The attorney/client collaboration forged during the fight to increase visitation, advocacy to locate a specialized foster home, reunite her with her son, and locate an appropriate education, built the trust essential to any collaborative policy agenda.

Angela's case reflects many of the policy issues she and the other girls in the 1996 discussions identified. Moreover, promoting her voice and mobilizing her and other girls in the juvenile justice system might yield programmatic change that could not be achieved by traditional lawyering. However, which strategies might be most successful or how client voices might be mobilized to effect system reform is less clear. Moreover, because Angela and many of the girls in the delinquency system move from one crisis to another, settling them to address system issues might be difficult. Nonetheless, promising next steps include: 1) employing participatory research methods to develop programs, 2) including girls in decisions over program design, 3) giving girls an economic stake in enterprises surrounding their programs, 4) freeing girls to mentor other girls to positively reinforce the relationships they form in institutional settings, and 5) introducing girls to the legislative and executive arenas in which policy is made.

PEDAGOGICAL ISSUES

Just as the Girls' Initiative was oriented through discussions with girls in the juvenile justice system, journals written by students enrolled in JRAP framed the pedagogy as well as the design of the advocacy agenda. Law students in the JRAP were asked to write their perceptions of their cases and of themselves as student lawyers. Just as the girls in the discussion group perceived the connections between individual and policy issues, students typically wrote about the challenges of individual lawyering in terms of concrete skills and theories as well as the systems issues raised by their cases. One student's evolving impressions of a client and her case illustrates the movement from single issue lawyer, to critical lawyer collaborating with her client and ultimately concerned with systems issues.

> *Week One:* I spent the majority of my time this first week getting acquainted with my two cases. I have had very little experience working in the delinquency system prior to this semester, yet what I noticed immediately upon reading Angela's file was the similarity in the life, the placements and the services that Angela had experienced relative to the juveniles that I had worked with in the CHINS and Care and Protection arenas. It amazes me that juveniles with parallel lives and experiences can find themselves on significantly different paths depending upon when a

state agency takes notice of a family and whether it is an "offense" or abuse situation that prompts the notice.

This became even more apparent to me when reading Jennifer's file, which had limited information about her history, and mostly information regarding her most recent crime. I noticed immediately that my perceptions of Angela and Jennifer were dramatically different. I do not think that the offense that Jennifer allegedly was involved with is very serious relative to most, yet absent the understanding of how she found herself with the group of individuals she did in Boston on that night, I find that I perceive her differently than Angela, someone whose crime was much more serious, yet within the context of her life I can understand how she wound up where she did.

Week Three: This week I spent a lot of time working on Jennifer's case. I am fascinated by how my perception of Jennifer has changed from last week when I did not have very much information about her life, and this week having a much fuller picture after reading her Department of Youth Services file and going to her home. Her DYS file reveals a "typical" juvenile female delinquent right down to the letter. Her past crimes, her family history, her experiences of being shuffled around within a system, and the status offense that initially brought her into the system.

My most memorable experience this week was meeting Jennifer's mother. As I drove up to her house I see the "welcoming" gang insignia and profanity on the door, then proceed upstairs to find a baby in a walker standing at the top of the stairs with the front door open. After safely stowing the child back in the home, I am instructed to come into the kitchen, which is almost as filthy as the children running around within the home. I have done many home visits in the last two years and the condition of this home was one of the worst. If the gang insignia and the party going on at the floor beneath us were any indication of what it was to live there at night, I can not even imagine what that experience would be like for Jennifer. I am used to doing Guardian Ad Litem work where I could walk out of a home like that and recommend to the court that some things change before the children are returned, yet in this case, representing the interests of Jennifer, if Jennifer insists on going home then that option will be explored. In a delinquency context, Jennifer has less of a chance of having the option of returning home at this time but when she does the issue will be Jennifer and not the suitability of the home. It does not make sense to me that because Jennifer wound up in the system because of an offense instead of the documented physical abuse by her mother that the system does not do more to stabilize the family as a whole.

Week Eight: The facts of Jennifer's case were interesting to sort out because they revealed a picture of someone who is only "delinquent" because of her family situation . . . To see her prior offense history primarily involve altercations within her family and the majority of her charges to span a period of about six months when her family was going through a lot of changes seems to cry out as someone who needs support services within the home . . . What amazes me is that once someone with her profile enters the delinquency system the perspective regarding her family seems to be lost . . . My experiences in court during Jennifer's pre-sentencing and sentencing hearings showed me just how much confusion the youthful offender statute has caused the system and how many issues remain unresolved in its application . . . In light of Jennifer's offense history, she appears to be one of those cases where the youthful offender statute is used to broaden the class of juveniles that are given longer commitments and suspended adult sentences as opposed to being a middle ground for juveniles that would otherwise have been transferred. This, to me, is a backward use of the statute and appears to be a very unjust disposition for someone like Jennifer. In light of this is would appear to be very useful to strategize ways to educate the juvenile courts on a more widespread basis about what the Department of Youth services offers to girls so that sentences are not based on misconceptions about the system. However, I am not sure how to convince a court that DYS can appropriately service juveniles when I have seen little evidence that this is the case.

Critical lawyers representing youth in the juvenile justice system must be reflective practitioners in a way that will permit them to go beyond short term, individual lawyering to see the cross categorical issues, collaborate with the client, and ultimately be open to innovative, client collaborative strategies aimed at system reform. This sort of reflective practitioner thinks about the systems in which she practices as she practices rather than assuming the systems exist as they should with little questioning. The practitioner must articulate her observations of the client, of the relationships among the clients and others significant to them (lawyer, case worker, family members, and so forth), of each system in which the client is involved, and of the relationships or lack of relationships among those systems. Through that articulation the student practitioner will begin to see the cross-categorical issues and devise strategies to address them.

The JRAP student journal illustrates that reflective practice. The student begins with a traditional lawyer's view of Jennifer, based on a typical delinquency case file focused on the circumstances of the offense. Once the student gathers the full Department of Youth Services and Department of Social Services background, she begins to see cross-categorically. Jennifer as the "typical juvenile female delinquent" who enters the delinquency system indirectly through the status offender system, was a victim of family violence and is reported to law enforcement by her family (girls, inc., 1996). She has educational issues and significant deficits in her home. By seeing in this way, the student lawyer can begin to see both the long term agenda for Jennifer and the system issues raised by Jennifer's case. The student lawyer properly notes that lack of attention to Jennifer's family situation will make return home problematic regardless of the delinquency treatment Jennifer may receive. She also recognizes the misapplication of the youthful offender law in cases like Jennifer's where the charge is serious but circumstances create broad service needs.

Too often law schools and other professional schools attempt to narrow the issues for students in their clinical experiences in an effort to focus them on specific tasks or skills. However, critical lawyering advises lawyers to humanize problems and resist the temptation to narrowly categorize. To do this, lawyers and students must see the complexities in the client's situation—see the case across categories (e.g., Bloch, 1982; Kegan, 1994). Cross-categorical seeing is facilitate by in depth lawyer/client collaboration working through "wicked" problems as they exist in the real world (e.g., King & Acklin, 1995; Waddock, 1999).

Just as critical lawyering is premised on lawyer client collaboration, pedagogy surrounding critical lawyering should involve collaboration between student and supervisor. Because new ways of seeing the issues develop through the representation, the supervisor learns with the student and together they can devise strategies. Unlike traditional academic approaches in which the professor knows the answer and the student's task is to come up with that answer, there are multiple answers to many of the issues posed by critical approaches to lawyering and many pathways that might be taken through the maze of issues and systems presented by the client. While this requires less structure than is typical of traditional teaching, it is that lack of tight structure that provides the room for experimentation needed to create collaborative solutions.

In keeping with the interdisciplinary direction of critical lawyering, literature on action learning (Raelin, 1997) and outreach scholarship (Lerner & Simon, 1998) is instructive. Action learning in management asks managers to undertake projects in the work setting and then bring their experiences back into the classroom for examination to promote their growth as professionals as well as reform of the organizations in which they work (e.g., Fisher & Torbert, 1995). Outreach scholarship brings the scholarly resources of universities to communities through collaborative projects in which communities define their needs and agendas and work collaboratively with professional schools who contribute expertise informed by the community. Because both action learning and outreach scholarship rely on community definitions of their problems, like critical lawyering, they demand cross categorical, interdisciplinary thinking and reflective practice in which solutions evolve through a cycle of action and reflection.

The following table developed with Professor Mary Walsh of the Department of Counseling Psychology at Boston College and Professor Sandra Waddock of the Carroll School of Management begins to develop a pedagogy for critical lawyering by contrasting traditional academic approaches with outreach approaches that are suggested by critical lawyering.

Table 12.1
Comparison of Traditional Academic Approaches
with those of the Outreach Scholar Practitioner

Traditional Academic Approaches	Outreach Scholar-Practitioner
Individual problem-solving model, based in single disciplines	Interdisciplinary team-based model, combining multiple disciplines
"Expert" model: "I teach, you learn." Passive learning, based on lecture, memorization, theory without practice. Power, status, turf maintained and amplified as the expert designs and delivers the educational experience individually. Community uninvolved.	"Co-learning" model: "We learn together through practice." Active learning, based on integration of practice with theory in the field, in conversation. Requires dropping of traditional power, turf, status roles for mutuality of input into process and outcomes. Working with students and community.
Faculty/expert driven: Faculty member defines the problem and appropriate questions, theory, and responses. Faculty member is the expert in the classroom, seldom ventures out into the field to test what is being taught.	Problem driven: Situation, client, community, or student define the problem and appropriate questions, theory, responses. Faculty member works jointly with students, community, or client to develop and implement projects, apply and use knowledge.
Learning outcomes: structured, closed-ended, neat, complete, and theoretical, based on exams and papers. Professor-led discussions with a specific end in mind, students may be dissociated from their learning. One perspective dominates (the faculty expert's).	Learning outcomes: open-ended, dialogic, messy and complex, linking theory and practice, based on application in the field of classroom learning. Professor-client-student-practitioner led dialogue, process oriented, iterative, involving for all. Multiple perspectives share the stage.
Learning occurs largely through one-way conveyance of theory, memorization and some discussion, listening to lectures. More theoretical than reflective or applied.	Learning occurs through interaction, practice, application of theory in the field, reflection on outcomes.

CONCLUSION

The mechanisms legal educators choose for educating attorneys depend on the sort of professional one hopes they become and the context in which one expects them to practice. The context of practice is to some extent defined by clients. In the juvenile justice context, clients see the connections between individual lawyering and the need for system reform, thus critical lawyering that promotes lawyer/client collaboration and walks the increasingly blurry line between lawyering for individuals and lawyering for causes, is a useful model. Law school clinics adopting this model must rethink pedagogy to model the approach to lawyering in order to create reflective practitioners who see and question the systems in which they operate in order to develop and implement strategies that will result in long terms solutions.

ENDNOTES

[1] As evidence of the lack of resources for girls in Massachusetts, a state known as a national model in community based juvenile corrections, the Department of Youth Services primarily relies on eight girls' facilities statewide. One of these is a hardware secure facility in which a girl can only be placed after her case has been presented to the Department of Youth Services' Classification Panel which hears discussion about the case history and determines length of secure treatment.

[2] With these intake criteria, we have represented girls presenting: disabilities, significant health issues; pregnancy; running away; prostitution; special educational needs; histories of family violence and many other complex problems.

[3] The maps are used to devise cross-categorical case strategies by providing lawyers with an overview of a client's significant life events, and involvement in social services, mental health, delinquency and educational systems.

[4] In October of 1996 Massachusetts implemented a youthful offender system which created a middle ground between delinquency and adult criminal charges. If the District Attorney proceeds along a youthful offender track, the juvenile might receive one of the following sentences: 1) commitment to the Massachusetts Department of Youth Services until 21 (delinquency commitments are until 18);
2) commitment to the Massachusetts Department of Youth Services until 21 and a suspended adult sentence; or 3) the adult sentence provided in the criminal law.

REFERENCES

Alfieri, A. V. (1988). The antinomies of poverty law and a theory of dialogic empowerment. *New York University Review of Law and Social Change*, 16, 659-712.

Alfieri, A. V. (1991). Reconstructive poverty law practice: Learning lessons of client narrative. *Yale Law Journal*, 100, 2107-2147.

Ansley, F. & Gaventa, J. (1997). Researching for democracy and democratizing research. *Change*, Jan./Feb.29-30, 46-53.

Bishop, D. M., Frazier, C. E. Lanza-Kaduce, L., and Winner, L. (1996). The transfer of juveniles to adult criminal court: Does it make a difference? *Crime and Delinquency*, 42, 171-191.

Bloch, F. S. (1982). The andragogical basis of clinical legal education. *Vanderbilt Law Review*, 35, 321-353.

Brustin, S. (1993). Expanding our vision of legal services representation—The hermanas unidas project. *American University Journal of Gender & Law*, 1, 39-59.

Buchanan, R. & Trubek, L. G. (1992). Resistances and possibilities: A critical and practical look at public interest lawyering. *New York University Review of Law & Social Change* 19, 687-719.

Fisher, D., & Torbert W. R. (1995). *Personal and organizational transformation: The true challenge of continual quality improvement*. London: McGraw-Hill.

girls, Inc. (1996) *Prevention and Parity: Girls in Juvenile Justice*. Washington, D.C: Office of Juvenile Justice and Delinquency Prevention.

Humes, E. (1996). *No Matter How Loud I Shout*: New York, Simon & Schuster.

Johnson, L. (1991). The new public interest law: From old theories to a new agenda. *Boston University Public Interest Law Journal*, 1, 169-191.

Kegan, R. (1994). *In over our heads: The mental demands of modern life*. Cambridge, MA: Cambridge

King, J. & Acklin, D. (1995). Creating common ground: A lesson from the past. *Journal of Business Ethics*, 14, 1-16.

Lerner, R. M. & Simon, L. A. K. (Eds.) (1998). *University-community collaboration in the twenty-first century: Outreach scholarship for youth and families*. New York: Garland.

Lopez, G. P. (1992). *Rebellious lawyering: One chicano's vision of progressive law practice*. Boulder, CO: Westview Press.

Matthews, M. (1996). Ten thousand tiny clients: The ethical duty of representation in children's class-action cases. *Fordham Law Review*, 64, 1435-1471.

Puritz, P. (1995) *A call for justice: An assessment of access to counsel and quality of representation in delinquency proceedings*. Washington, DC: American Bar Association.

Raelin, J. A. (1997). A model of work-based learning. *Organizational Science*, 8(6), 563-577.

Smith, A. (1995). They dream of growing older: On kids and crime. *Boston College Law Review*, 36, 953-1024.

Torbert, W. R. (1991). *The power of balance: Transforming self, society, and scientific inquiry*. Newbury Park, CA: Sage.

Trembly, P. R. (1992). Rebellious lawyering, regnant lawyering and street-level bureaucracy. *Hastings Law Journal*, 43, 947-970.

Trubek, L. (1991). Critical lawyering: Towards a new public interest practice. *Boston University Public Interest Law Journal*, 1, 49-56.

Trubeck, L. & Kransberger, E. M. (1998). Critical lawyers: Social justice and the structures of private practice. In A. Sarat & S. Scheingold (Eds.). *Cause lawyering: Political commitments and profession*. New York: Oxford University Press.

White, L. E. (1988). To learn and teach: Lessons from driefontein on lawyering and power. *Wisconsin Law Review*, 1988, 699-769.

White, L. E. (1994). Collaborative lawyering in the field? On mapping the paths from rhetoric to practice. *Clinical Law Review*, 1, 157-171.

Waddock, S. (1998) Educating holistic professionals in a world of wicked problems. *Applied Developmental Science*, 2(1), 40-47.

White, L. E. (1990). Subordination, rhetorical survival skills, and sunday shoes: Notes on the hearing of Mrs. G. *Buffalo Law Review*, 38, 1-58.

Dohrn, B. & Green, B. A. (1996). Special issue: Ethical issues in the legal representation of children. *Fordham Law Review*, 64, 1281-2074.

13 THE CALL TO BRIDGE KNOWLEDGE AND ACTION:
The Response of the Boston College Doctoral Program In Organization Transformation

William R. Torbert
Boston College

This chapter proposes that a new kind of social science, along the lines described as *Cooperative Inquiry* and *Developmental Action Inquiry* in Chapter 5, is necessary if we are to bridge knowledge and action in our real-time work and in our families in ways that contribute to human flourishing. The aim of this new kind of social science is not just to inform detached readers, but also to create conditions for transformation of the participants and/or the organization at the site studied (Bradbury, et al., 1998).

The chapter begins by describing some of the conceptual differences between this kind of social science and modernist social science. It then illustrates an early effort at this kind of science through the study of the first decade in the development of a doctoral program in Organization Transformation. This doctoral program does not just describe organization transformation at a distance, but is actively engaged in repeated and ongoing transformation itself. This illustration is particularly fitting, for, if social science is to change fundamentally from an "ivory tower" concern with knowledge separate from action, to a "real world" concern for integrating knowledge and action in real time, then doctoral programs in the social sciences must change fundamentally.

The author is a (senior, faculty) participant in the program, and he describes the ten-year evolution of the program in three distinct but interwoven "voices"—the common, impersonal, third-person voice of modernist social science, the direct second-person voices of colleagues (senior and junior, faculty and students), and his own first-person voice. The author describes how his own view and feelings about the program have changed as a result of the study. He also describes what conversations have recently been occurring in the department in relation to the study. Altogether, the study is meant to illustrate one way of creating a transformational social science, as described in greater detail in Chapter 5.

WHAT BRIDGES KNOWLEDGE AND ACTION?

The theme of the 1997 Academy of Management meeting, for which the original version of this study was prepared, was "The Call to Bridge Knowledge and Action." A marvelous critical review of the symposium asked bluntly, "What bridges knowledge and action? After reading these papers, I still don't know."

Hopefully, this question will startle all of us out of our continuing reveries long enough to realize that the true answer, at least 99% of the time is nothing.

Most of the time–moment-to-moment–our minds and our bodies are living in disconnected universes. We daydream as we drive to work. We speak earnestly about what we are thinking, not noticing that we are mumbling. Smilingly, we unilaterally insist on collaboration.

Sometimes, though, what bridges knowledge and action is a horrifying feeling-awareness that we are in self-contradiction–that we are pretending to be honest, or that we are advising someone not to take anyone's advice. Of course, we don't like this kind of bridge between knowledge and action, and we generally try to get off it as soon as possible, either by correcting the incongruity (that's the hard way), or by destroying the awareness of the incongruity (by far the easier and more common way, if my personal experience generalizes to you).

Thus, the call to bridge knowledge and action in a harmonious, aligned way is a call, first and foremost, to a new kind of *awareness*–a new kind of *attention*–that can interpenetrate our thinking, acting, and effects in real time. To cultivate and sustain this new kind of attention requires, in turn, a new discipline of suffering and loving. We must suffer our lack of awareness and love differences. For example, we must suffer and love incongruities, not turn away from them. Only then (check me on this!) can we cultivate an awareness within ourselves, in our significant relationships and communities of practice, and in the wider institutions in which we participate that gradually comes to harmoniously interweave four distinct "territories of experience" (see Figure 5.2; also, Torbert, 1991):

1)   our highest intuitions of mission ('attention'), with
2)   our best strategizing/theorizing ('knowledge'),

3) our most artistic performances ('action'), and some semblance of
4) our aimed-for results in the objecting, outside world ('assessment').

In other words, the call to bridge knowledge and action is a call not just for a bridge, but for a new kind of knowing, a new kind of research, and a new kind of acting. For example, knowledge in contemporary social science is primarily explicit, propositional theory and secondarily explicit, empirical data that are captured (hence, more accurately described as "capta" than as "data") via an analytic methodology intent upon minimizing incongruities between descriptive theory and descriptive data. Thus, it concerns territories 2 and 4 above in "analytic time," but not territories 1 and 3; and it engages none of the four territories in real time. In contrast, Heron and Reason (1997; Heron, 1996; Reason, 1995) describe four kinds of knowing–experiential, representational (artistic), propositional, and practical– ranging from the more implicit to the more explicit, with congruent bridging across all four necessary if our practical knowing is effectively to guide our action in the present. Although the specifics of their four kinds of knowing and what I call the four territories of experience are interestingly different in some ways, they both sketch a similar challenge to create a new kind of social science practiced by persons in the midst of their real-time action.

WHAT KINDS OF RESEARCH BRIDGE KNOWLEDGE AND ACTION?

Unlike Empirical Positivism which separates research from action and focuses exclusively on third-person research, research that cultivates bridging between knowledge and action will occur:

1) primarily *in real time* (for when else but now can the bridge exist?);
2) *within research/practitioners who cultivate self-and-other awareness as they act* [i.e., through what I call "first-person research/practice" (see Chapter 5 for more complete discussion of this and other methodological terminology in this chapter)];
3) *in meetings where participants develop the meta-norm that actions observed and norms inferred can be discussed at the time* (i.e., through "second-person research/practice"); and
4) *in organizations where visioning/strategizing /performing and assessment data and processes become co-created and co-interpreted* (i.e., through "3rd person research/practice");
5) *with increasingly timely single, double, and triple-loop feedback* see Figure 5.2 that:
    a.   tests the reliability, validity, and efficacy with which performance goals are actually achieved (i.e., the degree to which the learning system responds to single-loop feedback);

b. generates critical/creative dialogue that tests to what degree strategies are congruent with mission, to what degree the espoused strategies are actually being enacted, and to what degree new strategies are worth testing [i.e., to what degree the learning system seeks double-loop feedback in guiding itself (Argyris & Schon, 1974)];

c. reawakens active, inquiring visioning from moment to moment that both tests, and is supported by, philosophical/spiritual traditions that seek integrity across personal and organizational visioning, strategizing, performing, and assessing [i.e., triple-loop feedback (Bartunek & Moch, 1994; Nielsen, 1996; Torbert, 1994; Torbert & Fisher, 1992) across the four territories of experience]; and

d. invites change and transformation toward increasing inquiry and mutuality on the part of the initiating research/practitioners as well as other participants and their communities of practice and organizations.

DO UNIVERSITIES OR BUSINESS ORGANIZATIONS IN GENERAL, AND THE BOSTON COLLEGE Ph.D. PROGRAM IN PARTICULAR, SYSTEMATICALLY ENCOURAGE SUCH RESEARCH/PRACTICE AT PRESENT?

In response to this question, I am confident that the overwhelming majority of my readers (both in general and within our department) will intuitively agree with my assessment that the answer to this multi-pronged question is quite simply: *No.*

This is why some of the most expensive and popular scholarly consulting approaches today (e.g., Argyris, 1994; Nonaka & Takeuchi, 1995; Senge, 1990; Senge, et al., 1999) concern the question of how to integrate inquiry/research/action/ transformation in real time "learning organizations." Research findings in recent years (Lawler, Mohrman & Ledford, 1992; Niven, 1993; Total Quality, 1994), as well as many failed attempts at continual quality improvement and developmental organizational change to create learning organizations, confirm that for a manager or an organization to make a qualitative change toward learning orientation—where there is continual, timely interaction between inquiry and action—is a major challenge that requires a two to five year commitment of time, not to mention the commitment of rare facilitative, consultative, and leadership skills (Torbert, 1994; Fisher & Torbert, 1995; Rooke & Torbert, 1998). And all this . . . just to *begin.* Neither a semester-long university course, nor a typical six-month or one-year consultative relationship can possibly deliver such personal or organizational change. Moreover, there is no a priori reason to think that an "ivory tower" university department is any more likely to become good at balancing and integrating action and inquiry than a "real world" business department or a religious sect.

Indeed, over the past half century, even though a serious conversation has grown in Europe and the US over the nature of social science and its relations to social action (Argyris, Putnam & Smith, 1985; Bernstein, 1985; Gadamer, 1982; Reason, 1995; Reason & Rowan, 1981; Schumacher, 1977), doctoral programs in management in the United States that have attempted to bridge action and inquiry have found it difficult to survive. The program at Case Western Reserve University has probably been the most successful, but it long struggled with a reputation of not producing first rate academic researchers. The program at Yale was administratively destroyed. The program at UCLA bifurcated, and the action-theory-oriented faculty played a diminished role. At MIT, most of the action-focused faculty gradually left and were not replaced by others of similar commitment (and today the Senge-inspired Society for Organizational Learning is better described as tangential to MIT—indeed it has physically moved out this year).

In the case of the doctoral program in Organization Transformation at Boston College, the evidence that it does not systematically encourage the above-defined kind of real-time research/practice includes such data as: 1) only one of the six doctoral dissertations already completed explicitly and critically encompasses first-, second-, and third-person research/practice; and 2) although a number of faculty engage in various elements of real-time research/practice, only one of eleven explicitly engages in all elements of the type of research just defined in all the real-time institutions and communities in which he participates.

(As you may already have inferred, I count myself as that faculty member. This, in turn, makes it easy for my readers and colleagues to attribute bias, defensiveness, and offensiveness to my rhetoric here. Which, in turn, puts a special spotlight on whether and how I illustrate my claims and whether and how I introduce the voices of my departmental colleagues. For example, although I offer #2 above as a descriptive statement, one departmental colleague responds, "This sounds like you are making the others wrong, and that anyone who doesn't do your kind of research is a primitive nontransformed Neanderthal/positivist.")

Some qualities of the Organization Transformation doctoral program may initially make it seem surprising—even ironic—that the answer to this question should be "No" for our department in particular. First, four of the five senior faculty referenced above as contributing to the early development of the concept of triple-loop feedback and learning are members of the Boston College Organization Studies (BC OS) department (Moch is the exception) and all four are committed, not just professionally to conventional types of third-person social science research, but also personally to various forms of first-person research/practice. Second, the mission of the program as a whole is the study of organizational transformation. Third, many department members have pioneered innovative and eclectic combinations of quantitative, qualitative, and action research practices. And fourth, all four of the senior faculty referenced as contributing to the concept of triple-loop feedback have acted as Department Chair or Ph.D. Director (leading to the attribution that they are not a powerless minority).

Two years ago, I myself thought it ironic that members of our program were not more attracted to the new kind of research/practice I am describing here. But through this research on the history of the program my own point of view has transformed, so that the answer "No" now seems neither surprising nor ironic to me. I will describe below in my brief "first-person history" of the department how my view has changed, and then outline a second-person and third-person history of the department. But before these specifics, I offer a more general view.

WHY NOT? WHY IS RESEARCH THAT BRIDGES KNOWLEDGE AND ACTION NOT MORE PREVALENT?

Why are we—both we in general and we in particular in the BC OS Department—not in fact encouraging more real-time research/practice that bridges knowledge and action?

I have already mentioned the most general, third-person reason why we do not—neither in research nor in action, neither in universities nor in businesses or other organizations—encourage real-time research/practice that generates timely, transforming action. Namely, our modern paradigms of science and action *split* mind (visioning and strategizing/theorizing) from body (performing and empirically assessing)—*split* observer/researcher from participant/practitioner—in order to increase the validity of knowledge (make it more objective and dispassionate) and in order to increase the instrumentality of action (make it more technically efficient for achieving pre-determined ends) (Abram, 1996; Argyris, 1980; Berman, 1989; Mitroff, 1974; Needleman, 1975). As stated earlier, modernist social science treats reality as composed of two territories of experience [the map (mind) and the territory (the externally apprehensible world)], rather than four.

Over the past five hundred years, this modernist paradigm of science, technology, and economics has gradually (and not yet quite completely) supplanted traditional paradigms of reality. Traditional paradigms of reality intertwine the four territories of visioning, strategizing, performing, and assessing, but in ways that encourage introjection of, rather than inquiry about, the paradigm (in this avoidance of inquiry about the paradigm, they are no different from modern science) and in ways that do not reliably digest even single-loop feedback (Berman, 1981; Reason, 1995). By contrast, modern science, technology, and economics systematically encourage single-loop learning (empirical testing of propositions and market testing of products). During the past quarter century, the modernist paradigm has reached such maturity that it is increasingly being described and partially transcended by a Postmodern Interpretivist critique (Bernstein, 1985; Denzin and Lincoln, 1994; Pitkin, 1972; Spretnak, 1996).

A multi-paradigmatic, developmental theory that I have been studying and contributing to for thirty years (see Chapter 5) distinguishes seven distinctive paradigms of scientific inquiry. According to this view, modernist science covers only the first four paradigms. Hence, the next equivalent to the modern era (i.e., the next 500 years or so) can entail three paradigm transformations beyond the modernist paradigm boundaries, *if we wish* to develop persons, institutions, and sciences that support first-, second-, and third-person research/practice that generates transforming single-, double-, and triple-loop feedback and learning.

The emphatic "if we wish" in the previous sentence highlights some of the primary qualities of all postmodern paradigms: that they are not implicit paradigms that can be inculcated into children or other neophytes; but rather that they can be taken on only explicitly and voluntarily by adults with a concern for encouraging greater voluntariness in self and others, greater mutuality in relationships, and greater ability to transform toward one's own, continually revisioned version of a good life. Thus, the aim of this multi-paradigmatic developmental approach is not to create an implicit and imperial "grand design" that imprisons its readers and practitioners, but rather to create an explicit vision of a "grand design" that can be subject to continual testing in further personal and organizational research/practice and that requires all participants' full fledged partnership and leadership—not passive conformity. My point here is that the most general reason why we do not encourage real-time research/practice that bridges knowledge and action and encourages transformation (rather than certainty, stasis, conformity) is that we are just at the outset of envisioning what may well be a multi-generational, global effort to do so.

Some persons criticize developmental models on the grounds that they are "individualistic," "linear," "hierarchical," and "elitist"; and they further object to the claim I seem to be making that my work (Developmental Action Inquiry) represents the latest developmental form and hence the "best" kind of research/practice. I want to respond very briefly to these objections in the hope of encouraging such persons to "look again." First, it is true that much of the research on human development has taken place in psychology and has had an individualistic bias to it (Kohlberg, 1981; Piaget, 1965), but my own colleagues and I (Fisher & Torbert, 1995; Rooke & Torbert, 1998) have explicitly extended the developmental logic to the social level, as has recent psychological theorizing (Kegan, 1994; Overton, 1997), and Chapter 5 in this volume extends the developmental approach to epistemology and methodology as well.

Second, the initial appearance of developmental theory as linear and hierarchical is belied by actual experience within any of the later action-logics. As stated at the outset of this chapter, the increasingly intensive awareness generated by the later action-logics across four territories of experience and across the many interacting persons, groups, and organizations in real-time settings introduces one to suffering (and loving!) a chaos of interweaving and mutually interrupting actions and interpretations. At the same time, the later action-logics introduce one to the *in*efficacy of hierarchical, unilateral power for generating genuine transformation, voluntariness, and mutuality, which are increasingly prized. Thus, although only small minorities of humanity have pursued late-stage development to date, those who do are shown not to act in elitist fashion; they act inclusively rather than exclusively, collaboratively rather than hierarchically.

Third, the normative quality of developmental theorizing that makes the later positions in some way "better" is one that one can only commit to for oneself and offer as an invitation to dialogue with others. I commit to the awareness-and-action-challenge of the latest action-logic I can imagine (Developmental Action Inquiry) as an *aim*, not as an accomplished fact that makes me better than others. Indeed, both psychological measures and personal experience suggest that in personal developmental terms I am *at least* one transformation away from practicing the Developmental Action Inquiry action-logic. This aim shows me mainly my poverty. I experience this "poverty" in this research project, for example, as I struggle through revision after revision in an effort to write in a way that generates more dialogue with my colleagues.

So, let us turn to a brief and incomplete sketch of the actual state of affairs in the BC Organization Transformation doctoral program.

A FIRST-, SECOND-, AND THIRD-PERSON HISTORY OF THE BOSTON COLLEGE ORGANIZATION TRANSFORMATION DOCTORAL PROGRAM

I originally began to construct the ten-year history of our Organization Transformation Program in response to the invitation to participate in the Academy of Management symposium carrying the title of this chapter. I also began it as a first-person research/practice exercise intended to address, clarify, and possibly transform the mixture of pride and frustration I felt about my relationship with the program. The following two pages offer a summary of my personal experience in the department in a first-person voice. I offer this personal reflection for three reasons. First, this summary, in tandem with the later multi-voiced outline of our ten-year history, is intended to help readers disentangle the subjective, the intersubjective, and the objective aspects of this case (in order to appreciate more clearly how they are actually interwoven). Second, it is intended to show how this study transformed my understanding of, and feelings about, the department—transformation of the researcher being among the aims of Developmental Action Inquiry. Third, this first-person summary meets some of the validity demands of the Postmodern Interpretivist paradigm (namely, reflexive validity and situated validity, see Chapter 5).

After the first-person summary, I offer the ten-year history of the Ph.D. program, as developed with written and verbal input from well over half the members of the department.

ONE FIRST-PERSON HISTORY OF THE
ORGANIZATION TRANSFORMATION PROGRAM

As a twenty-year member of the department, I was among the founding faculty of the doctoral program. I had not suggested the Organizational Transformation theme near the outset of visioning the program, but was delighted when someone else did and when we rather easily achieved consensus on the idea. We have always been a department somewhat unusual in operating in a truly collaborative fashion and dealing well with single-loop feedback (for example, the entire faculty meets each year to develop the schedule of courses and times for the following year and does so in a friendly, fluid, adaptive fashion). At the same time, we had never worked closely together on an operating program and (perhaps for that reason, but in any event like most organizations) had never developed an organizational culture of double- or triple-loop feedback with one another.

I imagined that, like most of the MBA students I had ever worked with, many of the Ph.D. students would be deeply interested in the call to bridge knowledge and action. There is no question that many of them are; but, to my surprise and consternation, I found our early classes very cautious about engaging in action-oriented research. I gradually induced three reasons for this. A first reason was that, for the first time in a quarter century, management enrollments were declining and the market for new Ph.D.'s was frighteningly tight, encouraging conservative views of what kind of scholarship would "sell." A second reason was that the Ph.D. courses I taught did not entail as frequent or as encompassing action projects as my MBA courses, so instead of practicing *action inquiry in their own real situations and gradually developing an increasing taste for it, the Ph.D. students tended more toward* critiquing *what they imagined its premises to be and developing a distaste for it (and I was obviously less than facile at identifying and adjusting to this double-loop feedback).*

A third reason was that my most recent book at the time (Torbert, 1991), which had most fully embodied and illustrated my own efforts to integrate first-, second-, and third-person research/practices, had proven to be more controversial than I had expected. Although the book received generally superb reviews in many major journals in management and education and was a finalist for a national award, its foreword by my longtime colleague Donald Schon was uniquely confronting.

Both he and some of my departmental colleagues viewed the book as fundamentally unscientific because one of its three sections was explicitly presented in a first-person voice and some of the experiences described seemed shocking (as double-loop and triple-loop feedback sometimes is). Gradually, I came to recognize this reaction made perfect sense, given that (1) I have been attempting to develop and demonstrate an alternative paradigm that bridges knowledge and action, (2) different paradigms ordinarily seem illegitimate to one another, and (3) in the context of the doctoral program, with its explicit focus on methods of research and practice, I explicitly articulate the Developmental Action Inquiry paradigm as distinctive, rather than simply using it quietly to guide my own action, as I have through most of my prior career. This third reason for the disjunction between my sense of direction and that of most of my departmental colleagues reflects on a personal scale the more general phenomenon mentioned earlier that bridging knowledge and action requires a different paradigmatic approach to science from the modernist, positivistic, third-person approach. In any event, during the early years of the doctoral program, my work was viewed as outside the mainstream and perhaps dangerous, despite some indications that it "works" (e.g., research awards, teaching awards, consulting fees, documented organizational transformations, board positions, etc.). I was perceived as over-advocating this approach, and I felt more systematically frustrated and unsuccessful in communicating with departmental colleagues than ever before in my career (by contrast to more fulfilling relationships in other settings where I exercised, but did not explicitly advocate, Developmental Action Inquiry).

I was fortunate enough to be able to take on the Directorship of the doctoral program from 1994 to 1997. This gave me the opportunity for more real-time, organizational interactions with both faculty colleagues and doctoral students, and I experienced a gradual and partial transformation of my prior image within the department. In my role as director, I came to be viewed as reliable, as able to hear and address concerns, and as focused on helping students complete the program and market themselves successfully (though some of my colleagues have questioned whether I "spoiled" the students to some degree). During this time, students in the department won a wide range of national distinctions and awards, and these were obviously timely actions from the point of view of establishing a collective belief in the quality of our program as recognized from beyond its boundaries.

As director, it was prudent for me to reflect more about what was timely action in the context of our historical development. This reflection, along with the more disciplined and explicit effort to construct an outline of our history for the first version of this chapter, eventually opened me to the in-retrospect-blindingly-obvious realization of a fourth reason why our doctoral program was not instantaneously encouraging of single-double-, and triple-loop research/practice from its inception. Namely, in my own theoretical language, the program was evolving through the early developmental steps that eventually can lead to successful goal achievement based on single-loop feedback (the fifth stage in Table 13.4). Moreover, the senior faculty was simultaneously attempting to create fertile developmental conditions, not only for the doctoral program and students, but also for four, tenure-track junior faculty members. According to a developmental understanding, double- and triple-loop feedback may operate implicitly, within individuals or subgroups, during the early years of a new organizing process and new careers, but the organization as a whole can systematically choose to foster double- and triple-loop feedback processes explicitly and successfully only upon the foundation of single-loop feedback signifying relative success. For our doctoral program, this has happened only during the past year, when the first Ph.D's have been granted and our graduating students have received offers of university positions, as had been their and our aim. For our junior faculty, there are currently many positive interim signs of accomplishment, but their tenure decisions—the important single-, and double-loop feedback that transforms their status at the university—do not begin to occur until this coming 98-99 year (as this book goes to press, the two faculty members standing for tenure this year have won it).

Thus, my choice to study the history of our program eventuated in a transformation of my own intellectual and emotional appreciation for our department's accomplishments and direction. I am currently engaged in a continual recrafting of this chapter in response to departmental members' feedback in the hope that this process invites new insights for others as well.

A SECOND AND THIRD-PERSON HISTORY OF
THE BOSTON COLLEGE Ph.D. PROGRAM

My original historical outline of program events (see Table 13.1), divided into two-to-three year "eras," was based on: 1) my continual presence throughout that history (first-person data); 2) my at least relatively high ability to develop relationships of trust and confidentiality that generate valid data about others' views (second-person data); and 3) my own and the program's archival files (third-person data). Next, I asked five other members of the department (two faculty and three students) to respond and amend the outline (second-person validity test) before an initial paper was presented at the Academy of Management. Six months later—in order to explore and improve the validity of my initial history of the program, and simultaneously in order to encourage first- and second-person research/practice within the program itself around the questions of where we've been and where we're going–I circulated the original historical list of events to all department members. I asked for additions or revisions they would offer, with the promise of discussing this history and our present situation at an informal "brown bag" lunch seminar. This seminar will be described below.

Nine more students and one more faculty member responded in writing, providing the multi-voiced quotes in the current historical outline (see Table 13.1). Nineteen of twenty-one students and six of eleven available faculty attended the brown bag lunch seminar (it was noticed that none of the junior faculty were present; but while this may attest to their pressures and priorities, it does not reflect hostility or indifference, as I know from ongoing conversations with various ones of them). Fifth and finally until the present, I have received ten sets of comments on this paper from: two senior faculty members, two junior faculty members, four 3-6 year students, and two 1-2 year students, and all these have influenced the present manuscript in many ways, some of which become explicit below.

The following table (Table 13.1) results from these five iterations of history-construction. The table is not significantly different from the original in terms of sheer content. Indeed, it includes only one more item (a faculty member added "Board of Trustees support" to the 1989-91 period) other than student quotations and one date change. The change in voice resulting from the inclusion of student quotations is, however, a significant change. Quotes from individual students in italics (divided into two subgroups, "3-6 year students" and "1-2 year students") convey student experience of the program. The quotes are all from students because they were the prime contributors at this point in the research and because it seemed to me valuable for their colleagues and for the faculty to hear their perceptions and differences (e.g., the three final quotations in the 1996-98 period represent three quite different views). Each quotation is, of course, neither objective, nor representative, but rather one person's voice.

Table 13.1
Significant Events/Patterns during the First Decade of the
Boston College Organizational Transformation Doctoral Program

1987-89   1. University planning process "Goals for the Nineties" recommends
                Ph.D. in Management
              2. Initial design of possible Organization Studies program by
                department
              3. Department agreement on Organizational Transformation theme,
                balancing an action orientation (in research/consulting/teaching)
                with a strong quantitative and qualitative research emphasis

1989-91   1. Approval of program by School of Management faculty
              2. Delay in funding while Finance Ph.D. program goes forward
              3. Distinguished outside scholar calls department "Best Organization
                Behavior program in Boston"
              4. Board of Trustees support
              5. "Confrontative" meeting with Academic Vice President
                establishes funding for following year

1991-94   1. Recruitment of new and different faculty (more quantitatively
                oriented, but not hostile to multi-methods)
                *"New faculty are different from each other and from faculty
                already present. Is this a conscious choice? Is it a deviation from
                the transformation theme?"* (3-6 year student)
              2. Required courses in Change, Transformation, Consulting,
                Teaching & Qualitative Methods (as well as the more
                conventional Micro & Macro Theory, Statistics, and Quantitative
                Methods)
              3. Equal financial awards offered with admission (usually
                differential awards are offered separately from admission)
              4. Qualifying exam at end of first year (instead of Comprehensive
                exam after all course work is completed)
              5. Compete successfully with top tier doctoral programs recruiting
                students
              6. First director creates infrastructure and sense of legitimacy,
                working closely with Ph.D. Committee
              7. *"Move to St. Clements* (when Management School being rebuilt)
                *brings culture together through greater contact and more
                separation from others"* (3-6 year student)

1994-96
1. Tenured faculty change from 88% to 25% of department (with influx of new junior faculty and full complement of doctoral students)
2. Student-faculty participatory decision-making re guidelines, offices, assistantships (e.g., regular Director/Student meetings, faculty flexibility re student assistantship hours)
3. *"From my perspective as a member of the 2nd class, all "1sts" were crucial to the development of the program—e.g., 1st 2nd yr. research presentations, 1st Best Paper award (Benyamin), 1st dissertation defense (Go Karen!)"* (3-6 year student)
4. Marketing the program through annual newsletters & local and national student organization activism
"The proactive stance that Benyamin & Danna (& later Karen, Barbara, and Kate) took to the field (e.g., organizing students nationally into the Interdisciplinary Students Organization, creating the New Student Consortium at the Academy of Management) established a high profile for the BC program and encouraged others of us to 'seize the field'" (3-6 year student)
5. Intellectual Evenings for peer-like conversation of broad themes 4 to 6 times/yr.
6. Research on the program itself by students; concern among students about "undiscussables" among faculty
7. Second director nurtures both experiments and timely completion, with support of Ph.D. Committee
8. Every year at least one student drops out/leaves
9. June 1996: Entire class fails one or more parts of Qualifying Exam. (All who choose to retake the exam pass two weeks later.)

1996-98
1. Dissertation topics on change & transformation, using multiple research methods (quantitative, qualitative, participatory)
2. Five of six in first two classes win Best Paper Awards
3. First doctorate awarded 1997, in four years; first Ph.D. represents Carroll School of Management at university commencement
4. First three classes on 5 year average completion schedule, with four more doctorates achieved in 1998
5. First five on market receive multiple offers & placement at universities
6. *"The reality that some students will leave the program before finishing is better understood now than a few years back."* (3-6 year student)
7. Appointment of third Ph.D. Director
"The transition (of directors) has had an effect on community both salutory and negative and is evolving" (3-6 year student)

8. Concern among faculty that entering students are making a lower commitment to developing departmental synergies than earlier classes invites new conversation about the meaning, measurement indices, and ways of encouraging "community":

When I spoke with students here during the application process, one of the strong points about the program (they said) was the community. Boston University students, on the other hand, felt that the strong point of their program was its entrepreneurial spirit. "We could never adapt to that paternal culture at Boston College,' they said in so many words. BC appeared as an outsider to be a little more clubby, more of a neighborhood. Having been here for a while, I have not had a sense of community, in which we spend time together because we simply like each other. I expected more get-togethers, more collegiality with the faculty. The faculty keeps to itself. All are friendly one on one, but there is little group awareness.
(1-2 year student)

9. Some see movement from a balanced Action/Academic orientation to a focus solely on Academic orientation:

The Ph.D. program has promoted itself with a focus on organizational change and transformation and this label may apply to certain faculty but others have emerged. Action research/action science is the focus of Torbert's and Nielsen's work (a subcategory of change and transformation?). The students view it as a unique discipline. Stevenson, Jones, and Borgatti focus on social network analysis, and teaching is a major focus as well, which could be tied together into a multi-theme department. The scale has also been moving back toward the middle in terms of qualitative and quantitative research with the addition of new faculty (1-2 year student).

The current preliminary proposal to reconfigure the research methods courses and move the Consulting course from the first to the third year would send an important symbolic message about the role of action skills in the program. I have found that Consulting had an important influence on how I do my research and on how I teach and interact. I think a unique aspect of this program is getting us to develop experiential skills that enhance and complement other research skills (3-6 year student).

This table is by nature somewhat frustrating to read because its outline form raises many questions that are not answered in greater detail. The intent is: 1) to create just enough sense of the qualitative differences among the eras to permit the reader to compare each era to the characteristics of organizational structure and culture named later in Table 13.4; and 2) to invite members within the department to speak at greater length with one another and me about whichever incidents they wish. Here, we see a tension between a typical third-person history where the attempt is to offer a finished, authoritative account, and a history such as this which is meant to augment an ongoing second-person process of history-making-and-interpretation, as well as to serve as an illustration of this kind of scholarly work for third-persons.

CURRENT EVENTS (MARCH—AUGUST 1998)

After the "brown bag" lunch seminar had been planned and the initial draft of the history had been sent out for response (resulting in the expanded outline, with quotes, above), a faculty subcommittee circulated a preliminary proposal to amend the design of the program in an effort to strengthen the research methods sequence (this proposal was influenced by student input and is referred to in the next-to-last quotation in Table 13.1). Also, students called and held a student meeting about the program in response to faculty concern, expressed at a faculty meeting which includes a student representative, about students recently making a lower commitment to common activities (see #7 in 1996-98 section of Table 13.1).

So, the issue of how to interpret what is occurring in the program at present and how we wish it to evolve from here is currently "alive." The expansion of the list of historical events generated by the additional participation from the department, along with recent events, puts a stronger focus on the question of how to interpret current events and how to act in the coming days, months, and year. In order to indicate the level of controversy that such a list generates, I share the following comments offered by a junior faculty member and a senior faculty member after reviewing a draft of this (whole) chapter in July 1998:

> Junior faculty member: "I experience the junior faculty as somewhat demonized in this story–characterized as 'different' and as washing out a focus on change/transformation without a recognition of what has been brought in a positive way."

> Senior faculty member: "Why are all the quotes from students? I would think they would be the least informed informants concerning the history of the program. I think some of their

comments are misinformed. The most misinformed and perhaps inflammatory comment suggests the program has drifted from consulting to research. This appears to me to be a comment without any validity. From the start we have made it clear that this a research oriented program. This has been reaffirmed ad nauseam in faculty meetings. Bill, is there any faculty member who has seen this shift?"

I will respond briefly to each of these comments, not in an effort to have the final word, but rather in an effort to indicate the importance of a continuing second-person research/practice conversation about such matters. The junior faculty member's comment is certainly a plausible interpretation of the few references to junior faculty in a prior draft; it has influenced me to add: 1) the very-much-deserved positive comment about the junior faculty in my first-person historical summary above; 2) the explanatory parenthesis concerning the absence of junior faculty at the March 25 meeting; and 3) a brief interpretation below of the positive significance of having sought out "different" junior faculty.

In response to the senior faculty member's comment, I have now offered a brief explanation for having only student quotes before the table and have added the two faculty comments. In response to the senior faculty member's concluding inquiry, I would answer simply, "Yes, a few." But more important, the sense of a shift from a balance between action and research to an emphasis on research apart from action has been a continuing topic of student concern since the early days of the program. I think it is worth asking why. And I believe the response will reflect back on all of us in the program, refracting different lessons for each of us. Moreover, while I can see why student views of third-person research methodologies may in general be less developed and less valid than faculty members' views, it is not so clear to me why their versions of the history of the program are likely to be systematically less valid. It is true that none were present during the first two eras, but some have participated in it longer than some faculty. Also, students are required by their courses, papers, assistantships, and exams to interact repeatedly and rather intensively with most of the faculty and one another, whereas faculty have the freedom to conduct most of their interactions alone and in small subgroups, and their positions of relative power within the department can also potentially insulate them from valid data.

In any event, at the March 25 "brown bag" lunch seminar, I presented not only the outline of the program's history in Table 13.1, including the new quotes, but also the outline of personal, organizational, and scientific developmental paradigms shown in Table 5.2. Further, I suggested my view of how each of our short organizational eras represents an organizational transformation to a different operating paradigm (see Table 13.2, and compare names of eras to fuller descriptions in Table 13.4). Table 13.2 also highlights a few decisions or activity patterns of each era from Table 13.1. In my judgment, these events envision and/or enact themes and skills that reflect late developmental action-logics, indicating the potential for future evolution of the organization as a whole toward the later action-logics.

Table 13.2
Historical Events, by Developmental Era (as per Table 13.4), that Facilitate Further Transformation of the Boston College Organizational Transformation Doctoral Program

Conception **1987-89**
1. Department agreement on Organizational Transformation theme, with attention to both research and practice

Investments **1989-91**
1. 'Confrontation' with Academic Vice President

Incorporation **1991-94**
1. Recruitment of new *and different* faculty
2. Structural elements that empower students to operate relatively self-directingly (e.g., qualifying exam at end of first year; equal financial awards determined at admission)

Experiments **1993-96**
1. Student-faculty participatory decision-making re guidelines, offices, assistantships (regular director/student meetings)
2. Student activism in national student organizations
3. Research by students on the program itself

Systematic Productivity **1996-98**
1. Multiple offers to, & placement of, first five on the market
2. Five of six in first two classes win Best Paper Awards

Collaborative Inquiry **1999-2002???**

For example, the two items highlighted during the 1991-94 Incorporation era represent demonstrations of a willingness to encourage autonomy and difference among students and junior faculty. These structural commitments to valuing difference strike me as promising precursors for later-stage development of the program, when, not just single-loop feedback based on common standards of excellence, but also double- and triple-loop feedback based on different frames (such as this research explicitly introduces), become regular operating characteristics of an organization. The events highlighted in Table 13.2 can also often be construed as turning points in the program. For example, if the faculty had not initiated the characteristics of an organization. The events highlighted in Table 13.2 can also often be construed as turning points in the program. For example, if the faculty had not initiated the meeting with the Academic Vice President and pushed for a specific commitment at that meeting during the 1989-91 Investments era, the program might well never have achieved Incorporation.

Finally, in Table 13.3, I listed what seemed to me the foremost factors currently *facilitating* or *impeding* development by the Ph.D. program to the Collaborative Inquiry stage organizationally. (In response to an earlier draft of this paper, one faculty member suggests an additional "inhibiting" factor: the tendency toward social isomorphism through imitation of current high status programs.)

My only action recommendation to the participants at the "brown bag" seminar was for each individual energized to do so to initiate an evening of dialogue among a mixed group of perhaps four faculty and students, thus providing many local, decentralized occasions for relationship development and diverse conversation. This recommendation represents an attempt to address in a decentralized, voluntary, and mutual fashion (i.e., in a Collaborative Inquiry fashion) the final inhibiting factor identified in Table 13.3—the relative lack of visible cultivation of second-person research/practice among the faculty.

Figure 13.3
Most Significant Factors that *Support* or *Inhibit*
Further Transformation of the BC OS Ph.D. Program
(as adduced by the author to encourage further inquiry)

Support	*Inhibit*
1. Whole faculty actively involved in Ph.D.	1. Dominant paradigm(s) of field (see Table 5.1)
2. High profile of faculty and student 3rd-person research in field	2. Early stages of program until now & degree to which emphasis on successful market competition crowds out developmental time (see Tables 13.2, 13.3, and 13.4)
3. Lifetime dedication of three full professors to 1st-person research/practice (real-time, triple-loop learning)	3. Relative lack of visible cultivation 2nd-person research/practice skills among faculty
4. Engagement of about 1/2 of the students in interweaving 1st, 2nd, and 3rd person research/practice	

The second half of the "brown bag" seminar became a vivid illustration of the potential usefulness of such second-person research/practice in real time. A dialogue developed, led primarily by student contributions attesting to the significance for our good organizational health of: (1) having departmental members offering one another more direct feedback, so that one didn't learn of criticisms distortedly from third parties; and (2) recognizing and testing one's own attributions with the other participant(s) in occasions before reaching conclusions. One student offered a memorable "learning story" in this regard. She reported that she had been disturbed by reports that some students had acted rudely toward faculty members. Feeling that this very much hurt collective student credibility with faculty and committed to confronting whoever was responsible in as effective a manner as possible, she inquired about the particulars. To her astonishment, she discovered that she was one of the students alleged to have been rude. (She proceeded to discuss the incidents with the relevant faculty members.) There was some discussion about how this kind of daily second-person research/practice discipline could contribute to creating an atmosphere which, even more than at present, welcomes attempts, both informally and in formal written research products, to be explicit about and to interweave first-, second-, and third-person research/practice. [How differently this conversation could be interpreted by different participants is indicated by the comment of one senior faculty member afterwards that the students did not seem to care about my study of the department at all because they took the subsequent discussion (the one I have just reported) off in a different direction entirely.]

In the two months that followed, numerous small group dinners occurred. In addition, two junior students chose to conduct small interview research projects on department members' views about "feedback" and "community." Also, a small group of three advanced students who had been meeting for two years to develop their skills in "action science" [a second-person of research/practice (see Chapter 9, as well as Argyris, Putnam & Smith, 1985; Torbert, 1976)] invited others to form similar small groups, and twelve persons expressed initial interest. Meanwhile, the Consulting course has not been moved to the third year of the program; instead, a name-change to "Action Research Methods" has been approved, and it is to remain in the first year of the program. On a lighter note, students created, rehearsed, and performed a "departmental song" for the annual end-of-year departmental luncheon, thus directly and collectively making a generous and joyful contribution to the quality of second-person rhetoric in the department.

The junior student who studied department members' perceptions and conceptions of our "community" interviewed six of eleven faculty and nine of twenty-one students. She offered all members of the department the following executive summary of her findings:

> ". . . Results indicate many more similarities in our views than differences. (Shared) opinions about the characteristics of our community (included):

- positive aspects of the department: we are committed to and care about each other.

- negative aspects of the department: we are fractured by subgroups which are inherent in both the content and process of our work.

- the ideal type community: many would like more sharing, respect, collaboration, and engagement.

- barriers to the ideal type: we feel constrained for time and energy, and sense that the gap between our current community and ideal community is too big for us individually to impact.

"The biggest difference in our ideas deals with the normative definition of community and the requisite behaviors. Some indicated that community is singular, and that participation is a prime behavioral indicator of community. Others feel that there are multiple communities and that contribution, not participation, is the prime behavioral indicator of community.

"Regardless of respondents' positions on the normative definition, the most frequently mentioned descriptor of our community represented the idea of fragmentation (mentioned by 5 of 6 faculty and 7 of 9 students). Its prominence in interviews suggests that for some, there may be cognitive dissonance in thinking about the department as an oxymoronic 'fragmented community.' (Beatty, 1998, p.1)

FURTHER REFLECTIONS ON THE BOSTON COLLEGE DOCTORAL PROGRAM AND ON ORGANIZATIONS AND RESEARCH PARADIGMS MORE GENERALLY

During 1996 and 1997, tremendous emphasis was placed within the BC Organization Transformation doctoral program on helping students complete the program and obtain university-based positions. You can well imagine how different the program would feel to its members and how differently configured their sense of the challenges ahead would be, if we had *not* graduated our first student in May 1996, or if our first six students on the market had *not* received multiple academic offers, including pursuit and offers from top tier schools such as Texas A&M and Case Western Reserve University. These outside world results, along with the astonishing record of five of six members of the first two classes winning Best Paper Awards during the prior three years (not to mention a whole gamut of faculty successes), now provide the program with externally-validated confidence of its relevance to our field. In developmental terms, we appear to have reached the Systematic Productivity stage (see Table 13.2 and Table 13.4). This organizational action-logic parallels the Multi-Method Eclectic paradigm of science (see Table

5.2), which broadly encompasses the approach to dissertation research taken in five of the first six dissertations.

Table 13.4
Characteristics of Each Stage of Organizational Development
(drawn from Rooke & Torbert, 1998

Stage	Name	Characteristics
1	**Conception**	Dreams, visions, informal conversations about creating something new to fill need not now adequately addressed; interplay among multiple "parents"; working models, prototypes, related projects, or business plans developed; critical issues–timeliness and mythic proportions of vision.
2	**Investments**	"Champions" commit to creating organization; early relationship-building among future stakeholders; peer networks and parent institutions make spiritual, structural, financial commitments to nurture; critical issues–authenticity and reliability of commitments; financial investment appropriately subordinated to structural and spiritual investments.
3	**Incorporation**	Products or services produced; recognizable physical setting, tasks and roles delineated; goals and operating staff chosen; critical issues–display of persistence in the face of threat, maintaining or recreating consistency between original dream and actual organizational arrangements.
4	**Experiments**	Alternative administrative, production, selection, reward, financial, marketing and political strategies practiced, tested in operation and reformed in rapid succession; critical issues–truly experimenting, taking disciplined stabs in the dark, rather than merely trying one or two preconceived alternatives; finding a viable, lasting combination of strategy and structure for the following stage.
5	**Systematic Productivity**	Attention is legitimately focused only on the systematic procedures for accomplishing the pre-

defined task; marketability or political viability of the product or service, as measured in quantitative terms, is the overriding criterion of success; standards, structures, and roles are taken for granted as given and formalized, usually in deductive, pyramidal terms; reality is usually and most easily conceived of in deductive terms as dichotomous and competitive: win-lose, rational-emotional, leader-follower, personal-professional, practical-theoretical; critical issue: whether earlier development has provided a strong and appropriate analogical system that frames, and is not distorted by, the deductive systems developed during this stage.

| 6 | **Collaborative Inquiry** | Explicit shared reflection about the corporate dream/ mission and actuality/history in the wider social context; open rather than masked interpersonal relations, with disclosure, support, and confrontation of apparent value differences; systematic evaluation and feedback of corporate and individual performance on multiple indices; direct facing and creative resolution of paradoxes (which otherwise become polarized conflicts): inquiry-productivity, freedom-control, quantity-quality, etc.; interactive development of, and commitment to, unique, self-amending strategies and structures appropriate to this particular organization at this particular historical moment. |

| 7 | **Foundational Community** | Political friction within organization and with different norms of behavior in wider environments; regular, personal, shared research on relations among spiritual, theoretical, and behavioral qualities of experience; structure fails ('dies'), phoenix rises from the ashes, shared purpose (spirit) revealed as sustaining; transcendence of pre-existing cultural categories, appreciation of continuous interplay of opposites: action/research, sex/politics, past/future, symbolic/diabolic, etc.; new experiences of time: his-story becomes my-story: interplay of creative timeliness, timeless archetypes, and timebound needs. |

| 8 | **Liberating Disciplines** | Leadership practices deliberate irony; tasks incomprehensible and undoable without reference to accompanying processes and purposes; premeditated and precommunicated structural evolution over time; constant cycle of experiential and empirical research and feedback; leadership uses all available forms of power to support the previous four qualities, consistent with while also meeting the next three conditions; organizational structure open, in principle, to inspection and challenge by organizational members; leadership becomes vulnerable to attack and public failure in practice, if tasks, processes, and mission become incongruous and leadership does not acknowledge and correct such incongruities; requires leadership committed to, and highly skilled at seeking out, recognizing, and righting personal and organizational incongruities. |

As a Ph.D. program, we now have choices which we will make more or less explicitly and more or less collectively. Will we push ourselves to burnout repeating this successful systematic productivity performance, while losing our implicit transformational "feel"? Will we challenge ourselves toward further timely transformation by revisiting the question of whether we do or can share a vision? Will we relax just a little on our laurels and lose our edge? Will we define some fourth or fifth alternatives? Somewhat ironically, but not really very surprisingly if one steps back to reflect, the very success of the program in generating relatively high quality outcomes in the past year and a half has consumed energy that before was devoted to building some of our first- and second-person research/practice community infrastructure. This in turn means that our most recent two entering classes have in some respects been introduced to a more conventional and more pre-structured Ph.D. environment than those before them. The sudden spurt of student, faculty, and student-faculty meetings and departmentally-focused research projects at the end of the 1997-98 academic year, have in effect introduced our newest students to qualities of the department they had heard about but scarcely experienced (see Table 13.1). At the same time, the results of the student-initiated study of community within the department highlights a sense of fragmentation. Following the relatively centralized "corporate" reality of the Systematic Productivity stage, a sense of fragmentation is a necessary (though by no means sufficient) condition to motivate decentralized work on shared vision leading toward the next, Collaborative Inquiry organizational action-logic (see Table 13.4).

Thus, at this point, we have the possibility of developing from an *implicit* sense of community in building the organization to an *explicit* sense of a real-time community of inquiry that engages its members in the ongoing transformation of their sense of themselves, of the organization, and of the very institution of science. Such a community of inquiry is explicitly committed to exploring through first-, second-, and third-person research/practice how to manage the ongoing dilemmas of generating excellence and creativity, discipline and flexibility. In my understanding, we will not become a doctoral program that successfully bridges knowledge and action unless we take the step toward the later developmental action-logics. Nor can any other academic department, business organization, or not-for-profit agency bridge knowledge and action except through the later developmental action-logics. But the transformation from a Stage 5, Systematic Productivity organization, to a Stage 6, Collaborative Inquiry, organization is never mandated by an already constructed market. Nor are any of the postmodern action-logics blueprints that can simply be copied. The Collaborative Inquiry and other late stage action-logics always involve a voluntary, mutuality-enhancing restructuring of socially-received reality into unique configurations which share only the most abstract characteristics (see Table 13.4).

CONCLUSION

This chapter began with the notion that bridging knowledge and action requires a new kind of inquiring awareness that operates in the midst of real-time knowing and acting. The middle and end of the chapter concern a real-time process of inquiring into the knowing and acting of members of an organization, of whom the author himself is one. With all its incompleteness, my hope is that the work re-presented in this chapter can be of use to any person, group, or organization that values bridging inquiry and action and wishes to envision and enact organizing initiatives that integrate research and practice. At the same time, it matters even more to me that this rhetorical re-presentation of the underlying work engage the members of my own department in ways that are fruitful for them and for our episodic conversations. I have already commented briefly on the benefits of this historical and current work to this "first-person."

Does this work leave you with questions you will pursue? What do you see as the prospects for, and impediments to, paradigmatic, organizational, and personal transformation in your own social context toward serious engagement with research that bridges knowledge and action?

REFERENCES

Abram, D. (1996). *The spell of the sensuous.* New York: Vintage.
Argyris, C. (1980). *Inner contradictions of rigorous research.* New York: Academic Press.
Argyris, C. (1994). *Knowledge for action.* San Francisco CA: Jossey-Bass.
Argyris, C.& Schon, D. (1974). *Theory in practice: Increasing professional effectiveness.* San Francisco: Jossey-Bass.

Argyris, C., Putnam, R., & Smith, D. (1985) *Action science: Concepts, methods and skills for research and intervention.* San Francisco: Jossey-Bass.

Bartunek, J. & Moch, M. (1994). Third-order organizational change and the Western mystical tradition. *Journal of Organizational Change and Management,* 7(1), 24-41.

Beatty, J. (1998). Perceptions and conceptions of community in the organization studies department: a project designed to provide feedback about "community" to members of the community. Unpublished manuscript, Boston College, Chestnut Hill, MA.

Berman, M. (1981). *The reenchantment of the world.* Ithaca NY: Cornell University Press.

Berman, M. (1989) *Coming to our senses.* New York: Simon & Schuster.

Bernstein, R. (1985) *Beyond objectivism and relativism: Science, hermeneutics and praxis.* Philadelphia: University of Pennsylvania Press.

Bradbury, H., Bravette, G., Cooperrider, D., Ludema, J., Reason, P., & Torbert, W. (1998). "Creating a transformational science: dissertations that both inform and transform." Academy of Management Symposium, San Diego, CA.

Denzin, N. & Lincoln, Y. (1994). *Handbook of qualitative research.* Thousand Oaks CA: Sage.

Fisher, D. & Torbert, W. (1995). *Personal and organizational transformation: The true challenge of continual quality improvement.* London: McGraw-Hill.

Gadamer, H. (1982). *Truth and method.* New York, Crossroad Publishing

Heron, J. (1996). *Cooperative inquiry: Research into the human condition.* London: Sage.

Heron, J. & Reason, P. (1996). "A participatory inquiry paradigm." *Qualitative Inquiry* 3(3), 274-294.

Kegan, R. (1994). *In over our heads: The mental demands of modern life.* Cambridge, MA. Harvard University Press.

Kohlberg, L. (1981). *The philosophy of moral development.* San Francisco: Harper & Row.

Lawler, E., Mohrman, S. & Ledford, G. (1992). *Employee involvement and total quality management: Practices and results in Fortune 1000 companies.* San Francisco: Jossey-Bass.

Mitroff, I. (1974). *The subjective side of science: A philosophical inquiry into the psychology of the Apollo moon scientists.* Amsterdam: Elsevier.

Needleman, J. (1975). *A sense of the cosmos: The encounter of modern science and ancient tradition.* Garden City, NY: Doubleday.

Nielsen, R. (1996). *The politics of ethic.* New York: Oxford University Press.

Niven, D. (1993). "When times get tough, what happens to TQM?" *Harvard Business Review,* 71(3), 20-34.

Nonaka, I. & Takeuchi, H. (1995). *The knowledge-creating company.* New York: Oxford University Press.

Overton, W. (1997). Developmental psychology: philosophy, concepts, and methodology. In R. M. Lerner (Ed.), *Theoretical models of human development* (Volume 1 of W. Damon (Ed.-in-Chief) *Handbook of child psychology* (5th Ed.) New York: Wiley.

Piaget, J. (1965). *The moral judgment of the child.* New York: Free Press.

Pitkin, H. (1972). *Wittgenstein and Justice.* Berkeley CA: University of California Press.

Reason, P. (1995). General Medical and Complementary Practitioners Working Together: The Epistemological Demands of Collaboration. Paper presented at the Symposium on Transforming Self, Work, and Scientific Inquiry, Academy of Management national meeting, Vancouver.

Reason, P. & Rowan, J. (1981). *Human inquiry: A sourcebook of new paradigm research London*: Wiley.

Reason, P. (1995). *Participation in human inquiry.* London: Sage.

Rooke, D. & Torbert, W. (1998). Organizational transformation as a function of CEOs' developmental stage. *Organization Development Journal* 16(1), 11-28.

Schumacher, E. (1997). *A guide for the perplexed New* York: Harper & Row.

Senge, P. (1990). *The fifth discipline New* York: Doubleday Currency.

Senge, P., Kleiner, A., Roberts, C., Ross, R., Roth, G., & Smith, B. (1999). *The dance of change: The challenges to sustaining momentum in learning organizations.* New York: Doubleday Currency.

Spretnak, C. (1991). *States of grace: The recovery of meaning in the postmodern age.* New York: HarperCollins.

Torbert, W. (1976). *Creating a community of inquiry: Conflict, collaboration, transformation London*: Wiley Interscience.

Torbert, W. (1991). *The power of balance: Transforming self, society, and scientific inquiry.* Thousand Oaks: Sage.

Torbert, W. (1994). Cultivating post-formal adult development: higher stages and contrasting interventions. In M. Miller & S. Cook-Greuter (Eds.) *Transcendence and mature thought in adulthood: The further reaches of adult development.* Lanham MD: Rowman & Littlefield.

Torbert, W. & Fisher, D. (1992). Autobiographical awareness as a catalyst for managerial and organizational development. *Management education and development,* 23(3), 184-198.

"Total Quality" Special Issue of the *Academy of Management Review,* 9(3), 1994.

14 PRACTICE, PARTICIPATORY RESEARCH AND CREATIVE RESEARCH DESIGNS:
The Evolution of Ethical Guidelines for Research

Walter Haney
M. Brinton Lykes
Boston College

In this chapter we discuss dilemmas we have experienced as researchers within communities of action. We summarize briefly the guidelines and ethical standards for research with human subjects,[1] standards that formed the core of our socialization into the ethics of behavioral research. Until recently, these ethical standards and guidelines have evolved among various occupational groups with relatively little attention to the intersection of research methodology and ethical considerations. We describe how federal guidelines on research with human subjects have evolved and some of the effects these guidelines have had on research within the professions. Our personal experiences with ethical issues in research beyond university walls provide examples for discussing some of the inevitable dilemmas encountered in participatory and action-oriented research for change. Specifically, we explore the meanings of informed consent when one is engaged with communities in struggles for justice and/or in challenges to injustice within dominant institutions on behalf of those who are not being well-served by these institutions. Our experiences suggest limitations in applying abstract ethical guidelines and standards to such cases. We elaborate several dilemmas raised by creative research designs characteristic of much outreach scholarship for ethical standards and guidelines of selected occupational groups. Also, in an appendix we provide a summary of additional resources, both in print and on the World Wide Web, regarding ethical issues on social research.

It is worth noting that ethics, or moral philosophy, is concerned with the conduct and care of morals, that is, the study of principles and methods for distinguishing right from wrong, good from bad, and just from unjust. One of the first uses of the term "ethic," according to the Oxford English Dictionary came from Apol Poetrie (1581). "The Ethicke and politick consideration, with the end of well doing and not of well knowing only." This original use of "ethic" seems to convey much of the current concern for ethical consideration in research with human subjects—the need to balance not just the research aim of contributing to knowledge, but the moral aim of not just well knowing but well doing in one's dealings with other humans. In the work discussed here we are particularly concerned with issues of justice and how justice is articulated within and among diverse communities.

By way of introduction, we acknowledge also that we are not well versed in philosophy or the study of ethics in general. Despite this we hope it will be useful to describe some of what we have learned about the evolution of guidelines in research with human subjects and how contemporary institutional guidelines on research with human subjects stem quite specifically though indirectly from the most unfortunate Tuskegee syphilis study. After this review we summarize the manner in which we have sought to deal with ethical dilemmas in some of our own research. In particular we describe how we have dealt with issues such as informed consent when work that began as something other than formal research evolved into just that. Also, we describe how we have had to go beyond the normal boundaries of academic inquiry to use research not just to contribute to knowledge, but to effect social change. We hope that our discussion of our own dilemmas, and our perceptions of the limitations of ethical guidelines on research with human subjects, will inform ongoing consideration of ethical issues and future revisions of ethical guidelines.

ETHICAL STANDARDS AMONG OCCUPATIONAL GROUPS

Many professions have developed ethical codes or standards. Apparently the oldest code of ethics for an occupational group is the Hippocratic Oath, with its rules of conduct for physicians. It dates back to the fourth century BC and contains two major sections. The first specifies the duties of the physician to his teachers and his obligations in transmitting medical knowledge. The second provides rules to be observed in the treatment of diseases and is a short summary of medical ethics expressed in general principles. In a 1948 Geneva Convention, a modern version of the oath was drawn up by the World Medical Association and this was amended in 1968, as follows:

> At the time of being admitted a member of the medical profession swears:

> I solemnly pledge myself to consecrate my life to the service of humanity; I will give my teachers the respect and gratitude

which is their due; I will practice my profession with conscience and dignity; The health of my patient will be my first consideration; I will respect the secrets which are confided in me, even after the patient has died; I will maintain by all the means in my power, the honor and the noble traditions of the medical profession; my colleagues will be my brothers. I will not permit considerations of religion, nationality, race, party politics or social standing to intervene between my duty and my patient; I will maintain the utmost respect for human life from the time of conception; even under threat I will not use my medical knowledge contrary to the laws of humanity. I make these promises solemnly, freely and upon my honour.

In the twentieth century, many professional groups have developed their own codes of ethics; for example, codes of ethics have been developed by the American Psychological Association (APA), the National Educational Association (NEA), the American Federation of Teachers (AFT), and the American Educational Research Association (AERA). The oldest of these modern ethical standards of occupational groups is the ethical standards of psychologists (APA) promulgated in 1953. This original version of APA ethical standards for psychologists was 170 pages long, divided into six sections dealing with public responsibility, client relationships, teaching, research, writing and publishing, and professional relationships. The section dealing with research contained three specific guidelines dealing with the psychologist's responsibility (1) for adequately planning and conducting research, (2) for reporting research results, and (3) for relating to research subjects. The latter guideline outlined the psychologist's responsibility for protecting the subject's welfare, for preventing unauthorized identification of subjects and fulfillment of obligations to subjects. The 1953 APA standards made no mention specifically of informed consent as a general requirement. Specifically, under Principle 4.31-2 the psychologist is justified in withholding information from or giving false information to research subjects only when in his (sic) judgment this is clearly required by his (sic) research problem and when the provisions of the above principles regarding the protection of subjects are adhered to. A parenthetical comment followed this guideline noting that when the danger of serious after-effects exists, research should be conducted only when the subjects or their responsible agents are fully informed of this possibility and volunteer nevertheless. (Haney & Madaus, 1990).

Since 1953 the ethical guidelines of the APA have gone through several revisions. In 1958 they were revised and renamed *The Standards of Ethical Behavior for Psychologists*. The 1963 revision was entitled *The Ethical Standards of Psychologists*. It was revised again in 1977, 1981 and 1990. The most recent version of the APA's guidelines, issued in 1992, was called *The Ethical Principles of Psychologists and Code of Conduct*.

By 1981, Principle 9 of the Ethical Principles dealt specifically with research with human subjects and provided a much stronger guideline for informed consent, specifying the obligation of psychologists to gain informed consent of research subjects. Nonetheless, the following standard still held out the possibility of dispensing with informed consent under the following circumstances:

> Before determining that planned research (such as research involving only anonymous questionnaires, naturalistic observations, or certain kinds of archival research) does not require the informed consent of research participants, psychologists consider applicable regulations and review board requirements, and they consult with colleagues as appropriate.[2]

Continuing and increasing concern for ethical issues in research with human beings is reflected in the fact that in late 1998, the APA has circulated for public comment a new proposed revision of its ethical guidelines.

In contrast to the APA Ethical Standards, the American Educational Research Association (AERA) has only very recently issued ethical standards. In June 1992, the AERA developed and adopted *The Ethical Standards of the American Educational Research Association*. These standards were intended to be an educational document to "stimulate collegial debate, and to evoke voluntary compliance by moral persuasion. Accordingly it is not the intention of the Association to monitor adherence to the Standards or to investigate allegations of violations of the Code." The 1992 AERA Ethical Standards apprised: "Participants, or their guardians, in a research study have the right to be informed about the likely risks involved in the research and of potential consequences for participants, and to give their informed consent before they participate in research."[3]

Before analyzing some of our own research experiences in which these guidelines proved helpful but problematic, we backtrack to recount the manner in which federal guidelines on research with human subjects evolved. An understanding of this sociohistorical context will contribute to better understanding the limitations of current guidelines.

FEDERAL GUIDELINES ON RESEARCH WITH HUMAN SUBJECTS

As early as mid-century international guidelines for research with human subjects had been established; for example in the Nuremberg Code of 1947 (e.g., the Declaration of Helsinki issued in 1964 and amended in 1975, and the International Guidelines for Biomedical Research Involving Human Subjects proposed in 1982 by the Council for International Organizations of Medical Sciences (CIOMS) and the World Health Organization (WHO) (LaVertu & A.M. Linares, 1990). Increased attention to guidelines on research with human subjects in the United States was prompted in the United States by hearings in 1973 of the Senate Health Committee, then chaired by Senator Edward Kennedy. The Senate Health Committee held these hearings to investigate abuses in research with human subjects. Among the prominent cases dealt with in these hearings was the Public Health Service Tuskegee study in which 400 Black men with syphilis were studied from 1932 to 1972. They participated in this study for 40 years without ever being told that they had the disease or being treated for it, even though penicillin, a cure for the disease, had been discovered in 1943. The Tuskegee Study was terminated only after details of the study were uncovered by an intrepid newspaper reporter. Publicity given to the Tuskegee tragedy and other abuses led quite directly to the promulgation of federal guidelines. In 1974 the National Research Act mandated the National Commission for the protection of Human Subjects of Biomedical and Behavioral Research and the creation of Institutional Review Boards or IRBs in all institutions that were receiving federal research money. In 1975 the Department of Health, Education and Welfare ordered every institution applying for research grants to establish an IRB to evaluate grant submissions.

The 1979 Belmont Report, one of the key documents in the evolution of federal guidelines concerning research with human subjects, set out the Ethical Principles and Guidelines for the Protection of Human Subjects of Research. This was sponsored by the National Institutes of Health (NIH), Public Health Service (PHS), and the Health and Human Services Department (HHS). Specifically, the Belmont Report described the boundaries between research and practice as well as the basic ethical principles undergirding specific guidelines for research, namely respect for persons, beneficence, and justice. The third part of the Belmont report drew out the specific applications or guidelines motivated by these ethical principles: concern for informed consent, an assessment of risks and benefits, and care in selection of subjects. The federal guidelines evolved quite rapidly after this. The Code of Federal Regulations, with provisions dealing with research with human subjects was issued in 1981, March of 1982, July 1989, and again in 1991. Specifically, the June 18, 1991 Federal Register (10 C.F.R. part 27) set forth a common federal policy for protection of human subjects agreed to by sixteen federal agencies. In addition to elaborating standards for review by institutional review boards (IRB), this federal guideline also mandated establishment of procedures for dealing with cases of alleged misconduct. These federal guidelines have resulted in the establishment of IRBs in every research institution receiving or aspiring to receive, federal funding. In essence, Congressional and public outrage over the Tuskegee Study in the early 1970s led indirectly, but quite specifically, to the mandate for IRBs in universities and other research institutions in the 1990s.

ETHICAL DILEMMAS IN APPLIED AND ACTION RESEARCH

Like all seasoned researchers working beyond university walls, both of us have had personal ethical quandaries in conducting research. We grapple with our professional guidelines as we work on behalf of people who have been, not subject, but rather participants in our research. Even more difficult have been situations in which initiatives that began as something other than formal research evolved over an extended period into research. In some instances, for example, we have developed collaborative relationships over years of community-based activism that led us to seek to creatively design participatory research. As human relationships evolve, it is sometimes difficult to distinguish roles of researcher and subject, and hence to apply existing ethical guidelines that presume a clear and unchanging delineation of these roles. In a 1979 *American Psychologist* article Mirvis & Seashore, facing similar experiences within their own organizational research, proposed that role theory was a resource for analyzing such ethical quandaries. Rather than proposing prescriptive roles for the researcher they explored how critique of our own roles, norms that govern our roles and institutions themselves, can inform ethical decision-making within a field research process (Mirvis & Seashore, 1979). Our experiences suggest additional considerations in ongoing efforts to articulate ethical research guidelines.

Within this context, Walt Haney describes two of his experiences in trying to use research to effect social change. Brinton Lykes then discusses her experiences crossing cultural borders employing participatory research methods. What is common about these accounts, drawn from different research traditions and settings, is that they illustrate both the utility and the difficulty in applying abstract ethical guidelines to endeavors which are not just academic research *on* others as subjects but rather inquiry *with* others to improve practice (see Torbert, Chapter 5, on Cooperative Inquiry).

INSTITUTIONS AS OBJECTS/SUBJECTS OF INQUIRY

The first case began in 1991 when I was asked to help a young man who had, in effect, been accused of cheating on the Scholastic Aptitude Test (SAT) and was under threat of having his scores canceled. The young man, to whom I refer as John Smith, had taken the SAT twice. On the March 1990 administration he had received an SAT-Verbal score of 280. On the November 1990 SAT, he had received an SAT-V score of 500. This gain of 220 points, while unusually large, was not of sufficient magnitude to trigger screening by Test Security Office (TSO) of the Educational Testing Service (ETS). However, one of the recipients of John Smith's scores asked ETS about the unusual gain, and that inquiry triggered TSO review of the case. Among other things the ETS investigators compared Smith's answers with those of other test-takers in the same test center. Apparently, the large score gain combined with an unusual agreement of answers apparent in answer sheets of Smith and another test taker prompted ETS to accuse Smith of cheating and threaten to withhold his scores.

After a flurry of correspondence between ETS and Smith, Smith's parents contacted me and, due to my interest in the obscure subject of statistical methods for detecting possible cheating on tests (that is how the topic is often described in published literature, but I prefer to refer to the topic as statistical methods for identifying unusual answer concordance), I decided to look into the case. After a quick literature review, an analysis of the facts in the case, and statistical analyses to try to reproduce ETS's answer concordance results, I concluded that the statistical evidence against Smith was not at all persuasive, and that the manner in which ETS had handled the case was in violation of specific provisions of the 1985 test *Standards*. After a memo summarizing my findings was sent to the ETS Test Security Office by Smith's father, the case against Smith was dropped and his scores were released.

Concerned about what I had learned, I sought Smith's parents' permission to bring my concerns to the attention of top officials at ETS and to circulate a pseudonymous version of my memo. At this point in this story an ethical dilemma arises: A young man whom I had started out trying to help, turned into my research "subject," when I started sharing information (and eventually publishing accounts) about his case. Under the circumstances, I could not obtain informed consent before the research began (though some sort of consent might be imputed from Smith's request for help). As an alternative solution, I showed Smith and his parents my pseudonymous account of the case and obtained their approval before circulating the story.

The larger ethical dilemma occurred afterwards. Through the ETS officials to whose attention I had sought to bring my concerns thanked me for my observations, they left me with little confidence that the procedures I thought were severely flawed would be changed. However, in August 1992, I learned of a second test security case in which a young man named Brian Dalton had challenged ETS test security procedures in a New York court. In a trial lasting two weeks, several ETS security specialists had been called to testify. The trial court concluded that Dalton's legal challenge was meritorious and ordered ETS to release the questioned scores. ETS appealed this decision to a higher court. My reading of the transcripts of the Dalton trial led me to conclude that the TSO procedures were even more flawed than I had suspected from my work on the Smith case. Hence, in connection with a paper under preparation (Haney, 1993a), I formally requested that three professional organizations that had sponsored the 1985 test *Standards* (the American Psychological Association, American Educational Research Association, and the National Council on Measurement in Education) investigate what I suspected to be serious and ongoing violations of professional standards (Haney, 1993a; 1993b). Each organization responded by thanking me for my concerns, but declining to take on my request.

There are a variety of reasons that these organizations may have declined to do anything about my request, but one of the most obvious was that none of these organizations had a mechanism in place for investigating violations of professional standards by organizations as opposed to individuals. Although the APA has developed procedures for investigating violations by individual psychologists, the Association noted that in the case I had raised the alleged violations were the responsibility not of a psychologist but rather of an organization. The response indicated that the APA simply had no precedent or procedures for dealing with ethical transgressions, or alleged ethical transgressions, by an organization. This experience showed that only one of these three professional groups had developed mechanisms for adjudicating alleged transgressions of existing codes. As importantly it showed that while the APA had developed mechanisms to review ethical behavior of individual members of the organization, it had no way of dealing with acts by groups or institutions, such as corporations, government agencies or community-based groups.

The dilemma for me at this point was what to do next. I had tried direct communications with top officials of ETS, and had received in effect a polite "thanks, but no thanks." I had tried appeals to relevant professional organizations, but they told me there was nothing they could do. Instead of letting the matter drop, I decided to "go public" so to speak by writing an opinion/editorial on the topic (Haney 1993b), and by alerting newspaper reporters to the story, leading to coverage in newspapers such as *USA Today*. Subsequently, ETS did convene an independent panel to review and recommend changes in its test security procedures. Since 1995, ETS's test security procedures have been changed. I suspect that the review and changes were due more to ETS's loss of the Dalton trial (the first of some 20 test security cases the organization had not won) than to my own efforts. As a result of changes in test security procedures at ETS in the mid-1990s, I am hopeful that the concerns I raised about previous procedures, apparent in the Smith and Dalton cases, are no longer germane. However, this experience illustrates a lesson quickly learned by anyone engaged in action research. If one seeks to use research to effect social change, particularly if large organizations are involved, it is almost always necessary to go beyond the normal bounds of scholarly publications and communications.

USING STUDENT DRAWINGS AS A FORM INQUIRY AND RESEARCH

Work by Walt Haney and colleagues in the Center for the Study of Testing Evaluation and Educational Research in using student drawings as a form of inquiry has raised two quite different ethical dilemmas; how to contend with informed consent when a project that did not begin as formal research evolves into publishable work; and second, how should researchers help others use innovative but unproven approaches to social inquiry.

Our work with student drawings evolved out of two projects in which we helped middle schools to evaluate the progress of their own ambitious reform efforts (Haney, et al., 1998). As a result of our interest in using multiple modes of assessment, we helped schools develop surveys that included both multiple-choice type survey questions and open-ended written questions (e.g., "What is the most important thing you have learned in school this year?" "What do you think should be done to make your school better?"). An additional survey item read as follows: *"Think about the teachers and the kinds of things you do in the classroom. Draw a picture of one of your teachers working in his or her classroom."*

After the surveys (and other testing) were completed, we met with school staff to present the results and help them make sense of the results. Though we presented a wide range of assessment results (based on multiple-choice tests, written tests and performance assessments, and surveys of student attitudes), from the very first time we used student drawings in 1994, we were struck with how engaging the drawings were for teachers. When teachers discussed students' test results, conversations were typically brief and tended to focus on whether more or less of various subject matters should be taught. However, when stimulated by student drawings, discussions tended to be more extended and to focus not just on what was taught but also on how it was taught.

In 1995, we helped organize student surveys, including the drawing prompt, at five schools in three sites. Again we found that student reflection surveys, and the drawings in particular, were powerful in that they promoted reflection on the part of teachers about their methods of teaching, and analyses of these drawings were a simple but powerful way to document changes in the educational ecology of schools. Subsequent experience leads us to think that student drawings may be a powerful means for promoting reflection on instructional practices not just at school and district levels, but also among teachers and students.

More recently, in 1996 through 1998, we provided technical assistance to urban school districts funded under the Edna McConnell Clark Foundation's Program for Student Achievement. As part of this work we have helped close to three dozen schools undertake survey research, including student drawings. Again, we have often found that the drawings provide an unusually stimulating form of student generated evidence about what is happening in schools. For example, *Corpus on School Administrator* reported:

> . . . the survey had provided the most insightful information they had received regarding student perceptions of the academic standards and the strategies utilized by teachers, or the lack of such, in teaching the standards.

> . . . Analysis of the drawings and use of the rubric helped teachers to see the classroom through the eyes of students who "tell it like it is." (Lyons, 1997)

Another school principal reported that using drawings has been "especially helpful in allowing us to learn the feelings of our learning disabled students" and added that Middle school kids in general have a difficult time communicating with adults. The drawing lets us get some of the nonverbal communicators to give us their impressions" (quoted in Tovey, 1996, p. 6).

This work raised questions about informed consent stemming from outshift in roles. Our work with schools had begun as technical assistance aimed at helping them to examine their own educational practices. The results of the student surveys were intended primarily for internal school improvement efforts. We had not sought to obtain informed consent from the thousands of students who were being surveyed because we viewed the surveys as a routine form of educational practice with the schools and not formal research intended for external publication. However, as the work with student drawings proceeded with apparent success, we and others became interested in writing about it and including examples of student drawings.

To balance the research goal of contributing to the knowledge base on an important social issue with the need for fairness to one's subjects, we conceived of the subjects to the research more broadly. Since the drawings had been undertaken for the benefit of the schools with which we were working, we decided that it would be fair to reproduce drawings only with the permission of the schools involved. Most schools readily gave us permission, but in a few instances schools requested that none of their students' drawings be reproduced. This balance was justified, in part, because the student surveys, including the drawings, had been undertaken anonymously, leaving us and readers of the research no way to identify individual artists. However, in two instances, when we or an education writer wanted to reproduce individual drawings widely, we sought to track down the identity of individual artists to obtain their permission and potentially give them public credit for their drawings.

A second dilemma in our work with student drawings arose as we tried to help schools make sense of the drawings that are an unusual and unproven form of inquiry. We resolved this dilemma, through candor and full disclosure. For instance, we were often asked whether the drawings might simply represent students' stereotypes of teachers rather than the reality of teaching that students had actually experienced. Candidly, we responded that people in the schools from which drawings originated are in a much better position than we, as outsiders, to discern the meaning of the drawings, and we are uncertain about the meaning of the drawings and the extent to which they represent typical reality of teaching experienced, student stereotypes of teachers, and/or critical or memorable incidents that individual artists may have experienced in their classes. Because we have found the work with student drawings so promising, we have begun a more formal research study into the reliability and validity of drawings as means of documenting and changing the educational ecology of classrooms and schools (Russell & Haney, 1999). After several years' experience working with several dozen schools we are convinced that though unusual, drawings represent an extremely promising means of action research and social inquiry.

ETHICAL QUANDARIES IN PARTICIPATORY ACTION RESEARCH

Brinton Lykes has also had multiple experiences involving groups or collectivities of participants in community-based, participatory action research (PAR). PAR refers to a set of processes and practices whereby knowledge and action are produced by and for groups traditionally excluded from power and resources. Consciousness-raising ("a process of self-awareness through collective self-inquiry and reflection," Fals-Borda & Rahman, 1991, p.6) and sociopolitical action are achieved through genuine collaboration in research and education at the community level. PAR has a long tradition within committed social science and liberationist movement (Fals-Borda & Rahman, 1991; Gaventa, 1991; McTaggart, 1997) and has more recently been applied to work in Western organizations (Whyte, 1991; see also, Reason, 1994).

In this research the boundaries between researcher and research participant are often less clear than in traditional research. Moreover, because of the evolving nature of PAR, it is often the case that one may be engaged with individuals in a practice relationship long before the research aims of the collaboration evolve. In these cases, the exact manner by which one might adhere to prevailing ethical standards for informed consent is not altogether clear.

Several specific examples may clarify these points. The first involved an oral history project in which I collaborated with a local research center in Mexico City. The Center hoped to develop popular education pamphlets from the life stories/oral histories that I was gathering with a colleague (Lykes, 1989; 1996). In the design of the informed consent, I was particularly sensitive to power differentials, including language, culture, education, social class and racial/ethnicity. The human subjects review committee at my university underscored their concern that the women I hoped to interview have psychological or counseling resources, should their conversations with me and my colleague elicit negative psychological effects. I sought to "equalize" power, or at least articulate these differentials through the informed consent form, wanting it to reflect my attention to the ethical considerations of all research involving human subject (i.e., respect for persons, concern for beneficence, and justice).

Imagine my surprise when I encountered resistance on the parts of the participants not to the research itself, but to the informed consent form. These experiences (Lykes, 1989, Lykes, 1996) continue to inform how I think about the challenges facing university researchers seeking to collaborate with community-based participants in the co-construction of social inquiry and knowledge. Similar dilemmas have been explored by LaVertu and Linares (1990) in their discussion of the limits of ethical principles of biomedical research in working in some parts of the Third and Fourth (sic) worlds where concepts of informed consent may be difficult to articulate. This is particularly true in societies wherein the "life of each person assumes meaning in relation to his role in the community" (LaVertu & Linares, 1990, p. 74) and/or wherein the hierarchical relations within the community may dictate that consent is obtained from the local authority rather than the individual participant. The meaning of individuality and "freedom to choose" has cultural variability.

The reciprocal process of developing ties, building trust, and establishing rapport prior to beginning the research constituted "informed consent" and "ethical behavior" from their point of view. The introduction of a form, which required their approval and signature, shifted the developing understandings of power and powerlessness. As Robert Levine (1982, cited in LaVertu & Linares, 1990) suggested, the purpose served by informed consent and the document used to obtain it are not identical. In hindsight I also realized the extent to which the form itself was inscribed in a process designed to protect the researcher and her institution, not the participants within the developing relationship we were constructing. The very power differentials as researcher-participant that I was seeking to reorganize as we developed our relationships prior to beginning the interviews were thus undermined by the document. Since I authored the form as researcher, rather than co-authoring it with the "subjects", it reflected my voice including *my* voicing of what I anticipated to be *their* concerns. As importantly, I underestimated the complex meanings of asking for a signature rather than "one's word" as a commitment (LaVertu & Linares, 1990), especially among refugees of a war. The collaboration and trust that we developed and that contributed to their willingness to engage with me in the research process did not erase power differences between us. Rather, it enabled each of us to better understand our relative power and resources. Such understanding was critical for the Mayan women to agree to participate in the study organized by a Unitedstatesian researcher, from a country that was arming their government against its people. Yet, the informed consent form neither reflected that newly constructed understanding nor was it sensitive to the developing bonds between participants and researchers who provide many different resources for negotiating power differences.

ETHICAL CONSIDERATIONS IN PAR IN RURAL GUATEMALA

The power of differences in the developing relationships among participating researchers became clear when I sought to articulate the ethical considerations for a PAR project in which I have been engaged in rural Guatemala. I had worked with a local women's organization for nearly six years prior to our developing a PAR project. Within that context I had facilitated training workshops on organizational development, women's self-esteem, and the use of creative techniques for psychosocial work with child survivors of war. I had lived with the family of one of the women in the group and come to know many within the community as personal friends. As we worked together I became more and more concerned with the boundaries of what constituted my ethnographic observations of the process we were co-constructing and what was confidential conversation, not for sharing beyond the intimacy of our encounters. The ongoing war and the deeply complicated politics of the peace negotiations (broader social realities within which our relationships had developed) offered additional reasons for maintaining uncharacteristic silence about what I was discovering.

My own increasing concerns for sharing our developing understandings of women and children's lives in war torn countries and the eventual signature of Peace Accords between the URNG (Guatemalan National Revolutionary Unity) and the

Guatemalan government at the end of 1996, created a social space in which we were able to begin to collaborate in developing a research project. We sought to enhance our existing relationships in the co-construction of meaning making and action plans for change. I was particularly conscious, from my earlier research experiences with Maya women, to select research methods that enhanced control of the Maya Ixil women participants in both the knowledge construction and subsequent actions we sought to develop within their community and beyond.

The method we adopted to achieve our goals was used successfully in China with non-formally educated women who used their photographs as a tool for influencing local health and education policies (Wang, 1999; Wang, Wu, Zhan & Carovano, 1998). The focus of our work in rural Guatemala includes an analysis and re-presentation of the experiences of violence, displacement, and loss due to the war and their effects on the health and education of women and children now living in this rural town and its surrounding villages. Based on this documentation and subsequent analysis of the data gathered, participants will identify possible responses, communicate these to a wider community, and strategically plan additional community-based programs that they can coordinate to address their articulated needs.

Ethical considerations have been central to this ongoing two-year PAR project at multiple levels. We began the process by clarifying ethical issues that emerge in any research process and discussing parameters and guidelines for a project involving taking pictures of others (e.g., When would you not want to have someone take a picture of you? Should you ask someone permission before you take their photograph?). The methods for data generation and collection involve participation of all members of the team of twenty. In year one the women took multiple rolls of film based on a set of research goals and specific thematic content developed collaboratively through creative workshops. Once pictures were developed each woman told the story of between 5-7 pictures (per roll of 24) and these were recorded. We then met as a group of twenty participants and two technical assistants (including myself as principle investigator and a graduate student from the U.S. who was living in the community for year one). The gatherings were designed: (1) to discuss themes that had emerged, (2) to compare and contrast our initial understandings of what we have selected to photograph and our understandings of the pictures now that we had taken them, and (3) to analyze the reality of women and children based on these representations, (4) to discuss difficulties, and (5) to adapt our process to our developing understandings and needs.

This work draws on Freirian techniques of popular education and analysis (Freire, 1970), on photovoice (Wang, Burris & Ping, 1996), "talking pictures" (Bunster & Chaney, 1989) and participatory strategies we have used over the previous five years involving the use of indigenous creative resources including weaving, dramatization, and storytelling (see, e.g., Lykes, 1994,1996; Zipes, 1995). This iterative process of data analysis has been completed and we are currently engaged in the selection of photographs and text to develop a published presentation of these stories for a wider public. The methods adapted facilitate collaboration, not only in the co-construction of meaning making and action plans for change, but also in the exercise of more control by Maya Ixil women in the re-presentation of such knowing and doing to a wider public. As importantly, ongoing engagement of leaders among this group of twenty in training workshops to enhance skills in organizational development, accounting, and data management contributes to sharing additional aspects of power within the research process and to the development of ever-more collegial relations (Biggs, 1989). These participatory resources are catalysts for building cooperation, re-threading community, and enhancing problem-solving strategies among the participants, thereby enhancing understanding while also creating opportunities for sharing and for the development of skills and resources to confront some of the individual and collective effects of war, terror and violence. The data gathered and analyzed are the basis from which participants will design health and education programs for women and children in the participating communities. As importantly, they are acquiring skills that will enable them to evaluate these projects and generate new ones as the community develops and its needs change in relation to changing political and social realities. Photovoice offers an important alternative both at the level of the photograph and, more importantly, at the level of analysis. The photograph re-presents the photographer's perspective or point of view but then becomes a stimulus for the group's reflections, discussions, analyses and re-presentations. The fixed image offers a visual stimulus to ever-widening circles of women that can also be widely "read," providing the opportunity for a discussion of the differing views of reality that are present within these Maya Ixil communities.

The processual nature of the development of this PAR experience results in several ongoing ethical considerations. The ethical considerations raised here go far beyond those of the informed consent but suggest strongly that in PAR not only do the borders between who is a researcher and who is a participant easily blur but the multiple categories which inform critical understandings of power and powerlessness also begin to shift. Building relationships over time as one does in many participatory research processes heightens one's sense of mobile identities or multiple selves. For example, although I bring power and resources into this community, as a Unitedstatesian with a doctorate I do not know either the local indigenous language or the local culture and politics. As I begin to learn the latter I gain power and as the participants begin to develop as researchers they gain power. Within the local community their language skills give them access to power and decision making from which I am excluded. Within these continually changing relations, power is transformed and identity claims shift. However these developing relationships are constrained by wider community dynamics which sometimes do not recognize the micro changes within our research relationships and processes.

Significantly, many of these changes can be traced directly to research interventions that are constitutive of all PAR projects. For example, studies of photography in Central America and, more particularly, in Guatemala, reveal a "preference" for more formal rather than informal photographic representations (Parker & Neal, 1982). A picture is something very special for which one must dress appropriately and take on a serious demeanor. Photovoice, in contrast, records everyday experiences and thereby assumes spontaneity and informality on the parts of those being photographed, which may not be common among members of these rural communities. Thus, the methodology functions as a "cultural intervention" despite the fact that it is members of the "home culture" who themselves selected this strategy, thereby introducing the intervention. As the work has proceeded I have come to better understand that the "Western collaborators" and the "indigenous researchers/participants" share multiple concerns about justice, beneficence and respect in the operationalization of this project. However, it is clear that we have differently weighted priorities. Although I want very much to improve the quality of life (and the material resources) of this rural community I am deeply interested in better understanding how knowledge of the war, its effects, and responses to them, is co-constructed and represented at the local level among indigenous women. These latter concerns are deeply constitutive of my ongoing work within this community. They are of increasing interest to the Maya Ixil leadership within the group but of much less concern to young mothers seeking additional resources for feeding and caring for themselves and their children.

Secondly, this brief description illustrates the processual nature of PAR and the ways in which "participant" and "researcher" are mobile categories that re-present the realities of those involved in very differing ways in this process. We shared an articulated vision of the research when we "officially" inaugurated this research project, taping a conversation about our "informed consent" and dialoguing about risks to those within our research group, those whose pictures we would be taking, and those whose stories we would be recording. However, as the research is developing we encounter additional ethical challenges. For example, the costs of developing film and reproducing pictures are particularly noteworthy within a subsistence economy wherein the funding for this project could support many of the community's survival needs. For example, in some rural towns where few own cameras, a single entrepreneur can establish a "photography shop," offering services to photograph special events, including weddings, funerals, etc. Some women in our project with entrepreneurial spirit had hoped to use their cameras "after hours" to establish a similar business opportunity. The local mayor had initially resisted giving initial permission to the women for the project because he feared such a development. The limited financial resources of all participants made the idea of opening a business particularly appealing to many. I resisted the idea, reminding them of our earlier goals of developing a collective effort that would eventually benefit not only the women's organization that had generated the project but the wider community as a whole. Repeated group discussions helped clarify the distinctions between the camera as an individual resource for economic development and the camera as a resource for social change and justice. Together the women decided to suspend further discussion of picture-taking for income until they completed their two year PAR project, at which point the Association would entertain proposals from all of its members as to how best to use the resources of the cameras and their new found skills as photographers to benefit the Association and its members. This decision was made after considerable discussion and after weighing the individual and collective needs of all participants in this rural economy dominated by extreme poverty wherein women particularly have limited access to cash generating activities.

Thirdly, the strength of the photograph is also its weakness. Because it can be "multiply read" once presented to ever widening communities, the story of the women in this town will be multiply interpreted. For women who have been isolated in a rural community for generations this will present new challenges for which they are preparing themselves. As a Euro-American researcher I have found multiple interpretations to be resources for working through a process of meaning making, but the local realities of these communities place other kinds of constraints on that process. As importantly, years of war and armed conflict have created rigid ways of thinking that are frequently accompanied by dualism and rigid attachments to dichotomous thinking (see Martín-Baró, 1994).

Finally, and perhaps most importantly, I share with some local residents a deep concern about the threat posed to them if they photograph and critically analyze the realities of poverty and violence within their communities and re-present them to others outside the community. Similar agency among Maya and rural peasants has been interpreted as "revolutionary organizing" in Guatemala's all too recent past. The peace process within Guatemala is extremely fragile and experiences in many other countries suggest that war and organized violence may re-emerge. As this discussion suggests, ethical concerns are not once and for all decision-making points but rather ongoing processes wherein we encounter and re-encounter each other and ourselves as we are transformed and transform our contexts through the collaborative process.

CHALLENGES FROM COLLABORATIVE RESEARCH PROCESSES

The relationship of current ethical guidelines in research with human subjects and actual practice remains unclear. Collaborative forms of inquiry often blur the boundaries between research and practice. As importantly, these are not static relationships in research beyond university walls but processes wherein multiple selves and relationships are enacted. As significantly, organizations that have developed ethical guidelines and standards for research with human subjects often have not developed mechanisms by which they can examine cases of alleged misconduct. The AERA, in particular, has specifically eschewed any aspiration to enforce ethical standards or guidelines. As Arlene Kaplan Daniels has observed, "professional codes do not simply fulfill the function suggested by the professional ideology; rather, they are part of the ideology designed for public relations and justification for the status and prestige which professions assume vis-à-vis more lowly occupations (Daniels, 1973, p. 49)." In a sense this is not surprising for, according to the Oxford English Dictionary, the oldest meaning of the word standard in the English language refers to an emblem or symbol of a person, persons, or group. Thus we must be aware that occupational groups will sometimes promulgate standards not out of any clear-cut strategy for reforming practice but rather as a symbol or emblem of the professional aspirations of that particular occupational group.

Nonetheless, we are heartened by increased attention to issues of research with human subjects. The proliferation of Institutional Review Boards among universities is a sign of this increased concern. But in our experience, ethical standards of research often are not well served by sometimes-bureaucratic requirements of IRBs or other formal review mechanisms. They are better served, we think, through a concern for the underlying principles behind the guidelines for research with human subjects—as long ago as the Hippocratic Oath and, as recently as, the Belmont Report in the 1970s—respect for persons, concern for beneficence, and justice. As suggested in our own practices as researchers and practitioners, these are not static concerns but rather values that inform the multiple contexts in which researchers, practitioners, and participants encounter each other and in which roles and relationships shift over time. As participants in social inquiry we seek to remain faithful to these values while defining and redefining "good practice" within our variously defined communities of research and action. As definitions of what constitutes research and practice are stretched and redefined, criteria for evaluating the ethical aspects of those practices need to be reconsidered.

APPENDIX: Resources on Ethics in Research

World Wide Web Sites concerning ethics in research

Ethics in Research (overview)
http://trochim.human.cornell.edu/kb/ethics.html

Ethics in Science
http://www.chem.vt.edu/ethics/ethics.html

Annotated Bibliography on Teaching Research Ethics
http://www.indiana.edu/~poynter/tre-bib.html

Human Subjects and Research Ethics—pointers to information about ethical aspects of research involving human subjects as participants.
http://www.psych.bangor.ac.uk/deptpsych/Ethics/HumanResearch.html

Four publications on the evolution of ethical issues and standards in research with human subjects

1)   The chapter by Haney and Madaus entitled "Evolution of Ethical and technical standards" (1990) recounts the evolution of both AERA and APA ethical and professional standards giving particular focus to the way in which standards regarding educational and psychological testing have evolved.

2)   *Ethics in Psychology: Professional Standards in Cases* (1998) by Koocher and Keith-Spiegel recounts the current ethical standards of psychologists and also discusses a number of cases that have arisen among psychologists concerning their ethical standards.

3)   Fix and Struyk's volume entitled *Clear and Convincing Evidence: Measurement of Discrimination in America* (1993), by the Urban Institute Press argues for not requiring informed consent in the study of discrimination in public services. In addition to describing some very interesting research, Fix and Struyk help to document widespread existence of discrimination in housing and lending institutions. This book discusses the problems of carrying out research on discriminatory practices when informed consent might well make respondents behaviors different than they would be otherwise. The argument advanced in this volume is that when research focuses on public as opposed to private behavior, standards of informed consent should differ.

4)   Rosnow and Rosenthal's book entitled *People Studying People: Artifacts and Ethics in Behavioral Research* (1997) is a slender but elegant volume recounting a variety of research over the last several decades that helped document the way in which artifacts in research with human subjects can have unexpected impact on outcomes of social, and specifically psychological research as a result of the expectations of both researcher and subjects and as a result of the interactions between researcher and subjects. On the subject of ethics, this volume summarizes research indicating that ethically informed subjects clearly tend to behave and respond differently than those not so informed, thus suggesting that the process of obtaining informed consent may in and of itself affect the results of research with human subjects. In addition, the volume summarizes research indicating that there are different standards among groups, (i.e., men and women) in making ethical judgments about certain research procedures. In addition, Rosnow and Rosenthal point out that in addition to costs of doing research there are social costs that may be exacted from not doing research on important subjects.

ENDNOTES

[1] As social inquiry continues to be transformed by increasingly collaborative relationships between and among "investigators" and the "subjects" of research the labels that had previously been used to

describe the various participants are inadequate. Since ethical guidelines for research with human beings continue to refer to participants as subjects we use that term in referencing these guidelines. However we recognize the limitations of this language and use various, alternative terms in describing our own research experiences.

[2] The full set of the APA Ethical Standards is available at http://www.apa.org/ethics/code.html.

[3] The full set of the AERA Ethical Standards is available at http://aera.net/resource/ethics.html.

REFERENCES

AERA, APA & NCME (1985). *Standards for Educational and Psychological Testing.* Washington, DC: American Psychological Association.

Biggs, S. (1989). *Resource-poor farmer participation in research: A synthesis of experiences from nine national agricultural research systems.* OFCOR Comparative Study Paper 3. The Hague: International Service for National Agricultural Research.

Bunster, X., & Chaney, E. M. (1989). Epilogue. In X. Bunster & E. M. Chaney, *Sellers and servants: Working women in Lima, Peru* (pp. 217-233). Granby, MA: Bergin & Garvey Publishers, Inc.

Fals-Borda, O. & Rahman, M. A. (Eds.). (1991). *Action and knowledge: Breaking the monopoly with participatory action research.* New York: Intermediate Technology/Apex.

Fix, M. & Struyk, R. (Eds.). (1993*). Clear and convincing evidence: Measurement of discrimination in America.* Washington D.C: Urban Institute Press.

Freire, P. (1970). *Pedagogy of the oppressed.* New York: Seabury Press.

Gaventa, J. (1991). Toward a knowledge democracy. In O. Fals-Borda & M.A. Rahman (Eds.), *Action and knowledge: Breaking the monopoly with participatory action research.* New York: Intermediate Technology/Apex.

Haney, W. M. (1993a). *Cheating and escheating on standardized tests.* Paper presented at the annual meeting of the American Educational Research Association, Atlanta, Georgia.

Haney, W. M. (1993, September 29). Preventing cheating on standardized tests. *The Chronicle of Higher Education,* p. B3.

Haney, W. (1998, April). *The value of supplementary evidence in evaluating unusual answer concordance.* Paper presented at the annual meeting of the American Educational Research Association, San Diego, CA.

Hanet, W., et al., (1998). Drawing on education: Using student drawings to promote middle school improvement. *Schools in the middle,* Jan./Feb. 1998, 39-43.

Haney, W. & Madaus, G. (1990). Evolution of ethical and technical standards. In R. Hambleton and J. Zaal (Eds.) Advances in educational and psychological testing: Theory and applications. Boston: Kluwer Academic Publishers, pp. 395-425.

Koocher, G., & Keith-Spiegel, P. (1998). *Ethics in psychology: Professional standards and cases.* New York: Oxford University Press.

LaVertu, D.S. & Linares, A.M. (1990). Ethical principles of biomedical research on human subjects: Their application and limitations in Latin America and the Caribbean. *Bulletin of PAHO, 24*(4), 469-479.

Lykes, M. B. (1989). Dialogue with Guatemalan Indian women: Critical perspectives on constructing collaborative research. In R. Unger (Ed.), *Representations: Social constructions of gender* (pp. 167-185). Amityville, NY: Baywood. [Reprinted in Gergen, M., & Davis, S. (Eds.), (1996). *Toward a new psychology of gender: A reader.* New York: Routledge.]

Lykes, M.B. (1994). Terror, silencing and children: International, multidisciplinary collaboration with

Guatemalan Maya communities. *Social Science and Medicine, 38*(4), 543-552.

Lykes, M. B. (1996). Meaning making in a context of genocide and silencing. In M. B. Lykes, A. Banuazizi, R. Liem, & M. Morris (Eds.), *Myths about the powerless: Contesting social inequalities* (pp. 159-178). Philadelphia: Temple University Press.

Lyons, P. (1997). Memo to Ed Fierros, July 23, 1997 (personal communication).

Martín-Baró, I. (1994). *Writings for a liberation psychology: Ignacio Martín-Baró.* (A. Aron & S. Corne, Eds.), Cambridge, MA: Harvard University Press.

McTaggart, R. (Ed.). (1997). *Participatory action research: International contexts and consequences.* Albany, NY: State University of New York Press.

Mirvis, P.H. & Seashore, S.E. (1979). Being ethical in organizational research. *American Psychologist, 34*(9), 766-780.

Parker, A. & Neal, A. (1982). *Los ambulantes: The itinerant photographers of Guatemala.* Cambridge, MA: The MIT Press.

Reason, P. (1994). Three approaches to participative inquiry. In N.K. Denzin & Y.S. Lincoln (Eds.), *Handbook of qualitative research* (pp. 324-339). Thousand Oaks, CA: Sage.

Rosnow, R. & Rosenthal R. (1997). *People studying people: Artifacts and ethics in behavioral research.* NY: W. H. Freeman.

Russell, M. & Haney, W. (1999, April). *Validity and reliability of information gleaned from student drawings.* Paper presented at the annual meeting of the American Educational Research Association, Montreal, Canada.

Tovey, Roberta (1996). Getting kids into the picture: Student drawings help teachers see themselves more clearly. *Harvard Education Letter,* Nov./Dec, 5-6.

Wang, C. (1999). Photovoice: A participatory action research strategy applied to women's health. *Journal of Women's Health, 8*(2), 185-192.

Wang, C., Burris, M., and Xiang, Y.P. (1996). Chinese village women as visual anthropologists: A participatory approach to reaching policymakers. *Social Science and Medicine, 42,*1391-1400.

Wang, C., Wu, K.Y., Zhan, W.T. & Carovano, K. (1998). Photovoice as a participatory health promotion strategy. *Health Promotion International, 13*(1), 75-86.

Whyte, W.F. (Ed.). (1991). *Participatory action research.* Newbury Park, CA: Sage.

Zipes, J. (1995). *Creative storytelling: Building community, changing lives.* New York: Routledge.

INDEX